Chinese and English
Bilingual Version

A Study on Vocational Education Serving China-Africa Production Capacity Cooperation

African TVET Research Center

Compiled by Yufeng Liu, Yuwei Dai, Jun Li

Translated by Juan Wang

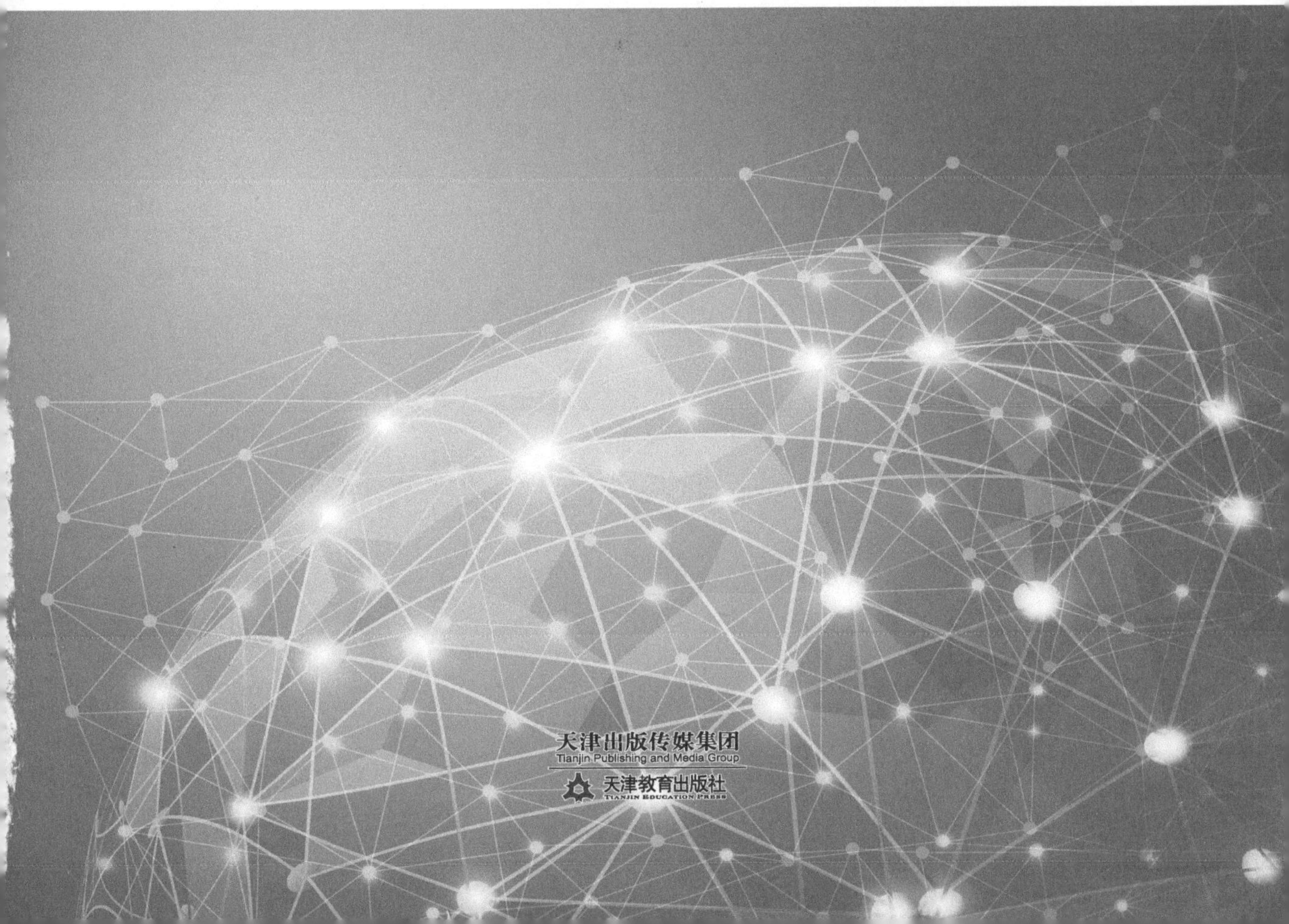

天津出版传媒集团
Tianjin Publishing and Media Group
天津教育出版社
TIANJIN EDUCATION PRESS

Editorial Board of African TVET Research Center

Directors: Liu Yufeng Dai Yuwei

Deputy Directors (*Sorted by last name strokes in Chinese characters*):

Mi Jing Yang Yan Chen Mingkun Zhang Jianxin

Chief Editors: Liu Yufeng Dai Yuwei Li Jun

Translator: Wang Juan

Editorial Board (*Sorted by last name strokes in Chinese characters*):

Ding Ran Ma Yan Wang Yan Wang Juan Wang Lu
Wang Danyang Wang Chunmei Kong Weijun Tian Zhetao
Zhu Mochi Liu Si Sun Jiangang Li Zhihui Li Shanshan Li
Guiyun Li Meihong Yang Can Yang Xiaodan Wu Weixin
Min Xueyang Shen Jie Song Jia Zhang Qin Zhang Ruyi
Zhang Menglong Chen Qing Chen Hairong Lin Lei Jin Yuejiao
Zhao Tong Zhao Hui Zu Xiaodong Yuan Yanxu Dong Simeng
Lin Yonggang Xian Jie Huo Lin

Preface

In President Xi Jinping's keynote speech at the Opening Ceremony of the 2018 Beijing Summit of the Forum on China-Africa Cooperation, he mentioned: We could both seize the opportunity created by the complementarity between our respective development strategies and the major opportunities presented by the Belt and Road Initiative. We need to see to it that the Belt and Road Initiative, the AU Agenda 2063, the UN 2030 Agenda for Sustainable Development and the development programs of African countries better complement each other. With these efforts, we could expand areas of cooperation, unlock new cooperation potential, consolidate our traditional areas of cooperation, and foster new highlights of cooperation in the new economic field.

Since its establishment in 2019, the Africa Technical and Vocational Education and Training (TVET) Research Center has been continuously conducting research on China-Africa vocational education cooperation, contributing to cooperation in education, economy and other fields between China and Africa. As the second batch of research outcomes of the research center, this book, Research on Vocational Education Serving China-Africa Production Capacity Cooperation was compiled through the collaborative efforts of center members. The book is edited by three prominent researchers: Researcher Liu Yufeng, Director of the Academic Committee of the Research Center for Africa Vocational Education and Director of the International Comparative Research Office of the Vocational Education Development Center under the Ministry of Education; Researcher Dai Yuwei, Director of the Research Center for Africa Vocational Education and Secretary of the Party Committee of Tianjin Light Industry Vocational and Technical College and Dr. Li Jun, Director of the Institute of Education Economics and Management at the College of Vocational and Technical Education, Tongji University.

In 2022, China-Africa economic and trade relations witnessed rapid development. According to the Report on Chinese Investment in Africa 2022 released by CCTV (China Central Television), by the end of 2021, China had consistently become Africa's largest trading partner for several years, with over 3,800 Chinese companies having invested in Africa. Chinese companies' investments in Africa cover various industries, including railway and highway transportation, bridges and ports construction, equipment manufacturing, steel and metallurgy, new energy, food processing, electronic information, rubber, building materials, and construction of buildings, etc. According to data from the Ministry of Commerce of China, by the end of 2020, China's stocks of Foreign Direct Investment (FDI) in Africa exceeded 47.4 billion US dollars, with investments spreading across more than 50 countries in Africa. Chinese enterprises' response to the national "Belt and Road Initiative" and the "going global strategy" have greatly promoted the economic and industrial development of African countries. To support the development of vocational education and enhance the level of youth employment in Africa, and to help enterprises' overseas expansion, Chinese vocational education has played a crucial role in serving the development of vocational education in partner countries and facilitating international production capacity cooperation. Currently, China has engaged in various forms of vocational education cooperation with multiple African countries. In Africa, 16 Luban Workshops have been established, and through the process of construction and practice, distinctive models of development and management have been explored, and a large number of locally skilled employees have been trained. Building upon the research achievements on the development of vocational education in African countries, this book conducts further research on vocational education cooperation in serving the international production capacity cooperation, and extracts exemplary and representative case studies as valuable references for China's vocational education assistance to African countries in this field.

Co-authored by seven schools, this book is divided into twelve chapters, containing with chapters one to six as the main part. This part was written by Dr. Li Jun and his team from the College of Vocational Education at Tongji University. His graduate student, Huang Meixue, and Ph.D. candidate, Li Dongshu, from Osnabrück University in Germany, also participated in the writing of several chapters. It includes the introduction background research, current and theoretical research, comparative studies of the internationalization of vocational education and suggestions for production capacity cooperation invocational education services between China and Africa. Chapters seven to twelve consist of six typical research reports on international production capacity cooperation in vocational education, focusing on Egypt, Djibouti, Ghana, Rwanda, Senegal and Uganda. These reports were co-written by research teams from Tianjin Light Industry Vocational Technical College, Tianjin Railway Technical and Vocational College, Tianjin Polytechnic College, Sichuan College of Architectural Technology, Weifang Vocational College and Jinhua Polytechnic. Zhang Ni and Xie Chaoai, graduate students from College of Vocational Education at Tianjin University of Technology and Education complied and proofread the book. Based on detailed country-specific research and guided by a problem-oriented principle, this book presents research reports that extensively elaborate on how Chinese vocational colleges have collaborated with Chinese enterprises in six African countries to provide support for the models, processes, achievements, and recommendations in international production capacity cooperation.

Till now, this book is the first research achievement aimed at the systematic study of China-Africa vocational education cooperation serving international production capacity cooperation in China, following the Research on China-Africa Vocational Education Cooperation by Africa Chinese—English bilingual edition TVET Research Center in 2022. Researcher Liu Yufeng provided detailed guidance for both the overall and individual reports, while Researcher Dai Yuwei, the Secretary of the Party Committee of Tianjin Light Industry Vocational and Technical College, conducted comprehensive planning and review for the monograph. During the writing process, this book received strong support and guidance from experts of the Center for Vocational Education Development of Ministry of Education, the Tianjin Municipal Education Commission, and the Academic Committee of Africa TVET Research Center. We sincerely appreciate their valuable contributions.

Research Board on Vocational Education Serving China-Africa Production Capacity Cooperation

October 2023

Contents

Chapter I
Introduction

1.1 Basic Concept Definition

The concept of "International Industrial Capacity Cooperation" was first seen in the important consensus reached between China and Kazakhstan on cooperation in steel, cement, flat glass, equipment technology and other fields on December 14, 2014, and has become a new way to promote international economic cooperation and innovate foreign investment. [a]

In March 2015, the Chinese government released Vision and proposed actions outhined on jointly building Silk Road Economic Belt and 21st Century Martime Silk Road, laying a strong policy foundation for international production capacity cooperation through the "Five-Pronged Approach", which refers to policy communication, facilities connectivity, smooth trade, financial and people-to-people connectivity, and the principle of joint consultation, co-construction and sharing.[b] In May of the same year, the "Guideline on Promoting International Production Capacity and Equipment Manufacturing Cooperation" was released, it was the first time to promote international production capacity cooperation in the form of a State Council document. The guideline emphasizes that developing countries with high equipment and production capacity, a strong desire for cooperation, good cooperation conditions and foundations will be taken as key countries and we should also actively explore the markets of developed countries. And a total of 12 major industries including steel, non-ferrous metals, building materials, railways, electric power, chemical industry, light textiles, automobiles, communications, engineering machinery, aerospace, ships and marine engineering will be taken as important fields for production

---

a Xia Xianliang. Build an institutional mechanism and policy system for international production capacity cooperation under the "Belt and Road" [J]. Intertrade, 2015(11): 26–33.DOI: 10.14114/j.cnki.itrade.2015.11.005.

b Website of the State Council Information Office. Vision and proposed actions outhined on jointly building Silk Road Economic Belt and 21st Century Maritinae Silk Road[EB/OL]. (2015–03–28)[2022–11–12].http//www.scio.gov.cn/31773/35507/35519/Document/1535279/1535279.htm.

capacity cooperation. [a]The guideline has become an important guiding document for advancing international production capacity and equipment manufacturing cooperation. In September of 2015, the late Premier of the State Council, attended the opening ceremony of the Summer Davos Forum, he further explained the concept of "international capacity cooperation" conterning the questions raised by Schwab, Executive Chairman of the World Economic Forum. He pointed out that the vast majority of countries that require international production capacity cooperation are still in the early or middle stages of industralization,and each country has its own comparative advantages in development, the global economy urgently needs to expand total demand, but trade protection is becoming more and more fierce. Therefore, it's an urgent need to apply the concept of win-win coorperation and promote the development of deep integration of the high, medium and low pends of the global industral chain. [b]

In summary, the international production capacity cooperation promoted by the Chinese government aims to realize a major transformation from product exporting to capital exporting relying on China's comparative advantages of its production capacity. It is a brand-new model that integrates investment, construction and operation through an overall output of the production line. It facilitates to revitalize China's existing assets and upgrading the industrial chain to the middle and high-end, and thus helps boost exports and employment in developed countries, and promote industrialization in less-developed countries. [c]

The academic community defines "international production capacity cooperation" as a joint action between two countries or regions with willingness and need to carry out cross-border or cross-regional allocation of production capacity supply and demand, and shift production capacity by means of product export or industry transfer[d]. Furthermore, the definition and interpretation in the Belt and Road Portal reflects the rich meaning of cooperation effectiveness of "helping importing countries to establish a more complete industrial system and manufacturing capacity". [e]Therefore, based on the previous research, this research defines international production capacity cooperation as a phenomenon in which countries in different positions in the global value chain realize the optimal cross-regional allocation of various production factors relying on their own comparative advantages, multi-party capital, technology and industrial cooperation, and

a China Government Network. Guideline on Promoting International Industrial Capacity and Equipment Manufacturing Co-operation[EB/OL]. (2015–05–13)[2022–11–12]. http: //www.gov.cn/gongbao/content/2015/content_2868464.htm.

b China National Radio. Li Keqiang Explains International Production Capacity Cooperation: Strengthen the win-win concept[EB/OL]. (2015–09–10)[2022–11–12].http: //china.cnr. cn/gdgg/20150910/t20150910_519838146.shtml.

c Chinese Government Website. Review and Interpretation of the Executive Meeting of the State Council (9) International Production Capacity Cooperation: 1+1+1>3[EB/OL](.2015–08–12)[2022–11–12]. http: //www.gov.cn/zhuanti/2015–08/12/content_2911547.htm.

d Guo Chaoxian, Liu Fang, Pi Siming. the "Belt and Road Initiative" and China's International Production Capacity Cooperation[J]. Global Review, 2016, 8(03): 17–36+143.DOI: 10.13851/j.cnki.gjzw.201603002.

e Belt and Road Portal. Silk Road Encyclopedia: International Production Capacity Cooperation[EB/OL]. (2016–10–25)[2022–11–07].https: //www.yidaiyilu.gov.cn/zchj/rcjd/2175.htm.

upgrading their respective levels in global market competition and value chain reconstruction through the transformation and upgrading of economic structure.

Based on this, China-Africa production capacity cooperation refers to the fact that China and African countries seize the opportunity of the fifth international production capacity transfer based on the actual industrial development needs of both sides, and transfer industries that China has almost lost its comparative advantage but still has excess production capacity to African countries, so as to promote the optimization and adjustment of industrial structures of both sides and advance the industrialization of African countries. Production capacity cooperation between the largest developing country and the continent, which is the largest aggregation of developing countries, new modalities has more consistent with South-South cooperation, and is more adaptable and equal in the transmission of development experience and the deepening of cooperation concepts. The current production capacity cooperation between China and Africa is mainly based on China's direct investment in Africa, with China-Africa trade as the premise, China's economic and trade cooperation zones in Africa as an important carrier, China's infrastructure connectivity in Africa as an important path, and China's aid to Africa and development finance as financial guarantees.[a] It has promoted the economic diversification and regional economic integration of African countries.

Therefore, to serve the China-Africa production capacity cooperation, vocational education aims to provide Chinese and African enterprises and local cooperative industries with local technical and skilled talents who meet vocational standards and professional standards. According to the actual development needs of China-Africa production capacity cooperation and the needs of local industrial structure, we tend to coordinate and integrate multi-party forces to integrate the institutional chain, knowledge chain and production chain. It would also promote the convergence, mutual recognition and promotion of Chinese standards and international standards at the industrial level.

1.2 Research Methodology

This study adopts the research method of field work. It is conducted research relying on China's vocational colleges and cooperation projects in Egypt, Djibouti, Ghana, Rwanda, Senegal and Uganda.

1.2.1 Methods of Data Collection

1. Interview

With the help of six vocational colleges, namely, Tianjin Railway Technical and Vocational

---

a China Social Science Network. Li Ronglin: Some Opinions on China-Africa Production Capacity Cooperation[EB/OL]. (2020–06–18)[2022–11–12]. http: // www.cssn.cn/jjx_lljjx_1/lljjx_gd/202006/t20200618_5144827.html.

College, Sichuan College of Architecture Technology, Weifang Vocational College, Jinhua Polytechnic, Tianjin Polytechnic College and Tianjin Light Inductry Vocational Technical College, the research conducted a semi-structured interview in Africa and thus to obtain information on the form and effectiveness of vocational education in Egypt, Djibouti, Ghana, Rwanda, Senegal, Uganda and other countries. Through interviewing key figures, this research tries to grasp the current production mode, employment demand evaluation and vocational education needs of Chinese-funded enterprises. This research helps to fully understand the current functions and missions of Chinese vocational education to the development of Chinese-funded enterprises.

2. Questionnaire

With the help of Tianjin Railway Technical and Vocational College, Sichuan College of Architecture Technology, Weifang Vocational College, Jinhua Polytechnic, Tianjin Vocational College of Industry and Tianjin Light Industry Vocational Technical College, a questionnaire was sent out to the Chinese-Funded enterprises in African industrial parks researching the production methods, employee structure, employment needs, local employee skills evaluation and job satisfaction of graduates.

1.2.2 Methods of Data Analysis

1. Case Study

Through country studies of Egypt, Djibouti, Ghana, Rwanda, Senegal and Uganda, this study analyzes the current situation of economic development, industrial development environment, international economic cooperation, vocational education and cooperative education and matching between vocational education and industries from a macro perspective. In the meso dimension, this study explains the development status of Chinese-funded enterprises and their demand for vocational education, this study explains the adaptability of vocational education in countries that they serving the development of Chinese-funded enterprises, and the effectiveness of vocational education in Chinese vocational education on other serving countries. At the micro level, it analyzes the school-running mode, institutional mechanism, effectiveness and future development direction of partner colleges who support the production capacity cooperation with countries. The step-by-step analysis of vertical integration from macro to micro is conducive to clarify the reasons for the differences in practice in China-Africa production capacity cooperation in vocational education services and the direction of future improvement.

2. Literature Analysis

Based on the databases provided by the World Trade Organization, the World Bank, the China Monetary Fund and other international organizations, this study gets information on the macroeconomic operation and development of the above six countries on the African continent.

Through the data released by the National Statistical Bureaus, Ministries of Finance, Investment and Free Zone Management and other official departments of Egypt, Djibouti, Ghana, Rwanda and Uganda, etc., information is acquired about the development status of industries, overall wage levels, the number of Chinese-Funded enterprises registered in Africa and the fields involved in these countries. Information about the distribution of vocational colleges in various fields and industries can be got from the Ministry of Education and Sports. Through the Ministry of Commerce, the National Bureau of Statistics and the State Administration of Foreign Exchange of PRC in China, we can learn about China's direct investment in Africa and China's labor dispatch to Africa.

In addition, this study also analyzes the policy texts of the above six countries on production capacity cooperation, such as documents issued by the Ugandan government, namely, Framework Agreement between the National Development and Reform Commission of the People's Republic of China and the Ministry of Finance, Planning and Economic Development of the Republic of Uganda on Industrial Capacity Cooperation, the Vision 2040 Development Strategy and the National Development Plan 2021–2025, Government priorities for FY2021/22, *COVID Response Plan and the industrialization policies formulated in 2020* etc.. This study also analyzes the data and reports related to the demand of Chinese-Funded enterprises and the quality of graduates from local vocational colleges in the six countries, such as the data released by the president enterprise of the Chinese Chamber of Commerce in Djibouti and the survey team of overseas Chinese enterprises of Yunnan University, the 2019 Report of the Uganda Higher Education Commission, etc. Detailed and rich literature provides strong support for this study to deepen the research on the basis of existing research results.

3. Comparative Research

This study compares the effectiveness and reasons of vocational education in these six countries, and the differences of the current situation of vocational education in China-Africa international production capacity cooperation and the reasons behind. By comparing the differences and reasons for the results of vocational education cooperation between China and other countries in these six countries, this study analyzes the advantages and shortcomings of the current internationalization of Chinese vocational education and service for industry capacity.

1.3 Fundamental Approach

The main content framework of this study is to analyze the mission, typical practice patterns, realistic development predicament, new theoretical construction, horizontal comparison and development strategies of services provided by Chinese vocational education for China-Africa production capacity cooperation. It has also clarified the current new requirements of China-Africa international production capacity cooperation for the coordinated development of vocational education by sorting out the historical origin of China-Africa industrial capacity cooperation, policy planning and deployment as well as challenges and new achievements and policy requirements. The practical patterns of Chinese vocational education serving production capacity cooperation between China and Africa are analyzed by sorting out the object, content, methods, results and problems of the service for production capacity cooperation among the six countries. With representative and exemplary typical cases, it aims to promote the counterparts in Africa. At the same time, the service practice of vocational education is summarised, generalised and abstracted, and raised to a theoretical level on the basis of six practical patterns, to guide the practical development of vocational education to improve its service for industries by theory. Through the comparative research on the vocational education serving for capacity cooperation, this paper also analyzes the operating mechanism of internationalized vocational education and the international cooperation of Chinese vocational education's service for international production capacity cooperation. Finally, based on the practical problems and theoretical basis, this paper puts forward suggestions on pertinent policies, practices and theoretical development.

1.4 Content Framework

This study focuses on elaborating the mission responsibilities, typical practice examples, current development challenges, new theoretical constructs, diverse cross-sectional comparisons and development strategies of China's vocational education serving for China-Africa industrial capacity cooperation.

Chapter 1 serves as an introduction, delving into the definitions of the basic concepts related to international industrial capacity cooperation, China-Africa productive capacity cooperation and vocational education serving China-Africa industrial capacity cooperation. It also outlines the data collection and analysis methods adopted in this study, as well as the fundamental research approach.

Chapter 2 provides a background research of vocational education serving China-Africa industrial capacity cooperation, which mainly discusses the historical origins, past policy planning and implementation, challenges and new initiatives of the production capacity cooperation between China and Africa. Additionally, it clarifies the policy requirements for vocational education servicing for China-Africa productive capacity cooperation and emphasizes the key demands and development directions outlined in policy documents.

Chapter 3 presents the research on the current situation of vocational education serving for China-Africa industrial capacity cooperation. Drawing from cooperation cases studies of China's vocational education in Egypt, Djibouti, Ghana, Rwanda, Senegal and Uganda, this section assesses the present scenario from the various perspectives, including target beneficiaries, service content, delivery methods, outcomes, as well as issues and challenges.

Chapter 4 focuses on the theoretical research in vocational education serving for China-Africa productive capacity cooperation. Building on the content of Chapter 3, this chapter aims to establish frameworks which is summarised, generalised and abstracted, and raised to a theoretical level based on the practical experiences of vocational education services, ultimately guiding the practical development of the production capacity cooperation between China and Africa.

Chapter 5 conducts a comparative study on the internationalization of vocational education. Its primary objectives is to compare and analyze the operational mechanisms of international vocational education and China's vocational education serving international capacity cooperation.

Chapter 6 offers the suggestions for vocational education serving for China-Africa industrial capacity cooperation. Based on practical issues and theoretical foundations, this section provides specific and targeted suggestions concerning policies, practices and theories.

Chapters 7 to 12 primarily consist of case studies illustrating vocational education cooperation between China and the six aforementioned countries (Egypt, Djibouti, Ghana, Rwanda, Senegal and Uganda), as well as the international capacity cooperation.

Chapter II

Background Research on Vocational Education Serving China-Africa Production Capacity Cooperation

According to the perspective of new structural economics, African countries can reduce the high input and high risks associated with technological innovation and industrial upgrading by importing, leasing, and acquiring licenses for mature technologies and entering mature industries. This allows them to leverage the advantages of being latecomers in the development process. Therefore, African countries need to participate in the fifth round of international industrial transfer, introduce labor-intensive industries, and follow the optimal industrial structure that aligns with their factor endowments and comparative advantages. This can ultimately lead to a transition in comparative advantages through capital accumulation. Throughout this process, it is necessary for the government to take the responsibility of improving the market environment, coordinating infrastructure development, and creating a favorable institutional framework. Similarly, China's economic structural transformation also requires adapting to the changed factor endowment structure. Utilizing the approach of "growth identification and facilitation", China can transfer industries that have almost lost their comparative advantages but still have surplus production capacity to African countries, helping them with industrial upgrading.

The tortuous development practice of African industrialization shows that premature deindustrialization under the influence of Western neoliberalism has shifted agricultural surplus labor to manufacturing and service industries with labor productivity far below, causing African countries to miss an important window of rapid economic growth relying on industrialization. By combing the history, policies and current situation of China-Africa production capacity cooperation, it shows that China, as the leader of the new concept and path of South-South cooperation, different from North-South Cooperation, is more adaptable in capacity cooperation, technical cooperation and parallel experience exchange.[a] China provides hardware guarantee for industrialization of African countries with investment, construction and operation of infrastructure and parks. China also provides them with a brand-new choice for realizing independent economic development with its own development experience[b], so as to deepen production capacity cooperation and promote economic diversification and regional integration in Africa.

At present, the most important factor constraining Africa's industrialization is the weak supporting capacity of human capital, and the key breakthrough lies in effective transforming demographic dividend into comparative advantages of industrial development. Under the strategic framework of the Forum on China-Africa Cooperation (FOCAC), China-Africa vocational education cooperation effectively serves the production capacity cooperation between the two sides. It tries to promote African countries' independent development ability by training technical and technical personnel in African countries.

2.1 Research on the History of China-Africa Production Capacity Cooperation

The economic structure of African countries is highly dependent on foreign countries, and most of their export products are primary agricultural products and energy resources, which are of high regional homogeneity. The industrial production capacity is weak and with a limited variety, together with poor infrastructure and many a trade barrier which have seriously hindered the formation of a regional production division of labor network. The regional industrialization process has been slow. As industrialization is the only way to promote Africa's independent development, economic diversification and regional integration, China and Africa undertake an inevitable mission in the process of industrial alignment and production capacity construction. The two are opportunities for each other and there is broad space for production capacity cooperation among them. China and Africa have achieved remarkable initial results through infrastructure construction, building up economic and trade cooperation zones and parks, clean energy cooperation and China-Africa Industrial Fund. These achievements effectively attract Chinese and other enterprises to invest productively in Africa, helping Africa to increase employment opportunities, promoting industrial upgrading and the transformation and human resources development, and effectively promoting Africa's industrialization process.

2.1.1 China's Assist Africa in Infrastructure Construction

The serious lag in infrastructure for industrial development in African countries has

a Zhou Jinyan. The Rise of New South-South Cooperation in the Changing International Cooperation System: Challenges, Missions and China's Solution[J]. Country and Area Studies, 2018, 2(05): 24–36+154.

b Zhou Jinyan. African Exploration of Industrialization Path and the Role of Chinese Solution[J]. Beijing Cultural Review, 2019(01): 74–81+143.

constrained the process of industrial development and regional integration in Africa. The cost of transporting commodities for intra-regional and foreign trade is too high. Energy supply is unable to support industrial production activities. Excessive costs hinder the possibility of international industry relocation to Africa and Western countries are generally absent in infrastructure consturcitons of Africa. However, the "Angola Model"[a] emerged, which features an integrated development mode of "resources-loan-infrastructure construction/production capacity cooperation". Such model has driven China's infrastructure construction, investment, operation and management in Africa, and has increasingly become one of the important models of China-Africa production capacity cooperation.

In 2012, on the Beijing Summit of the Forum on China-Africa Cooperation, the two sides adopted the China-Africa Infrastructure Cooperation Plan. Guided by the economic and social benefits of projects, Chinese government supported Chinese enterprises to participate in the integration of investment, construction and operation in Africa's transnational and cross-regional infrastructure construction. Since China formally put forward the "Belt and Road" Initiative in 2013, the plan of "three networks and one integration" (i.e., high-speed railway network, expressway network, regional aviation network and industrialization) has been carried out in an orderly manner. In 2015, China and the African Union signed a memorandum of understanding on cooperation in infrastructure construction, and China promised to strengthen mutually beneficial cooperation with African countries in the fields of transportation infrastructure and industrialization within the strategic framework of Agenda 2063. From 2016 to 2020, the total amount of infrastructure projects started in Africa is close to 200 billion US dollars, and 31.4% of projects has started to be implemented by 2020.[b] China encourages enterprises to adopt various modes such as "Build-Operate-Transfer", PPP (Public-Private Partnership) and "Build-Own-Operate" to expand investment scale and promote the sustainable development of infrastructure projects. It also supports the Programme for Infrastructure Development in Africa and the Presidential Infrastructure Champion Initiative. In 2022, facing the persistent infrastructure gap in Africa, China's cooperation with Africa will pay more attention to cultivating endogenous development momentum in Africa, strengthening docking China-Africa infrastructure cooperation and Phase II Priority Action Plan of Programme for Infrastructure Development in Africa (PIDA–PAPII) and other flagship projects.

Thus far, China has helped build several important railways in Africa, including the Mombasa-Nairobi Railway connecting Mombasa, a Kenyan port city to Nairobi, the capital; the Yaji Railway connecting Addis Ababa, the capital of Ethiopia, to Djibouti, and the railways built in

---

a Gao Jun. From the "Angola Model" to African Industrialization: China Africa Cooperation under the Transformation of Aid Model [EB/OL]. (2021–11–26)[2022–10–13]. https://www.sohu.com/a/254503269_260616

b The State Council Information Office of the People's Republic of China. China and Africa in the New Era: A Partnership of Equals[EB/OL]. (2021–11–26)[2022–10–12]. http://www.scio.gov.cn/ztk/dtzt/44689/47462/index.htm.

Angola and Nigeria. China also has trained a number of professional and technical workers and operation managers for African countries through infrastructure interconnection, created a number of jobs, droved the formation of commercial formats along the transportation infrastructure, and promoted the process of economic integration, which lay a solid hardware foundation for Africa's industrialization.

2.1.2 China Helps to Construct Economic and Trade Cooperation Zones and Industrial Parks in Africa

As the key of "One Body, Two Wings" of China Africa production capacity cooperation, infrastructure construction and park construction are interconnected as complementary economies of scale industries, providing basic conditions for the construction of economic and trade cooperation zones and industrial parks in areas along transportation infrastructure.

Relying on superior location conditions and compatible transferring industries, China's economic and trade cooperation zones and industrial parks have become an important platform for China-Africa production capacity cooperation, promoting important agglomeration and multi-dimensional radiation of industrial development. Since the 2006 Beijing Summit of the Forum on China-Africa Cooperation, the China Economic and Trade Cooperation Zone in Zambia, the Guangdong Economic and Trade Cooperation Zone in Nigeria, the Mauritius Jinfei Economic and Cooperation Zone and the China-Egypt Suez Economic and Trade Cooperation Zone in Egypt have successively been established in Africa[a]. Among them, the Suez Economic and Trade Cooperation Zone in Egypt is built by Tianjin TEDA. A high-standard modern industrial new city is built based on the experience of constructing Tianjin Development Zone[b], which actively undertakes China's industrial transfer, improves the industrial chain, and effectively attracts Chinese investment in Egypt. That cooperation zone has become an important path for China and Egypt to upgrade the level of industrial cooperation under the framework of the "Belt and Road".

By the end of 2020, 25 of China's economic and trade cooperation zones had been registered with the Ministry of Commerce of the People's Republic of China, and more than 580 enterprises had entered the zones, with a cumulative investment of more than US$7.3 billion[c]. According to the China and Africa in the New Era: A Partnership of Equals, released in 2021, China has established a production capacity cooperation mechanism with 15 African countries to attract

a He Wenping. China-Africa Cooperation Boosts African Development into Fast Lane[EB/OL]. (2018–08–25)[2022–10–13]. http: //www.gov.cn/ xinwen/2018–08/25/content_5316468.htm

b Ma Xia, Song Caicen. China-Egypt Suez Economic and Trade Cooperation Zone: New Oasis on "The Belt and Road"[J]. West Asia and Africa, 2016(02): 109–126.

c Guangming Online. Ministry of Commerce of PRC: The Overall Implementation Rate of the "Eight Major Actions" of China-Africa Cooperation Has Exceeded 85%[EB/OL]. (2021–01–14)[2022–10–13]. https: //m.gmw.cn/baijia/2021–01/14/1302036984.html.

investment in Africa in the form of *cooperative construction of cooperation zones and parks.* By the end of 2021, a total of 237 industrial parks of various types have been built by African countries or jointly built with other countries, among which nearly 60 of them have been planned, constructed and operated by Chinese enterprises. For example, the Lekki Free Trade Zone in Nigeria is a pioneer project of an industrial park jointly operated by China-Turkey Group and the African government under the PPP model. By August 2022, there are 54 enterprises operating in the park[a]. In the future, China will continue to support the China-Africa Industrialization Cooperation Plan. The Chinese government will support the China-Africa economic and trade cooperation zones to upgrade to demonstration zones for China-Africa Industrial Chain and Supply Chain Cooperation. Attention will be paid to the capacity building of African countries in the process of cooperating in the construction or upgrading of industrial parks. Continuous and effective training in basic vocational skills will be provided to them as well as efforts to cultivate vocational skilled talents compatible with industrialization.

2.1.3 China-Africa Cooperation on Clean Energy

Today, China has taken the initiative in the field of renewable energy. Clean energy investment ranks first in the world for many years, and the capacity of hydropower, wind power and photovoltaic power generation ranks first in the world.[b] China can effectively accelerate the green transformation of Africa's energy sector with its technology and services in the field of new energy. Dozens of Chinese-funded enterprises have built photovoltaic power stations cooperating with African enterprises, with a cumulative installed capacity of more than 1.5 GW, filling the gap in the African photovoltaic industry chain[c]. These stations effectively alleviate local power shortages and reduce low-carbon emission. Hereafter, the two sides will continue to promote the transformation of energy cooperation to clean, green and low carbon, increase the utilization ratio of clean energy, actively develop renewable energy, extend the industrial chain and expand the investment and construction of supporting infrastructure upstream and downstream of the industrial chain, so as to turn resource advantages into new driving force for economic development. In this process, China-Africa vocational education cooperation projects, especially Luban Workshops Project, have played an important role. These projects have cultivated a group of applied technical talents in the field of new energy for African countries, constantly upgrading the skills of African energy practitioners through training programs.

---

a Wang Jinjie. The Contribution of China-Africa Cooperation Industrial Park to African Industrialization[J]. World Affairs, 2022(17): 23–26.

b Kexun cable. Clean Energy Industry Will Maintain Medium and High-speed Growth in the Middle and Later stages of the 13th Five-Year Plan Period[EB/OL]. (2018–04–08)[2022–10–13]. https: //www.sohu.com/a/227526340_735708.

c The State Council Information Office of the People's Republic of China. China and Africa in the New Era: A Partnership of Equals[EB/OL]. (2021–11–26)[2022–10–13]. http: //www.gov. cn/zhengce/2021–11/26/content_5653540.htm.

2.1.4 China Investment and Financial Cooperation with Africa

China's investment and financal cooperation with Africa provides a strong and favorable financial guarantee for China-Africa production capacity cooperation. By the end of 2020, China's investment stock in Africa exceeded $43.4 billion, covering more than 50 African countries[a]. China has become the fourth-largest source of investment in Africa, and private enterprises have increasingly become the main investment force in Africa. The proportion of local employees employed by Chinese enterprises exceeds 80%[b], and local employment has been expanded and industrial development has truly benefited people's livelihood.

As an important outcome of the 2006 Beijing Summit of the FOCAC, the China-Africa Development Fund is China's first equity investment fund in Africa. The fund actively gives play to investment experience and talent advantages when providing investment and financing support. It provides intelligent services such as planning and consulting for Africa's industrialization development, and continues to create endogenous driving forces for African economic development. The China-Africa Development Fund, established in 2007, with an initial size of $5 billion, plays an extremely important role in encouraging and supporting Chinese companies' investment in Africa. The China-Africa Industrial Capacity Cooperation Fund was set up specifically at the 2015 Johannesburg Summit of FOCAC, and the first batch of funds was $10 billion. In 2021, the fund played the role of development finance in "planning investment and guiding investment", and invested 2.50 billion *yuan* to strategically support China Telecom and China Mobile's 14th Five-Year Plan for Africa[c], which effectively promotes China-Africa digital economy cooperation to empower the real economy. As of March 2021, the China-Africa Industrial Capacity Cooperation Fund has invested a total of 21 projects around Africa's "three networks and one system" construction, leveraging the industrial development of African countries with infrastructure construction. By the end of June 2022, the China-Africa Industrial Capacity Cooperation Fund had invested a total of 26 projects with an investment amount of $3.30 billion.

It has completed 28 contracted projects with an amount of $3.70 billion. and the total investment of projects leveraged by the funded projects has reached $18.6 billion[d]. By the end of August 2022, the China-Africa Development Fund had made more than $6.4 billion investment decisions in 37 African countries, which could leverage Chinese enterprises to invest and raise

---

a CCTV.COM. Ministry of Commerce: By the End of 2020, China's Investment Stock in Africa Exceeded $43.4 billion[EB/OL]. (2021–11–17)[2022–10–13]. http: //news.cctv.com/2021/11/17/ARTIUKpNpuPaxHg7wYaeNISG211117.shtml.

b Tian Shida. Sino-African Friendly Cooperation Deeply Rooted in People's Hearts.[EB/OL]. (2022–07–04)[2022–10–13]. https: //baijiahao.baidu.com/s?id=17 37371755629354610&wfr=spider&for=pc.

c Chi Jianxin. The Contribution of China-Africa Development Fund to the Industrial Capacity Cooperation between China and Africa[J]. West Asia and Africa, 2016(4): 15.

d cssn.cn. Tong Qing: China-Africa Industrial Capacity Cooperation Fund deepens investment-driven projects[EB/OL]. (2022–08–09)[2022–10–12]. http:

$31 billion in Africa. The investment projects covered various fields of production capacity cooperation and effectively provided financial guarantee for China-Africa production capacity cooperation.[a]

2.2 Policy Studies on China-Africa Production Capacity Cooperation

China-African economic and trade relations have a long history. China-Africa traditional economic and trade cooperation is a prerequisite for China-Africa production capacity cooperation, and thus the international flow of commodities, machinery and equipment, and other production factors could achieve industrial transfer and production capacity cooperation between the two. China is the largest developing country and Africa is the continent with the most concentrated developing countries. Since the beginning of Forum on China-Africa Cooperation (FOCAC), China-Africa production capacity cooperation has enjoyed the development opportunities of strategic aligning between the two sides.

The Forum on China-Africa Cooperation (FOCAC) was established in 2000 and currently contains 55 members, including China, 53 African countries that have established diplomatic relations with China and the African Union (AU) Commission. Ministerial meetings are held every three years alternately in China and African countries, and so far three ministerial conferences have been upgraded to summits, namely the Beijing Summit in November 2006, the Johannesburg Summit in December 2015 and the Summit in 2018 Beijing Summit in September[b]. FOCAC provides a direction and platform for China-Africa production capacity cooperation in the new era. It provides new impetus for Africa's development through the construction of a cross-regional cooperation mechanism, setting a new benchmark for South-South cooperation, and continuously enhancing the international influence of African countries[c]. The agreements and outcomes of the ministerial meetings that China and Africa have reached and the follow-up action plan strengthen the major deployment of China and Africa in the field of production capacity cooperation.

Under the framework of FOCAC, China-Africa production capacity cooperation and the promotion of Africa's industrialization have always been given top priority and prominence which are used to promote mutually beneficial cooperation in other fields. The Chinese government consistently encourages and supports Chinese enterprises to invest in Africa in traditional fields such as infrastructure and industrial manufacturing, and pays attention to the development and cooperation of new fields such as the digital economy and the marine economy. Compared with

---

a intl.ce.cn. China-Africa Development Fund: Join Hands with Chinese Companies to Promote Africa's Digitalization Process[EB/OL]. (2022–09–14)[2022–10–12]. http:intl.ce.cn/sjjj/qy/202209/14/t20220914_38103974.shtml.

b FOCAC. About US[EB/OL].(2019–08–31)[2022–10–13]. http://www.focac.org.cn/ltjj/ltjz/

c Zhou Yuyuan. Fifteen Years of Forum on China-Africa Cooperation: Achievements, Challenges and Prospects[J]. West Asia and Africa,2016(01): 4–21.

the construction assistance in the early days of the founding of the People's Republic of China, China nowdays pays more attention to the sustainability of projects under the framework of FOCAC, and makes the production capacity cooperation between the two sides a major part of foreign investment and profit-oriented business activities.

From the contents of China-Africa industrial capacity cooperation in Table 2–1, the two sides have continuously strengthened in the scale and extent of industrial capacity aligning and industrial capacity cooperation. Financial support has been continuously expanded, and more cooperative projects have been more suitable for the economic development needs of both sides. More emphasis is attached to strengthening capacity-building for African countries in policy orientation, so as to enhance the independent development capabilities of African countries, promote economic diversification and regional integration. Under the guidance of policies, the two sides have gradually formed a production capacity cooperation mechanism of "enterprise entities, market operations and government guidance", and have made great efforts to improve the level of clustering, scale, industrialization and localization of cooperation projects, effectively driving the development of African industries, and favorably supporting African countries to better integrate into the global and regional industrial chains.

Table 2–1 The Evolution of Production Capacity Cooperation Policies Based on FOCAC

FOCAC	Action Plan	China-Africa Relation	Important Measures for China-Africa Capacity Alignment and Capacity Cooperation
Beijing 2000 Ministerial Conference (2000)	China–Africa Economic and Social Development Cooperation Programme	a new-type long-term and stable partnership based on equality and mutual benefits	1. China is committed to continuing to provide free assistance, concessional loans and interest-free loans to African countries within its capabilities and within the framework of South-South cooperation. 2. China will run the "China Investment Development and Trade Promotion Center" in Africa, and establish the "China-Africa Chamber of Commerce and Industry". 3. China will provide special funds to support and encourage strong Chinese companies to invest in Africa.[a]

a www.gov.cn.Programme for China-Africa Cooperation on Economic and Social Development[EB/OL].(2006–10–31) [2022–10–10].http://www.gov.cn/ ztzl/zflt/content_428691.htm.

continued

FOCAC	Action Plan	China-Africa Relation	Important Measures for China-Africa Capacity Alignment and Capacity Cooperation
Second Ministerial Conference (2003)	Addis Ababa Action Agenda (2004 — 2006)	A new type of partnership featuring long-term stability, equality and mutuals benefits, and comprehensive cooperation	1. The Chinese government focuses on helping African countries build infrastructure projects such as roads and bridges by providing loans or free assistance to African countries. 2. China will further encourage and support eligible enterprises with various forms of ownership to invest in Africa, including investment through the establishment of China-Africa joint ventures aimed at encouraging technology transfer and creating jobs in African countries. 3. African countries are encouraged to sign bilateral Investment Protection Agreements and Double Taxation Avoidance Agreements with China.[a]
Beijing Summit and Third Ministerial Conference (2006)	FOCAC Beijing Action Plan (2007—2009)	a new type of China–Africa strategic partnership	1. China supports the Chinese banks to establish the China-Africa Development Fund, which will gradually reach a total of $5 billion. 2. China encourages and supports powerful and reputable Chinese enterprises to invest in Africa and set up projects conducive to improve the technological level of African countries, increasing jobs, and promoting sustainable local economic and social development. 3. China will support Chinese enterprises in establishing 3–5 overseas economic and trade cooperation zones in eligible African countries in the next three years.[b]
Fourth Ministerial Conference (2009)	The Sharm el-Sheikh Action Plan (2010—2012)	a new type of China–Africa strategic partnership	1. China has decided to increase the size of the China-Africa Development Fund to $3 billion, and support Chinese companies to expand investment in Africa. 2. China will continue to build overseas economic and trade cooperation zones in Africa, increase efforts to attract investment, encourage more Chinese enterprises to invest in the zone, and make access of these zones for African small and medium-sized enterprises easier. 3. China will increase investment and participation in Africa's infrastructure construction by providing loans or non-reimbursable assistance to African countries and encouraging Chinese enterprises to invest. In the next three years, China would provide $10 billion in concessional loans to African countries, mainly for infrastructure projects and social development projects.[c]

a www.gov.cn. Addis Ababa Action Agenda (2004—2006)[EB/OL]. (2006–10–31)[2022–10–10].http:// www.gov.cn/ztzl/zflt/content_428690.htm.

b China-Africa Business Council. FOCAC Beijing Action Plan (2007–2009)[EB/OL].(2006–11–15)[2022–10–10].https://www.cabc.org.cn/detail.php?cid=12&category_id=24&id=197.

c Embassy of the People's Republic of China in the Federal Democratic Republic of Ethiopia. The Sharm el-Sheikh Action Plan 2010–2012[EB/OL].(2009–11–12)[2022–10–10].http://et.china-embassy.gov.cn/chn/zgxx/policy/200911/t20091112_7213871.htm.

continued

FOCAC	Action Plan	China-Africa Relation	Important Measures for China-Africa Capacity Alignment and Capacity Cooperation
Fifth Ministerial Conference (2012)	FOCAC Beijing Action Plan (2013—2015)	a new type of China–Africa strategic partnership	1. China will continue to expand the scale of aid to Africa with non-reimbursable aid, interest-free loans and concessional loans. And will innovate aid methods, and improve the effectiveness of assistance. 2. Financial institutions from both sides are encouraged to provide financing support for China—Africa cooperation in energy, agriculture, processing and manufacturing, telecommunications and power, railways, highways, ports and other infrastructure. 3. China will expand cooperation with Africa in the fields of investment and financing, and will provide African countries with a loan quota of $20 billion, focusing on supporting infrastructure construction, agriculture, manufacturing and the development of small and medium-sized enterprises in Africa. 4. The Chinese government continues to encourage and support powerful and reputable Chinese enterprises to invest in Africa and guide Chinese enterprises to establish processing and manufacturing bases in Africa. It will increase investment in service industries such as commercial and trade services, transportation and consulting management. 5. China will establish a partnership with the African Union in the design, inspection, financing and management of projects in the "Infrastructure Development Plan for Africa" and "Presidential Champion Infrastructure Initiative".[a]
Johannesburg Summit and Sixth Ministerial Conference (2015)	FOCAC Johannesburg Action Plan (2016—2018)	the China–Africa comprehensive strategic and cooperative partnership	1. "Ten Major Cooperation Plans" has been reached, including the industrialization cooperation plan, infrastructure cooperation plan, green development cooperation plan, financial cooperation plan and trade and investment facilitation cooperation plan, etc. 2. With the establishment of the first batch of "China-Africa Industrial Capacity Cooperation Funds" with a capital of $10 billion, China will gradually increase the capital of the China-Africa Development Fund by $5 billion, so that its total scale will be expanded to $10 billion. 3. China will dispatch senior experts and advisors to African countries to provide consultation and assistance in industrial planning, policy design, operation management, and other aspects. 4. The two sides will jointly formulate the China Africa Railway Cooperation Action Plan (2016—2020) to promote the construction of the African railway network[b].

a Embassy of the People's Republic of China in the Republic of Rwanda. FOCAC Fifth Ministerial Conference (2012)—Beijing Action Plan(2013—2015)[EB/OL].(2012–07–24)[2022–10–10].http://rw.china-embassy.gov.cn/zt/zfgx/201207/t20120724_7122303.htm.

b The State Council Information Office of the People's Republic of China. FOCAC Johannesburg Action Plan (2016—2018)[EB/OL]. (2015–12–10)[2022–10–13]. http://www.scio.gov.cn/XWfbh/xwbfbh/wqfbh/44687/47454/xgzc47460/Document/1716759/1716759.htm.

continued

FOCAC	Action Plan	China-Africa Relation	Important Measures for China-Africa Capacity Alignment and Capacity Cooperation
Beijing Summit and Seventh Ministerial Conference (2018)	FOCAC Beijing Action Plan (2019—2021)	To build an even stronger China–Africa community with a shared future	1. Agreements on eight major initiatives have been reached, including industrial promotion, facility connectivity, trade facilitation, capacity building, etc. 2. China encourages policy financial institutions, development finance institutions, China-Africa Development Fund, China-Africa Production Capacity Cooperation Fund and Special Loans for the Development of African Small and Medium-sized Enterprises to increase support for China-Africa production capacity cooperation. 3. China will strengthen support for the development of African processing and manufacturing industries, special economic zones, industrial parks and other industries. It will support Chinese private enterprises in building industrial parks and carrying out technology transfer in Africa[a].
Eighth Ministerial Conference (2021)	FOCAC Dakar Action Plan (2022—2024)	"Building a China–Africa Community with a Shared Future in the New Era" was written into the *Dakar Declaration of the Eighth Ministerial Conference of the Forum on China-Africa Cooperation*	1. It announced the "Nine Projects" of China-Africa practical cooperation: trade promotion project, digital innovation project, capacity building project, investment-driven project, green development project and people-to-people exchange project. 2. China will assist Africa in implementing 10 industrialization and employment promotion projects. 3. China supports upgrading the China-Africa economic and trade cooperation zones to industrial supply chain cooperation demonstration zones. 4. China will promote a total investment of no less than $10 billion by enterprises in Africa in the next three years, especially to expand investment in areas such as manufacturing. 5. China will set up a "China-Africa Private Investment Promotion Platform" to encourage Chinese enterprises to invest in Africa[b].

Note: It is compiled by the author based on the relevant contents of production capacity cooperation in the action plans of the previous FOCAC sessions

2.3 Studies on Current Status of China-Africa Production Capacity Cooperation

According to the statistics of China-Africa economic and trade cooperation released by the Ministry of Commerce of China in 2021, the bilateral trade volume between China and Africa reached $254.2 billion, a year-on-year increase of 35%. Similarly, Chinese direct investment in entire African industries was $3.74 billion, a year-on-year increase of 26.1%. Chinses newly

a FOCAC. FOCAC Beijing Action Plan(2019–2021)[EB/OL].(2018–09–05)[2022–10–13]. http://www.focac.org.cn/zywx/zywj/201809/t20180905_7875851.htm.

b Jiangxi Provincial Government. FOCAC Dakar Action Plan (2022–2024)(2022–2024)[EB/OL].(2021–01–29)[2022–10–13. http://www.jiangxi.gov.cn/art/2022/1/29/art_5451_3850041.html.

signed contracts for contracted projects in Africa have amounted to $77.9 billion, a year-on-year increase of 14.7%[a]. China-Africa production capacity cooperation has entered a new stage under the "Belt and Road" Initiative and the building of a closer China-Africa community with a shared future. Chinese enterprises have carried out industrial, supply chain cooperation with African countries, continuously achieving breakthroughs in cooperation in traditional and emerging areas of manufacturing.

The economic structures and resources of China and Africa are highly complementary. The stages of industrialization are interlinked, and the development strategies and development concepts are mutually integrated. Therefore, China-Africa industrial capacity cooperation has a solid foundation and broad space. The total population of China and Africa accounts for more than one third of the world's total, and the total economic output for about 21% of the world's total[b]. China is the largest developing country and Africa the continent with the largest number of developing countries. Thus, the two sides could strategically link up under the framework of the implementation of the outcomes of FOCAC, and realize a high-quality China-Africa production capacity cooperation led by the "Belt and Road" and the African Union (AU) Agenda 2063. China and Africa will try their best to promote the strategic and close alignment of the China-Africa Cooperation Vision 2035, China's Vision 2035, and the 2030 Agenda for Sustainable Development of UN and the AU Agenda 2063. They aim to give full play to the role of the industrial capacity cooperation mechanism, strengthen the demonstration effect of major projects on China-Africa production capacity cooperation, so as to fully unleash the development potential of African countries, and accelerate the diversification, integration and modernization of African countries' economy.

2.3.1 Current Situations and Challenges Faced by China-Africa Production Capacity Cooperation

The structural downward pressure of the global economy is increasing. Headwinds such as trade protectionism and nationalism continue to emerge, while the market demand of China's traditional exporting countries and regions tends to be weak and Chinese domestic market saturated. For China, overcapacity in some manufacturing industries has become increasingly prominent. There are still some challenges induced by other difficulties in China-Africa production capacity cooperation. COVID-19 pandemic hindered personnel training and exchanges between the two sides, and also made African countries face difficulties such as

---

a Department of West Asia and Africa, Ministry of Commerce of the People's Republic of China. Statistics on China-Africa Economic and Trade Cooperation in 2021[EB/OL].(2022–04–28)[2022–10–06]. http://xyf.mofcom.gov.cn/article/tj/zh/202204/20220403308229.shtml.

b Phoenix TV. African Scholar: Although China and Africa Are Distant Neighbors, They Have Commonalities, and China's Achievements in Poverty Reduction have Brought Enlightenment to Africa[EB/OL].(2022–09–27)[2022–10–13.]https//baijiahao.baidu.com/s?id=1745114770863590316&wfr=spider&for=pc.

shutdown, production stoppage, shortage of intermediate inputs led by supply chain disruption, decline in orders and income brought by shrinking demand and declines in foreign capital inflows[a]. According to a questionnaire survey conducted by Chinese Academy of International Trade and Economic Cooperation of the Ministry of Commerce in 2021, the prominent problems faced by Chinese enterprises in Africa are the intertwining of local social problems and imported terrorist threats in Africa, the intensification of geopolitical games, the depreciation of currency exchange rates in African countries, and the international public opinion environment questioning and challenging China's investment and financing models[b], all of which have increased the uncertainty of the investment environment in Africa. Similarly, international cooperation with Africa is still in a rather competitive situation. The United States intends to introduce great power competition into Africa through "value recognition", European countries are increasing investment in Africa, and emerging powers are struggling to advance in African cooperation[c].

As an important platform for China-Africa production capacity cooperation, China's industrial parks in Africa also face developmental challenges. First, it is difficult for those host countries with frequent regime changes to support the lasting stability of policies, while the long-term park construction requires stable national financial capacity, coherent and effective policy, and strong policy implementation. Second, with the under-performance of the resource endowment and the insufficient quality of the labor force, it is difficult to effectively transform the demographic dividend into a strong driving force for industrialization development. And thus, it is difficult to complete the technology undertaking and transfer of international production capacity. The employment scale driven by the park economy is limited, too. Third, the regional synergy of African countries is insufficient. Most African countries are in the initial stage of industrialization and lack differentiated development ideas, so there are widespread investment difficulties caused by homogeneous competition.

At present, China-Africa relations will also enter a new era along with the transformation of the international system acceleration and the basic model of China's great rejuvenation. China-Africa production capacity cooperation also needs to be adjusted accordingly. After the period of rapid development, China-Africa cooperation is still facing significantly rising systemic exogenous pressures and endogenous pressures for sustainable development.[d] These challenges

---

a Institute of West-Asian and African Studies, CASS.Xu Zelai, Hao Rui: Impact of the COVID-19 Pandemic on Manufacturing in Africa[EB/OL].(2021–09–17)[2022- 10–1].http: //iwaas.cssn.cn/kycg/yjbg/202109/t20210917_5361259.shtml.

b Wang Heng, Zhou Xingcan, Lai Changming. Resilience of Economic and Trade Exchanges Between China and Africa, Leads to Mutual Benefit and Win-win Cooperation between China and Africa[N]. Guangming Daily, 2022–05–19(12).

c Yao Guimei. Characteristics of African Situation and Prospect of China-Africa Cooperation under the COVID-19 Epidemic[J]. Contemporary World, 2022(05): 55–60.

d Institute of West-Asian and African Studies, CASS.Zhang Chun, Zhang Zitong: The Strategic Positioning of China-Africa Cooperation under the Change of the Century Is Clear Again[EB/OL]. (2021–09–17)[2022–10–10].http//iwaas.cssn.cn/kycg/yjbg/202109/t20210917_5361263.shtml.

include problems such as how to consolidate the foundation for stable growth, how to deal with the pressure of interest-led model adjustment, and how to improve the current situation of insufficient capacity in areas with disadvantages.

2.3.2 New Initiatives in China-Africa Production Capacity Cooperation under the New Situation

The world is undergoing an unprecedented change, and the willingness of strategic cooperation between China and Africa will lead China-Africa relations into its prime. Sustainable development of production capacity cooperation is an important pillar of China-Africa cooperation at present. China and Africa should face up to challenges and actively adapt themselves to the new situation. They should seize new opportunities and expand new spaces for China-Africa production capacity cooperation through integrating fragmented markets of the African Free Trade Zone and enhancing the diversification of demand gradient levels.

With the arrival of a new round of scientific and technological revolution and the transformation of technologies, China and Africa will continue to expand new areas of production capacity cooperation such as digital economy, green economy and blue economy and continue to play the dominant role of financial services to the real economy so as to promote the high-quality development of China-Africa capacity cooperation.

1. Digital Economy Cooperation Facilitates the Real Economy

Under the background of global digital technology popularization and industrial digital transformation, the digital economy has sprung up as a new benchmark for economic growth and a strategic victory for countries in international economic competition. Digital technology could help the entire manufacturing industry chain to improve efficiency and promote transformation and upgrading. It will become the core advantage of African countries to participate in a new round of global industrial division of labor and competition. Chinese enterprises have expanded their investment in industrial Internet, digital economy and other industries in Africa, and effectively promoted poverty reduction with the transfer of information and communication technology, which provided a multi-dimensional path for African countries to achieve economic diversification.

China and Africa will build a China-Africa community with a shared future in cyberspace under the China-Africa Digital Innovation Partnership Program. The two sides will continue to expand digital economy cooperation. On the one hand, the two sides will encourage and support enterprises to participate in the construction, operation and services of communication infrastructure such as optical cable backbone networks in African countries. And on the other hand, two sides will promote cooperation in personnel training, innovation center construction, and new technology application fields, so as to narrow the digital divide and support the construction of smart cities in African countries. Relying on the construction of digital information platforms, the scattered and disorderly China-Africa production capacity cooperation projects will be linked into an industrial network. In this way, the efficiency of China-Africa enterprise cooperation will continue to improve, and China-Africa economic and trade cooperation will be empowered with scientific and technological innovation and industrial transformation.

2. Joint Response to Climate Change and Clean Energy Development

China and Africa have gradually focused their cooperation on new energy and green and low-carbon areas, jointly applying clean energy, tackling global climate change and achieving sustainable development. According to the China-Africa Cooperation Vision 2035, China-Africa energy cooperation will be transformed to be clean, low-carbon and green. As a staunch supporter of sustainable development for Africa, China has implemented hundreds of clean energy and green development projects within the framework of FOCAC. It has pledged not to build new coal-power projects abroad and expanded the scale of investment in Africa in low-emission projects such as renewable energy and green and low-carbon industries. China and Africa will gradually solve the energy accessibility of African countries and upgrade electrification in Africa under the framework of the China-African Union Energy Partnership. They would explore green and sustainable ways of energy cooperation.

China and Africa will continue to strengthen cooperation in trade, investment, technology and setting standards in the field of energy resources. China will extend assistance to improve and optimize the layout of energy resource industrial chains in African countries by investment, building and operation of energy resource projects, so as to enhance their product processing capabilities, and break the technical bottlenecks in the field of clean energy in Africa. At the same time, China will continue to pay attention to capacity building in the field of energy in African countries. China will help to improve the ability of African countries to build and manage their own energy systems by dispatching technical teams and providing professional training for energy management and operation personnel in African countries.

3. Marine Economic Development Cooperation

China and Africa have huge potential for cooperation in the field of marine economy. The two sides aim to promote the construction of the "21st Century Maritime Silk Road" through pragmatic and mutually beneficial cooperation in the marine economy. And thus, they could make positive contributions to global marine governance. Under the framework of the International Maritime Organization (IMO) Technical Cooperation Programme, China will provide funding, technical support and personnel training to African countries with special emphasis on capacity-building in the maritime field. China is willing to share its plans for the construction of marine special economic zones, ports and port industrial zones, as well as related plans for the marine industry. It also will intensify the exchange of experience in offshore aquaculture, marine transportation, offshore wind power and marine scientific research. In this way, the two sides will promote China-Africa Blue Economy investment and financing cooperation and cultivate new blue economic growth points for African countries so as to promote and achieve sustainable development of African countries.

2.4 Policy Studies on Vocational Education Serving China-Africa Production Capacity Cooperation

At present, African countries are still facing a relatively severe dilemma of human capital reserve when undertaking the transfer of labor-intensive industries. Rich and low-cost labor resources are even difficult to support industrial production efficiently, and the lack of vocational skills makes it difficult for their young and middle-aged laborers to meet the needs of the labor market. At the same time, due to the weak industrial base in Africa, its labor force has not established the values and disciplined work behaviors that adapt to industrial production, which leads to low production efficiency. Difficult staff management leads to additional transaction costs for enterprises.

According to the relevant survey[a], the biggest challenge facing 52.2% of Chinese enterprises today is the low productivity caused by employee's lack of professional skills and the difficult employee management. In a survey of more than 8,000 local African employees, less than 3% of them have received "secondary vocational/junior college vocational education". Obviously, the education system is insufficient to cultivate blue-collar workers. In another survey of 15 industrial parks in seven African countries-Egypt, Djibouti, Ethiopia, Kenya, Tanzania, Nigeria and Zambia, though more than 80 percent of local workers have junior high school education or above, they generally lack of techniques and skills to adapt to the development of industrialization. Therefore, the key to breaking the obstacle and releasing Africa's demographic dividend lies in promoting the upgrading of vocational skills of the African labor force and developing vocational education and technical training. Therefore, when accompanied by capital investment, China-Africa production capacity cooperation should focus on capacity building, combining vocational education and technical training with its industrialization development stage, thus promoting sustainable development in Africa relying on the development of human capital.

However, due to the lagging industrial development, limited economic development and the World Bank's focus on education funding shifting to primary education and non-formal education, vocational education in Africa was stagnant or even regressive for nearly half a century at the beginning of its independence, and then had been gradually paid attention. In its Decision on a Second decade of education for Africa (2006—2015) and Strategy to Revitalize Technical

---

a Yuan Li, Li Qiyan, Wang Jinjie. Facilitating Africa's Industrialization: Exploring China-Africa Cooperative Industrial Park[M]. Beijing: China Commerce and Trade Press, 2020.

and Vocational Education and Training in Africa, the African Union emphasizes the significance of vocational and technical education to individuals and countries. It hopes to promote vocational education in African countries with an integrated policy framework.[a] Then, AU approved the Roadmap on Harnessing the Demographic Dividend through Investments in Youth, trying to increase investment in African youth through technical and vocational education and training. However, the development of vocational education in Africa still faces many challenges in its development.

In 1980s, Omdurman Vocational Training Center in Sudan was the first vocational education institution aided by China to Africa[b]. Since the second FOCAC, China has carried out systematic vocational education assistance to Africa. The vocational education cooperation mode between China and most African countries is gradually market-oriented and enterprise-oriented. Such kind of vocational education and technical training are independent of the local vocational education school mode. However, there are still some problems, such as the difficulty in standardizing training and examination, the limited mobility and social recognition of the training talent market, and the lack of concept and brand building[c], which make it difficult for Chinese vocational education brands to "going global".

From Table 2–2 that under the framework of FOCAC, China pays attention to the capacity building of various fields of economic and social development of African countries, especially in labor-intensive areas such as agriculture, manufacturing and energy. It focuses on the cultivation of the employability of African youth, especially women. China has provided African countries with a large number of education and training opportunities through a variety of short-term and long-term training programs, educational infrastructure construction, the establishment of special scholarships, and the support for outstanding young people to visit China and the increase in the scale of capital investment. In this way, it also helps cultivate personnel with technical skills to enhance the capabilities of independent development in African countries.

---

a Liang Kedong. Concept and Path of Sino-Africa International Cooperation in Vocational Education[J]. Vocational and Technical Education, 2020, 41(06): 69–74.

b Chen Mingkun, Zhang Xiaonan, Li Junli. Development of Practice and Strategic Significance of Aid to Africa and Cooperation between China and Africa on TVET[J]. International and Comparative Education, 2016, 38(08): 1–6.

c Zhou Jinyan. New opportunities for Trilateral Cooperation between China and Germany in Vocational Education in Ethiopia[J]. Deutschland-Studien, 2018, 33(04): 18–34+139–140.

Table 2–2 China's Policy Requirement on Vocational Education to Facilitate China-Africa Production Capacity Cooperation

FOCAC	Action Plan	Important Measures of Vocational Education Serving Production Cooperation
Beijing 2000 Ministerial Conference (2000)	China Africa Economic and Social Development Cooperation Programme	China had set up the African Human Resources Development Fund, which has been especially used to train African human resources and has held various forms of training courses for African talents. The two sides agreed to develop country-specific training programs to develop and facilitate specific cooperation projects through appropriate channels.
Second Ministerial Conference (2003)	Addis Ababa Action Agenda (2004—2006)	1. The Chinese government would further increase capital input on the basis of the existing size of the "African Human Resources Development Fund", and strive to train and 10,000 African personnel of various types. 2. To strengthen educational cooperation between the two sides, they would exchange teachers and give each other new scholarships, and establish communication channels between institutions of higher learning and schools of skills and vocational education and training. China will continue to help African institutions of higher learning and schools of vocational education and training to strengthen discipline and professional construction.
Beijing Summit and Third Ministerial Conference (2006)	FOCAC Beijing Action Plan (2007—2009)	1. China would strengthen cooperation with Africa in practical technology and human resources development in agriculture. 2. China would help African countries train a certain number of educational administrators, principals and key teachers of universities, primary and secondary schools and vocational education schools for African countries every year. 3. China pledges to increase its investment to provide training of various types for 15,000 personnel in African countries within three years on the basis of the existing African Human Resources Development Fund.
Fourth Ministerial Conference (2009)	The Sharm el-Sheikh Action Plan (2010—2012)	1. The scholarship programs and various seminars and training courses provided by China have made positive contributions to the development of human resources in Africa. 2. The Chinese government will continue to train all kinds of talents for Africa in accordance with the needs of Africa, and pay attention to improving the quality of training. A total of 20,000 talents will be trained for African countries over the next three years. 3. They proposed to implement the "20+20 Cooperation Plan for China-Africa Universities", which aims to select 20 Chinese universities (or vocational education colleges) to establish a new model of "one-to-one" inter-university cooperation with 20 universities (or vocational education colleges) in African countries. 4. China would expand efforts to train teachers for primary and secondary schools and vocational colleges in African countries. It also plans to train 1,500 principals and teachers in African countries over the next three years.

continued

FOCAC	Action Plan	Important Measures of Vocational Education Serving Production Cooperation
Fifth Ministerial Conference (2012)	FOCAC Beijing Action Plan (2013—2015)	1. China will send agricultural vocational education and training teachers to African countries to help Africa establish an agricultural vocational education system. 2. China will continue to implement the "20+20 Cooperation Plan for China-Africa Universities" and further improve the inter-school cooperation mechanism between Chinese and African universities. 3. China will continue to help African countries build education and training facilities, and provide more short-term, medium-and long-term training and scholarship opportunities to train vocational and technical personnel for African countries, especially to help African youth and women improve their employment skills. 4. The Chinese government will implement the "African Talent Plan" to train 30,000 African talents of various types in the next three years, and provide 18,000 government scholarships. It also will pay attention to optimizing the training content and improving the training quality. 5. China and Africa reaffirm their commitment to strengthening the human resources capacity building of African countries. The scholarship programs and various training and seminar programs offered by China cover agriculture, industry, health, education, communication, media, science and technology, disaster prevention and mitigation, administration and other fields.
Johannesburg Summit and Sixth Ministerial Conference (2015)	FOCAC Johannesburg Action Plan (2016—2018)	China will support African countries in renovating existing or building more vocational and technical training facilities, set up a number of regional vocational education centers and a number of capacity-building colleges in Africa, train 200,000 local vocational and technical talents in Africa, and provide 40,000 training opportunities in China to help young people and women improve their employment skills and enhance Africa's self-development capabilities.
Beijing Summit and Seventh Ministerial Conference (2018)	FOCAC Beijing Action Plan (2019—2021)	China will implement the "China-Africa Industrialization Cooperation Plan" to provide effective and sustainable basic vocational skills training for the African working population. A tailor-made program will be carried out to train 1,000 high-caliber talents for Africa, provide 50,000 Chinese government scholarships for Africa, and 50,000 training opportunities for African talents and train more professionals in various fields for Africa.
Eighth Ministerial Conference (2021)	FOCAC Dakar Action Plan (2022—2024)	1. China will implement "Future of Africa — a project for China-Africa cooperation on vocational education", start the "employment through a train scheme for African students in China" and hold the China-Africa Education Ministers Forum. 2. China will continue to provide short-term training opportunities for African countries and cooperate with African countries to set up the "Luban Workshop". It encourages and supports Chinese-funded enterprises to carry out vocational training in African countries, and provide no less than 800,000 local jobs in Africa. 3. China will increase vocational training for youth, especially women in areas related to the African Infrastructure Connectivity Initiative, including engineering project development management, power station construction and operation, high-speed rail network management, shipping, investment projects and financial management.

Note: It is compiled by the author according to the relevant contents of vocational and educational cooperation in the action plans of the previous Forum on China-Africa Cooperation. See Table 2–1 for references to the document.

Under the framework of the Forum on China-Africa Cooperation, Luban Workshops Project has played an important role in China's assistance to African countries in vocational education, exploring new models of China-Africa vocational education cooperation. According to China and Africa in the New Era: A Partnership of Equals, China has built "Luban Workshops" with local colleges and universities in Egypt, South Africa, Djibouti, Kenya and other African countries since 2018. China has shared the Chinese vocational teaching model as a whole, and also provided advanced teaching equipment, professional standards and teaching resources. It will extend continuous support in training teachers for cooperative countries, so as to cultivate technical and skilled personnel needed for industrialization development in African countries, while serving China-Africa production capacity cooperation. As a demonstration zone for China's vocational education reform and innovation, Tianjin pioneered the Luban Workshop International Brand Cooperation Project, providing vocational and technical training for African youth, and played an important role in China-Africa cooperation. By June 2023, China had established 27 Luban workshops in 25 countries, laying a solid foundation for high-quality cooperation in vocational education between China and Africa. The construction of Luban Workshops closely cooperates with the human resources needs of Chinese enterprises in Africa and the China-Africa production capacity cooperation. The workshops gradually build an international cooperation system for vocational education that covers all aspects of vocational education from secondary vocational schools to colleges and universities, from skills training to academic education[a]. However, there are still many external uncertainties and internal coordination problems, and it is necessary to continue to track, evaluate and improve the implementation of the project.

---

a Institute of West-Asian and African Studies, CASS. Gan Zhenjun: New Explorations in China-Africa Vocational Education Cooperation: Luban Workshop[EB/OL]. (2021–05–10)

Chapter III

Studies on Current Status of Vocational Education Serving China-Africa Production Capacity Cooperation

Chinese-funded enterprises are faced with severe bottlenecks in human resources in Africa. There are problems such as a shortage of professional and technical personnel, difficulty in recruitment caused by low comprehensive skills of local employees, and difficulty in achieving stable production. However, the training provided by enterprises themselves is not enough to cope with the refined operation of facilities and equipment maintenance. The local vocational education system is even more unsuitable for the needs of Chinese-funded enterprises. Therefore, Chinese vocational colleges should provide necessary human resources and technical support for China-Africa production capacity cooperation, so that these enterprises can improve their productivity through educational assistance. This chapter will look into and present the current states of vocational education serving China-Africa production capacity cooperation through five parts, namely target beneficiaries, service content, service modes, service effect and existing obstacles.

3.1 Target Beneficiaries

China and Africa have a solid foundation and broad space for production capacity cooperation due to the convergence of the development stages of industrialization and development strategies, as well as the complementarity of production resources. Moreover, the Chinese-funded enterprises in Africa are at the forefront of China-Africa production capacity cooperation. They have created a large number of employment opportunities for the host countries with advantages in their field, promoted technology transfer in the form of skills training and new technology introduction, and helped these countries achieve industrial transformation and upgrading.

Contracting projects of Chinese-funded enterprises in Africa are mainly distributed in three major business areas as transportation construction, general construction and power engineering construction. In 2020, the contracted turnover of the above three major industries accounted for

68.7%, and the newly signed contracts accounted for 71.9%[a]. Water conservancy construction, communications engineering construction, petrochemical projects, industrial construction, scientific research and technology service are also important investment business areas. For example, the government of Uganda also regards real economies such as agriculture, oil, energy, transportation, mining, manufacturing and others as key industrial areas, and plans to promote industrialization by strengthening infrastructure construction, industrial upgrading and diversification (See Figure 3–1 and Figure 3–2).

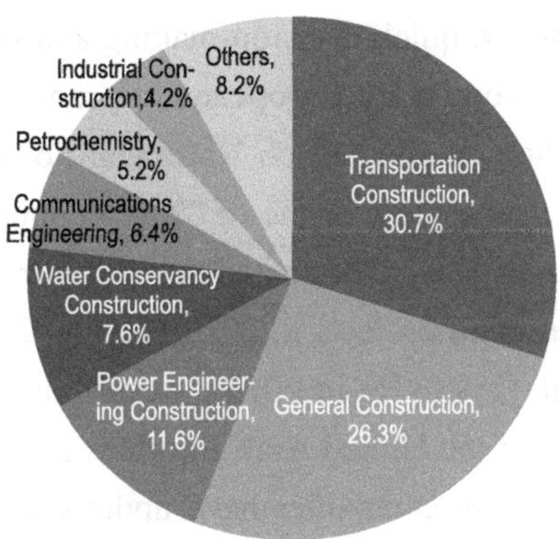

Figure 3–1 Completed Turnover of Chinese Enterprises in Contracted Projects in the African Market by Sectors in 2020 (in $100 million)

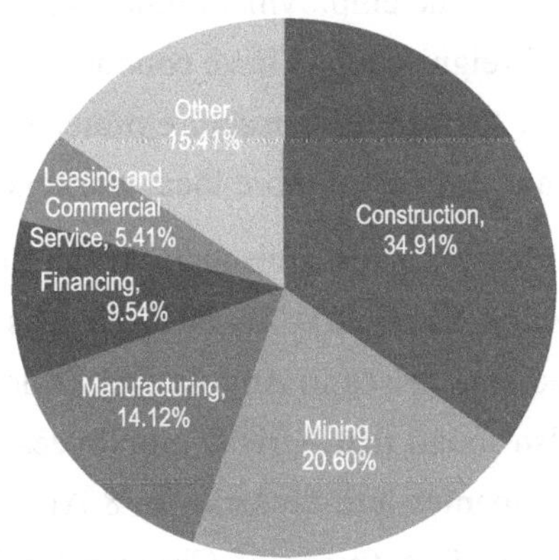

Figure 3–2 China's Stock of Direct Investment in Africa by the End of 2020 (in Industries)

Note: Figure 3–1, Figure 3–2 from released by the China–Africa Economic and Trade Expo Secretariat Report on Economic and Trade Relations between China and Africa (2021).

a The China—Africa Economic And Trade Expo Secretariat. Report on Economic and Trade Relations between China and Africa.2021[R/OL] (2021–09–24) [2022–12–23]. https://www.investgohn.com/ueditor/jsp/upload/file/20210924/1632478576207046328.

Cross Regional Economic Network, a Kenyan think tank in 2022, conducted a poll targeting more than 1,000 policymakers in 25 African countries. According to this poll, these African policy makers are concerned with the fierce competition between the European Union and China in Africa. The report points out that China surpasses European countries in terms of speed and reliability of large-scale infrastructure construction projects such as highways, hydropower stations, railways and bridges, while Europe has advantages in abstract areas such as soft power exchanges and climate change awareness. More than 85% of the respondents agree with the statement that "China supports infrastructure construction in Africa", for China's meeting Africa's priority development needs, quick decision-making and fast implementation of projects. "These are more concrete than projects by Europeans to promote democracy, human rights or sustainability", said Stefan Schott, the Friedrich Naumann Foundation in East Africa Project Director.[a] According to an article on the website of "The Economist" in 2022, titled "Chasing Dragons: How Chinese Companies Have Dominated African Infrastructure", Chinese companies built 31% of all African infrastructure projects in 2020 (12% in 2013), while western companies were responsible for only about 12% (37% in 2013).[b]According to another article published on the website of the "Gulf Necos" of the United Arab Emirates in 2022, "How China Is Outpacing the United States in Africa", Chinese companies have updated modern technologies and know-how for African countries. Especially, investment in infrastructure has increased the overall production capacity of African countries[c].

The financing and development of key infrastructure led by Chinese-funded enterprises in Africa has led to a western review of the employment models and procedures of Chinese-funded enterprises. Based on this, many foreign scholars have conducted surveys and found that Chinese-funded enterprises participating in African infrastructure projects have created a large number of local employment opportunities and employed more local workers than Chinese workers.

For example, based on a survey by a research team at the School of Oriented and African Studies, the University of London from 2016 to 2017, it was found that 74% and 90% of employees in the Chinese-funded enterprises in Angola and Ethiopia were natives respectively[d]. Similarly, in 2017, McKinsey also found that African employees accounted for 89% of the total labor force in 1,000 Chinese companies and factories in 8 African countries, providing nearly 300,000 jobs for African workers. Two-thirds of Chinese-funded enterprises provide skills

---

a huanqiu.com.Kenyan Think Tank report: China Clearly Outperforms EU in Meeting Africa's Priority Needs [EB/OL]. (2022–07–22)[2022–12–23]. https: //baijiahao.baidu.com/s?id=1739005834874133682&wfr=spider&for=pc.

b cankaoxiaoxi.com. British Media: How Chinese Companies can Dominate Africa's Infrastructure[EB/OL]. (2022–02–22) [2022–12–23]. https: // baijiahao.baidu.com/s?id=1725459922891535478&wfr=spider&for=pc.

c Guangming Online.Arabian Media: China's Influence in Africa Is Overtaking That of the United States[EB/OL]. (2022–12–02)[2022–12–23]. https: //m.gmw. cn/baijia/2022–12/02/36205337.html.

d cankaoxiaoxi.com. . U.S. Media: Chinese Companies' Hiring Patterns in Africa are Unquestionable[EB/OL]. (2021–04–07) [2022–12–04]. https: //baijiahao. baidu.com/s?id=1696380033016935651&wfr=spider&for=pc.

training for local people, one-half of them provide internships for local people, and one-third of Chinese-funded companies have introduced new technologies for local people.[a]

3.1.1 Overview of Chinese-Funded Enterprises' Development in Africa

According to the report titled Market power and Role of the Private Sector: Report on Chinese Investment in Africa released in 2021, the investment and operation activities of Chinese-funded enterprises in Africa have gone through three major development stages. The first stage is from 1980 to early 1990. Only a few private enterprises took the initiative to conduct small-scale trade with Africa. The second stage is the last decade of the 20th century. More and more Chinese-funded enterprises entered the African market, and commodity trade in light industry, food, chemical industry and other fields grew rapidly. The third phase marks the period since the beginning of the 21st century, with the Forum on China-Africa Cooperation covering more regions. Investment in industries and diversified fields has grown rapidly. China's new investment in Africa covers 47 African countries, and investment by Chinese private enterprises in Africa accounts for about 70% of China's foreign direct investment. With their sensitivity to the market, private enterprises effectively identify and manage risks. Thus, they could quickly grasp market opportunities and control innovation costs. They are active in manufacturing, service, communications, media and other fields. State-owned enterprises tend to undertake projects funded by the Chinese government in the form of foreign aid or cooperation and assistance. Their investment and operation decisions are subject to accountability, economic feasibility and profitability. They also need to bear the pressure to balance national strategic goals and corporate financial interests, maintaining an international image in a long-term operation.

Chinese state-owned enterprises have a greater impact on industries such as large-scale infrastructure construction, while many private enterprises mainly work in light manufacturing and other fields. As existing policies favor the supply side of the labor market rather than the demand side, Chinese-funded enterprises often face the problem of a lack of skilled workers in Africa. For example, Chinese-funded enterprises in the Uganda Mbale Industrial Park are in need of more than 2,000 skilled workers in the fields of electronic and electrical appliances, metallurgy, textiles, construction, chemicals, packaging materials, etc.. The shortage of skilled workers in Rwanda is mainly in the fields of construction, trade, and communications, specifically for personnel of construction site supervision, water and electricity installation, equipment installation and commissioning, TV network installation, operation and maintenance, advertising, logistics and warehousing, as well as drone operators, construction machinery teachers, basic coders and other. (See Table 3–1)

---

a scio.gov.cn. Foreign Ministry's Q&A on U.S. Media Reports that Chinese Companies' Investment in Africa has Created a Lot of Jobs, etc.[EB/OL].(2018–08–31)[2022–12–23]. http: //www.scio.gov.cn/xwfbh/gbwxwfbh/xwfbh/wjb/Document/1636699/1636699.htm.

Table 3–1 Service Beneficiaries' Listings

Countries served	Chinese Vocational College	Industries	Service Beneficiaries and Their Features
Egypt	Tianjin Light Industry Vocational and Technical College Luban Workshop in Egypt	Petroleum equipment, textile industry, building materials industry, household appliances and machinery, manufacturing industries	Enterprises in China-Egypt TEDA Suez Economic and Trade Cooperation Zone, CCCC First Highway Engineering Group, Hanergy Mobile Energy Holding Group, Himile Mechanical Science and Technology (Shandong) Company, Tianjin Shengna Science And Technology Company, Yingli Energy Development Co., Ltd.
Djibouti	Tianjin Railway Vocational and Technical College Luban workshop in Djibouti	Infrastructure construction industries (such as railways, wharf construction, cross-border water supply projects and industrial park construction and operation projects)	There are a total of 19 Chinese-funded enterprises in Djibouti. 61% of them are industrial enterprises and 39% are service enterprises; 28% are large enterprises, 22% are medium-sized enterprises and 50% are small enterprises. 39% are state-controlled and 61% are private.
Ghana	Weifang Vocational College	Industries of agriculture, fishery, real estate, building materials, furniture, food and beverage, ceramics, steel, pesticides, shoemaking, wood processing, textiles and clothing	Sinohydro Group, CGGC, Hunan Construction Engineering Group, Shenzhen Energy Group, Sinopec, China Railway Construction Engineering Group etc.
Uganda	Tianjin Polytechnic College, Luban Workshop in Uganda	Agricultural product processing, iron and steel, equipment manufacturing, textile, construction	There are about 50 enterprises, such as CCCC, Sinohydro Group, CIWE, China Gezhouba Group International Engineering Co. Ltd., China Railway No.5 Engineering Group, China Railway No.7 Engineering Group, CIOC, CHICO CJIC ZTE Cooperation and Huawei, etc. And most investors in industrial parks are private enterprise.
Rwanda	Jinhua Polytechnic	Communication electronics, construction, infrastructure, digital television, e-commerce	There are about 30 enterprises, including China Civil Engineering Construction Corporation, China Geo-Engineering Corp., Beijing Construction Engineering Group International Co. Ltd., Huashan International Engineering Co. Ltd. CHICO, CJIC, Zhejiang China Commodities City Group, Beijing Forever Technology Co. Ltd. Sinohydro Group, C&D Garment Factory, Guangdong CHINESTAR Steel Structure Co. Ltd. and Sinohydro Tianjin Engineering Co. Ltd. etc. Most of them are state-owned, supplemented by private enterprises, and mainly construction enterprises, there are a small number of clothing enterprises, trading companies and communications enterprises.

These Chinese-funded enterprises have created a large number of employment opportunities and provided technical training guidance for host countries. These have brought obvious technological spillover effects, effectively promoted the development of related industries, and advanced the industrialization process in Africa. For example, with the construction of the Addis Ababa–Djibouti Railway, the demand for localization of railway-related technical talents has grown. The number of operation personnel in Ethiopia and Djibouti increased from 50.3% in 2016 to 97.1% in 2021, and the net increase of localized employment is 3.5 times as much as before.

3.1.2 Insufficient Adaptation of Local Vocational Education System to the Talent Needs of Chinese-Funded Enterprises

Constrained by the economy and the tendency of education capitalization, the local government invests less in vocational education. The purpose of vocational education is not to protect the right to education of the most vulnerable groups, but to become a tool to meet certain specific economic needs. The relatively backward local vocational education system in Africa has made it hard to help African youths accumulate vocational skills to meet employment needs. The vocational skills structure is difficult to match the labor market structure, triggering a serious shortage of high-quality technical and management talents and hindering the localization of staff in Chinese-funded enterprises.

At present, Chinese-funded enterprises are facing the problem that the local vocational education system is not adapted to the needs of their local technical and skilled talents. Especially, the learning content is not consistent with the skills required in the employment field, and it takes too long to transit from school to work. The reasons are mainly reflected in the following aspects:

1. Relatively Backward Basic Education has Limited Support for the Development of Vocational Education

According to the “Transforming Education in Africa: An evidence-based overview and recommendations for long-term improvements” released by UNICEF in 2021, three-fifths of African population is under 25 years old, and half of the population is between 3 and 24 years old. Such a large youth group has brought great pressure to the education systems of African countries. In addition, the educational systems of African countries are faced with increasing demand for education, relatively low quality of education, uneven access to education and relatively high dropout rates. Although some African countries set a legal framework for nine years of compulsory education, the completion rate is still difficult to reach. This is due to multiple problems, such as insufficient supply of qualified teachers affecting students’ learning and skills development, illiterate parents hindering students’ enrollment, serious defects in teachers’ administration and teaching management, insufficient investment in education public funds, low efficiency of education expenditure and disjointed education planning, which lead to limited support for vocational education in the education system. For this, the quality of students and the educated groups in vocational education have been seriously affected. On average, only 3 percent of young Africans aged 15 to 24 have access to vocational education, with little technical and vocational education and training available at the secondary level, where technical and vocational education enrolment accounts for an average of only 1.6 percent of the total secondary school enrolment rate. In the Continential Education Stragtegy for Africa, the African Union has made expanding the supply of vocational and technical education and training as its eighth strategic objective. It aims to expand access to education at the secondary and high levels and strengthen the links between employment and the education and training system. However, in fact the coverage of technical and vocational education and training (TVET) in Africa is still narrow. Vocational education in African countries is constrained by its economic and social factors. It either lacks sufficient financial support, or coordinating management across government departments. And thus the quality of its achievements is not high.

2. Imperfect Mechanism of Vocational Education and Insufficient Guarantee Function of External System

Some African countries lack a channel between vocational education and general education, and the entrance system has not yet been opened. There are a large number of secondary vocational colleges, but the employment rate of graduates is low and the training quality is not high. The number of higher vocational colleges is very small, and the vertical training system of secondary and higher vocational talents is not connected.

The imperfect mechanism of vocational education stems from the insufficient support of the external security system. It is obvious that local vocational education lacks legislative support, financial assistance and social recognition. At the same time, most vocational colleges can not be effectively managed, and are unable to purchase teaching equipment and hire high-caliber trainers. The persistence of the above difficulties makes vocational education in African countries less attractive, and also makes it difficult for Chinese vocational colleges to run schools in Africa.

3. Poor Quality of Students and Insufficient Teaching Faculty and Teaching Resources

Restricted by the economy, the basic education in some African countries is weak and depends on educational assistance from European and American countries and international organizations, which makes the number and quality of students enrolled in vocational education fail to meet the requirements.

The imbalance between supply and demand for teachers, low quality and poor allocation of vocational education teaching staff also restrict the cultivation of technical talents. The teaching quality still needs to be improved. At the same time, the limited teaching conditions, insufficient and backward teaching resources lead to more theoretical learning than practical operation. The outdated courses and skills training failing to update make it only stay in the teaching of traditional skills, which makes their graduates unable to meet the technical requirements and basic digital skills for employment. For example, only about 30% of the graduates trained in Djibouti for the primary needs of the traditional simple business sector have successfully entered the labor market.

4. Insufficient School-Enterprise Cooperation Leads to Mismatch between the Market Demand and Employability of Graduates

Due to the low level of local industrialization, the number of large and medium-sized enterprises is small in Africa and most of them are controlled by foreign capital. With the influence of differences in the political system and national culture, the coupling degree of these enterprises with local vocational education is low. In the process of recruiting local employees, it is easy for foreign enterprises to find that the quality of graduates trained by vocational education system is not adaptable to job requirements, and thus it is difficult to obtain recognition from these enterprises.

For the weak connection between local vocational education and labor market, graduates trained in vocational colleges are out of touch with the actual needs of industrial economy. This could be mainly reflected in the lack of consistency between learning content and actual working field, and the long transition from school to work. In addition, the lack of communication mechanism between local vocational colleges and enterprises makes vocational colleges fail to get access to the skills needed by enterprises in time.

3.1.3 Predicaments in the Development of Chinese-Funded Enterprises in Africa

Chinese-funded enterprises have created many jobs for host countries in Africa. They have promoted the transfer of know-how and new technologies by means of skills training, and promoted infrastructure construction and capacity building of African countries. However, there are also many business difficulties in the process of localization.

According to a survey conducted by the Chinese Academy of International Trade and Economic Cooperation of the Ministry of Commerce in 2021, the most prominent problems faced by Chinese-funded enterprises are local security issues, political risks, exchange rate fluctuations and international public opinion environment[a]. Because the business environment of African countries is complex and their economy and society are still at the primary stage of industrialization, there are many loopholes in laws and regulations due to the governments' inadequate capacity. These Chinese-funded enterprises, which are at the forefront of China's exchanges with Africa, inevitably have problems in the process of interaction with local

a Guangming Online. China-Africa Economic and Trade Exchanges Show Resilience, Leading China-Africa Cooperation to Mutual Benefit and Win-Win Results[EB/OL]. (2022–05–19)[2022–12–04]. https:// m.gmw.cn/baijia/2022–05/19/35746227.html.

governments and residents' communities. All these put forward higher requirements on dealing with labor relations and environmental disputes for these enterprises.

1. Facing the Unstable Political Environment and Security Situation

Affected by religious, political, local social issues and foreign terrorism, some African countries have serious security problems. Under the COVID-19 Pandemic, the problem of youth unemployment has gotten worse. Social contradictions and conflicts have accumulated, and the number of coups in 2021 has reached a new high in nearly 20 years, which has affected the normal business activities and investment interests of Chinese-funded enterprises. The unstable political environment has become the biggest obstacle to investment and operation for Chinese-funded enterprises.

2. Volatility in Local Business Environment and Unstable Investment Policies

Due to the frequent regime changes in some African countries, their business policies have fluctuated greatly, which has exacerbated the instability of the investment environment. In addition, due to the weak economic foundation and high external dependence, the exchange rates of African countries are greatly affected by the international economic situation. Even worse, some US and European development financial institutions question and interfere with China's investment and financing model. More than 70 percent of the engineering and investment losses surveyed were caused by the depreciation of currencies in African countries, and the investment outlook is relatively uncertain.

The complex and volatile business environment, inadequate government capacity and relatively early stage of industrialization in African countries make Chinese-funded enterprises face great pressure in environmental protection and labor relations. There are some problems in African countries, such as the lack of relevant laws and standards, mismatch between copying EU standards and their own development stage, mistakes in law enforcement by the government, and corruption of officials. If Chinese-funded enterprises exercise self-restraint to implement higher standards, they will raise their costs and reduce their market competitiveness[a]. In the primary stage of industrial development, the environmental pollution caused by relatively primitive processes and skills is also larger, and labor-intensive enterprises are faced with the challenge of workers' labor intensity and working environment. For example, the Rwandan government takes various measures to encourage investment, but the legal requirements and enforcement of taxes and environmental protection are strict, and the fines imposed on foreign enterprises are especially heavy. The heads of relevant examination and approval departments change frequently. The lack of stability in government policies and internal coordination leads to policy risks.

---

a guancha.cn. Interview with Tsinghua scholar Tang Xiaoyang: What is the Real Situation of Chinese Enterprises in Africa?[EB/OL]. (2021–08–02)[2022–12–23]. https: //m.thepaper.cn/baijiahao_13855584.

3. Various Segmentations of Languages and Cultures and Great Pressure from the International Negative Public Opinion

There are 54 countries in Africa, most of which usc English, French and Portuguese as official languages. However, the African continent has also formed many languages based on its own civilization and national characteristics, which makes it difficult to communicate in the process of interaction between Chinese-funded enterprises and local systems. There are local traditional religions, Islam and Christianity in the African continent. The strong religious cultures have natural sensitivity and xenophobia[a], which puts forward higher requirements on community interaction for Chinese-funded enterprises.

Problems encountered by Chinese-funded enterprises in African community mainly include misunderstanding of local residents due to their lack of understanding of China (42.6%) and negative media coverage (24.6%)[b]. In the process of localization, Chinese enterprises are faced with the inherent ideological prejudice in the western world, but what makes it worse is that they rarely deal with local media because of their closeness.

4. Weak Supporting Conditions for Industrial Development and Insufficient Infrastructure Construction

Some African countries are still in the primary stage of industrialization and lack some natural resources. For this, the cost of production factors is relatively high. At the same time, due to the lack of supporting industrial chains, dependence on imported machinery and equipment and expensive production materials, costs for the industrial construction and production are rather high. The seriously lagging infrastructure construction of power, roads, bridges and communications has hindered the operation of Chinese-funded enterprises and increased their transportation costs. For example, the lag of infrastructure construction, and shortages of talents and funds are still bottlenecks restricting Djibouti's economic and social development. Even the introduction of a large amount of foreign capital has failed to bring the expected spillover effects.

5. Some Small and Medium-Sized Enterprises Tend to Have Short-Term Interests and Damage the Image of Chinese-funded enterprises

Many small and medium-sized enterprises tend to operate for short-term benefits. Because they have been outside the supervision of the Chinese government for a long time, it is relatively easy for them to violate laws and regulations in Africa. They produce low-priced and inferior products, damage the image of Chinese-funded enterprises, and hurt the quality recognition of

---

a Liu Yufeng, Dai Yuwei. Study on China-Africa Cooperation in Vocational Education (Chinese-English bilingual edition) [M]. Wang Juan, trans. Tianjin: Tianjin Education Press, 2022.

b Wang Heng, Zhou Xingcan, Lai Changming. China-Africa Economic and Trade Exchanges Showed Resilience, Leading China-Africa Cooperation to Mutual Benefit and Win-Win Results[N]. Guangming Daily, 2022–05–19(12).

Chinese products in Africa. In addition, enterprise administrators also need to pay attention to the relationship between Chinese employees and their local employees. They should properly handle the demands of local employees, and enhance mutual communication and understanding.

3.1.4 Severe Human Resource Bottlenecks Faced by Chinese-Funded Enterprises in Africa

Chinese-funded enterprises have experienced three major explorations, namely: going to Africa, settling in Africa and taking root in Africa. However, there are still certain difficulties in getting talents for development in the interaction with local African systems. In the process of localization, they have an increasing demand for local technical employees as the demand for management localization increases, considering labor availability and costs. They also need to provide skills training to alleviate the shortage of technical and technical talents. At the same time, due to the different technical standards between China and African cooperation countries, while the entry condition for recruitment involves the qualification certificate, the skills of local employees are quite different from the job requirements of Chinese-funded enterprises.

Chinese-funded enterprises assume the dual roles of demand driver and skill training supplier in vocational education, forming a mode of cooperation between Chinese-funded enterprises and Chinese higher vocational colleges, and an expansion mode where enterprises promote vocational education industry through carrying out relevant skills training according to their own business needs. For example, China & South Africa Technical and Vocational Education Cooperation Alliance is a typical form of cooperation between Chinese enterprises and higher vocational colleges, which gathers various forces of cooperation among higher vocational colleges, local enterprises and local governments. However, such vocational education and training carried out by enterprises based on their own business and interests tend to neglect the docking to African local education system, where problems may arise when it emphasizes the short-term training effect and neglects the long-term human resources training.

1. Shortage of Local Skilled Workers, Difficult Management and High Operating Costs

Foreign workers are strictly restricted from entering the domestic labor market in some African countries. Faced with localized management, Chinese-funded enterprises need to consider the problem of labor ratio, mainly hiring local employees. However, the local labor market lacks skilled and semi-skilled workers and managers at present. For example, skilled workers in Rwanda even need to be imported in large quantities from Kenya, Tanzania, Uganda and other countries. According to the feedback from Chinese-funded enterprises there, it is difficult to recruit local skilled workers and professionals with Chinese literacy, the cost for domestic technicians to go to Africa has increased many times during the COVID-19 pandemic, and they often face flight fuse. Therefore, there is an urgent need for vocational education to cultivate management talents and technical talents who understand Chinese products and technologies and recognize Chinese culture, in order to provide stable support for the output of the industry.

According to the survey of Chinese-funded enterprises in industrial parks in Africa, local employees and vocational school graduates need to receive second training before taking up their posts because they lack vocational skills and professionalism suitable for their jobs. Reasons include that their weak vocational skills foundation is out of touch with the actual work scene, with narrow technical knowledge and weak practical ability. Especially, these graduates usually lack knowledge related to professional background of the industry characteristics and relevant regulations and standards. In addition, due to the colonial history, local employees in some African countries are deeply influenced by the culture of the former suzerain, and thus their work scope and time limit are clearly defined. Therefore, for these Chinese-funded enterprises, they should not only rationally and meticulously allocate the work responsibilities for each post, but also allocate these work contents in advance to ensure daily production and reduce operating costs.

2. Short-term and Unsystematic Employee Training for Their Specific Aims

The local staff training carried out by Chinese-funded enterprises include self-run training institutions, entrusting domestic or local colleges to conduct employee training, on-the-job training of mentoring system, and selecting outstanding employees to train in China. For local employees, on-the-job training is mostly adopted, which is carried out through a combination of expert lectures, practical internships and field visits. This method pays more attention to the cultivation of basic vocational skills and the improvement of basic professional qualities. Although this form is flexible, easy to organize and practical, it is difficult to guarantee a good training effect and the training skills provided are only at the entry stage. This kind of internal training is usually followed by on-the-job training with mentors to quickly by satisfy job requirements. However, for jobs such as facilities and equipment operation and maintenance, which involve refined skills, higher requirements should be imposed on local employees. It is necessary for these enterprises to cooperate with vocational colleges to provide formal and systematic training. Sending outstanding employees to China for training could intuitively show Chinese standards, Chinese technologies and Chinese equipment, and thus improve the comprehensive quality and skills of local employees. But the training cost is too high and it is unstable for the pandemic.

3.2 Practices

Due to the lack of self-organized staff training by enterprises, the local vocational education system is not adaptable to the talent development needs of Chinese-funded enterprises. It is urgent for Chinese vocational colleges to cooperate with Chinese-funded enterprises to enter Africa, serve China-Africa capacity cooperation, and train technical and skilled talents who are familiar with Chinese technology and craftsmanship.

3.2.1 Basic Approach of Vocational Education Serving Production Capacity Cooperation

In the reform for modernization, China's vocational education has gained a series of experience and reached practical achievements. The common problems faced by vocational education — lack of people, money and system, have been solved by the practical paths such as cultivating "double-qualified" teachers, establishing model schools, industrial colleges and vocational education groups, engaging industrial enterprises in vocational education governance and exploring apprenticeship with Chinese characteristics.[a] These practices provide conditions for building a brand of vocational education with Chinese characteristics. However, at present, it is urgent to sort out and refine the experience, objectively explain the reasons, regularity and application conditions, and thus to improve its reproducibility and transferability. In this way they could try to solve similar problems faced by different countries[b]. Now, China's vocational education has the ability to "going global" and we should also take the opportunity of serving international production capacity cooperation to continue to improve its quality and optimize the system of school-running elements. And thus it could provide sound service for China-Africa production capacity cooperation with foreign school-enterprise cooperation.

When serving China-Africa production capacity cooperation, the Chinese vocational education should adhere to the demand orientation. They should sort out the social economic and industrial development of African cooperation countries, and the demand for technical and skilled talents of Chinese-funded enterprises in these countries. Based on this, through selecting majors with advantages and international high-quality resources, these colleges could adopt different forms of school running according to local conditions. When selecting local partners, they should choose those institutions that understand and recognize China's vocational education model, which can cope with the local adaptation. These Chinese vocational colleges could carry out special enrollment, exchange information and resources with local partners, coordinate and interact with the local national education system, and make the local partner play an active host role. Second, the types and majors of vocational education cooperation will be determined on the basis of demand-orientation. The professional standards and curriculum standards of the cooperation in running schools should be made jointly by all parties involved, such as Chinese vocational colleges, cooperative African vocational colleges, Chinese-funded enterprises in Africa, and Chinese and African government departments. The results and processes of personnel training should be under the influence of a multi-evaluation mechanism involving Chinese and African vocational education colleges and Chinese-funded enterprises. Third, with a large number of active Chinese-funded enterprises, vocational education could directly meet the needs

---

a Liu Yufeng. Objectives and Path of Internationalization of Vocational Education——Based on the Analysis of International Education Strategies in Australia, New Zealand and UK[J]. Chinese Vocational and Technical Education, 2022(12):53–62.

b Liu Yufeng. Discussion on the Construction of Vocational Education Brand with Chinese Characteristics[J]. Chinese Vocational and Technical Education, 2022(34):27–36.

of technical training and labor market. In this process, they could strengthen the participation of enterprises in this foreign school-enterprise cooperation, aiming to make these enterprises, not the ones only providing training venues and internship opportunities.

3.2.2 Practical Experience in Vocational Education Serving Production Capacity Cooperation

These Chinese-funded enterprises are also deeply involved in the process of vocational education cooperation. They participate in the whole process of personnel training, training base construction, technological skills innovation, and teaching construction and quality evaluation. College-enterprise cooperation jointly trains technical and skilled personnel, showing a variety of cooperation modes.(See Table 3–2) For details, please refer to the subsequent chapters.

Table 3–2 Models of China's Vocational Education Serving for China-Africa Production Capacity Cooperation

Countries Served	Service Mode	Cooperative Entities	Majors
Egypt	Government-Industrial Park-Enterprise-College	Tianjin Light Industry Vocational Technical College, Tianjin Transportation Technical College, Ain Shams University, Cairo Advanced Technical School for Maintenance Technology	CNC equipment application and maintenance, new energy application technology, automobile application and maintenance technology (senior level), CNC machining technology, automobile maintenance technology (secondary level)
Uganda	College-College-Enterprise-Industrial Park	Tianjin Polytechnic College, Uganda Technical College Elgon, Tiantang Group, Sino-Uganda Mbale Industrial Park	Ferrous Metallurgy Technology Mechatronics
Djibouti	Government–Government–Enterprise–College–College	Tianjin Railway Technical and Vocational College; Tianjin The First Commercial School; Djibouti Business School, China Civil Engineering Djibouti	Railway Transportation Operation Management; Railway Engineering Technology; Business; Logistics
Rwanda	Government and college–College and Enterprise–College and College	Jinhua Polytechnic; Musanze Integrated Polytechnic Regional College, Rwanda Polytechnic	E-commerce Automation
Gana	Joint Talent Cultivation and Overseas Training Program for Teachers	Weifang Vocational College, Rizhao Polytechnic, Kumasi Technical University	Mechatronics Technology, Architectural Engineering Technology

3.3 Service Models

Generally speaking, when vocational education serves China-Africa production capacity cooperation, there are various ways, which include the mature and systematic cooperation carrier such as Luban Workshop, as well as other models that are relatively flexible and have a rich variety of participants. It should take into consideration comprehensive factors such as the local characters, need priorities and cooperation stage of the African partner countries to find out an appropriate cooperation model.

3.3.1 Luban Workshop

Possible participants in China-Africa vocational education cooperation projects include Chinese vocational colleges, African institutions, Chinese-funded enterprises in Africa, Chinese industrial parks in Africa, education departments of governments, Chinese embassies in Africa, etc. The project leader-duty system could strengthen individual responsibility at all levels. The leaders at every level are responsible for specific affairs such as communication and liaison, implementation, and teaching affairs. The leaders at the top are responsible for top-level design, determining the concept of cultivating technological and skilled talents and the way of school-enterprise cooperation. Leaders at the guidance level are responsible for talent training programs, curriculum standards, staff technical level standards, etc., and those at the executive level are responsible for the specific implementation of school-enterprise cooperation plans such as teaching resource construction and training base construction and operation. The China-Africa vocational education cooperation project set up a special overall coordination body jointly by multiple participants. They determine the responsibility list mechanism, the extensive consultation and sharing mechanism and the comprehensive guarantee mechanism. The projects aim to jointly introduce talent training standards, professional standards and curriculum standards following up the new process, new technology and new standards of "going global" enterprises as well as combining the changes in the economic and social development of African countries. Participants jointly build teaching venues and training bases, equip corresponding teaching equipment, integrate resources and share information as so to improve the teaching qualities of both sides. At the management level, a series of management systems are jointly formulated by multiple parties to provide a solid institutional guarantee for the smooth operation of the project, and can also standardize the use of teaching equipment and training bases.

Luban Workshop Project is a cooperative organization established overseas to implement academic education and technical training. It takes the teaching form of the "Engineering Practice Innovation Project (EPIP)", adopting the international professional teaching standards developed by Tianjin Vocational Colleges. Relying on the high-quality competition equipment of national competitions and industrial enterprise competitions, it makes the training of teachers and the development of teaching materials and teaching resources for joint cooperative vocational colleges as its necessary guarantee.

1. The Rights, Responsibilities and Obligations of Chinese Vocational Colleges

Chinese vocational colleges are mainly responsible for providing specific construction plans for Luban workshop, taking the overall lead in promoting the standard construction and operation of Luban workshop. They are responsible for organizing the team to formulate training programs, professional standards and curriculum standards. They should prepare teaching facilities, share and develop teaching resources, and carry out teacher training and skills training. Their work also includes summarizing and making timely adjustments. The aim is that the foreign partners could independently operate the school and fulfill teaching and training, while the Chinese side is responsible for guiding and supervising to achieve sustainable operation.

At the operational level, firstly the Chinese side needs to build a communication mechanism. It aims to enhance technical exchanges and sharing through communication between Chinese and African teaching staff. With this mechanism, the two sides could utilize various resources in a sound way and review education and teaching experience and problems. It also could realize aligning with enterprises in terms of new processes, new technologies, new standards, and talent demand scale and quality through communication. The second is to build an evaluation system of indicators. This system should assign weights according to the importance while taking into account the overall, sustainable, systematic and summarizable nature of the projects. They also establish a dynamic monitoring index system to achieve quarterly dynamic adjustment. This evaluation system will comprehensively evaluate all aspects of the operation and management of the cooperation projects, focusing on evaluations on the achievements of students, enterprises response, social influence and other dimensions back to the whole process of talent training. Chinese vocational colleges can give full play to the advantages of talents and techniques. They could hold academic education and carry out staff training in line with the talent needs of Chinese-funded enterprises, as well as provide technical support services and consulting on operation and equipment maintenance for these enterprises. They could assist these enterprises in formulating post grade standards, and assist African countries in formulating vocational qualification standards.

2. The Rights, Responsibilities and Obligations of Local Vocational Colleges

Local vocational colleges are mainly responsible for teaching venues and infrastructure. They should arrange student recruitment and teaching. They also should send a group of teachers with relevant professional backgrounds to participate in teacher training and then teach. Their work still includes to assist Chinese corresponds to formulate relevant talent training models, talent training programs, curriculum standards and develop teaching materials according to local education and teaching standards. At the same time, local vocational institutions need to maintain smooth communication with Chinese partners and adjust the operation of the Luban workshop according to the actual situation. They work to keep the assets and equipment and should regularly inspect and keep maintenance of the equipment for the safety of the assets.

3. Rights, Responsibilities and Obligations of Chinese-Funded Enterprises in Africa

These enterprises are mainly responsible for providing training base venues, and jointly building professional standards and resources. They will assist in the construction of venues and teaching equipment and instruments. They work to coordinate all parties such as recommending enterprises and entrepreneurs, providing internships and employment, and guiding training.

At the specific operation level, Chinese-funded enterprises need to assist in completing customs clearance and transportation of training equipment, and provide as much help and support as possible for teachers and managers of Chinese vocational colleges. At the same time, it is necessary for them to discuss the majors setting with cooperative colleges considering the talent capability the host countries need, production practice ability and new processes, new technologies, new ideas and new standards of industries. They also should assist in formulating relevant personnel cultivating models and training programs. It is necessary to assist Chinese vocational colleges in the construction of the Luban Workshop, such as purchasing decoration materials, carrying out basic decoration, providing corresponding teaching equipment, installing and debugging, etc., and the completed Luban Workshop can be used as a staff training base. It is necessary for them to provide the support of personnel, training equipment and places for the construction of teaching resources of cooperative colleges, and assist Chinese vocational colleges to carry out the training of local teaching staff.

3.3.2 Other Models

Compared with the fixed and mature model of Luban Workshop, other models are more flexible and changeable, serving a wider range of people within a wider radius. Taking its own professional training advantages as an important breakthrough, Chinese vocational colleges have established an increasingly professional and systematic training system. They conveyed the value concept of Chinese vocational education, and shared Chinese standards, technologies and services. Other forms of VET cooperation between Chinese vocational institutions and Africa include overseas school building, joint training programs for specialized talents, training programs for overseas teachers, short-term technical training programs, and assistance in the construction of vocational education institutions and educational infrastructure.

1. Overseas School Building and Joint Training Programs for Specialized Talents

Relying on the "Future of Africa — a project for China-Africa cooperation on vocational education", Chinese vocational colleges continue to deepen China-Africa vocational education cooperation with the help of high-quality resources from various cooperation alliances, as well as taking overseas school building and joint training programs for special talent as important tools.

In 2016, Jinhua Polytechnic signed a contract with the Ministry of Labor of Rwanda to set up an overseas branch school in Musanze, a Northern province. This is Musanze Integrated Polytechnic Regional College. Facing the industrial layout of the key development of Rwanda, Jinhua Polytechnic took the lead to "going global" with the breakthroughs of the two advantageous majors of e-commerce and automation. It has explored the Jinhua Polytechnic Model of the collaborative vocational education program in the form of a synergistic mechanism of "government-school, school-enterprise, school-school". Similarly, Weifang Vocational College cooperated with Uganda Petroleum Training Institute in 2018 to build a technical training center in Uganda, transferring teaching equipment and sharing high-quality teaching resources. These vocational colleges are catering to the manpower needs of Chinese-funded enterprises in Africa that are "going global", systematically cultivating internationalized specialists and effectively promoting technology transfer.

Joint training programs for specialized talents are mostly aimed at special professional fields, cultivating technical and skilled talents for host industries. They are featured in a fast, effective, flexible and targeted way. Weifang Vocational College, Rizhao Polytechnic College and Kumasi Technical University in Ghana have adopted the "1+2+1" mode to carry out joint cultivation projects for students majoring in mechatronics technology and construction engineering technology, which effectively responds to the demand for human resources in the initial stage of Ghana's infrastructural construction and industrialization, as well as the requirements of Chinese enterprises. Tianjin Railway Technical and Vocational College serves the Addis Ababa-Djibouti railway, a "Belt and Road" landmark project, providing six-month skills training for 100 employees of the Djibouti Railway Company for four majors, including railway engineering, railway signaling, rolling stock maintenance and railway transportation, in 2015. The practice of running schools coordinated at the national level has been highly recognized by the Ministry of Transportation of Djibouti and Djibouti Railway Company, and it has explored the sustainable development of localized talent cultivation.

2. Overseas Training Programs for Teachers

Chinese vocational colleges use overseas training or technical guidance for teachers to improve their partners' teaching standards. This practice conveys the concepts of Chinese VET, and has assisted the implementation of a number of national standards. For example, Weifang Vocational College hosted the first "Training for Managers and Key Teachers of African Vocational Colleges", providing online and offline training for teachers of Kumasi University of Technology in Ghana. The project has upgraded the practical training and professional and technical skills of 25 people, including leaders, teaching staff and leaders of relevant majors of these Ghanaian colleges, involving theoretical knowledge, cutting-edge professional and technical skills, educational concepts, teaching methods, curriculum design and evaluation, etc. It has also sent three teachers specializing in electromechanical and automobile to Ghana to conduct technical training on computer drawing, CNC lathes and other skills for teachers at the Kumasi University of Technology and other colleges and universities, expanding the extent and scale of cooperation between China and Africa in vocational education.

3. Short-term Technical Training Programs

Short-term technical training programs are mostly targeted at areas in short supply in the host countries, with a view to promoting the know-how transfer and upgrading the skills of local personnel. In Djibouti, Chinese vocational colleges have organized training and teaching resource-building activities, including training courses on the railroad industry, maintenance and repair of monitoring equipment, IT engineering, railroad operation technology, maintenance of bridges and pavements, and administrative management. The vocational education and training project between Wuhan, China, and Entebbe, Uganda trained 40 Ugandan trainees in the fields of pre-school education, tourism service skills, automobile maintenance, aquaculture, solar power generation (maintenance and repairs) and e-commerce. It has become an important element of the friendly exchanges between the Wuhan Municipal People's Government and the Municipality of Entebbe.

4. Assistance in Building Vocational Education Institutions and Teaching Infrastructure

There are other forms for China-Africa cooperation in VET, such as assistance for the construction of vocational education institutions, vocational education and training upgrading projects, and assistance for vocational education and training equipment and infrastructure, all of which have helped to provide better facilities for the development of vocational education in the host countries. In 2014, China assisted in the construction of an upgrade project for the Ghana Vocational and Technical College, providing assistance for educational infrastructure, and completed the project to upgrade Vocational Education and Training Center in Ghana in 2022. The project has been provided by a Chinese-funded enterprise involving the construction of one examination center and 15 training centers for vocational colleges and the provision of assistance for modernized vocational education and training equipment for 5 specialties, namely machining, electrical and electronic engineering, welding, automobile repair and civil engineering. The project has been widely recognized by the leaders of the two countries for its assistance in capacity building, industrial development and economic transformation of the partner countries in Africa.

3.4 Service Achievements

Under the framework of the "Belt and Road" Initiative and the Forum on China-Africa Cooperation, a series of innovative and exploratory actions of vocational education, schools and enterprises to "going global" have been formed to serve China-Africa production capacity cooperation, such as Luban workshops, talent joint training programs for talents and overseas teachers to achieve the synergy of the system chain, knowledge chain and production chain to provide a strong human resource guarantee for China-Africa production capacity cooperation. Especially in Africa, Luban Workshop has become a "bridgehead" for the integration of international industry and education between China and Africa, providing technical and talent support for the development needs of Chinese enterprises in Africa.

3.4.1 Nurturing Local Technical and Skilled Talents to Provide Human Resource Support for Chinese-Funded Enterprises

As of now, the Luban Workshop, talent joint training projects, and overseas teacher training projects have trained a large number of local technical and skilled talents in related fields based on the development needs of China's industries among African partners, effectively improving the professional and technical skills of African youth and achieving sustainable development of localized talents. At the same time, the cooperation in vocational education between China and Africa attaches great importance to the cultivation of high-quality teachers. They have held multiple teacher training exchanges and themed lectures to introduce advanced teaching concepts, methods, and resources to teachers from African countries, enhance the international teaching ability, equipment operation ability, and vocational skills training ability of local teachers, and also strongly support the implementation of professional teaching standards. In addition, the cooperation will benefit the talent development needs of Chinese-funded enterprises in Africa by recording and broadcasting course-teaching videos in various professions.(See Table 3–3)

Table 3–3 Achievements of Vocational Education Serving for China-Africa Production Capacity Cooperation

Major Educational Institutions	Internationalized Professional Teaching Standards	Curriculum Resources/Educational Teaching Resources	Talent Cultivation Scale
Egypt Luban Work-shop Partnering with: Tianjin Light Industry Vocational Technical College	The internationalized professional teaching standards for five majors has been developed: CNC equipment application and maintenance, new energy application technology, automotive operation and maintenance technology, CNC machining technology, and automotive repair technology.	1. The establishment of 5 training labs that reflect international advanced levels, and 11 sets of comprehensive training equipment have been completed; 2.A complete set of virtual simulation systems that are at the forefront domestically has been sharing, creating an integrated "virtual-simulation-real" teaching and training system; 3. Twelve course standards has been developed and 12 bilingual textbooks has been published.	Training tasks or over one thousand people has been completed.

continued

Major Educational Institutions	Internationalized Professional Teaching Standards	Curriculum Resources/Educational Teaching Resources	Talent Cultivation Scale
Uganda Luban Workshop Partnering with: Tianjin Polytechnic College	The majors of mechatronics technology and Blacksmithing technology have obtained local certification and recognized within the local education system.	Internationalized curriculum standards for 9 core courses have been achieved, with a total of 9 bilingual textbooks and 1 bilingual training textbook published.	Forty-five African employees has been trained for Uganda Tiantang Group, whose satisfaction rate is over 80% regarding the equipment and training at the Luban workshop.
Djibouti Luban Workshop Partnering with: Tianjin Railway Technical and Vocational College	The majors of railway engineering technology, and railway Traffic operation and management have been certified by the Ministry of Education in Djibouti. Additionally, the majors of commerce and logistics have received the confirmation letter for Secondary Vocational and higher vocational education in the fields of commerce and logistics from the Ministry of National Education and Vocational Training in Djibouti.	A total of 150 internationalized standards, textbooks, and practical training guidebooks have been compiled, out of which 3 textbooks have been officially published, and online resources of 1,412 class hours have been developed and recorded.	The training has involved 148 students and 69 teachers. It has also benefited over 800 employees with a projected impact on over 2,000 employees during the advancement phase.
Jinhua Polytechnic	The Teaching Standards for E-commerce Majors (Level 6–7) and Teaching Standards for Electrical Automation Technology Majors (Level 6–7) have been locally certified and have been incorporated into the education qualification framework system in Rwanda.	1. A Moodle course learning platform has been established, providing dedicated learning services on the "learning in the Jinhua Polytechnic" APP for international college students. 2. Resources developed include 36 bilingual courses, 16 bilingual textbooks core teachers, and 9 skill training packages.	Approximately 5,000 people have received urgently needed vocational skills training in the local area; and more than 43 backbone teachers have been trained and cultivated.
Weifang Vocational College	Internationalized Course Standards for Mechatronics category have been achieved.	A "one-on-one" training program for African vocational colleges administrators and backbone teachers has been completed.	Training of 30 students majoring in Mechatronics and architecture has been completed. And more than 100 individuals have been trained in operating specialized equipment related to the respective professions.

3.4.2 Building a New Platform for School-Enterprise Cooperation to Serve the New Development Needs of Chinese-Funded Enterprises in Africa

Luban Workshop has established a new platform for sustainable development through school-enterprise cooperation, where schools and enterprises jointly develop talent cultivation plans. Enterprises directly participate in the entire process of talent cultivation, achieving the integration of course contents and professional standards, as well as the integration of teaching and production processes. Schools and enterprises jointly build training and employment bases, expand new internship and employment fields, and create new cooperative education models. The current exploration and practice of Luban Workshop have better achieved the integration of industry and education, making it a "bridgehead" to serve and support Chinese-Funded enterprises in "going global". For example, Uganda Luban Workshop trained 45 African employees for Uganda Tiantang Group in 2022, and their satisfaction with Luban Workshop's equipment and training reached over 80%, effectively supporting the training for technical and skilled talents and human operation construction of Chinese-funded enterprises in Africa.

The establishment of the Luban Workshop Industry Education Integration Development Alliance has expanded the professional construction of the Luban Workshop, reflecting the close cooperation of the newly added Luban Workshop. Following the basic principle of "joint construction and promotion, and sharing achievements", it has gathered national, non-profit cooperative organizations and other forces involving enterprises, universities, scientific research institutions, and social organizations to go out. Also, it explores and deepens the international production and education integration development model of Luban Workshop that "serves the construction of the 'Belt and Road', assists enterprises in overseas development, and expands school cooperation space", thus providing a platform and resource support for the high-quality sustainable development of Luban Workshop, as well as skilled personnel training and technological innovation services for overseas development of Chinese-funded enterprises in Africa.

3.4.3 Fostering Mutual Understanding and Recognition to Facilitate the Entry of Chinese-Funded Enterprises into Africa

The effectiveness of Luban Workshop's joint talent training programs in Africa and overseas teacher training programs has been recognized, supported and appreciated by the Chinese Embassy in Africa, and has won high praise from the principals of the local partner colleges and the mainstream media at home and abroad.

By sharing professional and technical standards, conducting training for local teachers assisting in the construction of modern vocational college training centers, and providing modern vocational education and training equipment, these vocational education cooperation projects have improved African vocational education capacity in both hardware and software, and promoted the local school-enterprise cooperation and the integration of industry and education in African countries to a new height. In the process of "going global" according to professional standards and the national education system of African partner countries, local educators can truly feel the concept of Chinese vocational education and China's advantages, thus enhancing the image of Chinese products and Chinese-funded enterprises in Africa. For example, the Luban Workshop in Djibouti assists local vocational schools in establishing technical and management standards required for the development of railway and commercial industries, and helps Djibouti Business School to establish a railway and commercial higher vocational education system and vocational skill appraisal system suitable for the country. Luban Workshop in Egypt is the first to establish two different levels of Luban workshop in one country, forming a progressive training model for the integration of vocational and secondary education.

These vocational education cooperation projects are not only conducive to enhancing the positive understanding of Chinese vocational education, Chinese products, Chinese technology, and Chinese-funded enterprises among African countries, but also provide a bridge for serving Chinese enterprises entering Africa, for example, taking advantage of the opportunity of the Egypt Luban Work Industry Education Integration Work Conference to carry out Cloud Investment Promotion Meetings. After the meeting, ten companies expressed their intention to invest in Egypt on the spot. The convening of the Egypt Luban Workshop in Education-Industry Cooperation—New Energy Chinese-Funded Enterprises' Investment Inspection and Negotiation Conference in Egypt, aims to build a bridge for Chinese enterprises interested in investing in Egypt, achieving the integration of industry and education.

3.5 Service Challenges

At present, the service awareness and service ability of vocational education for China-Africa production capacity cooperation are still slightly insufficient, and the overall layout is still lacking, so the mechanism and platform centering on the integration of international industry and education between China and Africa have not been completely established. The main manifestation is that the vocational education cooperation between China-Africa vocational colleges and Chinese-funded enterprises is limited to projects, and the depth and breadth of cooperation need to be improved.

3.5.1 Problems of Adaptability of Local Adaptation in Cross-Border School-Enterprise Cooperation

Based on the practice of China-Africa production capacity cooperation in vocational education services mentioned above, it can be found that the current cooperation between foreign schools and enterprises is still in the exploratory pilot stage. From the current local practice in Africa, there is still a lack of formal, systematic, and campus-oriented vocational education. The depth and breadth of school-enterprise cooperation and industry-education integration still need to be improved. For example, the key deployment industries in Egypt do not have a high degree of matching with the majors offered by vocational education institutions. This virtual state of industry-education integration makes it difficult for vocational college graduates to fully support the development of enterprises. Djibouti's vocational education cooperation projects and teaching resource construction are still in the initial stage of exploration, and the goal of talent cultivation is not yet clear. Enterprises lack awareness of participating talent cultivation in vocational college, and participation in curriculum development is also limited because of lacking deep and effective support. There is no specialized system to support communication and coordination between schools and enterprises. The serious disconnect between vocational colleges and the labor market in Rwanda has resulted in a significant mismatch between the actual demand for skills by enterprises and the skills provided by vocational colleges. Due to insufficient financial resources, vocational colleges are unable to hire highly skilled trainers, lack necessary resources and equipment, and lack effective supply and updating of skills, making it difficult to cultivate digital literacy skills. The attractiveness of vocational education in Uganda is weak, and the quality of training is not recognized, which makes it difficult for Chinese vocational colleges to enter the local market. The outdated education system makes it difficult to make up for the huge gap in skilled talents in the existing industrial structures. The vocational education cooperation projects in Ghana are still relatively scattered and have not formed a joint force. The cooperation between schools and enterprises outside the region is limited to projects, and the depth of cooperation needs to be improved.

3.5.2 Challenges in Leveraging School-Enterprise Cooperation to Support China-Africa Production Capacity Cooperation

1. Lack of Theoretical Guidance and Government Operational Rules

Domestic vocational colleges have insufficient experience in international education and are in the stage of deep exploration of overseas education. They lack targeted theoretical guidance of abstract concepts and government implementation rules. The lack of theoretical research has constrained the pace of China's vocational education's "going global", resulting in a lack of theoretical guidance. The relevant policies on the internationalization of vocational education are clearly insufficient, resulting in a lack of comprehensive plans and operational implementation rules for "going global" in various universities. In terms of communication channels, equipment sharing, and cooperation mechanisms, cooperation between Chinese vocational colleges and Chinese-funded enterprises requires government's specific operational rules to guide both parties to jointly "going global".

2. Overall Management and Top-level Design is Insufficient, with Funds Scattered and Underutilized

At present, there is no specialized and unified management agency established to coordinate the cooperation between China and Africa in vocational education. Instead, it is managed by multiple departments such as the Ministry of Commerce, the Ministry of Foreign Affairs, the

Ministry of Education, the Bureau of Economic Cooperation and the Scholarship Council. This can easily lead to negative phenomena such as departmental segmentation, management gaps, or multi-management that may compromise the overall and coherent cooperation, and even undermine the educational synergy formed by the current China-African vocational education cooperation.

African vocational education resources are widely distributed but scattered, and independent breakthroughs are sought among various vocational colleges, but there is a lack of normalized cooperation and exchange mechanisms between colleges. Overseas education still faces vastly different external environment and education systems, making it difficult to effectively integrate the strength of colleges and universities to form a vocational education brand with Chinese characteristic.

3. Insufficient Support in the Guarantee System for Serving China's Vocational Colleges' "Going Global"

Due to differences in economic developments, legal systems, business practices, technical rules, and other aspects among target countries in African cooperation, the supporting measures for vocational education serving China African production capacity cooperation are relatively insufficient. Firstly, there is insufficient policy support in the countries, like relevant supportive policies for investing funds and equipment overseas to support vocational education's "going global", seriously constraining the internationalization of vocational education. Secondly, the funding guarantee mechanism is insufficient. Overseas education projects led by enterprises or vocational colleges often face problems such as large initial investment, long construction cycles, and poor sustainability due to the shortage of strategic project funding. Thirdly, the platform support is not enough, and the introduction and participation of domestic vocational colleges' platforms are insufficient, which restricts the high quality and efficient promotion of overseas education. Fourthly, the intellectual property protection mechanism is not perfect, especially the protection of relevant intellectual property rights in the construction and operation process of Luban Workshop, a national vocational education brand, which is slightly insufficient.

4. Unclear Rights, Responsibilities and Obligations of Relevant Parties in Cooperation, and Insufficient Interaction with Local Systems

In the initial stage of the construction and operation of the Luban Workshop, most of the agreements signed between vocational colleges and cooperative Chinese-funded enterprises were letters of intent, meaning that the purpose of cooperation was only to cultivate local technical and skilled talents who met the requirements of the cooperative enterprise, without conducting a comprehensive cooperation layout. At the same time, there is less consideration of the interests of enterprises, less exploration of the common interests of both sides, and the lack of clear elaboration of the rights and obligations of Chinese-funded enterprises in cooperation, which leads to the insufficient role of enterprises in running colleges and affects the enthusiasm of enterprises to participate in projects. The lack of awareness of enterprise participation causes the lack of depth and effectiveness in supporting professional construction and curriculum development. Due to the different orientation of cooperation interests and the lack of special incentive mechanism to support school-enterprise cooperation, only the human resources department contact or send personnel to participate in communication and coordination in the short term, the school-enterprise cooperation to build teaching resources is stuck in a shallow level.

Due to the lack of international education experience and international vision, and immature international thinking, vocational colleges have an incomplete understanding of the laws, regulations and industrial-economic development of the target countries of vocational education cooperation in Africa, and their shortcomings are prominent compared with "going global" Chinese-funded enterprises. Most of the "going global" vocational colleges that consider the cooperation demands of both Chinese and African institutions, do not have a clear understanding of the needs of Chinese-funded enterprises in the target countries. They do not cooperate with local enterprises and not accurately connect with the local development needs of African countries. Most of them have not established interactive mechanisms for in-depth cooperation with trans-regional organizations, local international organizations and regional organizations.

5. Imperfect Local Vocational Education System, Leading to Difficulties in Introducing Vocational Education into Africa

Due to the limitations of economic development and education development in African countries, vocational education in the post-basic education stage is facing numerous difficulties. Firstly, the education funds used for vocational education are significantly lower than those for higher education, far lower than those for basic education, and unable to meet the domestic development needs of African cooperation partners. Secondly, the scale of vocational education in the target countries is small, with a small number of higher vocational colleges, serious shortages of teaching equipment, textbooks, and other teaching resources. The teaching teams and enterprises lack practical experience, the channels for capacity improvement are not smooth, and the rights and interests of teachers often cannot be guaranteed. Thirdly, the curriculum is developed by a committee composed of all stakeholders. Local vocational colleges lack the right to speak and have limited practicality in curriculum content, causing low flexibility. The standards for talent cultivation are seriously disconnected from local enterprise standards and the professional settings are not well-matched with regional industrial needs. Fourthly, the vocational education system and vocational qualification framework of African partner countries are not perfect enough, and the channel between vocational education and general education has not yet been established.

Chapter Ⅳ

Theoretical Research on Vocational Education Serving China-Africa Production Capacity Cooperation

Vocational education serving China-Africa production capality cooperation not only involves the internal tension of the optimization of the elements system of overseas vocational education, but also includes the external subdivision requirements of international production capacity cooperation for this field. Therefore, this section will start with education internationalization theory, industrial transfer theory, global value chain theory, and symbiosis theory to analyze the internal logic of Vocational education serving China-Africa production capality cooperation.

4.1 Theory of Internationalization in Education

The most relevant theory of vocational education serving for China-Africa production capacity cooperation is the internationalization of vocational education, which is an important part of the internationalization of education. Therefore, analyzing from the perspective of education internationalization theory is conducive to a profound understanding of the internal driving force and innovative practical patterns of optimizing the overseas education elements system of Chinese vocational colleges.

4.1.1 Overview of Internationalization in Education

According to the *Dictionary of Education*, the internationalization of education refers to the trend of communication, discussion, and collaboration among countries around the world since World War II to solve common problems faced by educational development. It emphasizes the use of a cross-border, cross-cultural, and global perspective to view and examine the functions and goals of education, and promotes the interaction and integration of multiple elements of education, thereby promoting the common development of education worldwide. The internationalization of education is caused by economic globalization, reflecting the two-way needs of China's education reform and development, as well as international education exchanges and cooperation. The manifestations of education internationalization include cooperation in running schools, hiring experts, exchanges and cooperation between governments and schools, exchanges of students, cooperation with international organizations, introduction of foreign educational theories and translation of academic works, running schools outside the borders, training of international talents, etc. However, In the process of cultural and educational integration, there is an inevitably conflict between foreign culture and local culture, as well as the anxiety of local culture being soaked by foreign culture[a]. Nowadays, with the acceleration of globalization, the internationalization of education has greatly expanded in terms of educational perspective, participating members, activity contents, communication forms, driving subjects, institutional rule and value pursuit. It has shown an overall development trend from small-scale, single-dimensional and shallow to large-scale, all-round and deep-seated. The basic role of education in human development, the universal problems faced by education and the special problems in the process of education internationalization are highlighted, and the common value of education, the common responsibility of global education and the common interests of international education are more focused[b].

The concept and connotation of internationalization of vocational education vary in different languages and contextual conditions. Firstly, we need to determine the conceptual boundary of the internationalization of vocational education discussed in this section, which is to leave the perspective of a single country, in order to determine the common themes of vocational education internationalization research in different institutional backgrounds of different language countries. In such international studies, informal education and training need to be taken into account in addition to the usual vocational education, education in the acquisition of vocational qualifications or education and training in the field of work. But if international vocational education involves different educational systems and organizational structures, does it have systematic comparative significance? Hörner (1996) explained the possibility of comparing different systems, believing that there is comparability and comparative value between two things, not in structural similarity, but in a certain relationship established between two variables, but this relationship does not conflict with the establishment of similarity. Therefore, the prerequisite for comparability is to find meaningful comparison criteria. In this chapter, this article will review the main contribution of German and English Speaking Countries, as the main promotion countries, they did a lot for the internationalization of vocational education. It will find a communication bridge between the two languages and establish a Chinese conceptual context for the internationalization of vocational education.

---

a Gu Mingyuan. Internationalization and Localization of Education. [J]. Journal of Central China Normal University (Humanities and Social Sciences Edition), 2011, 50 (06): 123–127.

b Zhang Junzong. Internationalization of Education: An Important Force in Building a Community with a Shared Future for Mankind. [J]. Higher Education Management, 2020, 14 (02): 21–28+36

Under the advocacy of several major German vocational education and international cooperation departments in German-speaking country, the concept of "Internationalization of Vocational Education and Training" (IBBF) has been established, and the concept and research significance have been fully recognized. In recent years, multiple funding projects on this topic have been promoted and extensive international cooperation has been carried out. The Federal Ministry of Education and Research (BMBF) proposed in the document that research on the internationalization of vocational education will focus on achieving three objectives: (1) Promoting the practical refinement and professional knowledge acquisition of universities and other institutions in international vocational training projects; (2) Integrating relevant professional knowledge more closely into BMBF's international vocational training cooperation projects; (3) Enabling international partners to obtain research results to promote a shift towards more practical vocational education and training. To this end, BMBF has promoted 11 international partner programs for vocational education in Europe, Central America, South Africa and Asia, attempting to establish a systematic and cross-national research network to achieve the goal of international promotion of vocational education. In a series of activities aimed at promoting the internationalization of vocational education, the concept of "internationalization" is no longer based on the conceptual connotations of vocational education and training, but also involves a broader diplomatic level of funding significance. Tran et al. (Tran, Dempsey, 2017) proposed that the internationalization of vocational education should not only be understood as a response to external challenges, but also as a national strategic product. In addition to international aid projects, German vocational education internationalization services should participate in cooperation with international organizations to serve the economic and cultural motivations of national development. Frommberger et al. (2020) proposed that the concept of internationalization of vocational education should include three levels: determining the main driving forces of domestic vocational education, adjusting the content of vocational education in the context of economic globalization, and conducting international cooperation in vocational education. At present, Germany's research on the internationalization of vocational education mainly focuses on six themes: international cooperation and development of vocational education, international policy (mode) transfer in vocational education, regional cooperation and governance in vocational education, vocational education research in the context of service-oriented education, vocational education research in the context of enterprises, and research networks on vocational education internationalization (Gessler et al., 2020).

In the context of English-speaking countries, "internationalization of vocational education" usually refers to the concept of symbiosis with international students or globalization or labor markets in similar contexts. (Altbach, Knight, 2007; Marginson, 2007; OECD, 2012; Tran, 2008, 2013) The international enterprises that crosses national economic boundaries and the multicultural labor world have given rise to the emergence of internationalization of vocational education. Australia's Going Global (2013) strategy points out that the development of a knowledge-based economy and globalization requires students to have a global perspective and multiculturalism, and the job mobility of young workers is enhanced. This international educational activity occurs simultaneously in the fields of higher education and vocational education. Internationalized education requires the absorption and cultivation of domestic and foreign students, the improvement of international training programs, the promotion of global mobility of employees, the realization of cross-cultural exchanges with international partners and institutions, and the promotion of multi-dimensional dynamic connections with industrial partners to achieve interactive exchanges with more developing countries. In English-speaking countries, the concepts of internationalization and international mobility were already used as early as the colonial period in the 18th century. For example, in educational activities, Britain emphasized that civic education and student development in colonial countries should be global. In the trend of neoliberal market economy, there were a large number of international education aid programs for vocational and higher education in the past 30 years (Rizvi 2009). Knight et al. (Knight, de Wit, 1997) proposed that economic, political, socio-cultural and academic factors have promoted the internationalization of education, which has humanitarian, developmental, cooperative and trade characteristics. The internationalization of education in English-speaking countries attempts to view this internationalization as a market-oriented trade activity. The internationalization of education in English-speaking countries is usually achieved through international cooperation or agreements, based on the principle of market dominance (Marginson, 2007; Mattews, Sidhu, 2005). In English-speaking countries such as Australia and the United States, the internationalization of vocational education emphasizes cultivating students in a globalized platform to possess international and multicultural work abilities (Tran et al., 2014). In the 1980s, Australia launched its first internationalization plan for vocational education, the Colombo Plan, which introduced a large number of international scholars into the fields of technical education and continuing education (Raby et al., 2014). As a symbol of the nationalization of vocational education in Australia, this plan was replaced by the "Overseas Student Policy" in 1985, a more practical policy for internationalization of education (Hall, 2011). As a new trend, the internationalization of vocational education will cultivate more flexible and skilled labor forces for developing countries.

In the consensus of this interactive learning society, more English-speaking countries have exported their own vocational education models and carried out international partnership activities for vocational education. In 2012, public vocational education institutions in Australia exported 533 international vocational education projects, involving over 70,000 students. There are negative doubts in the international community about the export model of vocational education internationalization in English-speaking countries from the perspective of neocolonialism (Australian Government, 2012). In this model, the curriculum simply copies the vocational education institution system of the exporting country to the teaching staff who teaches the students of the importing country, without actually considering the needs and cultural differences of the importing country. This "donation" program is not effective in improving the skills and employment protection of the labor force in the importing country, and has many negative impacts (Steiner Khamsi, 2004). In recent years, more scholars from English-speaking countries have been discussing how this "aid" should be changed (Steiner Khamsi, Waldow, 2012; Leask, 2004; Shams, Huisman, 2012).

4.1.2 Examination of Vocational Education Serving China-Africa Production Capacity Cooperation

A joint study by officials and scholars from the Ministry of Education has pointed out that the practical basis for the internationalization of vocational education in China is reflected in the need to support the implementation of the country's opening-up strategy, promote the high-quality development of vocational education, and establish and consolidate different types of education. Chinese opening-up policy of vocational education is highly in line with the development needs of vocational education in African countries, which is reflected in the role of compulsory tools, the improvement of regulatory tool systems, the use of diversified mixed tools, the highlighting the effectiveness of market tools and so on[a]. Therefore, the internationalization of vocational education should follow the three basic principles, including two directions of "top-level design" and "grassroots innovation", two ways of "rule-making" and "following rules", and two axes in "bringing in" and "going global"[b]. Based on the theoretical foundation and foreign practices of the internationalization of vocational education, the following measures are required: the formulation of a systematic and scientific strategic development plan, the establishment and improvement of specialized policies and regulations to promote the internationalization of vocational education, the implementation of a guarantee and support system. These measures are good for promoting the internationalization of vocational education, and the establishment of a scientific and effective quality evaluation system with diversified participation for the internationalization of vocational education[c].

In the process of "going global" of Chinese vocational colleges and serving China-Africa production capacity cooperation, a series of innovative and exploratory actions have been formed. More strengthen has been placed on integrating various forces to go out, realizing the optimization of the overseas education system of Chinese vocational colleges, and providing

---

a Wang Xinxin, Ding Hengxin. Research on China's Vocational Education Opening-up Policy towards Africa [J] China Vocational and Technical Education, 2022 (30): 52–59

b Qiu Yi, He Zhengying, Yang Yong. Steadily Promoting the Internationalization of Vocational Education: Fundamentals, Adherence and Reference [J] China Vocational and Technical Education, 2022 (29):34–41

c Shi Weiping. Improving the Internationalization and International Competitiveness of Vocational Education: Strategic Focus and Specific Strategies [J] Modern Education Management, 2018(01):72–76. DOI: 10.16697/j.cnki.xdjygl2018.01.012

strong human resources guarantee for China-Africa production capacity cooperation with the coordination of institutional chain, knowledge chain and production chain. It also explored and deepened the international development model of integrating industry and education to serve the building of the "Belt and Road". The Luban Workshop, the talent training programs for talents and oversea teachers have trained a large number of local technical and skilled talents in related majors, improved the ability of vocational education to serve the "Belt and Road", and promoted the social and economic development of cooperative countries around the domestic industry development needs of African partners and the needs of African industrial parks. Especially in the African Luban workshop, a new platform has been established for sustainable development through school-enterprise cooperation, and innovative school-enterprise cooperation education models have been developed to achieve the integration of industry and education and to serve and support Chinese-funded enterprises in Africa.

The practical form of the Luban Workshop has achieved the overall sharing of China's vocational education program in Africa, and its advocated concepts and educational experience are widely recognized by the international community. On the basis of grasping the needs of Chinese-funded enterprises, in Africa, Luban Workshop is guided by the sharing of professional course standards to promote the profound construction of professional connotation and teaching resources. By cultivating high-quality teachers and supporting the implementation of professional teaching standards with African partner countries, we aim to enhance their vocational education capabilities and levels, and promote capacity building as well. For example, the Egypt Luban Workshop became the first to establish two different levels of Luban workshops in a country, carrying out a progressive training model for the integration of higher vocational education and secondary vocational education. The Egypt Luban Workshop completed the international professional teaching standards for five majors: CNC Equipment Application and Maintenance, New Energy Application Technology, Automotive Application and Maintenance Technology, CNC Machining Technology and Automotive Maintenance Technology. The Luban Workshop in Uganda has completed international professional teaching standards for two majors: Mechatronics Integration Technology and Ferrous Metallurgy Technology, and incorporated them into the local education system. Such achievements of vocational education serving of China-Africa production capacity cooperation reflect the significant improvement of the internationalization of China's vocational education and the level of vocational education overseas, thus sharing China's vocational education brand and China's vocational education standards, and expanding the international influence of China's vocational education opening to the outside world.

4.2 Theory of International Industrial Transfer

4.2.1 Overview of the Theory of International Industrial Transfer

The broad connotation of industrial transfer refers to the overall restructuring of the spatial location of industries due to the comparative advantages and disadvantages among different countries or regions. The narrow connotation emphasizes the behavior of enterprises to detach and transfer some production functions from the original location based on cost-benefit analysis[a]. Currently, the theory of international industrial transfer is mainly based on the perspectives of industry, enterprises, or countries, revealing the inherent laws of national industrial transfer[b].

Research on the theory of international industrial transfer from the perspective of industry mainly involves the theories of flying geese pattern, product life cycle, marginal industry expansion, and labor-intensive industry transfer. The theory of the flying geese pattern was proposed by Japanese scholar Akamatsu Yoichi and was used to explain the international industrial transfer trend of Asian countries with East Asia as the core. Its core viewpoint is that the typical industrial development mode of backward countries is "import-domestic production-export", which is similar to the formation of a flying geese pattern. The product life cycle theory was proposed by Raymond. Vemon, and its core viewpoint is that a complete product life cycle includes four stages: innovation, development, maturity and decline. Due to the different stages of industrial production, the different emphasis on production factors is different, it is necessary to transfer product production among countries with different levels of factor abundance[c]. For example, when the product is in the mature stage, it can be considered to transfer out through technology transfer or direct investment. The theory of marginal industry expansion was proposed by Kiyoshi Kojima, and its core viewpoint is that foreign direct investment should be carried out in the industries that are already or about to fall into comparative disadvantages in the home country. Industrial investment in developing countries should focus on comparative costs and their variability and shift sequentially from technologies with small technology gaps and easy transfer[d]. For example, Japanese manufacturing is carried out in the order of labor-intensive industries, basic industries, and processing and assembly industries. The labor-intensive industry transfer theory was proposed by W. Arthur Lewis on the basis of the H-O factor endowment theory, and its core viewpoint emphasizes that the difference in the abundance of unskilled labor between developed and developing countries is the fundamental reason for the transfer of

---

a Zhang Qianxiao, Li Jialin. Optimizing the Evolution Path of Industrial Transfer and Constructing a New Development Pattern of Dual Circulation in the New Era: An analysis Based on the Perspective of Industrial Symbiosis Under the Background of the Belt and Road Initiative [J]. Journal of Northwest University (Philosophy and Social Sciences Edition), 2021, 51(01): 124–136. DOI: 10.16152/j.cnki.xdxbsk.2021–01–013.

b Zhang Lili, Ma Wenbin. A Review of Theories and Research on Domestic and International Industrial Transfer. Jianghuai Forum, 2010(05): 23–29. DOI: 10.16064/j.cnki.cn34–1003/g0.2010.05.028.

c Gong Xue, Gao Changchun. A Review of the Theory of International Industrial Transfer [J]. Productivity Research, 2009(04): 157–160. DOI: 10.19374/j.cnki.14–1145/f.2009.04.057.

d Wang Xue. Research Status and Development Trend of the Theory of International Industrial Transfer [J]. Industrial Technology & Economy, 2006(10): 110–112.

unskilled labor-intensive industries[a].

Research on the theory of international industrial transfer from the perspective of enterprises mainly involves internalization theory and international production compromise theory. The internalization theory was proposed by Peter Buckley and Mark Casson, and was expanded by A. Rugman. Its main point is that due to the imperfect market mechanism, trade barriers, cost factors and other limiting conditions, the transaction costs of enterprises increase, and internalization is generated in the form of outward direct investment; the enterprise management mechanism replaces the market mechanism, and the internal market replaces the external market[b]. The theory of international production compromise was proposed by John Dunning, who believed that developing countries could change the one-way flow of international industries by actively engaging in foreign direct investment and deepening their connection with their own economic development stage[c].

The research on the theory of international industrial transfer from the perspective of national interests is mainly based on Rau'l Prebisch's theory of "center-periphery". The main viewpoint is that the "peripheral" countries are subject to the interests of the "center" countries due to their dependence on the technology and capital of the "center" countries, and thus fall into an unfavorable international division of labor system, losing the opportunity for their own industrialization[d]. This theory overly emphasizes the negative impact of international industrial transfer on the "peripheral" countries while ignoring its promotion of their economic development.

4.2.2 Examination of Vocational Education Serving China-Africa Production Capacity Cooperation from the Perspective of International Industrial Transfer

From the perspective of national industrial transfer, the key to vocational education serving China-Africa production cooperation lies in grasping the needs of industrial development, clarifying the laws of human resource utilization in industrial development, and improving the industrial service capabilities of local labor force from the supply side of talent cultivation. By enhancing effective interaction with Chinese-funded enterprises, it promotes the optimization of Chinese vocational colleges in the African education system, and enhances the competitiveness and comparative advantages of undertaking international industrial transfer through the improvement of human capital.

---

a Gong Xue, Gao Changchun. A Review of the Theory of International Industrial Transfer [J]. Productivity Research, 2009(04):157–160.

b Buckley, F. , Carson, Translated by Feng Yahua and Chi Juan. The Future of Multinational Companies. [M]. Beijing: China Financial Publishing House, 2005.

c Dunning J. H. The Paradigm of International Production [J]. Journal of International Business Studies, 1988, 1–31.

d Rau'l Prebisch. Commercial Policy in the Underdeveloped Countries J. American Economic Review, 1959, 49, 251.

In the process of industrial transfer, Chinese-funded enterprises in Africa have gone through three stages of exploration and practice, from "going to Africa" to "settling in Africa" to "rooting in Africa", facing survival difficulties and challenges such as local political conflicts and turbulence, complex commercial legal systems, diverse ethnic cultures, religious and colonial cultural legacies, language systems, localized management pressures, fluctuating exchange rates, increasingly fierce homogenized competition among Chinese-funded enterprises, unfriendly international public opinion environment, insufficient local technical workers and difficult management. The abundant and cheap labor resources have become an important comparative advantage for African countries to attract the transfer of national production capacity, but Chinese-funded enterprises still face prominent human resource bottlenecks, with insufficient local technical workers and difficult management, which increased the operating management costs and reduced operational efficiency due to the employment of local employees under the pressure of localized management. In some African countries, such as Ghana, local employees are deeply influenced by the culture of their former colonial powers due to their colonial history, and they divide their work scope and time limits very clearly. Therefore, Chinese-funded enterprises need to allocate work tasks and responsibilities for each position reasonably and carefully, and also need to adjust all work content in advance to ensure daily production efficiency.

4.3 Theory of Global Value Chain

4.3.1 Overview of Global Value Chain

The concept of Global Value Chain is based on the concept of value chain. This concept was proposed by Michael Porter in his book Competitive Advantage in 1985. It describes the value creation process of a single enterprise being subdivided into several independent but functionally related production and operational activities, which are then linked together to form the initial form of the "value chain". With the increasing frequency of communication and collaboration between enterprises, Porter further proposed the existence of a "value chain system" that includes upstream suppliers and downstream distributors, expanding the value chain from within a single enterprise to different enterprises. In the field of management, this vertical cooperation between enterprises is called "supply chain management"[a].

The idea of this global value chain is rooted in the production fragmentation theory proposed by Jones & Kierzkowski in 1990, and the concept was first proposed in the discussions of the "Global Value Chain Initiative" (2000—2005) sponsored by the Rockefeller Foundation. Scholars such as Gereffi have further conceptualized this concept through research on the structure and mechanism of value distribution among countries. With the prevalence of research on intermediate goods trade, Baldwin more precisely defined key concepts in the global value

a Yang Cuihong, Tian Kailan, Gao Xiang, Zhang Junrong. Overview and Prospects of Global Value Chain Research [J]. Systems Engineering-Theory & Practice, 2020, 40(08): 1961–1976.

chain based on the research conducted by Feenstra and Hanson in 1995 in 2006. Grossman and Hansberg and other scholars believe that countries can fully utilize their resource endowment advantages and maximize the economies of scale in different stages of the production process to enhance the efficiency of economic development, thereby achieving more specialized division of labor and economic growth and benefits[a]. Some scholars point out that global value chain analysis should focus on the inter-country system, world production structure, world labor structure, human welfare model, social cohesion and knowledge structure of each country[b].

The global value chain theory has been used to analyze international production capacity cooperation. Scholars have found that the United States, Europe, and ASEAN have integrated into the global value chain in different ways, forming different models of production capacity cooperation[c]. The United States has formed a vertically open global value chain through international production capacity cooperation, with overseas suppliers having greater autonomy and flexibility, resulting in higher value-added production. US product manufacturers improve supplier capabilities by providing technical guidance and support to overseas manufacturers, allowing more outsourcing. US companies themselves are turning to higher value-added product research and development, system integration and software upgrades, constantly improving the competitiveness of domestic companies in core technology fields, leading the direction of international production capacity cooperation, and increasingly becoming the core driving force of the global value chain. European countries adopted the way of economic integration and ceded some rights to the EU, a supranational organization, to ensure economic cooperation and common development among countries with a common market, currency and industrial policy. ASEAN is based on intergovernmental industrial cooperation agreements, planning production division of labor, specifying trade of goods produced after division of labor within the region, and providing tariff preferences. ASEAN encourages member countries to import goods from each other, promoting the circulation of goods and the construction of value chains in the region, and driving trade development in the region.

Scholars have conducted special research on China's participation in international production capacity cooperation from the perspective of the global value chain theory. The research found that since the reform and opening up in 1978, China has continuously integrated into the global value chain, going through three major stages: capital introduction, capital output, and industrial output. However, it still faces the monopoly of developed countries in the research and

---

a Ren Zhong, Song Shentong. A Review of Global Value Chain Theory and Empirical Research [J]. Journal of Hangzhou Dianzi University (Social Sciences Edition), 2020, 16(04): 16–21.

b Ding Tao, Jia Genliang. A Preliminary Exploration of the Global Value Chain Theory of New List Economics. Social Science Front, 2017(08): 23–32.

c Jin Renxian. Experience and Enlightenment of International Production Capacity Cooperation from the Perspective of GVC [J]. Economic System Reform, 2021(06):148–155.

development, design, and marketing of products[a]. Therefore, China should actively leverage the complementary advantages of enterprise groups and clusters to achieve "going global" in groups, and actively build a regional value chain with China as the leader. It should absorb innovative elements from host countries and promote Chinese standards in advantageous areas[b], to shape a value chain with China as the core.

Under the global value dual circulation mode, the building of the "Belt and Road" provides China with the possibility of actively integrating more developing countries into international economic cooperation. China, as an intermediate link, has played a role in improving the production and economic efficiency of a country by importing a large number of intermediate goods from developing countries, promoting the transformation and upgrading of the value chain in countries along the "Belt and Road"[c]. At the same time, Sino-foreign production capacity cooperation faces prominent risks and challenges, such as the need to clarify the relationship between strategic orientation and economic incentives, the poor political environment leading to difficulties for Chinese-funded enterprises, the serious lag in the construction of public service systems for capacity cooperation, the incompetence of coping with social risks in the cooperating countries, and the unfavorable direction of international public opinion. Some scholars have proposed that one of the measures to enhance the status of global value chain in the "Belt and Road" production capacity cooperation is to upgrade the factor endowment structure. In particular, developing countries that rely on the advantage of low labor costs can enhance the industrial service ability of labor force by increasing investment in education and training[d] and guiding the transfer of international production capacity cooperation to the high-end link of the value chain.

4.3.2 Examination of Vocational Education Serving China-Africa Production Capacity Cooperation from the Perspective of Global Value Chain

From the perspective of the global value chain theory, the key to China-Africa production cooperation lies in seizing the opportunity of capacity cooperation to establish a new global value chain network and production service system, and promote the common improvement of China and African countries' positions in the global value chain. The key to vocational education serving China-Africa production cooperation lies in cultivating technical and skilled talents through

---

a Wang Jiarong. Research on the Chinese International Production Capacity Cooperation in Manufacturing Industry [D]. Capital University of Economics and Business, 2016.

b Wu Fuxiang, Duan Wei. International Production Capacity Cooperation and Reshaping China's Economic Geography. Chinese Social Sciences, 2017(02): 44–64+206.

c Wang Yonghong. New Changes in the International Economic and Trade Pattern from the Perspective of Global Value Chain Theory: A Case Study of the "Belt and Road" Cooperation Area [J]. Commercial Economic Research, 2019(22):162–165.

d Liu Min, Zhao Jing, Xue Weixian. The "Belt and Road" Production Capacity Cooperation and the Promotion of Developing Countries' Global Value Chain Status. [J] International Economic and Trade Exploration, 2018, 34(08): 49–62. DOI:10.13687/j.cnki.gjjmts.2018.08.004.

vocational education and training, improving labor productivity, and enhancing the positions of China and African countries in the global value chain.

Due to the constraints of the economic development level, dependence on international organization aid, and the trend of education capitalization in African countries, the local governments invest very little in vocational education. At this point, the purpose of vocational education is no longer to protect the most vulnerable groups' right for education, but to become a training tool to meet some specific economic needs. Due to the low local industrialization in African countries, the number of large and medium-sized enterprises is small and most of them are foreign-controlled. Influenced by political systems and cultural differences, the coupling degree between enterprises and local vocational education is not high. Even in the process of recruiting a large number of local employees in foreign-funded enterprises, the quality of graduates trained by the vocational education system does not match the job requirements. The inadequate vocational education system in Africa is driven by supply rather than demand, making it difficult for African youth to accumulate vocational skills that meet employment needs and match the labor market structure, which seriously hinders the localization of employees of Chinese-funded enterprises in Africa. The reason for this result is that the connection between the local vocational education system and the labor market is weak, and there is a lack of communication mechanism between local vocational colleges and enterprises in Africa, which makes the mismatching the professional setting, curriculum setting, skill imparting and current industry development needs and labor market-related skills. The learning content and employment field lack consistency, and the transition time from school to work is too long. For example, the proportion of technical colleges in Egypt is 47%, but the employment rate of its graduates in industrial industries is only 12%, and the talent cultivation of local vocational colleges is disconnected from the needs of industrial and economic development. Although Rwanda is striving to develop a knowledge-based economy oriented towards modern services, the majors and practical training equipment that match industrial development are seriously insufficient, and the practical operation ability of the trained students is limited and their employment ability is insufficient.

Under the guidance of the global value chain theory, the improvement path of vocational education serving China-Africa production capacity cooperation should focus on emphasizing needs-oriented industrial development, following the laws of the market economy, and exerting effective government utility and deepening the cooperation mechanism between China and Africa. Firstly, Chinese vocational colleges should conduct comprehensive investigations on African partner countries in terms of politics, industrial economy, culture, and religion when establishing schools in Africa, and regard serving China-Africa production capacity cooperation as an important support. Through equal and in-depth communication and consultation, the demands of all parties should be clarified, and efforts should be made to reach a consensus on the specific forms, contents, behaviors and responsibilities of cooperation, ensuring joint participation and achievement sharing within the framework of mutual consultation. Secondly, the government should play a good role in guiding, promoting and coordinating, specifically by advocating the establishment of cooperation platforms and channels and providing institutional guarantees and directional guidance for China-Africa production cooperation. Thirdly, enterprises, as the specific implementers and executors of China-Africa production cooperation, should actively cooperate with Chinese vocational colleges in improving their own technical level and international management capabilities, as well as in exploring new connotations, trends, and measures of integration between production and education through employee vocational skills training and local vocational talent cultivation. Fourthly, Chinese vocational colleges should effectively serve the economic and social development of African partner countries and the needs of Chinese-funded enterprises in Africa, combining the development of vocational education with production, economic, and social development, actively exploring new models of school-enterprise cooperation to cultivate localized technical and skilled talents to high standards, continuously promoting and expanding the recognition of educational achievements and vocational qualifications, and jointly cultivating international skilled talents.

4.4 Theory of Symbiosis

4.4.1 Overview of Symbiosis

The term "symbiosis" first appeared in the field of biology, proposed by German mycologist De Bary in 1879. In 1986, Ahmad jian defined it as a relationship in which substances of different species are connected together to form a symbiotic unit, which can lead to mutual survival, co-evolution or inhibition[a]. The three elements of symbiotic relationships are symbiotic units, symbiotic patterns and symbiotic environments. Among them, symbiotic units are the fundamental elements, which are the units of energy production and exchange in symbiotic organisms or relationships. Symbiotic patterns reflect the way and strength of interaction between symbiotic units, as well as the relationship of material, information exchange and energy exchange. The symbiotic environment is composed of all other factors outside the symbiotic units, and it is an important external condition in symbiotic relationships. The three elements of symbiosis interact with each other and reflect the dynamic direction and laws of the symbiotic system[b].

From the perspective of symbiosis theory, international production capacity cooperation can be understood as the symbiosis between different countries. The symbiotic mode reflects the way in which cooperating countries interact or combine with each other in terms of production factors, product exchange and interests and it is the specific combination of symbiotic organizational and

---

a Ahmadjian, V. Symbiosis AnIntroduction to Biological Association. England University Press Of New England,1986.

b Yuan Chunqing. Theory of Symbiosis: On Small-scale Economy [M]. Economic Science Press, 1998.

behavioral models[a]. China's research on symbiosis theory is mostly related to energy-exporting countries, such as the sustainable economic growth characteristics of symbiosis theory in the field of China-Cambodia production capacity cooperation and the trend of continuous evolution from asymmetric symbiosis to symmetric symbiosis, which requires optimization of symbiotic environment from policies, facilities, trades, funds and other aspects[b].

There is a balanced complementary relationship between China and ASEAN countries, and three production capacity cooperation models of fund and technical support, industrial chain division of labor cooperation, and advantage production capacity gradient transfer are implemented. Under the concept of symbiosis, the optimal symbiotic system is constructed by optimizing the information exchange function of symbiotic interface, expanding the material exchange channel of symbiotic interface, establishing a reasonable symbiotic interest distribution mechanism, constructing a multilateral exchange mechanism within the symbiotic system, and constructing an efficient symbiotic environment optimization mechanism[c].

4.4.2 Examination of Vocational Education Serving China-Africa Production Capacity Cooperation from the Perspective of Symbiosis

From the perspective of symbiosis theory, the key to China-Africa productive cooperation in vocational education services lies in promoting the formation and improvement of symbiotic relationships between different countries through vocational education and training, enriching the symbiotic models in industries, energy, and other fields, and continuously optimizing the distribution of production factors, products, and interests among cooperating countries.

Starting with the construction of an optimal symbiotic system of vocational education servicing for China-Africa production cooperation, it is essential to first identify the cooperation points of convergence between the two sides. Chinese vocational colleges should mobilize various forces to create a cognitive and action community, actively cooperate with the key industries under the "Belt and Road" Initiative and meet the development needs of Chinese-funded enterprises in Africa. They should explore the establishment of professional, industry, and curriculum teaching standards applicable to African cooperative countries, and promote the alignment of talent training standards with degree certification standards. The practice of Luban Workshop demonstrates the attention to the construction of a reasonable distribution mechanism for symbiotic benefits and a multilateral communication mechanism within the symbiotic system.

---

a Zhang Hong, Liang Song. Analysis and Mechanism Construction of International Production Capacity Cooperation from the Perspective of Symbiosis Theory: Taking China-Kazakhstan Production Capacity Cooperation as an Example [J]. Macroeconomic Research, 2015(12): 121–128.

b Li Yiding. Research on China-Cambodia Production Capacity Cooperation Based on Symbiosis Theory [J]. Modern Business, 2019(26): 31–35. DOI: 10.14097/j.cnki.5392/2019.26.013.

c You Hongbing, Yang Lei. Research on China-ASEAN Production Capacity Cooperation Based on Symbiosis Theory [J]. Economic Research Reference, 2018(02): 44–54. DOI: 10.16110/j.cnki.issn2095–3151.2018.02.005.

It involves the signing of cooperation agreements by Chinese vocational colleges, local vocational colleges in Africa, and Chinese-funded enterprises in Africa. These agreements clarifies the rights, responsibilities, and obligations of each party involved, forming a management system and operational mechanisms for vocational education cooperation in the form of a responsibility list. For example, the Egypt Luban Workshop establishes a communication mechanism between Chinese and Egyptian teachers, providing a communication platform for the professional teacher teams of both sides, and promoting the technical exchange and sharing of knowledge among the teams. Additionally, one teacher from each side in each specific field is selected, forming a Luban Workshop professional teacher exchange group, which holds regular meetings every quarter to conduct training, summarize experiences of equipment usage and discuss existing issues. Similarly, it is particularly important to build an efficient and optimized symbiotic environment, and it requires supporting measures for vocational education servicing for China-Africa production cooperation. National policy support, a robust intellectual property protection mechanisms, a platform for overseas vocational education, and targeted funding, is essential due to the contrasting economic development environments, legal systems, and technical faced by Chinese vocational colleges and Chinese-funded enterprises in Africa.

In summary, based on the theories of internationalization of education, industrial transfer, global value chain, and symbiosis, the talent training standards of internationalized vocational education should shift from supply-driven to industry demand-oriented. Efforts should be made to break through the human resource bottlenecks of Chinese-funded enterprises in the process of industrial transfer in Africa, enhance the training of local technical and skilled talents, and improve the position of both China and Africa in the global value chain, optimize the symbiotic system of Chinese vocational colleges in Africa and better serve China-Africa production capacity cooperation.

Chapter V

Comparative Study of Internationalization in Vocational Education

The relationship between vocational education serving international production capacity cooperation and vocational education internationalization is twofold. On the one hand, vocational education internationalization can be seen as a component of vocational education service international production capacity cooperation. In this context, vocational education internationalization is a means, and serving international production capacity cooperation is the goal. It is through vocational education internationalization that the goal of promoting international production capacity cooperation can be achieved. On the other hand, vocational education serving international production capacity cooperation can be seen as a component of vocational education internationalization. Vocational education internationalization itself has a rich connotation, including many practices and measures, and serving international production capacity cooperation is one of the many practices of vocational education internationalization.

It is precisely because of this rich relationship between the two that we will provide a systematic introduction to the internationalization of vocational education in this chapter, and then based on this, we will propose insights into vocational education serving for China-Africa production capacity cooperation.

In general, different countries have adopted different models and strategies to promote vocational education internationalization, which is based on the characteristics of vocational education itself. Due to the richness of cultural, institutional, and vocational education traditions among different regions and countries, research on vocational education internationalization is still extremely limited (Evans, 2020; Pilz & Li, 2020). Existing research is mostly from the perspective of countries and regions to deal with the theme of "vocational education internationalization", or from a single dimension of discipline and professional fields to organize and analyze the framework, still lacking a systematic explanation of this theme.

5.1 Primary Models of Internationalization in Vocational Education

5.1.1 Germany: Internationalization Model of Vocational Education Based on the Dual System

Although the German dual system of vocational education faces many difficulties in international promotion, "Training-Made in Germany" is still considered a brand of vocational education internationalization that has achieved success (Wiemann et al., 2019; Wolf, 2017; Hilbig, 2019). In order to support the internationalization of the dual system in Germany, BMBF has established funding projects and research programs for different target countries, trying to make each specific project more compatible with the institutional environment of the target country in terms of design and implementation. (Internalization of Vocational Education and Training, IBB) With the promotion of organizations such as Germany's internal and OECD (2015; 2020), the dual system apprenticeship model in Germany is still regarded as an effective solution to reduce youth unemployment and to improve national technological competitiveness by many developing countries, who choose to introduce the dual system apprenticeship model from Germany and revise their own existing vocational education systems.

The migration of Germany's dual system apprenticeship model is usually accompanied by the establishment of new institutions of German multinational companies and possible projects for deeper cooperation with Germany. Germany's vocational education and training sector promotes the dual system apprenticeship model as an "export commodity" and provides "customized" support services (BEX, 2010–2017). As an important project of the BMBF, the Federal Ministry of Education and Research has developed a guidebook and an international marketing strategy for vocational education (International Marketing of Vocational Education (iMOVE). The guidebook contains two meanings, the internationalization of vocational education services and the development support for the internationalization of vocational education services (BMBF, 2017). Currently, Germany is a research field for the internationalization of vocational education services, which is a newly emerging field supported by BMBF. In recent years, the main research topics in this field include: (1) the prerequisites and possible obstacles of bilateral cooperation projects in vocational education; (2) the implementation models and support measures for bilateral cooperation in vocational education; (3) the development models of vocational education and training oriented towards the demand of the international training market (BMBF, 2017). The key supported projects of the German vocational education export strategy (Berufsbildungsexport, BEX) are transferable business education models and the driving forces and possible obstacles for the internationalization of vocational education and training (MOEZ, 2012).

Pilz (Pilz, Wiemann, 2020) and others analyzed the possible obstacles to the international transfer of the dual system apprenticeship model in Germany. Whether the dual system apprenticeship model in Germany can enter a new institutional environment depends first on the local training market regulatory conditions in the importing country, and second on the migration strategy of the project. When in a regulated market environment, the migrated project needs to be localized, or the company directly introduces training services. When the company introducing training services has some kind of connection with German companies, the migration process of the project will reduce the necessary adaptability and increase the possibility of successful migration. The differences in education systems and traditional training market differences between different countries are obstacles that migration projects must overcome (Posselt et al., 2019; Eckelt, 2018). The prerequisite for the successful migration of the project is that the two countries reach a consensus on the prerequisites such as institutional differences and training tradition differences (Porter, 2013). Within Germany, researchers and practitioners have been exploring solutions for achieving consistency and realizing international cooperation in vocational education and training led by a single country (Dybowski et al.).

There are many points of controversy in the German academic community regarding the international migration of the dual system apprenticeship model. The debate mainly focuses on critical research on the implementation of "good" migration projects and the analysis of conditions for successful migration (Barabasch, Wolf, 2012 & 2016; Pilz, 2017). In comparison to previous decades of German vocational education cooperation, in recent years, the promotion of the dual system apprenticeship model has been more about considering how to achieve a systematic migration of German vocational education in the specific economic, political, institutional, and training traditions of the target country, rather than modular transplantation (Euler, Wieland, 2015).

Germany has over 60 years of international vocational education cooperation experience aimed at helping partner countries develop vocational education and training (Erdsach, 1992). Long-term international cooperation in the field of vocational education and training has enabled Germany to accumulate rich curriculum transformation paradigms and project migration strategies. As an important theme of German international cooperation, vocational education and training aid projects involve Germany's development cooperation strategy (bundesdeutschen Entwicklungszusammenarbeit, EZ) (Arnold, 2006; Greinert, Heitmann, 1995; Wallenborn, 2006). For example, BIBB's iMOVE program attempts to open up the international market by providing initial and continuing training services for the labor market in importing countries. Another example is the AWE (Agentur für Wirtschaft & Entwicklung) program, which began in 2016, as well as other vocational training partner programs, who target at actors related to enterprises, business associations, enterprise associations, or industry enterprises.

In these programs, experts and managers from companies will be hired as vocational education cooperation experts, such as the Senior Experten Service (SES) project, where the foreign activities of German companies are the main support and important operational medium (MOEZ, 2012). After analyzing the vocational education internationalization projects of BEZ from 2010 to 2017, possible attraction points for promoting the internationalization of the German dual system apprenticeship model were proposed: (1) market dynamics: the quality of German manufacturing industry has strong appeal to target countries, and the recognition of German industry and industrial products worldwide; (2) modular vocational education and training services: practical education content and outcomes provide possibilities for vocational education services to adapt to emerging markets; (3) high-level political marketing capabilities: cross-departmental integration capabilities provide guarantees for continuing education services; (4) school-enterprise cooperation in overseas vocational education services: reliable enterprise partners inside and outside the project, participation of large multinational German companies, and internal structure and development strategies of school-enterprise cooperation.

5.1.2 Australia: Competency-Based Internationalization Model

In the 1950s, the Colombo Plan initiated by Commonwealth countries made vocational education an industry for aiding developing countries. Although Australia provided vocational education for overseas students at that time, it did not regard vocational education as an export industry. However, it laid an important political foundation for the internationalization policy of vocational education after the 1990s. The report Cross-border Learning: Internationalization of Vocational Education and Training Staff Development was published in 1997, summarizing the internationalization of Australian vocational education as "a process of vocational education responding to the challenges of the new international order in economic, technological, social and cultural aspects. This process enables vocational education students and teachers to have skills, attitudes and values that are effective for living and working in a diverse world, and it is closely linked to Australia's multicultural society, making contributions to Australia's industry in international economic competition." The report also condensed vocational education internationalization into five specific dimensions: curriculum internationalization, staff development internationalization, strengthening the connection between vocational colleges and the world, becoming the best international practice, and promoting international student mobility[a]. Specifically, Australia has formulated corresponding policies for overseas marketing of its vocational education curriculum, accelerated the recognition process of Australian vocational education qualifications in foreign countries, cooperated with industries to jointly develop development strategies and marketing plans for vocational colleges, incorporated influential industry associations and enterprises into regional working groups and determined phased expansion plans, and promoted the connection between its own qualification framework and relevant foreign qualification frameworks. The National Quality Strategy for Transnational

a Kearns. P, Kaye. S. Learning across frontiers: report on the internationalisation of staff development in vocational education and training [R]. Melbourne: ANTA, 1997.

Education and Training was released in 2005[a], which identified the most important principle of ensuring that the quality of cross-border vocational education cooperation in Australia is equivalent to that of domestic vocational education. This requires that Australia's quality assurance framework be fully understood and recognized both domestically and internationally[b].

Since the 1990s, the Australian Qualifications Training Framework project has been exported to 45 countries worldwide. As one of the most active suppliers of vocational education internationalization, the Technical and Further Education (TAFE) system, a public vocational education system in the state of Victoria, Australia, has undertaken over 70% of Australia's overseas vocational education projects (Australian Government, 2016).

As the Australian public vocational education sector, TAFE provides vocational qualification certification and degree certification services to multiple countries around the world. Unlike most Australian public vocational education sectors, TAFE has a high degree of independence and autonomy. Therefore, TAFE is able to seek oversea expansion and global cooperation more spontaneously and actively, and has an awareness of the internationalization of vocational education earlier than other vocational education and training departments in Australia. The vocational education and training courses provided by TAFE are designed, revised and managed based on the needs of domestic students in Australia. The management system of its overseas programs is also based on domestic policies and regulations in Australia. In overseas vocational education programs in Australia, over 70% of the courses are taught in English, while the rest are a mix of local languages and English. Over 80% of the teaching takes place in classrooms. Approximately half of the overseas courses are taught by local teachers, while the other half are taught by teachers from Australia. Over 60% of the courses are short-term courses within 12 months, but over 60% of the students participating in the programs will receive vocational education and training for more than 12 months. If the overseas programs are implemented in non-English-speaking countries, vocational education institutions may organize short-term English language training before the start of the program. TAFE consists of 16 vocational education institutions, and its overseas programs are discussed by all association members to ensure the quality of the programs and compliance with Australian vocational education audit supervision. TAFE has developed an overseas personnel supervision framework and overseas program audit system, which allows flexible implementation of the programs while respecting the local vocational education environment in the host country. (Dempsey, 2009) Quality Assurance in Transnational Vocational Education Provides regulatory guidelines and quality assurance for TAFE's internationalization activities in vocational education. Overseas TAFE activities must

---

a Department of Education, Science and Training. A national quality strategy for Australian transnational education and training: a discussion paper [R]. Canberra: DEST, 2005.

b Liang Shuai, Wu Xueping. Analysis ofthe Policy of Vocational Education Internationalization in Australia. Chinese Higher Education Research, 2019 (05): 97–103.

be conducted within the regulatory framework and aligned with domestic vocational education and training programs in Australia. However, in recent years, with the increase in the number of international vocational education programs, the participating regions or countries have also increased, and the Australian authorities are facing new challenges. Teachers of TAFE's overseas programs must have the Australian vocational education teaching qualification certificate; the curriculum of the programs must include Australian environmental units; when teaching qualifications in the host country are not recognized, all courses must be conducted in English.

Australian higher vocational education internationalization takes the TAFE model as its brand and has distinct characteristics in terms of curriculum, qualification framework, and quality supervision system. The curriculum consists of standardized course training packages that are nationally recognized and uniformly implemented. The packaging and classification of course training packages also facilitate the learning and application of other vocational colleges in other countries, promoting the standardization and replicability of Australian higher vocational education TAFE courses. The Australian Qualifications Framework (AQF), which has unified standards, covers 15 types of qualifications, including TAFE, ensuring wide recognition and providing guarantees for global market integration. Strict regulation of training institutions increases the credibility of this model as an educational brand and enhances its competitiveness in the international market. This model is not only continuously improved and summarized from domestic practices but also becomes the driving force and brand reliance for the internationalization of vocational education in Australia[a]. In this regard, the Australian government actively promotes the internationalization of higher vocational education through continuous, diverse, complementary policy measures and a harmonized policy environment, making TAFE colleges an important force in promoting the development of Australia's international education industry. With the guidance and regulation of the Australian government in education decision-making, scientific management, and support for research activities, Australia has now built a unique and comprehensive vocational education and training system, becoming one of the countries with a high degree of internationalization in vocational education in the world[b]. Both the "2025 Australian Vocational Education International Strategy" and the "2025 Vocational Education International Participation Strategy" reflect the provision of high-quality vocational education products based on demand orientation, and strive to obtain high recognition from the international community, more countries, employers, and governments for Australian vocational education. At the same time, it also proposes to "expand high-quality education products to online and offshore markets at different price points", mainly through expanding online learning, establishing overseas campuses, establishing partnerships with

a Pan Haisheng, Sun Yirui. Strategy Analysis and Enlightenment of Australian Higher Vocational Education Internationalization [J]. Education and Occupation, 2020 (07): 85–92.

b Mai Linyan. Historical Changes and Analysis of Internationalization Policies in Australian Vocational Education. Vocational Education Forum, 2017 (01): 80–85.

overseas institutions, and expanding the overseas delivery of Australian qualifications and non-qualification training, etc., to continuously improve the international status of Australian vocational education[a].

Although Australia's internationalization of vocational education and training has been ongoing for more than 30 years and has been recognized internationally, this overseas curriculum system cannot be well integrated with the education system and training market of the recipient countries. The competency-based vocational qualification certification system has an insufficient understanding of the complexity of the education environment in the recipient country. Due to the fact that some teaching qualifications in the recipient country cannot be certified by the Australian system, many teachers in the recipient country must reapply for the Australian teacher qualification certificate or conduct teaching activities under the supervision of Australian-certified trainers in order to participate in Australian overseas courses.

5.1.3 The United States: Internationalization Model of Remote Vocational Education and Training Based on Community Colleges

With the rise of neoliberalism and globalization, American community colleges embarked on a global educational activities and the training of students to meet the skill demands of the multinational labor force in the late 1980s. This further influenced national vocational education policies and the development of a nationwide skilled workforce in the United States. Community colleges, educational institutions that emerged in the 19th century, mainly focus on postsecondary education and training as well as academic, vocational, and adult education at the pre-baccalaureate degree level. Since the 1960s, American community colleges have expanded their educational functions, emphasizing open access, comprehensive curriculum offerings, and community oriented principles. While community colleges in the United States have close ties to the training market, they are not driven by labor market skill demands in the market (Quiggin, 2010). It was only in the 1980s, with the rise of neoliberal thinking that American community colleges began to explore marketization. For example, they incorporated certification processes to meet employers' demands for skill assessment (Levin et al., 2009). In the 1990s, American community colleges started offering more programs focused on job preparation and responding to the changes in labor market skills. They also established international partnerships and utilized the internet and information education technologies to implement distance learning. American community colleges reflect changes in US global competitiveness policies and the goals of a knowledge-based society. As part of the US strategy for global expansion, American community colleges have increasingly promoted the use of the internet in more countries since the 21st century, enabling the international implementation of their vocational education and training

---

a Liu Yufeng. The Goal and Path of Internationalization of Vocational Education: Based on the Analysis of the Australia-New Zealand-UK International Education Strategy. China Vocational and Technical Education, 2022. (12): 53–62.

programs from a remote distance. The internationalization of vocational education programs in American community colleges primarily operates on market-oriented principles and does not rely on government financial support (Ball, 2012). The establishment of vocational education and training programs closely aligns with the labor market demands of the private sector (Olssen, Peters, 2005). After the 2008 financial crisis, the quality of vocational education and training programs at community colleges declined, leading to increased tuition fees.

Under the strategic objectives in the US where "higher education is a tool to enhance national productivity and global competitiveness," presidents such as Obama and Bush proposed reform initiatives addressing the issue of "performance" in American community colleges. They introduced an evaluation system based on economics, efficiency and effectiveness, as well as funding projects for community college tuition (The White House, 2015).

Obtaining tuition revenue is an important driving force for the promotion of vocational education internationalization in American community colleges. The participation of more international students in vocational education and training programs can bring more funds to community colleges.

Most internationalization programs at American community colleges are run by individual colleges, with a focus on internationalized courses, creating opportunities for interactive learning of international students to interact and learn, and cultivating students' global work abilities. The organizers of the program are entirely composed of faculty and staff from the community college. If the resources are limited and the internationalization program does not serve the best interests of the community college, the program may face the possibility of being suspended.

5.1.4 United Kingdom: Market-Oriented Internationalization Model

Since the 21st century, the UK has elevated the international education industry and cross-border education services to the national strategic level. The growth in value brought by education exports and the capture of the global market are important driving forces for the implementation of the UK's education internationalization strategy. It also aims to serve its political and economic interests through the enhancement of cultural soft power. The two major strategic guidelines, International Education Strategy: Global Potential, Global Growth and International Education Strategy: Supporting Recovery and Driving Growth, provide important guarantees for the internationalization of UK education, clearly defining the goals of increasing the number of international students and promoting international education to bring economic benefits by 2030. Education exports are an important aspect of the UK's economic development, and vocational education is also one of the areas for increasing exports in the International Education Strategy: Supporting Recovery and Driving Growth. It is the great interest of the international community in vocational education reform that makes the UK an important partner in the international community[a]. Under the above-mentioned two major strategic guidelines, the UK markets educational products in the international community, expand the types of educational products, appoint international education ambassadors to expand the international education market, focus on researching the education product market to identify potential markets and key markets, establish a comprehensive government approach to ensure education exports, establish an international education advisory group composed of cross-government and senior officials to jointly find ways to address challenges, provide funding and financial support, strengthen and promote trade in education services in free trade agreements, and build a global network and education partnerships to enhance the sustainability of education exports. Specifically, the UK focuses on exporting teacher training courses, teacher training standards and methods, and takes effective actions to support transnational online education[b].

In the past decade, the education internationalization strategy implemented by the United Kingdom has followed the logic of "context-goal-tool", and adjusted the policy goals and tools of vocational education internationalization in response to changes in the symbiotic environment. The government has provided financial support mainly through incentive tools to promote education exports and expand international markets. The government's responsibility has also gradually shifted from formulating normative systems to promoting multi-party participation. The education internationalization strategy involves different entities, such as the Ministry of Education, the Ministry of International Trade, the Ministry of International Development, student loan companies, international clearing banks and local universities, which use their respective resource advantages to undertake different responsibilities to achieve common goals. Similarly, the UK government has improved the institutional environment through capacity-building tools, such as analyzing global education market trends and regional development trends through education export data, and using this information to develop measurement indicators and set market shares. They also focus on the operation of transnational education and the training of international teachers, promote overseas English training, and regulate the operation of British overseas schools through quality assurance standards.

The UK also regards overseas education as an important tool for its education internationalization policy. It promotes English language training through various international education programs and considers some African countries as "potential growth areas" and future partners for international education goals, continuously expanding its strategic layout[c]. Currently, the UK faces fierce competition from countries such as the US, Australia, and Germany in the

a Liu Yufeng. The Goal and Path of Vocational Education Internationalization: Based on the Analysis of the Australia-New Zealand-UK International Education Strategy. China Vocational and Technical Education, 2022 (12): 53–62

b Li Zhitao, Qu Yinjiao. The Direction and Inspiration of the UK's International Education Strategy in the Post-epidemic Era [J]. Heilongjiang Higher Education Research, 2023, 41(02): 92–98.

c Zhang Fengjuan, Wu Jiaxin. Research on the Internationalization Strategy of British Education from the Perspective of Policy Tools [J]. Comparative Educational Research, 2023, 45(02): 96–102+112. DOI: 10.20013/j.cnki.ICE.2023.02.10.

international education export market. It urgently needs to implement an overall development strategy to improve the quality of its overseas education system and enhance its level and ability of education export. This can be achieved through establishing a sound quality assurance mechanism, reshaping and promoting higher education brands, integrating existing education resources, and carrying out diversified overseas cooperation projects, such as setting up overseas campuses, developing overseas business relationships, and establishing joint research topics to build an overseas cooperation network[a].

5.2 International Comparative Analysis of Internationalization in Vocational Education

Compared with Germany and the United States, Australia defines internationalization of vocational education as "Transnational/Offshore Provider", which emphasizes the crossing-border and overseas connotations and the identity of providers. The German concept of international vocational education uses the words "Internalisierung/Transfer", which emphasizes the action tendency of "change" and "transformation", implying the initiative of active cooperation with the target country. The terminology used in the United States, "Internalization", is more neutral in semantics, but implies the neoliberal trend that has emerged with the rise of internationalization. In the training market of the United States, educational institutions' primary goal is to provide vocational education and training services to obtain tuition fees.

In the three typical models of Germany, Australia and the United States, the promotion entities of vocational education range from the macro level of international organizations, to the intermediate level of state and public education alliances, to the micro level of community colleges and individuals. The differences reflect the different development strategies of the three countries for the internationalization of vocational education. Although there are huge differences in the size of the promotion entities, there is no significant difference in the global influence of their vocational education models, the number of students involved in internationalization projects, and the regional scope. In some target areas, the three internationalization models coexist, which has enlightening significance for the development of China's vocational education internationalization.

Due to different promotional entities, there are also differences in the organizational participants of the project. In the German dual system model, the industry association power in the traditional German dual system apprenticeship model is introduced, which does not exist in the international vocational education and training projects of the other two countries. American community colleges use online platforms more flexibly to promote vocational education and

a Miao Qing, Jin Bo, Qi Tianci. The Internationalization of British Higher Education and Its Enlightenment to China [J]. Heilongjiang Higher Education Research, 2021, 39(03):66–71.

international training, thereby meeting their inherent needs to attract as many students as possible and obtain tuition. The State Education Alliance in Australia is integrated with its members to jointly formulate project supervision standards and seek target country partners.

In terms of market flexibility, community college courses in the United States are the most prominent, as they can tailor their education and training courses to the skill demands of the target country's labor market or enterprises. The ways of obtaining course resources and funding are also more diverse. Overseas companies can support community college teachers in developing courses after conducting on-site research. In Germany's dual system project, the participation of enterprises is highly valued, and many projects are jointly established with the overseas branches of German multinational companies, thus possessing relatively flexible market skill adaptability. Australia's competency-based model is designed based on the skill demands and qualification standards of Australia's domestic market. To meet the actual needs of different regions, a certain proportion of the content in the training package can be adjusted according to the actual situation in different places.

The biggest feature of vocational education and training internationalization project in Germany is the apprenticeship training. In vocational education and international training, Australia exports a unique national qualification framework. Skills assessment and certification of qualifications within this framework are the characteristics of this model. Meanwhile, American community colleges can choose very flexible ways to carry out international teaching and training activities, and distance learning is their characteristic, attracting international students.

In international vocational education and training projects of the three countries, the role of the government is not the same. The German government supports foreign projects through political and diplomatic means at the national level, helping to establish cooperation with target countries and integrate into the local culture and political environment. The Australian government plays more of a regulatory role, and the main body of foreign activities is the public education sector. Due to frequent changes in international diplomatic policies, although the U.S. government has provided some tuition assistance/loan programs in the process of internationalizing education, it sometimes has played a negative and limiting role in the development of U.S. education internationalization.

Regarding the participation of overseas corporate departments, the dual system apprenticeship model in Germany has a high level of involvement from overseas enterprises. In some projects, overseas companies are closely related to international projects. In Australia and the United States, overseas corporate departments did not appear to be significantly involved in the projects, but American overseas companies may provide financial support for some project courses.

All three countries face difficulties in terms of their systems and cultures, and funding and equipment issues cannot be avoided. Australia urgently needs to explore a locally appropriate solution for internationalizing vocational education and training. American community colleges need to properly handle the internal conflicts of "serving the community" and "cultivating global workforce" when facing funding and resource shortages. The German internationalization project attempts to coordinate with target countries to solve the difficulties encountered in system transfer, which may require obtaining multiple resources and support. Australia is still innovating its overseas vocational education system. American community colleges need to integrate internationalization strategies into their school charters and development strategies, resolving the conflict between "community" and "global" goals. However, to a certain extent, this conflict is a common issue in American politics and ideology.

5.3 Enlightenment for Vocational Education Serving China-Africa Production Capacity Cooperation

China-Africa Production capacity cooperation and the internal development dynamics of Chinese-funded enterprises in Africa have put forward new requirements for the internationalization of Chinese vocational education, requiring Chinese vocational colleges to play a more active role in manpower coordination in this new field environment in Africa. From the above international comparative analysis of typical governance models for vocational education internationalization, it can be seen that Germany's governance model for vocational education internationalization has significant accompanying advantages in terms of the integration of the education system and training market of the cooperating country, as well as interaction with German multinational corporations, which can provide more reference experience for China's overseas vocational education practice. Therefore, this section focuses on analyzing the governance model of Germany's vocational education internationalization, in the hope of drawing positive factors from it and providing reference for vocational education serving China-Africa production capacity cooperation.

The internationalization of German vocational education is mainly based on economic and cultural motivations, and is established in the form of a national strategic product alongside the foreign departments of German multinational enterprises. At the government level, effective intervention is provided to support vocational education in Germany, which is more in line with the institutional environment of the target country in terms of macro design and underlying operations. The participation of German multinational corporations has also been preserved as a key element of the dual apprenticeship model, serving as both a target for vocational education services and an important operational medium for vocational education. The systematic migration of vocational education in Germany requires continuous cross-departmental support, reliable cooperation among German multinational enterprises, as well as strong willingness and joint support from target countries for cooperation.

Benefited from its global influence of industrial manufacturing and embedded in the dynamic process of its multinational corporations adapting to emerging overseas markets, relying on the complete and clear structure of its vocational education system, the internationalization of vocational education in Germany is rooted in the internal willingness of its partner countries to address youth employment, improve their own vocational education system and promote technology transfer (Li Jun, 2018). According to the reform content of the internationalization of German vocational education, the international conversion of the degree system ensures the equivalence of diplomas and improves the transferability of vocational education. The international recognition of the credit system maintains its compatibility. The establishment of a lifelong learning qualification framework promotes the transformation between different levels and qualification systems, and enhances the versatility of vocational education (Xiao Fengxiang, Zhang Rong, 2017).

The export of vocational education mode is related to the local adaptability of vocational education transfer strategy. That is, whether the partner country has the corresponding conditions of other systems determines whether the mode can be transplanted smoothly after leaving the endogenous social and cultural enviroment. Based on its vocational education cooperation practice in Ethiopia as an example, Germany formed a special international aid agency responsible for technical assistance, financial assistance, and professional consulting, participating in the design of the country's vocational education system with a top-down organizational structure. The vocational education mode is exported through various methods, such as sending German vocational education experts to provide teacher training, cooperating with local five major vocational education institutions to foster talents, providing opportunities to visit Germany, offering professional consulting services, and setting up vocational education centers in local universities. However, the absence of German companies in Ethiopia weakens the German vocational education aid's self-interest motivation and commercial driving factors. Even with the efforts of German institutions, there is still insufficient participation of local companies. The export of the German vocational education mode has lost the important supporting condition of corporate participation. Another development dilemma is that the local area cannot establish cultural values that are compatible with industrial development and vocational education development in a short period. In contrast, Chinese vocational education has a significant advantage in directly connecting with the real labor market demand under the favorable opportunity of China-Africa production capacity cooperation. However, this bottom-up approach is independent of the local vocational education system, and its impact is limited. It also lacks iterative upgrading of abstract concepts and vocational education brand dimensions (Zhou Jinyan, 2018).

Currently, the service awareness and ability of vocational education for China-African production capacity cooperation is still insufficient. The root cause behind this is that the quality of vocational education in China still has room for improvement, and as there is currently no unified management institution, the policy guarantee system for vocational education internationalization is also incomplete. These factors have led to a lack of overall layout for China-African vocational education cooperation, and the quality of school-enterprise cooperation needs to be improved. There is also a lack of connection with the vocational education systems of African partner countries, as well as insufficient interaction with local institutions, relevant international organizations, and industry associations in African countries. Obviously, the above practical difficulties have undermined the integrity and coherence of China-African vocational education cooperation. It is difficult to effectively integrate and form a Chinese-style vocational education brand by relying solely on independent breakthroughs of various vocational colleges to cope with different foreign environments and education systems.

Based on the practical experience of German vocational education internationalization serving German multinational corporations, we propose the following suggestions.

The entry of Chinese vocational education into the new field of Africa requires a focus on standard-led construction, refining the core characteristics and connotations of Chinese vocational education, and then completing the formulation of vocational education standards in major construction and curriculum. Then, targeted efforts can be made to improve the transferability and replicability of the vocational education system. All the work depends on both the internal construction and quality improvement of Chinese vocational education and the provision of strong support for the internationalization of Chinese vocational education.

First, we need to establish a policy framework for the internationalization of China's vocational education, fill in the obvious gaps in the overall plan and operational implementation rules for Chinese vocational colleges to "going global", and establish a cross-departmental unified management agency to provide support services. Secondly, we need to explore the construction of a theoretical system for the internationalization of vocational education, using leading theories to promote Chinese vocational colleges to "going global" based on their own advantages; we also need to explain the Chinese vocational education model to partner countries to promote their understanding, mastery, and learning from it. Finally, in the process of China's vocational education "going global", we should first study the institutional environment and vocational education ecology of African partner countries, carefully evaluate the risks that may be encountered, and strengthen interaction with local systems to fully acquire local knowledge.

In addition, Australia, the United States and the United Kingdom, as countries with relatively high levels of internationalization of vocational education, all regard increasing the number of international students and economic benefits as important goals of their international education strategies. They attach great importance to building vocational education brands, developing and marketing education products such as online education and language teaching through multi-departmental cooperation, researching the international education market, focusing on improving the quality assurance of vocational education overseas output, and laying a foundation for the internationalization of vocational education[a]. Based on their own development practices of vocational education, these three countries have formed unique models of internationalization of vocational education. The enlightening significance of China's vocational education serving in China-Africa production capacity cooperation is to promote the adaptability of vocational education overseas schooling by improving internationalization of vocational education, and then enhance the ability to respond to the human resource needs of Chinese-funded enterprises in Africa. That is, we need to clarify the goal of internationalizing China's vocational education, summarize and refine China's vocational education reform and development experience to form a Chinese vocational education brand, improve the recognition of our qualification framework, adopt regional differentiation strategies to strengthen local education research in African countries along the "Belt and Road", give full play to the regional political advantages of local governments in carrying out vocational education cooperation, and take advantage of the communication and negotiation advantages of vocational education international exchange institutions in carrying out vocational education cooperation, enhance the enthusiasm of domestic vocational colleges to provide human resources support for the building of "Belt and Road", improve the quality of overseas cooperation schools with good quality standards, and pay attention to cross-cultural training for outbound faculty and staff.

---

a Liu Yufeng. Internationalization Goals and Pathways of Vocational Education: Analysis Based on the Australia-New Zealand-UK International Education Strategy [J]. China Vocational and Technical Education, 2022, (12): 53–62.

Chapter Ⅵ

Recommendations for Vocational Education Serving China-Africa Production Capacity Cooperation

Based on the overseas practice of vocational education serving for China-Africa production capacity cooperation, the service awareness and capabilities of vocational education still need to be improved as the mechanism and platform centered on the integration of China-Africa production and education have not yet been fully established.

Starting from the internationalization theory of vocational education, industry transfer theory, global value chain theory, and symbiosis theory summarized in the previous chapters, through analyzing the internal logic of vocational education serving China-Africa productive cooperation, it can be seen that in order to better serve China-Africa production capacity cooperation, the talent cultivation standard for overseas vocational education should be shifted from supply-driven to demand-driven and targeted to meet the demand for local technical and skilled talents of Chinese-funded enterprises in their industrial transfer process in Africa. In this process, China's vocational colleges should continuously optimize the symbiotic system of overseas schools, and promote internal and external compatibility with the local systems.

This requires strengthening the internal construction and quality improvement of vocational education by optimizing the elements of the school system, enhancing its transferability and replicability with an international perspective and thinking, as well as improving the overseas school-enterprise cooperation to promote the local adaptation of China's vocational education internationalization process. Therefore, this section focuses on providing strategic suggestions for improving vocational education services for China-Africa production capacity cooperation from three levels: macro, intermediate, and micro.

6.1 Macro Level: Providing Upper-Level Support in Institutional Design

The localization adaptation of China's vocational education "going global" initiative first needs to face significant differences in economic development, legal system, business practices, and technical rules with African cooperation countries. Currently, vocational education serving for China-Africa production capacity cooperation faces the problems of insufficient layout and lack of support system, requires overall intervention from both theoretical research and top-level design, with the aim of obtaining sufficient upper-level support.

6.1.1 Research-Driven Approach: Advancing Prudently with Controlled Risks

Currently, China's vocational education "going global" and international cooperation require not only leading with theory to grasp the laws of development and learn from the experience of other countries, but also identifying and effectively avoiding many risks that may be encountered. It also requires controlling the work arrangements of current vocational education cooperation projects at an appropriate pace. Starting with small-scale and lightweight pilot projects, and flexibly adjusting them according to the development of practice, to gradually increase the scale and depth of cooperation in an orderly manner.

1. To Implement and Refine African Regional and National Studies and Conduct Targeted Interdisciplinary Clusters

To bring Chinese vocational education to Africa, it is first necessary to develop a comprehensive understanding of the regional economic and social development and educational system characteristics of the cooperating countries to formulate cooperation plans, with assessments of the risks and challenges as comprehensive as possible. First, strengthen the research on regional countries of vocational colleges, promote the establishment of African regional vocational education research centers in Chinese cooperative colleges, and systematically and deeply study the economic and social development status, trade union system, tax system and labor system, and vocational education system policies of cooperating countries. Second, form a joint working group composed of researchers from existing research institutions related to Africa, and conduct special research on economic, trade, cultural research and vocational education serving production capacity cooperation for a certain African country through interdisciplinary cooperation. Through international comparative research on vocational education, improve China's vocational education service capabilities for overseas industries. Third, attempt to transfer the research base to African countries, in order to deepen understanding of the specific human resource needs and overseas teaching and learning environment of China-African production capacity cooperation through in-depth investigation and frontline experience, focusing on optimizing industrial production processes and innovation in technology and skills. Fourth, strengthen the construction of African research think tank alliances, continue to optimize the research layout of African regional countries based on the "one province + one country" cooperation model currently being explored, and focus on forward-looking policy consulting research on the current China-African vocational education cooperation and production capacity cooperation content, providing theoretical support and intellectual services for China-African cooperation.

2. To Strengthen the Construction of Vocational Education Brand with Chinese Characteristics, and Objectively Interpret the Application Conditions and Rules

Firstly, there is a need to enhance theoretical research on the internationalization of vocational education, clarify the current development stages and characteristics of vocational education internationalization in China. In particular, providing a systematic exposition of the Chinese vocational education model can promote the understanding, mastery, and reference by partner countries, ultimately achieving theoretical innovation in the internationalization of vocational education and driving innovative practices abroad. Secondly, based on the examples of Chinese vocational colleges establishing overseas campuses, it is important to build a case database for the internationalization of Chinese vocational education. By analyzing and deconstructing the logic of practice operations, this can promote theoretical innovation, and further guide Chinese vocational colleges to leverage their advantages in professional fields and engage in educational collaborations in Africa. Thirdly, it is necessary to further summarize effective practices in improving industry-education integration in China's vocational education reform practice. Additionally, objective explanations of the regularity, scientific basis, and application conditions of China's vocational education brand could be explores. Efforts should be made to enhance the replicability and transferability of the Chinese vocational education model.

6.1.2 Top-Level Design: Establishing an All-Encompassing Support System

The government should have clear goals and strategies for the current China-African vocational education cooperation, especially in terms of serving Chinese-funded enterprises in Africa and sharing Chinese education. International rules and standards should be respected, and innovative models for Chinese vocational education and Chinese-funded enterprises to jointly "going global" should be explored. Top-level internationalization strategies for vocational education should be developed to achieve Chinese standards, effectively share Chinese vocational education concepts, and promote mutual understanding and respect between world cultures and education through the dissemination of traditional Chinese culture. Therefore, building a comprehensive guarantee and support system has become a key factor in Chinese vocational colleges' overseas education and service for China-Africa capacity cooperation.

1. To Establish a Comprehensive Management System and Mechanism for the Internationalization of Vocational Education

A specialized unified management agency should be established to achieve deep collaboration across departments, gathering policy support from education, human resources, commerce, foreign affairs and finance departments. Local governments should establish a scientific and effective supervision and evaluation system, promote the landing of international vocational education outside the country, and cultivate technical and skilled personnel targeted to the needs of Chinese-funded enterprises in Africa. Chinese vocational colleges should establish and improve international exchanges and cooperation management agencies, and integrate and mobilize positive forces to improve the ability and level of vocational education to run schools overseas.

In the construction of the legal system, the government needs to promote the legislation of international vocational education, as well as to introduce specific operational guidelines and standards for vocational education services in international production capacity cooperation. Especially, it is necessary to make specific requirements for the behavior of Chinese vocational colleges serving international production capacity cooperation, and to manage and regulate the internationalization of Chinese vocational education.

A specialized institution should be set up to operate and execute the formation of China-African vocational education cooperation projects. This institution will lead the early-stage research, market exploration, project development and implementation, and it will accept the supervision and evaluation of third-party agencies commissioned by the government to enhance project efficiency and governance and to mitigate political risks posed by the government as a pioneer in internationalizing vocational education. Third-party forces should be supported and encouraged to participate in international vocational education exchanges and cooperation in a lighter, more convenient, localized manner through civil cooperation. They will become a powerful supplement to internationalizing vocational education.

2. To Improve the Funding Mechanism for Overseas Cooperation of Vocational Education

In terms of funding mechanisms, the government needs to provide special policy and project plans for vocational education aid in Africa to support vocational education overseas, and try to build a funding source security mechanism to address the problems of large initial investment, long construction period, poor sustainability, and relatively low proportion of input of African countries in vocational education cooperation construction projects. Specifically, Chinese vocational colleges that "going global" should seek funding support to alleviate the shortage of insufficient mid-and-long term development funds. For example, they can use national and provincial special funds such as the "High Level Vocational Colleges and Majors with Chinese Characteristics" Scheme to ensure investment and apply for relevant non-profit fund projects of UNESCO and the World Bank, establish a school-enterprise cooperation mechanism with Chinese-funded enterprises in Africa to attract enterprise funds, and so on.

3. To Strengthen the Construction of Overseas Alliances for Industry and Education Integration

Through the official policy communication mechanism of the China-Africa Cooperation

Forum, enterprises or institutions are encouraged to establish a cooperation platform between transnational non-governmental organizations, in order to strengthen the connection between non-governmental organizations, think tanks, and vocational education institutions in both China and Africa, and to provide a suitable symbiotic environment for vocational education cooperation and school-running projects. Based on the established China-Africa cooperation regional platforms, active efforts are made to seek cooperation forces, such as the China-Africa Economic and Trade Expo held every two years, the China-Africa Economic and Trade Cooperation Vocational Education Industry-University-Research Alliance initiated by Hunan International Business Vocational College, the China-Africa Vocational Education Alliance, etc. A cross-border production-education integration alliance will be established to lead the formation of a transnational cooperative organization for production-education cooperation, which will bring together various forces, including Chinese high-level vocational colleges, Chinese-funded enterprises in Africa, vocational education institutions in partner countries, and Chinese industrial parks in Africa. Through the production-education integration alliance, companies and vocational colleges that have the intention to "going global" but have not yet achieved it will be introduced into the platform, which can be used to share information and cooperation resources, reduce cooperation costs, optimize the reasonable allocation of current key element resources and seek united development.

6.2 Intermediate Level: Strengthening Responsibilities of Collaborative Entities in Cooperation Mechanisms

At the intermediate level, it is mainly reflected in the interactive relationship and operation mechanism between Chinese-funded enterprises in Africa and Chinese vocational colleges under the top-level institutional design. The cooperation between schools and enterprises overseas faces major problems such as China's dispersed and underutilized resources in Africa, the need to deepen their cooperation, and differences in local system interests and demands. To efficiently serve China-Africa production capacity cooperation, it is necessary to seek common interests on the basis of clarifying the demands of all parties, reach a consensus on specific cooperation content, and participate in construction together within the framework of joint consultation to achieve shared results.

6.2.1 Enhancing Platform Establishment: Improving the Construction and Operational Mechanism of the Luban Workshop

As an important carrier of China-Africa cooperation in education, the Luban Workshop needs to continue to improve its construction and operation mechanisms, conduct research and construction simultaneously to improve it scientifically and rationally, and promote the innovation of construction mode standards with theoretical innovation. On the timeline of its construction, it is necessary to conduct detailed research on the industrial and economic conditions, symbiotic environmental factors, and talent needs of Chinese-funded enterprises in partner countries in Africa, and formulate risk prevention plans to effectively identify and avoid risk factors. The common core interests of all parties will be clearly identified and potential cooperation partners will be cultivated before practice to avoid independent project operation and lay a good foundation for the sustainable development of the project. In the process of cooperating with Chinese-funded enterprises, Chinese vocational colleges should first refine and clarify the rights and obligations of all parties, fully tap into the development benefits, actual needs of the enterprises, and common interests of both parties, continuously optimize professional layout and scope, and improve the participation enthusiasm of all parties through the innovation of cooperation mechanism, striving to form a comprehensive, sustainable, and long-term cooperation. The Luban Workshop also needs to continue to expand its service functions, and build a cooperation platform for talent training, employee training, technical collaborative innovation, product and equipment promotion, and other projects. The workshop should also focus on formulating professional, industry, and curriculum teaching standards that are adapted to the local conditions, promote the recognition of academic and degree certification standards through the recognition of talent training standards, promote the overseas landing of Chinese standards with the internationalization of China's high-quality vocational education resources, and pay attention to the protection of national vocational education brands' intellectual property rights in the construction and operation process.

6.2.2 Addressing Industry Needs: Establishing Local School-Enterprise Cooperation Alliances

Based on the regional industrial development needs of African partner countries and the human resource needs of Chinese-funded enterprises in Africa, establish a local school-enterprise cooperation alliance based on a certain country, select the best partners in both directions, and determine cooperation models, mechanisms, and quality evaluation requirements. Through cooperation with local vocational education institutions, actively try to incorporate the results of cooperative education and the international professional teaching standards formed into the national education system of the cooperative country. The selected majors should meet the regional economic development trends and technical needs, such as the international logistics and management professional group in the China-Africa Economic and Trade Cooperation Zone and the engineering technology professional group in the China-Africa Industrial Park. Chinese vocational colleges, based on the local knowledge obtained by Chinese-funded enterprises in Africa, actively explore new models of overseas education, establish deep interactive school-enterprise cooperation relationships, and form a normalized mechanism for proactive docking between Chinese-funded enterprises and vocational colleges. They cooperate to carry out school-enterprise scientific research projects, and provide internship and practice platforms, facilities, and funding support for the training of local technical and skilled talents under localized management needs. In the future, knowledge cooperation focused on experience and technology transfer can promote investment cooperation and try to establish relevant industrial colleges in industrial parks, focusing on providing solid guarantees for international technical and skill education. Build a multi-party and diversified quality evaluation mechanism, score and certify the theoretical learning and practical operation of local students, and regularly review and supervise the teaching quality of vocational colleges, etc.

6.2.3 Optimizing Resource Connections: Enhancing Interaction with Local Systems

Moreover, the overseas practices of Chinese vocational colleges should continue to strengthen their connection with external resources. Under the tension of universal knowledge, the internationalization of vocational education requires effective responses to common challenges faced in vocational education development. Hence, Chinese vocational colleges need to enhance communication and cooperation with local educational institutions. This can be achieved by establishing exchange centers and forming dedicated teams to overseas external collaborations. At the same time, Chinese vocational colleges should actively engage with local systems. Cooperation with various Chinese institutions abroad and international organizations is essential to facilitate the smooth implementation of projects. Establishing mechanisms for in-depth cooperation with cross-regional organizations, local international organizations, and regional bodies helps to gather support and promote effective interaction.

6.3 Micro Level: Promoting Mutual Communication in Education and Teaching

The internationalization of vocational education is to validate not only the transferability and replicability of China's vocational education model, that is, whether China's vocational education experience is clear, mature and systematic, but also the overseas implementation ability and level of curriculum standards, that is, whether it is supported by corresponding strengths for the landing of educational and teaching activities.

6.3.1 Enhancing Key Educational Capabilities and International Mindsets of Chinese Vocational Colleges

The key educational abilities of Chinese vocational colleges should be enhanced to strengthen its foundation for internationalization. It is necessary to focus on the innovative achievements of Chinese vocational education and strengthen their overseas promotion, such as industry colleges, integration of work, class, competition and certificates, and 1+X certificates, etc. We should also fully exploit the rich experience accumulated due to the differences in gradient development, systematically comb and refine the development strategies and measures that adapt to different levels of industrial development, and share targeted solutions for the industrial development needs of African countries. Therefore, Chinese vocational colleges need to improve their international thinking, expand their international perspectives, and strengthen their international capabilities. They should also attempt to develop the educational resources of their advantageous professional fields internationally and actively participate in the practice of China-African production capacity cooperation.

6.3.2 Deepening the Development of Internationalized Faculty Team and Curriculum

Currently, there are few professional teachers in China who can teach directly in English or French, and few full-time teachers with internationally recognized professional qualifications. The insufficient international teaching staff leads to difficulty in effectively undertaking international teaching tasks. To address this issue, an effective path has been explored: cultivating a Chinese international teacher team to train local teachers in African partner countries, who will train local students. Therefore, a teaching team with international thinking, familiar with Chinese technology and equipment as well as the environment of African countries has become the key to serving Sino-African capacity cooperation. Establishing a qualified teaching staff requires professional teachers to strengthen their language learning. This can be achieved by collaborating with foreign language colleges to provide language training so as to improve the ability of professional teachers to share with the world. It can also be achieved by employing Chinese employees of companies involved in African affairs as part-time teachers in vocational colleges to develop training courses related to Africa and improve the adaptability of projects to local conditions. Chinese vocational colleges should also strengthen their international thinking, build distinctive and strong majors, develop new courses that reflect ability-oriented and action-oriented approaches, and create an international curriculum system. Instead of focusing on the imported curriculum system, a linked course development mechanism should be established to optimize the curriculum structure and form an international curriculum and training system that integrates industry and education for China-Africa cooperation.

6.3.3 Building Local Support through Local Faculty Training and Curriculum Development

Efforts should be made to continuously optimize the system of overseas education elements of Chinese vocational colleges, especially by clarifying talent cultivation objectives, expanding course resource construction, strengthening local teacher training and construction of the practical training base. To address the problem of insufficient teaching skills of local vocational education teachers in African countries, training programs for local teachers should be conducted to improve their practical training and professional technical ability, and to convey Chinese vocational education experience and concepts regarding theoretical knowledge, cutting-edge professional technology, educational philosophy, teaching methods, curriculum design and evaluation. At the same time, outstanding teachers from African partner countries can be selected to come to China for systematic and practical learning, and backbone teachers can be sent to African partner countries to carry out teaching training. To address the shortage of teaching resources in African countries, on the one hand, teaching resources in advantageous professional fields should be internationalized, namely the completion of international curriculum standards, development of bilingual textbooks and course materials, and construction of online course learning platforms, truly realizing the internationalization of Chinese professional standards; on the other hand, African teachers should be involved in developing teaching resources and setting up teaching platforms to promote the localization of Chinese vocational education teaching concepts.

Chapter Ⅶ

Reports on Vocational Education Collaboration Serving China-Egypt Production Capacity Cooperation

Located at the confluence of Asia, Europe and Africa, Egypt holds the strategic hub of the 21st-Century Maritime Silk Road; the Suez Canal Corridor connects the South China Sea and the Indian Ocean to the Red Sea and the Mediterranean Sea; geographical proximity to Europe and the Middle East has attracted an increasing number of overseas investors. By virtue of the foregoing, Egypt has a natural geographical advantage in synergizing with the "Belt and Road" Initiative. On the whole, the situation of political stability and economic growth in Egypt will not fundamentally change. With the widespread support of the International Monetary Fund (IMF), the World Bank and other international organizations, as well as major global economies such as the United States, the European Union and China, Egypt's economic development prospects remain promising. In addition, Egypt was the first Arab and African country to establish diplomatic relations with China, and China and Egypt regard each other as reliable friends and sincere partners.

7.1 Overview of Egypt

7.1.1 Economic Development

According to the African Development Bank, Egypt is the only country in North Africa to have maintained GDP growth of 3.6% in 2020. In its *April 2021 World Economic Outlook*, the IMF predicted that Egypt's economy would grow by 2.5% in 2021 and 5.7% in 2022. Over the past five years, Egypt's GDP has shown a steady upward trend, and its economic situation is sound (See Table 7–1 and Figure 7–1). Although Egypt's economic growth slowed down due to the impact of the COVID-19 pandemic in 2020, its actual GDP growth rate still reached 3.57%, ranking first in the African region.

Table 7–1 Egypt's GDP Over the Past Five Years (billion US dollars)

Year	2017	2018	2019	2020	2021
GDP	236.53	250.25	302.33	364.02	402.84

Note: Data is sourced from the Global Economy Database.

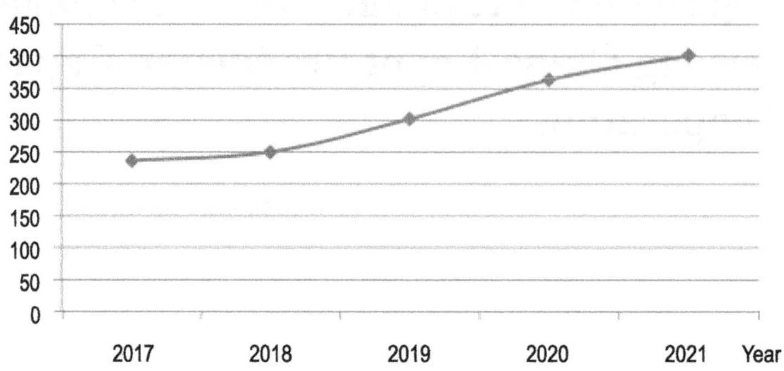

Figure 7–1 Egypt's GDP Over the Past Five Years

CPI is a relative number that reflects the trend and extent of price changes for consumer goods and services purchased by urban and rural residents over a specific period. As can be seen from Table 7–2 and Figure 7–2, the CPI in Egypt has been on an upward trend over the past five years, with values ranging from 2% to 4%, and the inflation levels have remained stable.

Table 7–2 Egypt's CPI Over the Past Five Years

Year	2017	2018	2019	2020	2021
CPI	2.311%	2.644%	2.886%	3.031%	3.199%

Note: Data is sourced from the Global Economy Database.

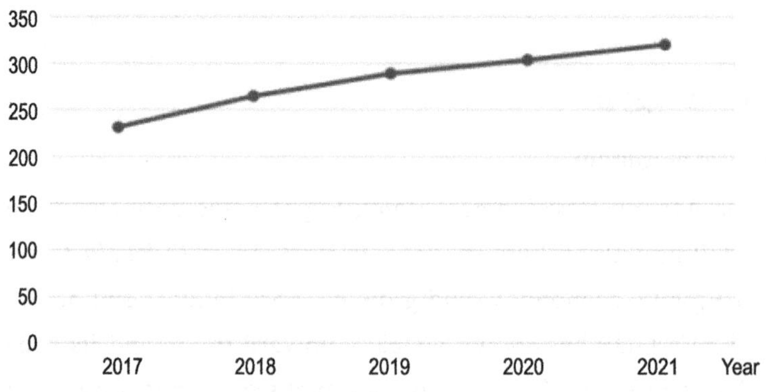

Figure 7–2 Egypt's CPI Over the Past Five Years

Egypt, South Africa, and Nigeria are the top three economies in Africa in terms of total GDP (Refer to Tables 7–3 and Figure 7–3). As the third largest economy, Egypt has maintained its economic growth momentum over the past five years, achieving the highest growth rate among these three countries and gradually narrowing the gap with the other two. Egypt ranked first in the report Where to Invest in Africa 2021 released by South Africa's Rand Merchant Bank, being rated as Africa's top investment destination. Despite the severe impact of the pandemic, Egypt was one of the first countries to return to economic growth while maintaining its top ranking in Africa in terms of GDP and remaining the largest consumer market in the Middle Eastern and Northern African (MENA) region. Its investment and legal business environment has also improved considerably.

Table 7–3 GDP of Africa and Its Three Major Economies Over the Past Five Years (billion US dollars)

Year	Africa's Total GDP	Egypt's GDP	South Africa's GDP	Nigeria's GDP
2017	2,261.58	236.53	381.32	375.75
2018	2,320.00	250.25	404.67	421.74
2019	2,400.00	302.33	387.85	448.12
2020	2,390.00	364.02	335.34	429.42
2021	2,703.50	402.84	418.02	440.80

Note: Data is sourced from the Global Economy Database.

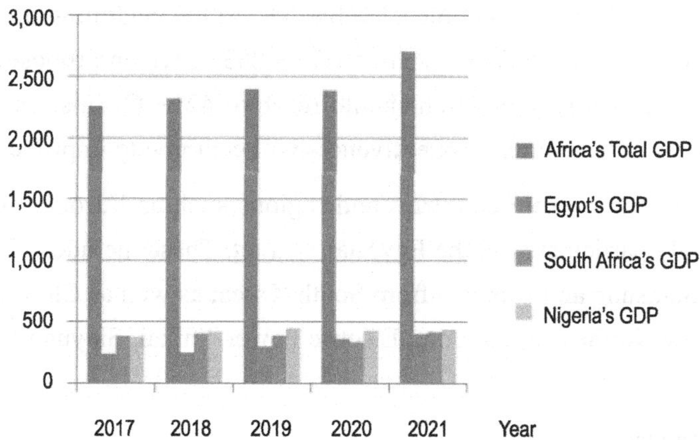

Figure 7–3 GDP of Africa and Its 3 Major Economies Over the Past Five Years

7.1.2 Industrial Environment

1. Pillar Industries and Specialty Industries

(1) Electric Power

Egypt's construction capacity for power projects is competitive in Africa and the Arab region, where local enterprises are capable of manufacturing power transmission and transformation equipment ranging from 380 V low voltage to 500 kV high voltage. Furthermore, according to statistics provided by the Egyptian Electricity Holding Company (EEHC), Egypt's total installed electricity capacity in FY2019/2020 was 59,530 MW, representing a year-on-year growth of 2%, of which, the installed capacity of renewable energy, specifically wind and solar, experienced the greatest increase of 34.2% (See Table 7–4).

Table 7–4 Statistics of Egypt's Installed Electricity Capacity in FY2018/2019 and 2019/2020 (MW)

	FY2018/2019	FY2019/2020	Change Rate (%)
Total installed capacity	58,353	59,530	2
Hydroelectric power	2,832	2,832	0
Thermal power	51,226	51,634	0.8
Renewable energy (wind and solar)	2,247	3,016	34.2
Private sector's BOOT power generating project (thermal power)	2,048	2,048	0

Source: Egyptian Electricity Holding Company (EEHC)

As one of the most active countries in the North African region in developing renewable energy, Egypt is committed to converting its abundant solar energy into clean electricity to boost economic development and improve people's livelihoods. At the beginning of 2020, Egypt issued the *Integrated Sustainable Energy Strategy 2035* (ISES 2035), which proposed that by 2035, the proportion of renewable energy generation should reach to 42%. Of this, photovoltaic power is expected to account for 22%, and its competitiveness will continue to improve.

Equipment manufacturers from countries and regions such as Europe, South Korea, China and India have actively participated in the Egyptian market. These include GE Alstom, ABB, and Siemens; Hyundai, Samsung and Daewoo from South Korea; as well as China XD Group, TBEA, Pinggao Electric, New Northeast, Shandong Electric Power, Taikai, Sieyuan Electric and CHINT from China.

(2) Oil and Gas Industry

Egypt is an important producer of oil and gas in Africa, and the oil and gas industry constitutes one of the main pillars of the Egyptian economy, accounting for 13.6% of the total GDP. According to BP's *Statistical Review of World Energy 2020*, as of the end of 2019, Egypt had oil reserves of 3.2 billion barrels (400 million tons), ranking sixth in Africa and accounting for 0.2% of the global total; it also had natural gas reserves of 2.1 trillion cubic meters, which is the third largest in Africa and accounts for 1.1% of the global total. The main gas reserves are distributed as follows: approximately 40% in the Western Desert, 25% in the Mediterranean coastal area, and 15% in the Nile Delta; other producing areas include the Gulf of Suez, the Eastern Desert, Sinai, and Upper Egypt.

From 2016 to 2019, foreign companies invested $35 billion in Egypt's oil and gas sector, with fuel and energy accounting for 27% of Egypt's GDP, as depicted in Figure 7–4. Currently, 21 Chinese-funded enterprises are involved in the development of Egypt's petrochemical industry, covering the entire oil and petrochemical industry chain. This involvement includes exploration and development, oil engineering services, equipment manufacturing, material trade, as well as refining and chemical engineering.

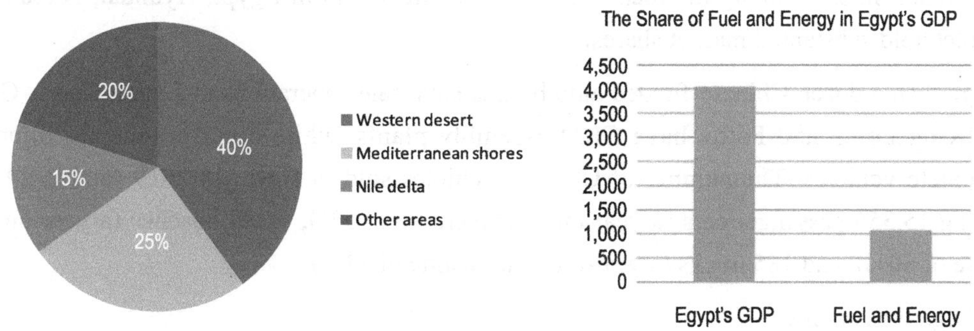

Figure 7–4 Distribution Map of Egypt's Oil and Gas Industry

(3) Textile Industry

Egypt boasts the largest cotton and textile industry cluster in Africa, with a relatively complete industrial chain ranging from cotton farming, spinning, weaving, to clothing manufacturing. Egypt has a strong capacity in clothing manufacturing but is relatively weak in weaving and dyeing, which require heavy imports.

Currently, there are over 7,000 textile enterprises in Egypt, 90% of them are small and medium-sized enterprises. These enterprises employ approximately 1.5 million people, accounting for one-third of the country's industrial workforce. Meanwhile, the textile industry contributes around 3% to the GDP. In recent years, textile exports (including clothing manufacturing) have accounted for approximately 10.6% of the total export volume, with Europe, the United States, Türkiye and Italy being its main export markets. About 1,000 firms are eligible for Qualified Industrial Zones (QIZ) qualifications, which allow them to export duty-free products to the United States. Egypt has an active private textile industry. Oriental Weavers Carpet Company is the world's largest manufacturer of woven carpets, with an annual production of 110 million cubic meters. Its production accounts for 85% of the Egyptian carpet market, 25% of the American carpet market and 20% of the European market.

Chinese textile companies have been increasingly focusing on the Egyptian market in recent years, with some leading companies having tested the Egyptian market through joint ventures and planning to expand their investment.

(4) Automobile Industry

Without its own automobile production lines, Egypt relies on imports, and local assembly for vehicle supplies. The France brands (Peugeot, Renault), Italian brand (Fiat), German brands (Mercedes-Benz, BMW), Japanese brands (Toyota, Honda, and Mitsubishi), and Korean brands (Daewoo, Hyundai, and Kia) have a high market share in Egypt. In recent years, Egypt's automobile assembly industry has experienced rapid development with 12 car assembly plants (14 production lines), 8 coach assembly plants (8 production lines), and 5 truck assembly plants (9 production lines). Among the local assembly manufacturers in Egypt, Hyundai, Nissan, and Chevrolet hold substantial market shares.

More than a dozen Chinese-funded auto brands have sales operations in Egypt. Chery, Geely, BYD, King Long, and Foton have CKD assembly plants, while other brands are imported as complete vehicles. The number of Chinese vehicles sold in Egypt in 2019 totaled 24,725, including 15,356 passenger cars (a year-on-year increase of 5%); 9,184 coaches (a year-on-year increase of 60%); and 185 trucks (a year-on-year decline of 13%).

(5)Digital Economy

The Information and Communication Technology (ICT) industry has experienced rapid growth. For the fiscal year 2019/2020, the total output value of Egypt's ICT industry amounted to $69.5 billion, marking a year-on-year increase of 15.5% and contributing 4.4% to the country's GDP. ICT exports reached approximately $4.1 billion, an increase of 13.8% year-on-year. Total investment in the ICT sector reached $3.08 billion with year-on-year growth of 35.8%.

The e-commerce industry is experiencing significant development. Egypt's total value of goods and services traded online was approximately $9.83 billion in 2019, indicating an average annual growth rate of nearly 35%. According to the latest data released by the United Nations Conference on Trade and Development (UNCTAD), Egypt ranked 13th in the Arab world and 109th globally in the 2020 Global E-Commerce Index.

The percentage of e-payments needs to be increased in Egypt. Eygpt has the largest online consumer market in the MENA region. Currently, cash-on-delivery is the main way of online shopping. However, the proportion of e-payment is relatively low in Egypt, with 60% of online transactions relying on cash, 25% using credit cards, 8% using bank transfers, and 7% using e-wallets or other means (See Figure 7–5). Egypt is the second most dependent country on paper money and ranks among the top three countries in the world with a high proportion of "unbanked" citizens.

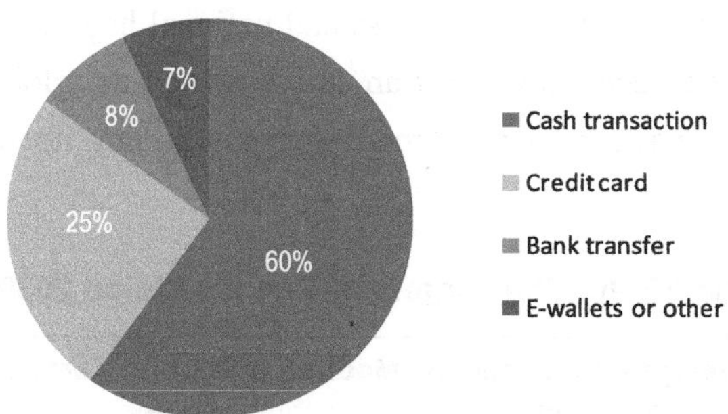

Figure 7–5 Percentage of Online Transaction Methods in Egypt

(6) Tourism Industry

Tourism accounts for 13% of the Egyptian economy and directly or indirectly creates 12% of the country's jobs, according to the World Travel & Tourism Council (WTTC). Egypt's tourism industry has recovered strongly since 2018, with tourism revenues reaching $11.4 billion in 2018 and $13 billion in 2019, attracting over 10 million tourists. However, the tourism industry suffered a significant blow in 2020 due to the COVID-19 pandemic, with revenues plunging by 69% to only $4 billion (See Table 7–5).

Table 7–5 The Income of the Tourism Industry in Egypt Over the Past Three Years (hundred million US dollars)

Year	Tourism Revenue
2018	114
2019	130
2020	40

2. Relevant Industrial Policies

In February 2016, the Egyptian government released *Sustainable Development Strategy: Egypt's Vision 2030* (hereinafter referred to as Egypt's Vision 2030), aligning it with the United Nations' 2030 Agenda for Sustainable Development and the African Union's Agenda 2063. It outlines three core elements of economic development policies: maintaining macroeconomic stability and reducing the fiscal deficit, improving the investment climate and actively attracting foreign investment, and implementing large-scale national projects in various fields such as the New Suez Canal.

According to *Egypt's Vision 2030*, the Egyptian government will continue to devote itself to developing a diversified, private sector-led, competitive and knowledge-based market economy (specific indicators are shown in Table 7–6). Egypt's stable macroeconomic environment, sustained inclusive growth, and maximized added value will create sufficient employment opportunities. By 2030, Egypt envisions being ranked among the top 30 economies of the world while also aiming for its national competitiveness and national happiness index to be among the world's top 30. The Egyptian economy seeks an active role in the global economy by adapting to the requirements of international development and positioning itself among middle-income countries.

Table 7–6 The Targets of Egypt's Vision 2030

Targets	Development Goals for 2018–2022	Medium and Long-Term Tar-Gets	Scheduled Target for 2030
Real GDP growth rate	From 5.8% to 6%	Average annual GDP growth rate	7%
Real GDP growth rate per capita	From 3% to 6%	Contribution rate of investment to economic growth	30%
New employment post created each year	From 750,000 to 870,000	Contribution rate of exports to eco-nomic growth	25%
Natural population growth rate	From 2.65% to 2.1%	Services-to-GDP ratio	70%
Inflation rate	From 14.3% to 8.5%	Debt-to-GDP ratio	Not more than 50%
—	—	Inflation rate	3%–5%
—	—	Fiscal deficit ratio	Reduced to below 5%
—	—	Unemployment rate	Reduced to below 5%

3. Overview of Economic Parks in Egypt

The economic zones available for foreign investment in Egypt mainly include industrial zones, investment zones, science and technology parks, free zones, and special economic zones. Among them, investment zones, science and technology parks, and free zones are governed by the *Investment Law*; special economic zones are governed by the *Special Economic Zones (SEZ) Law No.83*; and industrial zones are governed by the general domestic investment mechanism without any special requirements.

The industrial zones are uniformly administered by the Industrial Development Authority of the Egyptian Ministry of Trade and Industry. At present, there are 119 industrial zones. The infrastructure and supporting facilities of industrial zones are relatively well developed; however, there are no special preferential policies available. If there are no explicit legal restrictions, investment projects of any sector can be settled in industrial zones after consulting either the Industrial Development Authority or the Industrial Zone Management Committee.

Investment zones are utilized for establishing one or more types of investment and related projects, with the property developers of these zones being responsible for developing and equipping the necessary infrastructure. The prime minister has the authority to establish special investment zones in various sectors, including but not limited to logistics, agriculture and industry. Each investment zone is governed by a board of directors that enables private companies to develop and manage the zone or attract investments. The General Authority for Investment and Free Zones (GAFI) serves as the regulatory body of these investment zones.

Science and technology parks mainly involve the ICT industry, which includes the design and development of electronic products, data centers, OEMs, software development and updates, technology education, and other related complementary activities. The General Authority for Investment and Free Zones is the regulatory body responsible for these parks. Egypt currently has seven science and technology parks distributed across six governorates, including Alexandria and Beni Suef.

Currently,there are 11 free zones in Egypt, including Alexandria Free Zone, Nasr City Free Zone, Suez Free Zone, Ismailia Free Zone, Damietta Free Zone, Port Said Free Zone, and Al Rahmaniyah Free Zone. The supervising authority is the General Authority for Investment and Free Zones. Free zones have played an important role in promoting Egypt's exports and employment. These zones have created 1 million direct and indirect jobs, accounting for 24% of Egypt's total exports. As of April 2019, investment projects in the 11 free zones reached a total of 1,095, attracting foreign investment worth $12.5 billion and infrastructure investment of $26.3 billion, while providing 194,000 direct employment opportunities.

4. Overview of Local Enterprises in Egypt

The light industry of Egypt is predominantly occupied by textile and food processing industries, whereas the heavy industry is dominated by petrochemical, machinery manufacturing, and automobile industries (Refer to Table 7–7). Over the past decade, industries such as garment and leather products, building materials, fertilizers, and pharmaceuticals have experienced significant growth. The industries of petroleum, iron and steel, electricity, fertilizers, cement, electromechanical, pharmaceuticals, tanning, and ceramics have developed at varying levels. Among these, the automobile manufacturing and assembly sector is experiencing rapid growth, while the oil and gas industry, particularly the petrochemical industry is rapidly developing.

Table 7–7 Representative Enterprises in Egypt

Company Name	Industry Involved	Business Scope	Talent Demand
Infinity Group	Africa's largest company for renewable energy	Providing solar, wind and garbage power solutions. Developing utility-scale solar and wind projects	Workers who are familiar with technology and engi-neering
Orascom Construction Industries	One of Egypt's most famous construction companies and building material suppliers	Construction, building materials, petrochemicals, transportation, port construction, etc.	Engineering technicians

continued

Company Name	Industry Involved	Business Scope	Talent Demand
Elsewedy Electric	Leading enterprise of the electric meter and instrument industry	Instruments and apparatus, industrial automation	People proficient in various languages and technologies
GB Auto	The largest car assembler in the country	Assembling line	Production workers, assembly workers, and parts R&D technicians
Oriental Weavers Carpet Company	The world's largest manufacturer of woven carpets	Carpets and textile production, modernization of the textile and garment industry	Applied technology talents

7.1.3 Status of Vocational Education

Egypt's general education system consists of basic and higher education. Basic education includes education in the kindergartens, primary and secondary schools. Elementary education lasts for 6 years. Junior high schools offer either general preparatory education or vocational preparatory education, each lasting for 3 years. Vocational preparatory education adds vocational skills courses to the basic cultural curriculum and is equivalent to vocational secondary schools in China. There are two types of senior high schools: regular high schools with a 3-year school system and secondary technical schools with either a 3- or 5-year school system. Regular high school students can enroll in colleges with a 4-year course or higher vocational schools with a 2-year course of study. Graduates from secondary technical schools can also be admitted to higher vocational schools (See Tables 7–8).

Table 7–8 The Education System in Egypt

<table>
<tr><th>Grade</th><th colspan="2">Educational Level</th><th>Regulatory Agency</th></tr>
<tr><td>2</td><td colspan="2" rowspan="2">Doctor</td><td rowspan="8">Ministry of Higher Education & Ministry of Science and Research</td></tr>
<tr><td>1</td></tr>
<tr><td>2</td><td colspan="2" rowspan="2">Master</td></tr>
<tr><td>1</td></tr>
<tr><td>4</td><td rowspan="4">Universities and higher education institutions</td><td rowspan="2">—</td></tr>
<tr><td>3</td></tr>
<tr><td>2</td><td rowspan="2">Higher vocational education schools</td></tr>
<tr><td>1</td></tr>
</table>

continued

<table>
<tr><th>Grade</th><th colspan="2">Educational Level</th><th>Regulatory Agency</th></tr>
<tr><td>12</td><td rowspan="3">General high schools (3years)</td><td rowspan="3">Secondary vocational education schools (3 or 5 years)</td><td rowspan="12">Ministry of Education and the Technical Education</td></tr>
<tr><td>11</td></tr>
<tr><td>10</td></tr>
<tr><td>9</td><td rowspan="3">General preparatory education (junior middle schools)</td><td rowspan="3">Vocational preparatory education (junior middle schools)</td></tr>
<tr><td>8</td></tr>
<tr><td>7</td></tr>
<tr><td>6</td><td colspan="2" rowspan="6">Primary schools</td></tr>
<tr><td>5</td></tr>
<tr><td>4</td></tr>
<tr><td>3</td></tr>
<tr><td>2</td></tr>
<tr><td>1</td></tr>
<tr><td>Kindergarten 2</td><td colspan="2" rowspan="2">Kindergartens</td><td rowspan="2">Ministry of Social Solidarity</td></tr>
<tr><td>Kindergarten 1</td></tr>
</table>

There are not many higher vocational institutions in Egypt; the training system for secondary- and higher-vocational personnel has failed to cohere. Additionally, the vocational education system is relatively inadequate to meet the demand for training a large number of high-level technical personnel. The establishment of the Egypt Luban Workshops compensates for these weaknesses in the Egyptian vocational education system and provides a channel for technical and skilled talents to improve their academic qualifications and technical skills. The simultaneous establishment of two Luban Workshops for secondary and higher vocational education respectively further enhances the strength of running higher vocational schools, optimizes the Egyptian vocational education system, meets the needs for developing vocational education, and contributes to the reform and development of vocational education in Egypt.

7.1.4 Vocational Education and Industry

Egypt has a population of more than 100 million, making it the third most populous country in Africa. With a workforce exceeding 29 million, Egypt possesses ample labor resources. Egypt's overall GDP index has demonstrated steady growth over the past five years, and the prospects for economic development are promising. Continued recovery in sectors such as manufacturing, agriculture, telecommunications and IT is expected to attract more investment and create a large number of job opportunities. Egypt is a major exporter of labor services, with abundant labor resources and little demand for foreign workers. Due to the dire domestic employment situation, the Egyptian government has imposed severe restrictions on the entry of foreign labor into the country. Additionally, due to average production efficiency, particularly the shortage of skilled and semi-skilled workers as well as management personnel, wages in Egypt are relatively low (as shown in Figure 7–6).

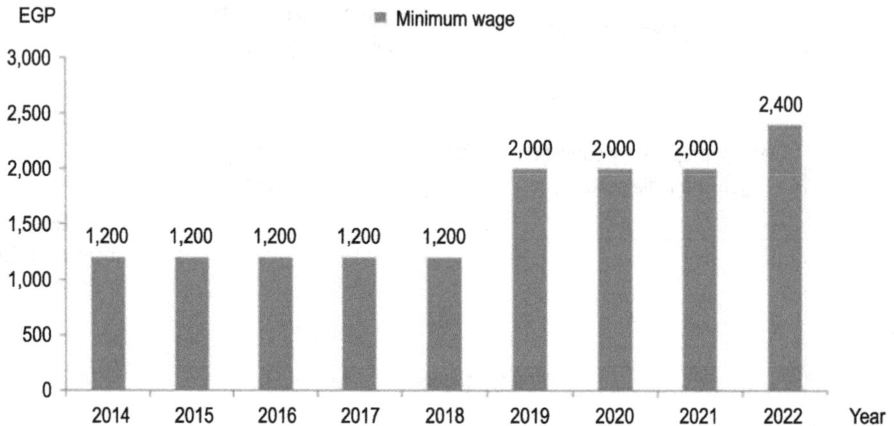

Figure 7–6 Changes in Egypt's Minimum Wage Standard (EGP / month)

Source: CAPMAS (Egypt)

The development of vocational education in Egypt has been relatively slow. The limited number of higher vocational institutions makes it challenging to satisfy the demand for skilled workers in the labor market. Currently, there is not only a situation in Egypt where the skill level fails to meet employment demands but also a mismatch between the skill structure and labor market structure, leading to a shortage of highly qualified technical and managerial personnel.

In the case of the new energy sector, Egypt lacks of personnel with relevant experience and technology in the photovoltaic industry. Additionally, due to the impact of the COVID-19 pandemic, the suspension and reduction of international flights have hampered personnel exchanges, making it difficult for overseas personnel to arrive in Egypt promptly to carry out their work. Currently, the Egyptian PV industry is accelerating its development with a planned installed capacity of 43 GW by 2035. On October 28, 2022, Power Construction Corporation of China and AMEA Power held a signing ceremony for the 500 MW Gulf of Suez II wind farm project, the largest wind power project in Egypt in terms of capacity. The construction phase could provide over 1,000 direct jobs as well as a significant number of jobs related to materials, transportation and other auxiliary services. Once completed, it is expected to generate approximately 2.7 billion kWh of clean energy per year. However, there is currently a huge shortage of technical and managerial personnel in the new energy sector.

7.1.5 International Economic Cooperation

Egypt is one of the United States' key partners in the Middle East and the second-largest recipient of U.S. direct investment in Africa. In 2004, Egypt, the United States and Israel signed an agreement on Qualified Industrial Zone, which has further strengthened their economic relations. The European Union is one of Egypt's most important economic and trade partners, with bilateral trade accounting for 40% of Egypt's total foreign trade, and the two sides have extensive and in-depth cooperation in political, economic and security spheres. Since 2009, Egypt's relations with Russia have developed steadily through frequent exchanges of high-level visits and good military cooperation. In 2020, Egypt accounted for 40% of the total trade volume between Russia and Africa, making it Russia's main partner in Africa and the Middle East.

Egypt has signed various multilateral and bilateral trade agreements with the United States, the European Union, as well as Middle Eastern and African countries. Under these agreements, the majority of Egyptian exports to the agreed areas enjoy a free trade policy with zero tariffs and have access to major markets, providing security for manufacturers based in Egypt. Positioned as a global and regional hub for services, production and transit, Egypt has created numerous jobs and contributed to economic growth by opening up new markets for domestic products, attracting direct investment from foreign enterprises, and taking advantage of unique preferential trade agreements, competitive labor and utility costs, along with convenient proximity to major global markets. These advantages make Egypt as an ideal export logistics hub for Europe, the Arab world, the United States and Africa.

7.2 Chinese-Funded Enterprises and International Production Capacity Cooperation

7.2.1 Egyptian Industrial Development and Its Demand for Foreign Investment

China and Egypt are engaged in all-round cooperation in industries, energy, telecommunications and infrastructure construction. Chinese companies have successfully won bids for national projects such as the Central Business District at the new administrative capital, and the 10th of Ramadan Light Rail Transit (LRT). The operation of Chinese-funded enterprises have been somewhat affected during the COVID-19 pandemic, but the overall situation is under control. After the normalization of the epidemic, production has basically resumed without any major shutdowns or divestments, and investment and cooperation projects have maintained their normal operation. The ongoing projects are progressing steadily without significant impact. China and Egypt have also collaborated to establish the first production lines for medical masks and vaccines respectively. Egypt has offered extensive support in terms of finance, taxation, industry and enterprises.

China has been Egypt's biggest trading partner for many years. In 2020, the bilateral trade in goods between China and Egypt stood at $14.53 billion. Bilateral trade in goods between China and Egypt reached $19.97 billion in 2021, showing a year-on-year increase of $5.444,197,5 billion or 37.3% compared to the same period in 2020 (Refer to Figure 7–7).

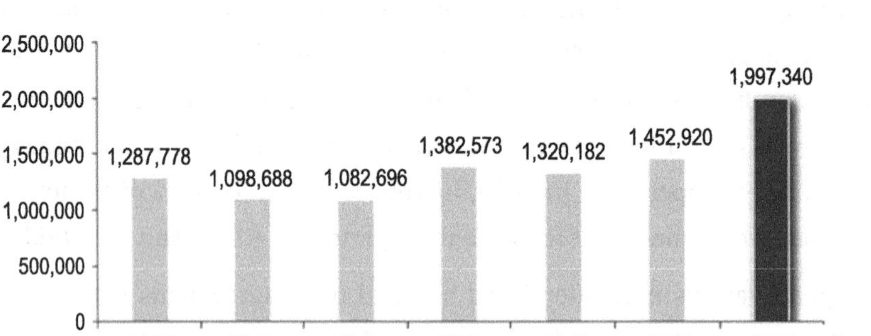

Figure 7–7 The Import-Export Volume of Bilateral Trade in Goods Between China and Egypt, 2015—2021

7.2.2 Status Quo and Development of Chinese Enterprises

1. An Overview of Chinese Investments in Egypt

According to China's Ministry of Commerce, the direct investment flow from China to Egypt reached $27.34 million in 2020. By the end of 2020, the stock of China's direct investment in Egypt amounted to $1.19 billion (See Table 7–9).

According to the General Authority for Investment and Free Zones, there are over 1,500 Chinese-funded enterprises registered in Egypt, with investments concentrated in oil and gas extraction, manufacturing, construction, IT and services. More than 140 Chinese-funded enterprises are registered at the Economic and Commercial Office of the Chinese Embassy in Egypt, engaging in economic and trade activities. Among them, 80 are officially registered in Egypt while the rest consist of informal institutions such as liaison offices and project departments (see Table 7–10).

Table 7–9 China's Direct Investment in Egypt, 2016–2020 (ten thousand US dollars)

Year	2016	2017	2018	2019	2020
Flow	11,983	9,276	22,197	1,096	2,743
Stock(by the end of each year)	88,891	83,484	107,926	108,580	119,172

Source: *2020 Statistical Bulletin of China's Outward Foreign Direct Investment* jointly issued by China's Ministry of Commerce, the National Bureau of Statistics, and the State Administration of Foreign Exchange

Table 7–10 China's Key Investment Enterprises and Business Scope in Egypt

Name of Chinese Investors	Name of Overseas Enterprises (Institutions)	Business Scope
Sinopec Star Petroleum Company	Sino-Tharwa Drilling Company, Egypt	Land and offshore drilling, workover engineering, and rig equipment trade

continued

Name of Chinese Investors	Name of Overseas Enterprises (Institutions)	Business Scope
ZhenHua Oil Co., Ltd.	North Petroleum International Company Limited	Oil and gas exploration and production
China-Africa TEDA Investment Co., Ltd.	EGYPT-TEDA Investment Company / EGYPT-TEDA SEZONE Development Company	Development, construction, operation and management of industrial zones
Jushi Group Co., Ltd.	Jushi Egypt for Fiberglass Industry S.A.E	Manufacture and sale of fiberglass products
Huawei Technologies Co., Ltd.	Huawei Egypt	Communication equipment, IT products and related services
China XD Group Co., Ltd.	XDEGEMAC HV Electric Equipment Co., Ltd.	Manufacture, sale and service of power transmission and transformation products such as high-voltage switches, transformers, capacitors, and arresters
Angel Yeast Co., Ltd.	Angel Yeast (Egypt) Co., Ltd.	Production of dry yeast, baking powder, bio-fertilizer
New Hope Liuhe Co., Ltd.	New Hope Egypt Co., Ltd.	Production and processing of feed, and breeding poultry
Midea Group Co., Ltd.	Carrier/Midea Joint Venture (Miraco)	Manufacture and sale of air conditioners
Konka Group Co., Ltd.	KONKO Technologies Co., Ltd.	Manufacture and sale of televisions and other home appliances

Source: Economic and Commercial Office of the Chinese Embassy in Egypt

2. Current Situation of Chinese-funded Enterprises in Egypt

(1) China-Egypt Suez Economic & Trade Cooperation Zone

The main economic and trade cooperation zone constructed by Chinese-funded enterprises in Egypt is the China-Egypt Suez Economic and Trade Cooperation Zone. Founded in 2008, it is a state-level overseas economic and trade cooperation zone guided by China's Ministry of Commerce and promoted by the Tianjin municipal government. It is jointly funded by Tianjin TEDA Investment Holding and China-Africa Development Fund, and operated by China-Africa TEDA Investment Co., Ltd. (hereinafter referred to as China-Africa TEDA). After more than a decade of development and construction, it has gradually become one of the main platforms for economic and trade cooperation as well as cultural exchanges between China and Egypt. The cooperation zone is located in the Suez Canal Economic Zone (SCZone), which serves as the golden triangle connecting Asia, Africa and Europe. It is adjacent to the Suez Canal, just 2 km away from Ain Sokhna, Egypt's third-largest seaport, with a highway connecting it to Cairo. The cooperation zone mainly focuses on industrial projects in processing and manufacturing, logistics, bonded warehousing, technology development, commerce and trade, and modern services.

It is also an international industrial base and a modern new city that integrates residential, commercial, financial and other functional areas. The cooperation zone covers an area of 7.34 square kilometers with an initial area of 1.34 square kilometers and a cumulative investment of approximately $146 million. All development and construction have been completed to form four leading industries: new building materials, petroleum equipment, high and low voltage equipment, and machinery manufacturing. The expansion covers an area of 6 square kilometers with a planned development investment of $230 million. The first phase of infrastructure construction in the expansion area has been completed while being divided into four leading industries: passenger vehicles, textiles, building materials and chemical engineering.

The cooperation zone is governed by the *Egyptian Special Economic Zone Law* and benefits from the policy of returning 50% of investment costs to companies in Zone A under the *Investment Law*. By the end of April 2021, the zone has attracted 102 enterprises, with actual investment exceeding $1.25 billion, cumulative sales surpassing $2.5 billion, tax payments approaching $176 million, and creating over 30,000 jobs. Key enterprises include Jushi Group, Famsun Muyang Group, XD Group, etc. (Refer to Table 7–11).

Table 7–11 Representative Chinese-funded Enterprises in the China-Egypt Suez Economic and Trade Cooperation Zone

Company Name	Affiliated Industrial Park	Business Scope	Talent Demand
Egyptian Petroleum HH Rig Manufacturing S.A.E Co.	Petroleum Equipment	local manufacturing of oil rigs in Egypt	Skilled and well-trained workers
XDEGEMAC HV Electric Equipment Co., Ltd.	High and Low-Voltage Electrical Appliances	500 kV ultra-high voltage transformer manufacturing, electrical equipment	Over 500 jobs provided, Local engineering and technical personnel can participate in the product design, production, site operation, installation and commissioning
Egypt CTMC Nonwovens Co., Ltd.	Textile and Garments	Production of PP spunbond non-woven fabrics and non-woven products	Provide over 500 jobs, transfer technology and train technical personnel to Egypt
Jushi Egypt for Fiberglass Industry S.A.E	New Building Materials	Africa's only fiberglass production base	Provide 2,000 direct employment opportunities
Muyang Warehousing Co., Ltd.	Machinery Manufacturing	Construction of production lines specialized in grain storage steel silos, and feed machinery	Skilled and well-trained workers
TBEA Xinjiang Sunoasis Co., Ltd.	The largest solar project in Africa	Installed capacity of 186 MW	Provide 5,000 jobs and require a large number of Egyptian workers and engineers

continued

Company Name	Affiliated Industrial Park	Business Scope	Talent Demand
Zhejiang CHINT New Energy Development Co.,	The largest solar project in Africa	Installed capacity of 165.5 MW	Provide a large number of employment opportunities
Haier Smart Home Co., Ltd.	Home appliances	Production of air conditioners, washing machines, folding screens, refrigerators, freezers, etc.	Skilled and well-trained workers

Enterprises settled in the cooperation zone benefit from tax exemption, duty-free policies, and bonded policies under the bonded zone system, thus enjoying more favorable and superior conditions for their import and export activities. To support Chinese enterprises in "going global", the Chinese government has launched a $40 billion Silk Road Fund, while the Asian Infrastructure Investment Bank offers financial backing for the "Belt and Road" Initiative.

(2) The 500 kV Transmission Kine Project of State Grid

The project was undertaken by the Egypt branch of China Electric Power Equipment and Technology Company (a subsidiary of State Grid) in the form of "EPC+F". The project construction includes fifteen 500 kV double-circuit AC lines on the same tower, with a total length of about 1,210 km. In January 2016, the project officially started with a scheduled construction period of 18 months and a contract value of $757 million. Egypt's Ministry of Finance has provided a sovereign guarantee. The project is the first to be signed, executed and financially closed under China-Egypt Production Capacity Cooperation. It also has been the largest transmission line project in Egypt for many years.

(3) Projects at the Benban Solar PV Park in Aswan, Egypt

TBEA Xinjiang Sunoasis, along with Spanish power developer Acciona and Dubai-based Swicorp, has jointly invested in three 50 MW photovoltaic projects in Egypt, in which TBEA holds a 24% stake, while undertaking the EPC execution of these three projects. This is the first time for Chinese-funded enterprises to participate in investment in Egypt's PV sector, and it is also their first investment in power generation in Egypt (See Table 7–12). Financing for the projects was jointly provided by an international consortium of banks, including the International Finance Corporation (IFC) of the World Bank, the Industrial and Commercial Bank of China (ICBC), and the Asian Infrastructure Investment Bank. Additionally, Egypt has become the first Arab and African country to receive financing support from the Asian Infrastructure Investment Bank. The total EPC amount for these three projects is approximately $130 million.

Table 7–12 Projects at the Benban Solar PV Park in Aswan, Egypt

Company Name	Business Scope	Talent Demand
TBEA Xinjiang Sunoasis Co., Ltd.	Installed capacity of 186 MW	Provide 5,000 jobs and require a large number of Egyptian workers and engineers
Zhejiang CHINT New Energy Development Co., Ltd.	Installed capacity of 165.5 MW	Provide a large number of employment opportunities
Acciona, Spanish developer of renewable energy projects	Jointly constructed three large PV plants with a total installed capacity of 186 MW	Skilled workers and engineers
Dubai-based Swicorp	Jointly constructed three large PV plants with a total installed capacity of 186 MW	Skilled engineering technicians

(4) The 10th of Ramadan Light Rail Transit (LRT)

The project is to construct a double-track electrified light rail line with a design speed of 120 km/h, connecting the urban areas of Cairo, the 10th of Ramadan City and the new administrative capital. There will be 11 stations covering a total mileage of about 66 km. The project's estimated cost is approximately $1.29 billion, and it is funded by China.

(5) Haier Home Appliances and Food Industrial Complex in the 10th of Ramadan City

On August 4, 2022, Egyptian Prime Minister Moustafa Madbouly attended the signing ceremony of the Memorandum of Understanding between the General Authority for Investment and Free Zones and China's Haier Smart Home Company at the government headquarters in Al 'Alamayn New City. According to the plan, Haier Group Corporation will invest in the construction of a 200,000-square-meter home appliances and food industrial complex in Egypt's 10th of Ramadan City, with a total investment estimated at $130 million. Haier Group will introduce advanced technology into its planned projects, thereby helping Egypt become an investment center for the home appliance industry and attracting new investors in the home appliance processing industry. The project creates more than 2,000 jobs for Egypt while achieving a production capacity of 900,000 devices annually, aimed at meeting the needs of the local market and as a center for exporting products to African and Asian countries.

7.2.3 Chinese-Funded Enterprises' Demand for Vocational Education

The majority of Chinese-funded enterprises "going global" belong to industries such as petroleum equipment, textiles, building materials, home appliances and machinery manufacturing. With an increasing number of Chinese-funded enterprises "going global," comes a significant rise in jobs for partner countries. Consequently, there is a growing demand for skilled local workers and engineers. However, in Egypt, the vocational education professions do not align well with its industrial development. Despite accounting for 47% of all educational institutions, merely 12% of technical college graduates are employed by industrial companies. This discrepancy indicates that Egyptian vocational colleges fail to cater to the actual needs of its industrial economy, and the individuals they trained are struggle to fulfill industry and enterprise requirements, resulting in a persistent phenomenon of "educated unemployed". This is a common characteristic of the labor market in Egypt and across the MENA region.

7.2.4 Adaptability of Egyptian Vocational Education to the Development of Chinese-Funded Enterprises

Through systematic data collection and investigation, it was found that the development of vocational education in Egypt has been relatively slow. In order to improve the quality of vocational education in Egypt and better adapt it to industrial development, Egypt Vision 2020 puts forward the following goals for vocational education and training: implementing a world-standard quality and certification system to equip learners and trainers with the skills required by the job market; providing comprehensive and sustainable career planning for teachers and trainers; continuously improving curricula and learning programs; building a sound organizational system for vocational education (vocational, technical and training) that can adapt to development planning and the job market.

It can be seen that the Egyptian government has fully taken into account the importance of vocational education and training in the development of industries and enterprises. However, there are still many aspects of vocational education in Egypt that are not adapted to the development of Chinese-funded enterprises. They are as follows:

(1) The policy support for vocational education by the Egyptian government needs improvement. Over the years, fewer than a dozen policy documents on vocational education have been issued by the Egyptian government and its education authorities. The development of vocational education in Egypt lacks strong policy and legislative support.

(2) The recognition of vocational education by Egyptian citizens needs improvement. There is a prevalent phenomenon of "prioritizing general education over vocational education." According to statistics, the majority of students prefer attending high schools within the general education system and subsequently entering regular higher education institutions, while only a minority show interest in vocational colleges.

(3) The vocational education system in Egypt requires further improvement. A survey said that while there are over 800 secondary vocational schools, there is a shortage of higher vocational schools and the admission is not smooth. Additionally, inadequate facilities and a lack of practical experience among teachers in vocational schools severely impact the quality of education they provide.

(4) The participation of Egyptian industrial enterprises in vocational education needs to be improved. The integration of industry and education, as well as the cooperation between schools

and enterprises, is at a low level in Egypt. Vocational colleges lack corresponding professional standards, and their professional settings do not match the key and pillar industries of Egypt's current economic development. As a result, graduates of vocational colleges struggle to meet the needs of local and Chinese companies.

(5) The local labor force needs to receive additional vocational education and training. According to the survey conducted by China First Highway Engineering Co., Ltd., only 23% of local employees have received vocational education above the secondary level, a small number of employees are graduates of ordinary colleges and universities, and most employees are unemployed local residents who have not received any vocational education or training. This phenomenon is common in the employment practices of Chinese-funded enterprises in Egypt.

In short, vocational education in Egypt is at a relatively low level. There is a lack of a reasonably structured system for vocational education in Egypt, and there is no national framework for vocational qualifications. Professional setting and curriculum provision have lagged behind industrial development, and the quality of teachers in vocational colleges is subpar. Moreover, the integration of industry and education as well as the cooperation between schools and enterprises are also lacking, with the latter failing to play a guiding role in vocational education. Furthermore, Egypt lacks systematic research on vocational education and has fewer research institutions and specialized personnel. Therefore, it is urgent for Egypt to significantly develop its vocational education.

7.3 Chinese-Funded Enterprises Collaborating with Chinese Vocational Education for "Going Global"

7.3.1 The Necessity of Chinese Vocational Education Supporting Egypt's International Production Capacity Cooperation

China's investment in Egypt spans across a number of sectors, including petroleum equipment, high and low-voltage electrical appliances, new energy, textiles, new building materials, machinery manufacturing, and household appliances. Regarding household appliances, in August 2022, the General Authority for Investment and Free Zones signed a memorandum of understanding with Haier Group, a Chinese home appliances company, to jointly establish an industrial park for the production of household appliances and related products. In terms of new energy, China Energy Engineering Group Zhejiang Thermal Power Construction Co., Ltd. showcased its newly launched small-capacity wind-solar storage integrated solution at the China (Egypt) Trade Fair in June 2022. Egypt is considered a key country for Zhejiang Thermal Power's overseas expansion due to its focus on addressing the inconvenience and high cost of electricity consumption faced by Egypt's agricultural and animal husbandry bases located in the desert areas.

Against the backdrop of the strong demand for China-Egypt international production capacity cooperation and the inability of local vocational education in Egypt to meet the development needs of Chinese-funded enterprises, there is an urgent need for vocational education to cooperate with Chinese-funded enterprises in entering Egypt, serving China-Egypt international production capacity cooperation, and training technical and skilled talents who are familiar with Chinese technology and craftsmanship. Collaborating with Chinese vocational education in "going global" is of great importance for Chinese-funded enterprises.

7.3.2 Internationalization of Chinese Vocational Education in Egypt

1. Egyptian Chinese College for Applied Technology (ECCAT), the Egyptian Branch of Beijing Information Technology College

In 2016, to actively support the construction of the "Belt and Road" and assist Chinese enterprises in "going global", Beijing Information Technology College collaborated with Suez Canal University and Misr El Kheir Foundation (MEK) in Egypt to establish ECCAT. The college began admitting students from 2018 onwards. ECCAT provides a four-year vocational and technical education program with majors in electronic engineering technology, communications technology, and mechatronics technology, etc. The college currently accommodates 390 students and its first batch of graduates completed their studies in 2022. As the first high-level vocational education collaboration project between China and Egypt, ECCAT has introduced a new model of cooperation in the field of vocational education for both countries. Details of the partner organizations are as follows:

(1)Beijing Information Technology College

Beijing Information Technology College currently has several secondary schools offering more than 30 majors, including the School of Artificial Intelligence, School of Industrial Internet, School of Electronic Information, School of Digital Commerce, and School of Digital Art. The college is a construction unit for a distinctive high-level vocational college in Beijing as well as China's Double High-level Plan.

(2)Suez Canal University

Suez Canal University (SCU) is a government-affiliated comprehensive university and one of the well-known universities in Egypt. The university has branch campuses in Port Said and Al Arish, focusing on undergraduate education while actively developing graduate education. The university has the authority to award bachelor's and master's degrees. It comprises 25 faculties and departments, including liberal arts, economics, medicine, computer and information technology, agricultural sciences, business management, tourism and hospitality management, as well as Chinese language larguage and literature.

2. Luban Workshops in Egypt

The Luban Workshops in Egypt, jointly built by Tianjin Light Industry Vocational Technical College, Tianjin Transportation Technical College, Ain Shams University, and the Advanced Technical School for Maintenance Technology in Cairo, was officially unveiled on November 30, 2020. Among them, the campus of Ain Shams University covers an area of 1,200 square meters with three specialized training rooms for CNC equipment application and maintenance, new energy application technology, and automotive application and maintenance technology. The 620-square-meter campus of the Advanced Technical School for Maintenance Technology in Cairo has two specialized training rooms for CNC machining technology and automotive maintenance technology. It also includes a training area for intelligent MicroMouse. For the first time in Egypt, the Luban Workshop has implemented a vocational education system that connects middle and high vocational schools. This means that after students complete their secondary vocational studies at the Luban Workshop of the Advanced Technical School for Maintenance Technology in Cairo, they can be promoted to study at the Luban Workshop of Ain Shams University for higher vocational education. From there they can graduate with an undergraduate diploma. Details of the partner organizations are as follows:

(1)Tianjin Light Industry Vocational Technical College has four secondary schools, namely Mechanical Engineering, Electronic Information and Automation, Economic Management, and Art Engineering, offering 35 majors. It is a national excellent exemplary backbone higher vocational college, and one of the top 50 service contributors of higher vocational colleges in China. Additionally, it is a construction unit of the national Double High-level Plan and Tianjin's World Advanced Higher Vocational College, as well as the host of the National Vocational College Skills Competition for 12 consecutive years.

(2)With 7 secondary schools and 3 teaching departments, Tianjin Transportation Technical College offers 38 majors in 6 professional clusters, which include automotive application technology, modern logistics, traffic construction, rail transit, intelligent manufacturing technology, and transportation services. As one of the first batch of national backbone higher vocational colleges, Tianjin Transportation Technical College serves as a construction unit for the national Double High-level Plan and aims to enhance Tianjin's school-running capabilities in order to build world-class schools. Moreover, it has been hosting vocational skills competitions at both national and local level for many years.

(3)Founded in 1950, Ain Shams University is the third university established in Egypt. As an important scientific and cultural institution in Egypt, Ain Shams University plays an undeniable role in advancing Egyptian culture and science, and enriching human knowledge. Currently, the university has 8 campuses, 16 secondary schools, 3 research centers, and a total of 200 departments, and offers 952 learning programs. The school has an enrollment of over 200,000 students and employs more than 14,000 staff members.

(4)The Advanced Technical School for Maintenance Technology in Cairo was established in 1996. It is a five-year senior school located in Nasr City, Cairo Governorate, Egypt. The school offers majors such as mechanical equipment repair, electric grid, wood furniture repair, construction, plumbing, metal furniture repair, and renewable energy. It was first accredited by the National Authority for Quality Assurance and Accreditation of Education (NAQAAE) in 2009 and then successfully re-accredited in 2012 and 2014.

7.3.3 Forms and Achievements of Internationalized Education

1. Overview of Cooperation Between Germany and Egypt

(1) Cooperation Background

Germany has cooperated with Egypt in running schools and providing financial aid through vocational and technical training. In 2011, Germany implemented the Debt-for-Development swap, which reinvested Egypt's four-year debt to Germany totaling 300 million euros into development projects aimed at improving vocational education, enhancing employment of young people, and increasing investment in Egypt. In 2019, the Egyptian-German Technical Academy was established in the Suez Canal Economic Zone as the first vocational and technical training center in the region. The training center was jointly established by Siemens, the German Federal Ministry for Economic Cooperation and Development (BMZ), and German Corporation for International Cooperation GmbH (GIZ), with a total investment of 22 million euros. It planned to provide vocational and technical training for 5,000 people in the Suez Canal Economic Zone from 2019 to 2023. Additionally, Germany and Egypt signed an agreement on a dual education and training system known as the Mubarak-Kohl Initiative.

(2) Form of Cooperation

Relying on the model of German Universities of Applied Sciences (UAS), Egypt provides local support to establish a mutually beneficial and win-win cooperation model. In 2018, Professor Ashraf Mansour, who successfully founded the German University in Cairo (GUC) in 2001, proposed the establishment of the German International University of Applied Technologies (GIU-AS) in Egypt. Designed and operated by the Alliance of German Universities of Applied Sciences (UAS7), GIU-AS is primarily responsible for developing professional-level degree programs and providing support during their establishment process. The local partner, the German University in Cairo, supports this project by providing teaching buildings, classrooms, laboratories, IT technology, and other supporting services.

The establishment of the project GIU-AS, which is oriented towards practice and the needs of the local labor market, relies on the model of German Universities of Applied Sciences. It awards degrees (Bachelor's and Master's degrees) according to Germany's learning curriculum, academic standards, rules, and regulations. The project emphasizes hands-on professional training and aims to align graduates' competencies with the needs of the Egyptian labor market. Initially, it offered courses in engineering technology, business economics, information technology, and design.

2. Overview of Cooperation between Japan and Egypt

(1) Cooperation Background

Japan's foreign aid focuses on vocational and technical education and training in agriculture, engineering, and medicine, with an emphasis on developing skilled human resources for recipient countries. Major aid projects are related to mathematics, science and technology. Experts in these disciplines account for 31% of the total sent overseas by Japan, while funding accounts for 22% of the total allocation. For example, from 1997 to 2000, the Micro Project Technical Assistance for Innovative Curriculum Development in Primary Education was launched in Egypt with a focus on mathematics, science and technology education.

(2) Form of Cooperation

In 2006, Japan and Egypt collaborated to set up a skills training center. In 2010, they jointly inaugurated the Egypt-Japan University of Science and Technology (E-JUST) with the aim of introducing Japanese science and technology education, training technical and skilled talents proficient in Japanese science and technology skills as well as standards to Middle Eastern and African countries by conducting research on applied education according to standards in industrial enterprises. Additionally, Japan provided funding for the Entrepreneurship Curriculum Program (ECP) in Egypt, which seeks to impart theoretical and practical knowledge of entrepreneurship education while fostering an entrepreneurial culture among students in secondary technical colleges to meet local economic development needs.

3. Overview of Cooperation between China and Egypt

(1) Cooperation Background

In 2004, China and Egypt issued a joint statement on establishing a comprehensive strategic partnership. Within the framework of the joint statement, the two sides encouraged exchanges between higher education institutions, academic and scientific research institutions, vocational schools, and news media. They also promoted increasing exchanges of scholarships and academic grants. So far, Egyptian universities such as Suez Canal University, Cairo University, Alexandria University, and Ain Shams University have signed memorandums of understanding and engaged in joint projects with Chinese universities such as Peking University, Beijing Language and Culture University, Beijing Foreign Studies University, Shanghai International Studies University, and Anhui University.

(2) Form of Cooperation

The Egyptian Chinese College for Applied Technology (ECCAT) was officially established in 2017. ECCAT is jointly operated by Beijing Information Technology College, Misr El Kheir Foundation (MEK) and Suez Canal University. It mainly offers a four-year applied undergraduate education, focusing on three majors: mechatronics technology, electronic engineering, and communications technology. The goal is to cultivate high-quality applied engineering and technical personnel who can speak Chinese, understand technology, possess strong skills, and play a role as an expert in both technology and management in Egypt's economic construction. In November 2020, the Luban Workshops were officially inaugurated and put into operation in Egypt, making the first instance of "Two Workshops in One Country". These two workshops in Egypt were jointly built by Tianjin Light Industry Vocational Technical College, Tianjin Transportation Technical College in cooperation with Ain Shams University and the Advanced Technical School for Maintenance Technology in cairo, which is directly under the Egyptian Ministry of Education and Technical Education. Dedicated to providing technical skills training to Egyptian young people, they offer majors in CNC equipment application and maintenance, new energy application technology, automotive application and maintenance, as well as CNC machining technology. They have implemented systematic training combining vocational education and undergraduate applied disciplines.

7.4 Tianjin Light Industry Vocational Technical College's Support for Egypt's International Production Capacity Cooperation

7.4.1 Current Situation Analysis

The construction of the "Belt and Road" Initiative opens opened doors wider for Chinese enterprises to "going global", and vocational education seizes this opportunity to go abroad and keep pace with the world. Tianjin Light Industry Vocational Technical College actively serves the building of "Belt and Road" by assisting Chinese-funded enterprises to "going global" and actively participating in the development of China-Africa vocational education cooperation. In 2020, Tianjin Light Industry Vocational Technical College, Tianjin Transportation Technical College, Ain Shams University, and the Advanced Technical School for Maintenance Technology in Cairo jointly established Egypt Luban Workshops as a carrier and platform for China-Egypt international production capacity cooperation. Its aim is to enhance Egyptian vocational education's adaptability to Chinese-funded enterprises through professional construction, teaching materials development, teacher training, teaching equipment maintenance, and talent cultivation. Thanks to the efforts of Tianjin Light Industry Vocational Technical College, the African Vocational Education Research Center was set up in 2021, In recent years, Tianjin Light Industry Vocational Technical College has focused on serving international production capacity cooperation and has engaged in deep collaboration with leading enterprises at home and abroad. By learning from international advanced experience and standards, the college through the construction and operation of Egypt Luban Workshops has created a "bridgehead" for industry-education integration between China and Africa. During its international education, Tianjin Light Industry Vocational Technical College has explored and built a global vocational education community for a shared future through the combination of "Chinese Language + Vocational Skills". It aims to assist countries along the "Belt and Road" to training more high-quality skilled talents who possess an understanding of Chinese technology and culture.

7.4.2 Construction Model: College-Enterprise Collaboration and Industry-Education Integration

Since their establishment, Egypt Luban Workshops have undertaken the mission of serving China-Egypt international production capacity cooperation. Based on local economic and industrial development, they have trained and provided local technical personnel to Chinese-funded enterprises in Egypt, enhancing vocational education capabilities to serve international production capacity cooperation. Currently, Egypt Luban Workshops have established exchange and cooperation mechanisms with several enterprises, an overview of which is given below.

1. China-Egypt TEDA Suez Economic and Trade Cooperation Zone

The China-Egypt TEDA Suez Economic and Trade Cooperation Zone is a key and landmark project for China-Egypt cooperation, as well as a demonstration project for China-Africa cooperation, in the construction of the "Belt and Road". After more than 10 years of construction, the TEDA Cooperation Zone has become Egypt's industrial park with the best-integrated environment, the highest investment density and unit output, and the largest number of Chinese-funded enterprises. Currently, it has attracted 101 enterprises to settle in, with actual investment exceeding $1.25 billion, cumulative sales surpassing $2.5 billion, a localization rate of over 90% for employees, direct employment for nearly 4,000 people, and industry-driven employment for about 40,000 people. The TEDA Cooperation Zone is fully utilizing its role as a platform to accelerate industrial agglomeration while promoting economic and trade cooperation between China and Egypt. It also contributes to the new development pattern where the domestic grand cycle serves as the main body while domestic and international dual cycles promote each other.

2. China First Highway Engineering Co., Ltd.

China First Highway Engineering Co., Ltd., a subsidiary of China Communications Construction Co., Ltd., is the world's leading integrated services provider for mega infrastructure projects, mainly engaged in investing, designing, and constructing transportation infrastructure such as highways, waterways, railways and airports. Established in 1963 with total assets exceeding 60 billion *yuan*, China First Highway Engineering Co., Ltd. is recognized as a state-level "high-tech enterprise" and a well-known brand enterprise with strong comprehensive strength in frastructure industry.

3. Hanergy Mobile Energy Holding Group Limited

Hanergy Mobile Energy Holdings Group is a global multinational in the clean energy sector and the world leader in thin-film solar power generation. Headquartered in Beijing, Hanergy has branches in many provinces across China as well as in other in 32 countries and regions worldwide. Currently, it has evolved into a high-tech clean energy enterprise that integrates the entire industrial chain of thin film power generation, including technology research and development, high-end equipment manufacturing, component production, and mobile energy applications. Additionally, it pioneered the concept of "mobile energy" globally and opened up a new industry focusing on "mobile energy."

4. Himile Mechanical Science and Technology (Shandong) Co., Ltd.

Himile Mechanical Science and Technology (Shandong) Co., Ltd. mainly develops four categories of products: tire molds, special CNC machine tools for tire molds, HVAC machinery, and natural rubber processing equipment. In 1997, China's first special EDM machine for tire mold processing was born in Himile, marking the entry of China's tire mold industry into the era of CNC mechanized production. Since then, the company has developed a range of products, such as CNC lettering machines for tire molds, CNC lathes, and electrode processing machine tools to lead the development of China's tire mold industry. The company's tire molds are well sold in Europe, America, Japan, South Korea, Singapore, the Middle East and other countries and regions due to their high precision and short production periods.

5.Tianjin Shengna Science and Technology Co., Ltd.

Tianjin Shengna Science and Technology Co., Ltd. (hereinafter referred to as Shengna Technology) is a national high-tech enterprise specialized in the research and development, production, sales and service of educational equipment. By introducing foreign advanced talent training and education models, Shengna Technology has developed training equipment related to new energy vehicle inspection and maintenance, automobile application and maintenance, automotive electronics, automotive sheet metal spray, automobile marketing, and new energy vehicle maintenance and overhaul. The company offers training rooms to colleges and universities of all levels, including new energy vehicle training rooms, theory-practice integration rooms for complete vehicle inspection, and automotive sheet metal spray training rooms. Since its inception, Shengna Technology has been engaging in exchanges with Tianjin Light Industry Vocational Technical College, and jointly signed a cooperation agreement for an off-campus practice base in June 2011. Relying on the college's PV engineering technology, the company and the school have jointly developed professional curriculum standards and online teaching resources, compiled teaching materials, applied for scientific research projects, and conducted technical research and development and achievement transformations. The new energy vehicle developed by Tianjin Light Industry Vocational Technical College and Shengna Technology has been applied and promoted in five Luban Workshops abroad. Currently, newly developed intelligent networked new energy vehicles can achieve self-driving and intelligent driving capabilities. Typical cases, which are formed based on the practical training functions of such vehicles, have been incorporated into the teaching. Additionally, related courses, resources, and loose-leaf teaching materials have been developed.

6.Yingli Group

Since 1999, Yingli Group has undertaken the NDRC's first demonstration project with an annual output of 3 MW of polysilicon solar cells and application systems, filling a gap in China's commercial production of solar energy. With the mission of "Producing Affordable Green Energy for Ordinary People", Yingli Group is committed to the production, R&D, application, AIOps, and green recycling of the entire photovoltaic industry chain, covering its complete life cycle. In 2012, Tianjin Yingli New Energy Resources Co., Ltd. reached a consensus on strategic cooperation with Tianjin Light Industry Vocational Technical College. The two sides completed jointly the development of the PV rooftop project, established a PV-R&D technology center based on the college with the participation from the company, and set up an exhibition center to promote both solar energy technology and the groups corporate culture.

The Luban Workshops in Egypt are the first example of establishing two different levels of workshops within one country. It implements various forms of education and training according to the needs of Chinese-funded enterprises, and adopts progressive training models for secondary-level and higher-level vocational training. The China-Egypt Industry-Education Integration Alliance aims to promote the integration between vocational industry and education in Egypt. The alliance includes Luban Workshops, partner colleges in Egypt, relevant industry management departments in Egypt, Chinese-funded enterprises in Egypt, and local enterprises for establishing a dialogue and exchange mechanism among industries, enterprises and colleges. It aims to gradually form a closely integrated industry-education organization in line with Egypt's industrial development plan, especially addressing the needs of highly skilled workers required by enterprises. Colleges and enterprises "go global hand in hand, as education going abroad with industry." Exemplified by the fact that vocational colleges in China are collaborating with enterprises such as EGYPT-TEDA SEZONE Development Company and Shandong Himile Group through Egypt Luban Workshops to address the shortage of local technical and skilled personnel during their overseas development, while enhancing the international influence of vocational education.

Egypt Luban Workshop operates and conducts teaching and training independently as a foreign entity, while Chinese colleges are responsible for guidance and supervision. This has led to the birth of the construction and operation mode of "One Body, Two Wings, and Four Linkages". Among them, "One Body" refers to supporting the reform and development of vocational and technical education in Egypt by training technical personnel; "Two Wings" refers to building bridges between China and Egypt through cultural exchanges and international production capacity cooperation; "Four Linkages" refers to synergy among the "government, cooperation zone, enterprise and college." With their construction and operation mode, the Egypt Luban Workshops have become a benchmark for the establishment of Luban workshops in Africa.

7.4.3 Institutional Mechanism: Multi-Party Collaboration for Mutual Benefit and Win-Win Results

Tianjin Light Industry Vocational Technical College and its partner enterprises have adopted an institutional mechanism for multi-party cooperation, mutual benefit and win-win results, with each party assuming corresponding responsibilities, rights, and obligations in cooperation.

1. Tianjin Light Industry Vocational Technical College and Tianjin Transportation Technical College

Tianjin Light Industry Vocational Technical College and Tianjin Transportation Technical College have jointly set up two Luban Workshops in Egypt, offering three majors in CNC equipment application and maintenance, new energy application technology, and automotive application and maintenance technology at Ain Shams University in Egypt. They have also partnered with Advanced Technical School for Maintenance Technology in Cairo to offer two specialties: CNC machining technology and automotive maintenance technology. The two colleges collaborated on the construction and operation of the Egypt Luban Workshops, summarized their construction experience, promptly addressed and resolved operational issues, and established a coordination mechanism for the Egypt Luban Workshops.

(1)Standardization of the Construction of the Luban Workshops

After several years of practice, the construction procedure of the Egypt Luban Workshops is as follows: selecting high-quality partner vocational colleges overseas→ determining majors and sites →implementing curriculum standards and providing teaching resources → training foreign teachers → installing and debugging training equipment → unveiling and operating the Luban Workshops (as shown in Figure 7–8).

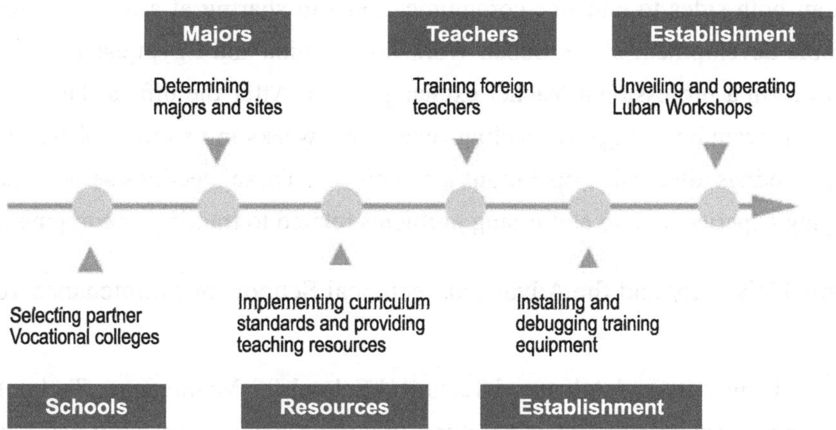

Figure 7–8 The Construction Process of the Luban Workshops

2. Standardization of the Operation of the Luban Workshops

① Management System. Let us take the Luban Workshops in Egypt as an example. China and Egypt have jointly established a coordination and management team for the Egypt Luban Workshops, adopting the 3+1+1+1 mechanism. This mechanism consists of two Chinese institutions, one Egyptian institution, the Chinese Embassy in Egypt, the Tianjin Municipal Education Commission, and the Egyptian education department. Its purpose is to coordinate and address any problems that may arise during the operation of the Luban Workshops in a timely manner. The team is responsible for coordinating and implementing workshop tasks with well-established management and overall planning. It comprises a liaison team and a working team. The liaison team handles communication with various matters related to the Luban Workshops while the working team takes care of concrete task implementation at the workshop. The Luban Workshops implement a system of quarterly meetings, semester reports, and annual reports after they officially begin operations.

The management structure of the Egyptian side of the Luban Workshops follows a person-in-charge system. Under the person-in-charge, there is an executive director who is responsible for the specific operation of the Egypt Luban Workshops and for liaising with the professional leaders in the three specialties. All full-time teachers at Egypt Luban Workshops hold bachelor's degrees or above in related majors and have received systematic professional and vocational education and training in China. In the workshops, Egyptian teachers are primarily responsible for teaching, while Chinese teachers do not participate in actual teaching work. This management model lays a foundation for the independent operation, management and development of the Luban Workshops.

② Liaison Mechanism. In order to promote the orderly operation of Egypt Luban Workshops, rationally and fully utilize the software and hardware resources of the workshops, and improve the quality of technical and skilled talent training, China and Egypt have established a communication mechanism for teachers. The aim is to build a platform for professional teachers from both sides to enhance communication and sharing at a technical level, ensuring the sustainable development of the Luban Workshops. China and Egypt each selects one teacher per major to form a professional teacher exchange team. After the official launch of the Luban Workshops, this team holds regular meetings every two weeks in its initial phase, which changes to quarterly meetings after stable operations are achieved. These meetings serve as an opportunity for exchanging experiences and addressing problems related to training or equipment use.

2.Ain Shams University and the Advanced Technical School for Maintenance Technology in Cairo

Ain Shams University and Advanced Technical School for Maintenance Technology in Cairo provided the necessary site and infrastructure, including water, electricity and heating, for the construction of the Luban Workshops. In addition, these institutions allowed a group of teachers with relevant professional backgrounds to participate in the teacher training at Luban Workshops. Teachers who have completed the training and passed the certification are eligible to teach in the training rooms and participate in the training tasks at the Luban Workshops. Foreign and Chinese institutions need to establish a smooth liaison mechanism to dynamically adjust the operation of Egypt Luban workshops based on actual situations to ensure their healthy operation.

3. Chinese-Funded Enterprises

Chinese-funded enterprises have provided teaching devices and instruments, and support for the construction of teaching resources, as well as other services. This has helped the Egypt Luban Workshops achieve "going global" and expand their international business.

7.4.4 Specific Measures

1. Supporting the Reform and Development of Vocational Education in Egypt, and the Training of Technical Talent.

Chinese vocational colleges have been collaborating with China-Africa TEDA and Shandong Himile in countries along the "Belt and Road" to train technical and skilled talents for enterprises involved in overseas development. These colleges cooperate with foreign enterprises that have been "introduced". For example, a molding industry academy has been jointly established with GF Casting Solutions of Switzerland, and a new specialty has been developed in partnership with Carl Zeiss AG of Germany to train highly skilled technical personnel for serving high-end industries. On the one hand, advanced standards, technologies, and equipment are introduced; the mold specialty draws on corporate standards; and the professional teaching standards developed by colleges have been recognized by enterprises at home and abroad to enhance the quality of personnel training. On the other hand, the colleges collaborate with leading Chinese enterprises to "going global" together, sharing high-quality vocational education resources worldwide, cooperating with the enterprises to explore overseas markets, training localized technical and skilled talents, and assisting Chinese enterprises and products in establishing a presence overseas.

2. Jointly Building the Egypt Luban Workshop Training and Employment Base

Tianjin Light Industry Vocational Technical College, Tianjin Transportation Technical College, Ain Shams University and the Egypt TEDA Special Zone Development Company jointly built the Egypt Luban Workshop Training and Employment Base, which was unveiled on December 30, 2021. The 2021 Annual Summary (Teacher Training Summary and Student Exchange) Meeting of the Egypt Luban Workshop was held simultaneously. Establishing a training and employment base is the correct approach to serving the development of local industries and enterprises. With the collaborative efforts of the four units, Egypt Luban Workshop Training and Employment Base will not only benefit Ain Shams University but also extend its influence throughout Africa.

3. Constructing and Developing Online and Offline Education and Teaching Resources Collaboratively

Relying on professional teaching faculties and personnal as well as Chinese high-quality education and teaching equipment companies, Egypt Luban Workshops have built 5 training rooms and 11 sets of comprehensive training equipment that reflect the international advanced level. These provide students with places and conditions for practical teaching and skill training. In addition to sharing materialized teaching equipment, the Egypt Luban Workshops also share a complete set of virtual simulation systems at an advanced level in China, providing a customized 3D virtual simulation training environment. The national new energy education resource library, teaching materials, and other online high-quality teaching resources are available, along with 24 online video open courses such as CNC machining technology. These resources provide the conditions for the combination of online and offline teachings. Despite the impact of COVID-19 on offline teaching in China and Egypt, the Luban Workshops have not been interrupted due to their excellent online teaching resources.

4. Establishing an International Exchange and Cooperation Platform to Facilitate Training for Chinese and Egyptian Enterprises

The Egypt Luban Workshops have established an international exchange and cooperation platform for Chinese-funded enterprises in Egypt and local Egyptian enterprises to train technical and skilled personnel. The platform includes a skilled talent-training center, a collaborative technology innovation center, a technology and product promotion center, and a staff-training center. These centers boast high-quality vocational education resources, and advanced technologies and products in related industries and professional fields from China. They also provide customized training based on the needs of enterprises, enabling the sustainable development of the Luban Workshops in Egypt.

5.Egypt Luban Workshops Integrate Education and Production, and "Going Global" Alongside Chinese-Funded Enterprises

In order to further deepen cooperation between China and Egypt in education and industry, an online meeting named "Egypt Luban Workshop Education Going Abroad with Industry: A Fair for China's New Energy Enterprises to Invest in Egypt" was held on October 11, 2022 by Tianjin Light Industry Vocational Technical College, Yingli Group, Shengna Technology, and EGYPT-TEDA Special Zone Development Company. During the meeting, Tianjin Light Industry Vocational Technical College shared information about the construction and operation status of the Egypt Luban Workshops as well as their cooperation with Yingli Group, Shengna Technology, and EGYPT-TEDA Special Zone Development Company which then briefed on the current situation and development prospects of the China-Egypt Suez Economic and Trade Cooperation

Zone while also sharing information about investment environment and policies in Egypt. Yingli Group, a world-renowned company in the photovoltaic industry, engaged in extensive discussions regarding specific issues and cooperation models for development in Egypt. After the meeting, both companies expressed their willingness to invest and cooperate in the China-Egypt Suez Economic and Trade Cooperation Zone.

7.4.5 Key Achievements

1. Precisely Assist Egypt in Training Technical and Skilled Personnel

In terms of the higher vocational education, Egypt Luban Workshops, organized by Tianjin Light Indstry Locational Techical College in cooperation with Ain Shams University, have set up three majors including CNC equipment application and maintenance, new energy application technology, and automotive application and maintenance technology. They have built three training rooms in China's first-class level, covering an area of 1,200 square meters. In collaboration with the Advanced Technical School for Maintenance Technology in Cairo, the college has established a 690-square-meter secondary vocational school which specializes in CNC machining technology and automotive maintenance technology. It has also constructed a MicroMouse training area of first-class standards in Egypt. Since their inauguration in 2020, the Egypt Luban Workshops have successfully completed training tasks for more than 1,000 individuals.

2. Elaborately Construct to Enhance the Vocational Education Level in Egypt

Tianjin Light Industry Vocational Technical College has deeply integrated itself with world-renowned and leading enterprises, and has developed international teaching standards for 5 majors based on the world's leading industry standards. These standards have been applied to Egypt Luban Workshops, elevating the construction of training bases and teaching standards to a world-class level. The two sides have collaborated in developing 12 curriculum standards and publishing 5 bilingual professional textbooks. A comprehensive Virtual-Simulation-Practical teaching system has been established, while two vocational schools (secondary and higher) have been built at the same time in Egypt. This marks the first time that China has established an integrated vocational education system at both secondary and higher level overseas.

3. Exquisite Craftsmanship of Luban Workshops Sets a Benchmark for Construction

From April to May 2021, ambassadors from 46 countries to China visited Tianjin Light Industry Vocational Technical College for investigation and exchange, which attracted significant attention from mainstream media at home and abroad. In December 2021, the only training and employment base for the Egypt Luban Workshop, was inaugurated, practicing the spirit of General Secretary Xi Jinping's speech at the Eighth Ministerial Conference of FOCAC. Tianjin Light Industry Vocational Technical College is the vice chairman unit of the China Light Industry International Production Capacity Cooperation Enterprise Alliance, and the Luban Workshop

Construction Alliance. It is also a member of the "Belt and Road" Alliance for Industry and Education Collaboration (BRAIEC), BRICS TVET Cooperation Alliance, and China-Africa Vocational Education Cooperation Alliance. Additionally, the college has taken the lead in establishing the Sino-Indian Vocational Education Alliance. Tianjin Light Industry Vocational Technical College, as the executive secretariat, is preparing for the establishment of the World Vocational and Technical Education Development Conference (WVTEDC) in 2022.

The China-Egypt vocational education cooperation has also received great attention in the media of both countries. Mr. Liao Liqiang, the Chinese Ambassador to Egypt, published a signed article entitled *China-Egypt Vocational Education Jointly Training Skilled Personel-Written on the Occasion of the Launching of the Egypt Luban Workshop* in the Egyptian newspaper *The Charter*. The Deputy Minister of the Egyptian Ministry of Education and Technical Education has visited the Egypt Luban Workshops several times, and a number of institutes have also visited them, which has also been reported several times in the Egyptian media. "In the long run, the Luban Workshops will help students better adapt to the job market and meet employment needs". The President of Ain Shams University told Xinhua News Agency. He believes that Luban Workshops' concepts and educational experience are worth promoting and learning from in today's globalization context.

4. Accurately Leading and Facilitating China-Egypt International Production Capacity Cooperation

The construction of the Egypt Luban Workshop has played a leading role in facilitating international production capacity cooperation. On November 30, 2020, the Luban Workshops were officially inaugurated in Egypt, marking a new phase of vocational education cooperation between China and Egypt. In February 2021, the "Egypt Luban Workshop Industry-Education Integration Work Conference and the Investment Promotion Conference for Chinese Enterprises in Egypt" were held online. After the conference, 10 companies expressed their intention to invest in Egypt on-site. In December 2021, the Egypt Luban Workshop Training and Employment Base was unveiled with a mission to expand into new areas of internship and employment, create a new model of cooperative education, and achieve significant progress in institution-business cooperation. In October 2022, "Egypt Luban Workshop Education Going Abroad with Industry: A Fair for China's New Energy Enterprises to Invest in Egypt" was held. Following the meeting, Yingli Group and Shengna Technology expressed their willingness to cooperate and invest in the China-Egypt Suez Economic and Trade Cooperation Zone. Through Luban Workshops in Egypt, Chinese-funded enterprises can better achieve industry-education integration and promote "education going abroad with industry", serving as a bridgehead or a bridge to support Chinese enterprises to "going global".

7.4.6 Development Enlightenment

The sustainable development of the Luban Workshops has become a key consideration in recent years, and it is mainly carried out in the following aspects. First, the Luban Workshop should enable partner countries to truly benefit from their project construction. Second, before building the Luban Workshops, it is necessary to investigate the political relations between the two countries and assess the willingness of institutes to cooperate. Strong support from governments and institutions is a prerequisite for access to the partner countries' academic education systems. Third, the Luban Workshop project should establish a sound management and operation system to ensure its normal operation. It is important to give full play to the role of Chinese-funded and local enterprises to integrate personnel training with industrial development needs. Vocational colleges and cooperative enterprises should reach a consensus that effective cooperation between both sides must meet the vocational colleges' requirements of personnel training while maximizing the interests of the enterprises. Fourth, information technology should be fully utilized to develop a diverse range of online and offline teaching resources for routine teaching in Luban Workshops. Take the Egypt Luban Workshops as an example. Customized bilingual digital resources compatible with physical equipment have been developed in line with internationalization and digital development needs in professional fields such as CNC equipment application and maintenance, and new energy, forming a 3D Virtual-Simulation-Practical teaching system at China's leading level.

7.5 Existing Problems and Development Recommendations

7.5.1 Existing Problems and Analysis of Causes

Egypt Luban Workshops have been in operation for several years and have achieved remarkable results. However, the project faces some common problems, such as the impact of the COVID-19 and the lack of a national-level surveillance and evaluation system for operations and effectiveness. In addition, there are still some issues with its development.

1. Although the Egypt Luban Workshops have cooperated with many Chinese-funded enterprises since their construction began, there are still issues in their actual operation, such as insufficient cooperation and a lack of momentum for collaboration. For instance, most of the contracts signed with enterprises are merely "letters of intent", where the responsibilities, rights and obligations of both parties are not made clearly and sufficiently detailed, and there is no comprehensive plan of cooperation that can meet the future development needs of the cooperative enterprises.

2. Although Egypt Luban Workshops have had a mature concept of construction standards since their inception, they have not yet formed a complete and mature model in the operation process, which needs to be summarized to complement and improve the operating system and standards. For example, the lack of a corresponding response mechanism in the face of an emergency at the Egypt Luban Workshops may lead to untimely resolution of problems.

3. The Egypt Luban Workshops are not deeply involved in facilitating international production capacity cooperation. The platform established on the basis of the Luban Workshops is relatively simple and lacks diversity. Although it has entered into various cooperation agreements with the Suez Economic and Trade Cooperation Zone, there have been few deals signed with enterprises within the zone. For instance, despite the urgent need for professionals in the new energy sector at the Benban Solar PV Park in Aswan, there is no close collaboration between the Part and the Luban Workshops. Furthermore, the Egypt Luban Workshopss face a shortage of technicians for routine equipment maintenance and upgrades, necessitating regular support from professionals from relevant Chinese-funded enterprises to carry out maintenance and debugging tasks.

7.5.2 Recommendations for Further Development

1. Establishing Standards and Constructing Models to Ensure the Sustainable Development of the Egypt Luban Workshops

The duties, rights and obligations of vocational colleges and cooperative Chinese-funded enterprises should be detailed and clarified in relation to the practical issues of serving the Egypt Luban Workshops. It is necessary to fully leverage the role of Chinese-funded and local enterprises in the construction process of the Egypt Luban Workshops to promote personnel training and meet industrial development needs. Consensus should be reached between vocational colleges and cooperative enterprises, meaning that effective cooperation between colleges and enterprises should meet the requirements for personnel training in vocational colleges as well as maximize the interests of enterprises. Operational standards and models that are in line with the actual conditions of Egypt Luban Workshops should be formulated to serve their sustainable development.

2. Multi-platform Construction, Two-way Empowerment, Broadening the Cooperation Platform and Enhancing the Functions of the Egypt Luban Workshops

Multi-platform construction serves as the foundation and bridge for international exchange and cooperation in vocational education. By relying on different platforms, such as the ones for advanced technology collaborative innovation, professional construction and resource development, interactive exchanges for teachers and students, vocational skills competitions, forums and conferences communication, as well as cultural exchanges and mutual learning. These platforms were jointly built by Egypt Luban Workshops, relevant government departments, domestic and foreign enterprises, foreign colleges, and social organizations. We can promote the integrated development of international exchanges and cooperation in vocational education across multiple fields, levels, and dimensions. In addition to that, the problem of insufficient internal impetus for the cooperative development of the Egypt Luban Workshops can be solved through two-way empowerment between China and Egypt. For instance, by relying on the platform, agreements can be signed with Chinese-funded enterprises in Economic and Trade Cooperation

Zones, and professional personnel can be arranged to regularly maintain and debug equipment in the training rooms. This will not only maximize the efficiency of equipment usage and reduce costs but also strengthen ties between vocational colleges and partner enterprises.

3. Education Going Abroad with Industry, Conducting Research and Practice Simultaneously to Support China-Egypt International Production Capacity Cooperation

The characteristic and fundamental path of international exchange and cooperation in vocational education is "Education Going Abroad with Industry". With the foundation of Egypt Luban Workshops, colleges and enterprises "Going Global Hand in Hand, as Education Going Abroad with Industry", and foster a harmonious partnership. The Egypt Luban Workshops are partnering with prominent domestic enterprises to achieve their goal of "going global", sharing high-quality vocational education resources around the world. Together, they are exploring overseas markets, providing localized technical and skilled talent training, and assisting Chinese enterprises and products in establishing a global presence.

At the same time, a series of research were carried out during construction to further deepen the functions of the Egypt Luban Workshops with the combination of research and practice. Through the Egypt Luban Workshops, enterprises can better realize the "integration of industry and education, and education going abroad with industry", making Luban Workshops a bridgehead or a bridge to serve and support Chinese-funded enterprises in global market expansion. China's vocational education will help promote international production capacity cooperation between China and Egypt as well as contribute to the development of Egypt's green economy.

Chapter Ⅷ

Reports on Vocational Education Collaboration Serving China-Djibouti Production Capacity Cooperation

The Republic of Djibouti is located in the northeast of Africa, bordering Somalia in the southeast, Eritrea in the north, Ethiopia in the west, southwest and south, and the Gulf of Aden in the north and east, and facing Yemen across the Bab el-Mandeb Strait. It is on the channel from the Red Sea to the Indian Ocean, so its geographical location has very important strategic value, enjoying the fame of "Oasis of Peace" in the Horn of Africa. Djibouti has a land area of 23,200 square kilometers and a coastline of 372 kilometers. The coastal areas are plains and plateaus, which boast mainly tropical desert climate, namely hot and dry all year round. The mainland is mainly composed of plateaus and mountains, with a tropical grassland climate. Under the influence of France, the former suzerain, Djibouti is a capitalist country with a presidential republic political system. Its current President, Guelleh, was re-elected in April 2021 for a fifth term as President of Djibouti. Djibouti pursues a foreign policy of neutrality, non-alignment, and cooperation with the rest of the world based on equality, mutual respect, and non-interference in the internal affairs of other countries. Djibouti participates actively in the maintenance of peace and stability in the region and attaches great importance to the development of good relations with the Arab States and neighboring countries. It took France and other Western countries, Saudi Arabia and other Middle Eastern countries, and Ethiopia and other North-East African countries as major partners for cooperation, but since the 21st century it has been actively looking for new partners, and its relations with China, Japan, South Korea and India have developed rapidly. Djibouti has also actively participated in the building of the "Belt and Road" and is an important pivot point of China's "Maritime Silk Road" in East Africa, as well as the location of China's first overseas logistics support base.

8.1 Overview of Djibouti

8.1.1 Economic Development

Djibouti is one of the least developed countries in the world. According to the International Monetary Fund (IMF), as of September 2022, Djibouti had a GDP of $3.836 billion, an annual GDP growth rate of 3 percent, a per capita GDP of $3,780, an inflation rate of 3.8 percent, a current account balance of –$180 million, a current account balance as a percentage of GDP of –4.7 percent, and general government debt as a percentage of GDP of 49.2 percent. The changes in the major economic indicators of Djibouti from 2018 to 2022 are shown in Table 8–1.

Table 8–1 Changes in Major Economic Indicators of Djibouti from 2018 to 2022

Major Economic Indicators	2018	2019	2020	2021	2022
GDP (billions of US dollars)	30.13	33.17	34.10	35.89	38.36
Ranking of GDP among 54 Countries in Africa	45	43	43	43	43
Annual GDP Growth Rate	8.5%	6.6%	1.0%	4.0%	3.0%
GDP per Capita (US dollars)	3,142	3,408	3,452	3,581	3,775
Ranking of GDP per Capita among 54 Countries in Africa	15	13	11	14	13
Inflation Rate	0.1%	3.3%	1.8%	1.2%	3.8%
Current Account Balance (billions of US dollars)	4.3	5.6	3.7	–0.4	–1.8
Current Account Balance as a Percentage of GDP	14.2%	17.0%	10.7%	–1.0%	–4.7%
General Government Debt as a Percentage of GDP	46.5%	39.1%	41.0%	43.2%	49.2%

In recent years, the Government of Djibouti has actively adjusted its economic policy by reducing the budget, raising taxes, encouraging foreign investment, and actively participating in the regional integration process, and has maintained a low rate of economic growth. Djibouti's annual GDP growth rate has been low for a long time. According to the World Bank, Djibouti's GDP growth rate remained at 5–7 percent from 2017 to 2019, and then dropped to 1 percent in 2020 due to the impact of COVID-19, so its economy is still resilient to a certain extent. Djibouti is one of the few countries in the world that maintained positive growth during the pandemic. The pandemic has also had a negative impact on Djibouti's public finances, with a decline rate of 0.8% in fiscal revenue and a growth rate of 0.3% in current expenditures in terms of the country's GDP. In 2022, Djibouti ranked 43rd in GDP and 13th in GDP per capita among 54 African countries. The comparison of GDP and per capita GDP between Djibouti and some African countries is shown in Figure 8–1.

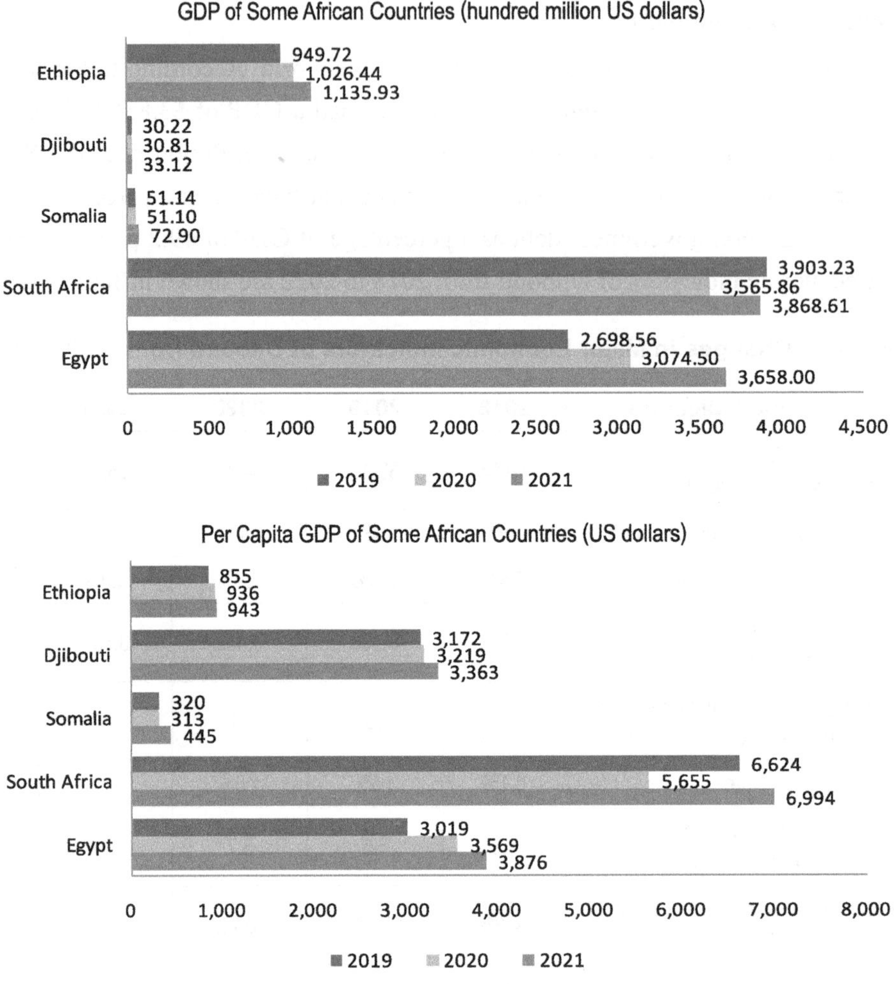

Figure 8–1 Comparison of Total GDP and GDP Per Capita between Djibouti and Some African Countries

In 2014, the Djibouti government released the *Djibouti Development Expectation Until 2035*, which is the long-term development plan of the Republic of Djibouti. The overall goal is to build Djibouti into a regional and international economic, commercial, and financial center by 2035 to enhance the well-being of the people in Djibouti. The specific objectives are twofold: one is to quadruple Djibouti's income per capita and increase its gross domestic product per capita (GDP) by 10 percent per year by 2035; the other is to improve social and human development indicators, alleviate social problems such as food scarcity, education inequalities, and poor health care, and strengthen the social security system.

8.1.2 Industrial Environment

1. Overview and Policies of Industrial Development

The foundation of Djibouti's primary and secondary industries is weak, with over 95% of agricultural and industrial products relying on imports. The tertiary industry dominates the Djibouti's economy, focusing on transportation, commerce, and services (mainly port services), accounting for approximately 80% of GDP. The added value and annual growth rate of Djibouti's industries over the years are shown in Table 8–2.

Table 8–2 Added Value and Annual Growth Rate of Djibouti's Industries Over the Years

Years	Added Value of Industrial (billions of US dollars)	Annual Growth Rate of Industrial-added Value	Added Value of Agriculture, Forestry, Animal Husbandry, and Fishery (ten thousand US dollars)	Annual Growth Rate of Agriculture, Forestry, Animal Husbandry, and Fishery Added Value	Added Value of Manufacturing (hundred million of US dollars)	Annual Growth Rate of Manufacturing Added Value	Added Value of Service Industry (hundred million of US dollars)	Annual Growth Rate of Service Industry Added Value
2020	4.75	2.00%	5,348	3.50%	1.4100	18.69%	24.58	0.11%
2019	4.51	9.40%	4,693	4.88%	1.1400	10.73%	23.78	6.82%
2018	4.08	7.23%	4,128	5.97%	0.9661	13.15%	22.58	4.72%
2017	3.43	2.71%	3,575	2.78%	0.8568	8.02%	13.26	3.76%
2016	2.95	4.56%	2,593	-4.36%	0.7387	11.35%	12.66	11.02%

In the early 1990s, Djibouti's economic situation deteriorated. In 1996, the Government of Djibouti began implementing an economic restructuring plan. In 1998, after the border armed conflict between Ethiopia and Eritrea, the goods originally transshipped by Ethiopia through Eritrea were transferred to the port of Djibouti, which significantly increased the income of the port and restored Djobouti's economy. Since 2010, the Djibouti government has actively adjusted its economic policies, sought foreign aid and investment, focused on developing the tertiary industry, stepped up infrastructure construction, and actively participated in the regional integration process. In 2013, the Djibouti government formulated a plan to 2035, focusing on the development of transportation, logistics, finance, telecommunications, tourism, fishing and other industries. Djibouti's economic growth in recent years has mainly benefited from foreign direct investment, especially that in transportation and logistics infrastructure, clean energy development such as wind and geothermal energy, and chemical industries such as sodium bromide in port-free trade zones.

2. Overview of Relevant Enterprises

(1) Djibouti Salt Company

In June 2017, CCCC (China Communications Construction Corporation) Djibouti Salt Investment Company launched the pilot production of industrial salt, which was praised by President Guelleh as an important industrial project of the "Belt and Road" in Djibouti, ending Djibouti as a non-industrial country. The sodium bromide produced by the project has also become Djibouti's first batch of industrial products exported overseas, helping to build a salt chemical industry base in East Africa, which has greatly changed the industrial structure of Djibouti. The first phase of the project created 2,000 jobs and earned $100 million in foreign exchange, doubling Djibouti's total exports volume.

(2) Djibouti International Free Trade Zone

The Djibouti International Free Trade Zone (DIFTZ) is jointly invested and operated by the Djibouti Port and Free Trade Zone Management Bureau, China Merchants Group, and Dalian Port Group. It covers an area of 48.2 km^2 and has attracted 165 enterprises from different countries to settle in, with a warehouse occupancy rate of nearly 100%. After completion, it will generates a GDP of over $4 billion, which is more than twice the current GDP of Djibouti. It can create over 100,000 jobs, exceeding one sixth of Djibouti's employable population.

(3) Djibouti Damerjog Industrial Zone

The Damerjog Industrial Zone is the first heavy industrial park planned and constructed by Djibouti, and is an important part of the development strategy of the "3+1", including three zones and one port in Djibouti. With the coordinated development of the international free trade zone, central business zone, and Damerjog Industrial Zone as the pillars, it lays the foundation for Djibouti to become an international shipping center port and has positive significance for promoting the development of Djibouti's national industry and economic structure transformation. The industrial zone is located near the border between Djibouti and Somalia, adjacent to the main road No.2 National Highway connecting the two countries, with convenient transportation. The park covers an area of approximately 30 square kilometers.

8.1.3 Status Quo of Vocational Education

1. Overview of Vocational Education

Djibouti's education system is divided into national quality education and vocational education, and national quality education includes basic education, secondary education and higher education, as shown in Figure 8–2. Basic education includes five-year education in primary school and four-year education in junior high school, and free compulsory education is provided to all young people between the age of 6 and 15. Secondary education refers to the three year education in high school, and those with excellent results can enter the University of

Djibouti, Djibouti Medical School, or universities and colleges in other countries, like Ethiopia and France, to receive higher education. Djibouti vocational education is mainly divided into a full-time vocational-technical education model and an apprenticeship vocational educational model. The former is primarily based on intermediate-level vocational training, accepting middle school graduates and carrying out vocational skills training in various industries. The latter is mainly organized by various industry associations, mainly in the handicraft industry, emphasizing practical training. Its training places are at the production sites of enterprises and apprenticeship training schools, which is a traditional primary dual-system vocational education model. The Ministry of National Education and Vocational Training is the highest educational administration institution in Djibouti and manages all the Djiboutian schools, colleges and universities, as well as, including higher education, secondary education, primary education and vocational training.

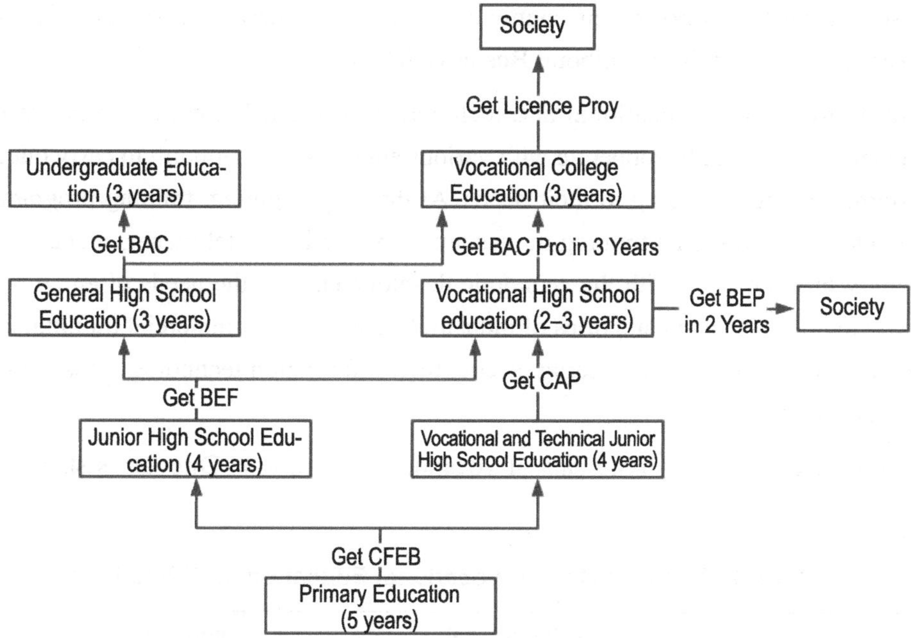

Figure 8–2 Djibouti Education System

2. Vocational Schools and Major Settings

There are three main types of full-time vocational and technical education schools in Djibouti, including vocational preparatory schools, secondary vocational and technical schools, and senior secondary vocational and technical schools.

Vocational preparatory school is a form of compulsory education and lasts for one year. It is designed to help students who have finished their compulsory education adapt to primary jobs. They offer majors in civil engineering, mechanical maintenance, office automation, service industry, and tourism. Students can practice skills in training bases at the school, factories, and other places, which plays a positive guiding role in students' future career choices.

Secondary vocational and technical schools mainly impart basic knowledge and vocational skills, with a 4-year academic system and full-time teaching. They are the main vocational and technical talent training institution in Djibouti. Their majors cover civil engineering, architecture, machinery, computer applications, and logistics management. Students can obtain a vocational license after graduation.

Senior vocational and technical schools have a duration of 2–3 years and implement full-time teaching. They offer higher vocational and technical majors such as mechanical engineering, business management, and computer application. After 2 years' studying, students can obtain a Vocational and Technical Education Certificate (BEP) and enter the workforce. Or after 3 years' studying, they can obtain a Vocational and Technical High School Diploma (BAC Pro) and then choose to enter the workforce or continue their studies. The largest senior vocational and technical school in Djibouti is the Djibouti Business School.

In addition to full-time vocational and technical education, Djibouti also has vocational training centers, which mainly cooperate with various enterprises in Djibouti to carry out medium and short-term training according to their needs. At the very begining, training programs of the centers include adult vocational training in masonry construction, hotel management, automobile and machinery maintenance. With the economic development and the needs of enterprises, they are gradually divided into two categories of industrial training and commercial training, including automobile maintenance, electric welding, accounting, information technology, business English and other training programs.

As of September 2022, the basic data of vocational education in Djibouti is shown in Table 8–3.

Table 8–3 Basic Data of Vocational Education in Djibouti

	Number of Schools	Educational System (Year)	Professional Talent Level	Number of Majors	Number of Students on Campus
Vocational Preparatory School	28	1	Primary	105	21,568
Secondary Vocational and Technical School	6	3	Intermediate	156	11,532
Senior Vocational and Technical School	4	5	Senior	65	3,815
Adult Training Institution	216	0.3–1	Intermediate and Senior	52	7,893

8.1.4 Vocational Education and Industry

Since the beginning of the 21st century, Djibouti has increased its efforts to attract foreign investment and strengthen infrastructure construction such as ports and transportation. The sustainable development of the tertiary industry requires the participation of local talents. Although the Djibouti government hopes to achieve a seamless connection between vocational education and the needs of the tertiary industry, and regards the development of vocational education as an important way to solve the problem of the country's high unemployment rate, the current vocational education cannot meet the needs of modern economic and social development. The main problems are as follows:

1. The Scale and Quality of Vocational Education Need to Be Improved and More Investment Is Required

Djibouti has a relatively small-scale economy and slow-development speed, with a government debt ratio of 40%-50% of GDP. The government's financial budget is mainly used to maintain the normal operation of the country, while less investment is used for vocational education. In recent years, Djibouti has actively promoted the diversification of education and investment, introduced foreign enterprises and vocational education resources, and achieved certain results in improving the quality of vocational education and the employment rate of students. However, to improve the level of vocational education on a large scale to meet the needs of enterprise development, the government still needs to carry out sustained investment.

2. A Weak Foundation in Vocational Education and A Shortage of Teaching Resources

In recent years, with a large number of foreign enterprises entering Djibouti, the shortage of vocational education teachers has become prominent. Due to the weak industrial and commercial foundation and insufficient talent reserves in Djibouti, there is a lack of teachers to provide vocational education in various industries. In vocational education schools in Djibouti, the average ratio of students to teachers is 70:1, with some areas even reaching 120:1. Due to the shortage of teachers, it is difficult to meet the teaching needs of the school. At the same time, many teachers of lack relevant professional skills and vocational and technical education qualifications, which affects the quality of teaching. Data shows that more than half of teachers don't have experience in professional technology used in relevant industries, and about 30% of them have short-term contract relationships with schools, resulting in insufficient motivation for some teachers to make long-term investments in skills growth and qualifications gaining.

3. Lacking Practical Equipment and High-Standard Training Conditions for Vocational Education

Due to the underdeveloped economy, insufficient education investment budget, and limited vocational education training equipment of Djibouti, it is not conducive to students' learning of professional knowledge and mastery of skills. At present, only 60% of vocational colleges in Djibouti have practical teaching areas, and the practical training equipment has an applicability rate of less than 30% for the majors. For various emerging industries in Djibouti, the existing training equipment is insufficient to cultivate the skilled talents needed by enterprises.

4. Poor Cooperation between Vocational Schools and Enterprises in Djibouti, Resulting in Limited Internship Opportunities for Students

The main reason why Djibouti vocational colleges and enterprises are not closely connected is that most of Djibouti's enterprises are foreign-funded enterprises, and their enthusiasm for localizing enterprise operations is not high enough. There are few communication channels between enterprise investors and Djibouti vocational schools. Therefore, there are not many opportunities for students to enter enterprises for job internships, which is not conducive to familiarizing them with professional skills and cultivating professional qualities.

The basic data on the development and changes of vocational education in Djibouti from 2008 to 2022 are shown in Table 8–4.

Table 8–4 Changes and Development of Vocational Education in Djibouti from 2018 to 2022

Main Indicators	2018	2019	2020	2021	2022
Number of graduates from vocational preparatory schools /person	15,695	16,782	17,708	18,513	18,756
Employment rate of graduates from vocational preparatory schools/%	29%	28%	33%	32%	35%
Number of graduates from vocational schools/%	7,563	7,685	8,978	9,012	9,282
Employment rate of vocational college graduates/%	48%	49%	53%	52%	56%
Number of adult training graduates/person	7,026	7,936	7,816	6,512	6,735
Employment rate of adult training graduates/%	70%	73%	75%	78%	76%

8.1.5 International Economic Cooperation

More than 80% of Djibouti's development funds rely on foreign aid, mainly from the African Development Fund, the Arab Economic Development Fund, the World Bank, the European Union, the Islamic Development Bank, France, Kuwait, China, the United States, and others. Among them, China and Arab countries' assistance to Djibouti is mainly reflected in infrastructure construction, while developed countries such as the United States, France, and Japan mostly provide assistance in materials and cash.

According to statistics from the World Trade Organization, the top five export destinations for Djibouti are Ethiopia (35.3%), the European Union (20.6%), Somalia (11.9%), Brazil (8.7%), and

Qatar (6.3%). The top four sources of goods import are the European Union (36.7%), the United Arab Emirates (18.5%), Saudi Arabia (6.0%), and Japan (5.5%).

In trading, port transit trade accounts for a large proportion. According to the statistics of the Central Bank of Djibouti, the country's imports and exports account for only about 0.5% of all imports and exports at its ports, and the rest are re-exported to Ethiopia, Somalia and other regions. The main imported goods include food and beverages, mechanical equipment, electrical products, cartel grass, transportation equipment, petroleum products, metal products, textiles, and footwear. While, the main export commodities include sodium bromide, salt, livestock, leather, etc. Also, the service trade mainly includes transportation services and tourism.

8.2 Chinese-Funded Enterprises and International Production Capacity Cooperation

8.2.1 Cooperative Country's Industrial Development and Its Demand for Foreign Investment

The Djibouti government encourages foreign investment and implements policies to attract foreign capitals and open up industries. Overall, it maintains an open attitude towards foreign investment, aiming to promote the domestic economic development and regional economic integration. In the Djibouti Version 2035 Development Plan, it is clearly stated the goal of building Djibouti as a logistics and information exchange platform connecting the three continents of Africa, Asia and Europe, as well as a regional financial center. In the water, electricity and telecommunications sectors, state-owned enterprises operate exclusively. However, in infrastructure construction such as ports, railways, roads, as well as project development and operations in energy, salt, chemicals and other fields, the Djibouti government doesn't set restrictions on the proportion of foreign investment, development modes, or operation modes.

In October 2021, Djibouti Prime Minister, Kamil, presented the government's policy priorities in the policy report, identifying education, healthcare, and the primary sector as priority areas. Transportation is a crucial driving force for economic development in Djibouti. Efforts will continue to be made to promote the construction of the Port of Doraleh and related infrastructure, while increasing the proportion of industrial and manufacturing sectors in the GDP. Djibouti will also establish regional banks, logistics, and telecommunications center, construct a second transmission line to connect Ethiopia, and build a new thermal power plant to meet the power supply demands as soon as possible. In November 2021, the Djiboutian government officially released the "Djibouti Sustainable Development Goals". These goals provide policy support and an introduction of 8 industries and 21 investment fields with sustainable development potential for investors themes, as shown in Table 8–5.

Table 8–5 Industries Sustainable Development Potential in Djibouti

Number	Industries	Main Content
1	Transportation	Djibouti's economic growth is mainly driven by maritime transport, and it plans to build a multi-modal infrastructure hub around Djibouti's ports by 2035.
2	Service Industry	Djibouti Tourism is eligible for concessional financing from Djibouti's State-owned Economic Development Fund. Hotel owners can apply for financing to implement environmentally friendly sustainable solutions, and eco-friendly tourism companies can apply for loans at preferential rates.
3	Renewable and Alternative Energy Sources	The government, in partnership with the African Power Company, plans to achieve an electricity supply only provided by renewable energy by 2035.
4	Financial Industry	The Micro-Finance can provide innovative financing solutions for small and medium-sized enterprises
5	Information and Communication Technology	The govement will improve the current situation of limited telecommunications and network services in Djibouti by investing in mobile Internet, and harness the potential of digital technologies to drive economic development.
6	Infrastructure	The govement will provide affordable and environmentally friendly housing for the Djibouti people.
7	Food and Beverage Industry	In the "Djibouti Development Expectation Until 2035", Promoting agricultural development can create jobs and help address food security concerns amid high dependence on imported food and rising levels of desertification in rural areas. This plan is to increase the contribution of agriculture to Djibouti's GDP from 3.7% in 2012 to 5.0% in 2035.
8	Medical and Healthcare	The National Health Development Plan from 2018 to 2022 allocates that 6.73% of total government expenditure will give to the Ministry of Health to provide high-quality care and accessibility services, as well as carry out disease prevention campaigns and strengthen governance and information management in healthcare.

8.2.2 Status Quo and Development of Chinese-Funded Enterprises

1. Overview of the Development of Chinese-Funded Enterprises in Djibouti

According to the data released by the Economic and Commercial Office of the Chinese Embassy in Djibouti, at present, the number of Chinese-funded enterprises in Djibouti is 19, as shown in Table 8–6, and excellent results have been achieved in infrastructure construction and China-Africa production capacity cooperation. In terms of industry attributes, 61% belong to industrial enterprises, 39% belong to service enterprises. In terms of size, 28% are large enterprises, 22% are medium-sized enterprises, and 50% are small enterprises. In terms of holdings, 39% are state-owned and 61% are non-state-owned. Besides, more than 80% of enterprises have been registered and operated in Djibouti since 2010. Chinese-funded enterprises have successively carried out infrastructure projects in Djibouti, including the expansion and renovation of old ports, the construction of the Doraleh multifunctional terminal, the Addis Ababa–Djibouti Railway, the Egypt-Djibouti cross-border water supply project, the Egypt-

Djibouti cross-border oil and gas transportation and liquefaction project, the national library and archives project, as well as the construction and operation projects of industrial parks, such as the Djibouti International Free Trade Zone and the Touchroad Djibouti Special Economic Zone. Chinese-funded enterprises have taken root in Djibouti and made certain contributions to reducing high unemployment rates and enriching industrial structures.

Table 8–6 List of Chinese-Funded Enterprises in Djibouti

Number	Enterprise Name	Business Scope
1	Jiangsu International Economic and Technical Cooperation Limited	International and domestic project contracting, real estate development, etc
2	Fortune Rich Cooperation Limited	Building industrialization, building construction, and real estate development, etc
3	China State Construction Co., Ltd. in Djibouti	Construction engineering, international engineering contracting, real estate development, etc
4	China Civil Engineering Construction Corporation in Djibouti	Domestic and foreign engineering general contracting and project management business, etc
5	China Harbour Engineering Company Limited	Port construction, etc
6	Hong Kong (China) Merchants Holdings (International) Company Limited	Investment and operation activities in ports and related services, etc
7	Huawei Technologies Co., Ltd.	IT, Radio, Microelectronics, Communication, Routing, IP PBX, etc
8	ZTE Corporation	Wireless, wired, core network, routing, switching, terminals, etc
9	CGC Overseas Construction CO., Ltd. in Djibouti	Engineering construction, trade leasing, investment and operation, etc
10	Sinotrans Container Lines CO., Ltd. in Djibouti	Comprehensive logistics and shipping, etc
11	China State Construction Engineering Corporation Limited (CSCEC)	Construction project contracting, real estate development, etc
12	Gcl-poly Group Office in Djibouti	Clean energy investment, intelligent energy information services, etc
13	China First Highway Engineering Co., Ltd.	Project general contracting, design and consulting, project management, etc
14	China Gezhouba Group Corporation Office in Djibouti	Water conservancy, power generation, roads, municipal services, real estate, port contract construction, investment, foreign trade, etc
15	China State Grid Office in Djibouti	Transmission, power supply, industrial investment and business management, etc
16	Djibouti Fisheries Company	Marine resource development, etc
17	Bondex Supply Chain Management Co., Ltd.	Maritime international cargo transportation agency, etc

continued

Number	Enterprise Name	Business Scope
18	China Muti-trans CO., Ltd. in Djibouti	Logistics planning, logistics operation, material trade services, etc
19	Hansun-Djibouti Free Zone	Import and export of engineering machinery and equipment, vehicles and related accessories, logistics business, etc

2. Main Problems Faced by Chinese-Funded Enterprises Based in Djibouti

Chinese-funded enterprises engaged in "going global" have been deeply rooted in Djibouti for many years, utilizing the enormous development potential of Djibouti ports and shipping industries, as well as the advantages of free foreign exchange and social stability. They actively promote projects that benefit people's livelihoods such as drinking water, education, and environmental protection, strengthen local development capabilities, and boost employment, which are highly suitable for the most urgently needed areas of Djibouti's economic and social development. But Chinese-funded enterprises are facing new challenges in Djibouti.

(1) High Production Costs and Incomplete Industrial Chains

Djibouti is relatively short of natural resources, and has a high cost of production factors. It is also has weak industrial and agricultural foundation, and lacks supporting industrial chains. All of these are not suitable for the development of manufacturing and processing and assembly industries.

(2) Rising Urbanization Rate and High Unemployment Rate

Djibouti's urbanization rate keeps rising annually. The young people account for more than 70% of Djibouti's labor force, but the unemployment rate remains high, as shown in Figure 8–3. While urbanization has been steadily improving, the corresponding demographic dividend and lifestyle changes have not been as effective as expected.

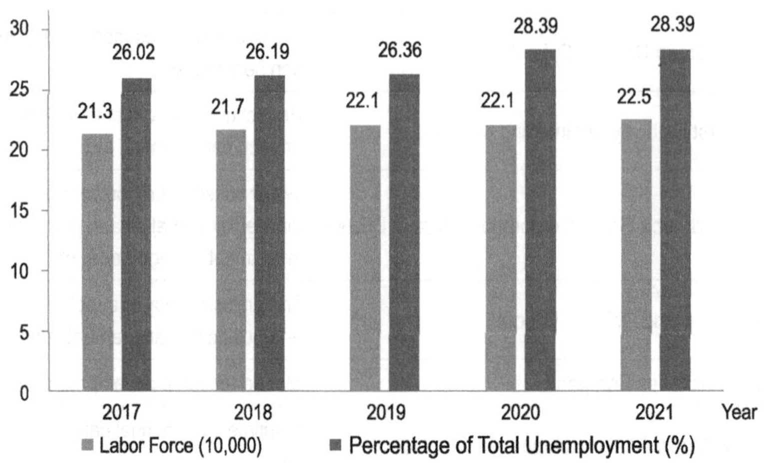

Figure 8–3 Ratio of Labor Force and Total Unemployment in Djibouti

(3) Lagging Infrastructure and Inadequate Funds

Problems such as lagging infrastructure construction, and shortage of talents and funds are still bottlenecks in Djibouti's economic and social development. For example, although the transportation efficiency of the Addis Ababa-Djibouti Railway has been greatly improved, and the employment opportunities brought by infrastructure construction and industrial parks have indeed made positive contributions to poverty alleviation and industrial restructuring. There are still lots of problems need to solve, due to the lack of urbanization strategy and local governance strategy. The introduction of large amounts of foreign capital has not produced the expected spillover effect and the skill level of workers has not been significantly improved, so local investors have failed to achieve capital accumulation.

(4) Increased Production Costs Caused by the COVID-19 Pandemic

The international implementation restrictions, poor international logistics, rising raw material prices, and difficult recruitment of skilled workers caused by COVID-19 Pandemic have all led to an increase in construction and operation costs. The transportation cost of domestic technical personnel to Djibouti has increased by three times compared with that before the pandemic, and there are often flight circuit breakers, which have prevented Chinese staff in Djibouti from returning home for a long time rest.

8.2.3 Chinese-Funded Enterprises' Demand for Vocational Education

At present, with the increasing number of Chinese-funded enterprises in Djibouti, the demand for technical skills is becoming more and more urgent. There is a serious shortage of skilled workers in Djibouti, but the Djibouti government has developed relatively strict labor policies in order to protect domestic employment. Although foreign labor is allowed to work in Djibouti, there are still certain restrictions on the types of work. Foreign laborers need to obtain approval from the National Agency for Employment, Training and Professional Integration (ANEFIP) before they can work in Djibouti. Except for high-level technical jobs that are easier to obtain approval, general jobs such as manual labor, drivers, and security guards are difficult to obtain approval. In addition, the procedure of getting job in Djibouti for professional and technical personnel associated with the contracted projects related to Chinese-funded enterprises is very cumbersome and the cost is expensive. The cost of foreign workers to handle the relevant documents is as high as $1,300 each person every year.

Due to the Djibouti government's restrictions on foreign workers, Chinese-funded enterprises need to fully consider the problem of labor ratio when hiring employees, that is, they need to hire a large proportion of local employees. However, the current situation of vocational and technical education in Djibouti cannot meet the urgent demand of the enterprises for localized technical talents.

For example, as a form of vocational education in Djibouti, Djibouti vocational preparatory schools are mainly aimed at the needs of the tertiary industry, training primary service talents, or providing vocational basic training for industry and commerce, and the professionalism and skills of talents are mainly targeted at the primary needs of traditional industry and commerce. However, due to the poor cultural foundation and low skill level, only about 30% of the professional talents trained by vocational preparatory schools can successfully enter to the labor market, which is seriously out of line with the needs of Djibouti's economic and social development.

For another example, at present, Djibouti mainly uses French vocational education textbooks, which leads to the lack of targeted vocational skills training. After hiring talents, enterprises need to conduct secondary training, which increases the cost of employing and reduces their enthusiasm for hiring talents. Due to the backward development of Djibouti's local industry, there are fewer number of large and medium-sized enterprises is small, and most of them are foreign-controlled, which makes less communication between the schools and the enterprises, and it is difficult for students to enter the enterprise for practice. At the same time, many enterprises that need localized employees, due to the differences in political system and culture, are not smoothly connected with vocational colleges, which also affects the absorption of local talents.

8.2.4 Adaptability of Vocational Education in the Cooperative Country to the Development of Chinese-Funded Enterprises

1. The Shortage of Highly Educated People

According to the data released by the president unit of China-Djibouti Chamber of Commerce and the Overseas Chinese-funded Enterprises Survey Project Team of Yunnan University, as for the composition of Chinese-funded enterprises in Djibouti, in terms of gender distribution, men account for 90% while women account for only 10%. In the age distribution of employees, 37% are aged 16–25, 38% are aged 26–35, and 25% are aged 36 and above. In terms of the educational level of employees, 30% don't have any education, 22% have primary school education, 34% have secondary school or junior college education, and only 15% have bachelor's degree or above. The distribution of education levels among employees of different age groups is shown in Table 8–7.

Table 8–7 Distribution of Education Levels of Employees of Different Ages

The Highest Educational Level	16–25 Years Old	26–35 Years Old	36 Years Old and Above
Uneducated	25.78%	27.48%	40.48%
Primary School Education	23.44%	18.32%	23.81%
Secondary School or Junior College Education	40.63%	32.82%	23.81%
Bachelor's Degree or Above	10.16%	21.37%	11.90%

As can be seen from the above table that the education level of localized employees is generally not high. Then, the reason for the lack of highly educated talents is that Djibouti's education development level is generally backward, including the lack of professional teachers and practical training equipment. Most employees lack professional vocational skills, so it is difficult to meet the needs of enterprise development, and employees cannot achieve long-term stable employment.

2. The Increasing of the Demand for Localized Talents

At present, China's large-scale investment projects in Djibouti include the Djibouti International Free Trade Zone and the Salt Chemical Industry Park project. The large-scale engineering contracting projects include the construction of the Djibouti section of the Addis Ababa–Djibouti Railway, the Cross-Border Water Supply project (Phase I) undertaken by CGC Overseas Construction CO., Ltd, the construction of the Doraleh Multi-functional Port jointly undertaken by China State Construction Harbour Construction Co., Ltd. and China Civil Engineering Construction Corporation, and the construction of the Assal Lake Salt Industry Export Terminal undertaken by China Harbour Engineering Company Limited. The Djibouti International Free Trade Zone project was jointly invested in and constructed by China Merchants Group, the Djibouti Port, and Free Trade Zone Management Bureau, and the East Africa International Business Zone project exhibition area was constructed by China First Highway Engineering Co., Ltd and CIMC Group. After large-scale investment projects and large-scale engineering contracting projects are put into operation, a large number of localized technical skills are urgently needed correspondingly.

Taking the Addis Ababa-Djibouti Railway as an example, it starts from the capital city of Ethiopia in the west and ends in the capital city of Djibouti in the east, with a total length of 752.7 kilometers and a total investment of approximately $4 billion. China Railway Erju Group Co., Ltd. (hereinafter referred to as "China Railway Erju"), a subsidiary of China Railway Corporation, has undertaken the construction of the Addis Ababa to Mieso section, with a total length of approximately 325 kilometers. China Civil Engineering Group Co., Ltd. (hereinafter referred to as "China Civil Engineering"), a subsidiary of China Railway Construction Corporation, undertook the construction of Ethiopia's Mieso to Djibouti, with a total length of approximately 428 kilometers. The design speed of the line is 120 km/h, and a total of 45 stations are set up along the line, adopting the "6+2" model, that is, the joint venture formed by China Civil Engineering and China Railway Erju will operate for six years, and then they will provide technical services for another two years.

Since its official operation in 2018, the railway has continuously developed the freight market, enriched the service scale, increased the capacity by 25% to 30% annually, shortened the freight time from 3–7 days to about 10 hours, and reduced the transportation cost by 30%. According to the Railjour nal website, the operating revenue of the Addis Ababa-Djibouti Railway in 2021 was $86.13 million, an increase of 37.5% compared to 2020. This line has sent a total of 449 passenger trains throughout the year, transporting approximately 300,000 passengers, and the total of 1,469 freight trains, with more than 70,000 transport containers.

With the continuous improvement of the transportation capacity of the Addis Ababa-Djibouti Railway, the demand for localization of technical and skilled talents on the railway is on the rise, as shown in Figure 8–4. In 2021, the net increase in localization labor compared to 2016 was 3.5 times. The proportion of the total number of Chinese operating personnel has been decreasing year by year. For example, in 2019, there were 80 Chinese employees and about 2,582 local employees, with localized employees accounting for 97% of the operating personnel of the Addis Ababa-Djibouti Railway.

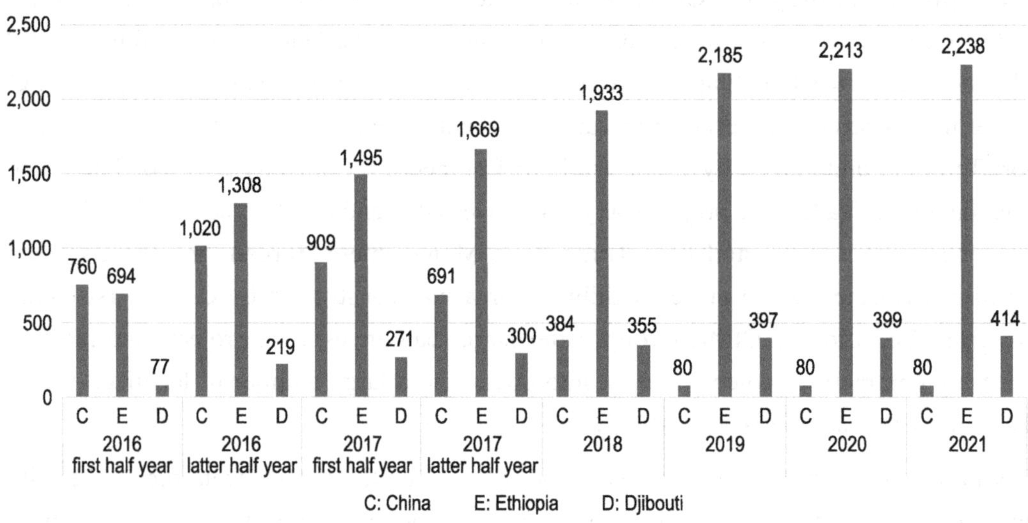

Figure 8–4 Requirements for Operating Personnel of the Addis Ababa-Djibouti Railway

3. The Most Scarce Talent in Technical Skills Positions

In terms of professional skills for local employees of Chinese-funded enterprises in Djibouti, taking the Addis Ababa-Djibouti Railway constructed by China Civil Engineering Corporation as an example, in 2021, the proportion of local employees who need to improve their professional skills reached 97%. Among them, there are a total of 411 employees in the Djibouti section, distributed in six first-level departments, including Infrastructure Management Department, Operations Management Department, Human Resources Management Department, Budget Management Department, Safety and Quality Department, and Capacity Building Department, covering 68 positions such as ET&ETS, equipment maintenance, and shunting. Figure 8–5 shows the distribution of main positions for local employees who need to improve their professional skills.

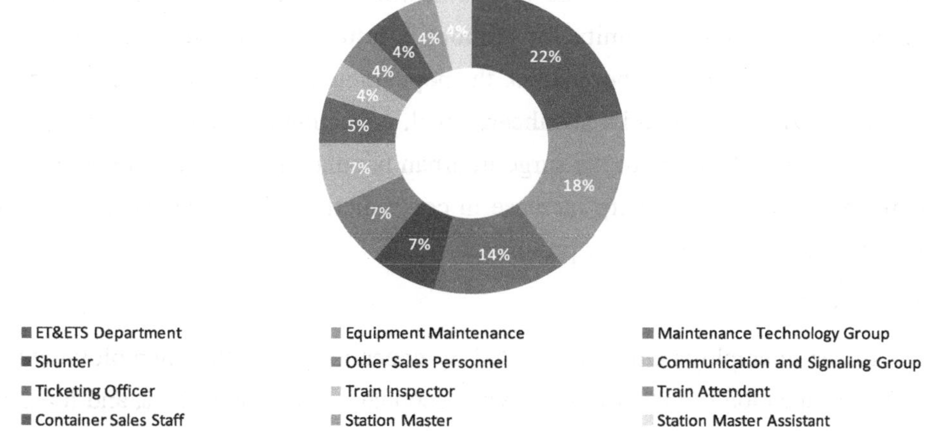

Figure 8–5 Distribution of Main Positions for Local Employees to Improve Vocational Skills in the Djibouti Section of the Addis Ababa-Djibouti Railway

4. Salient Supply-Demand Contradiction

On the one hand, the reserve of high-end skilled talents required for enterprise development is insufficient, resulting in the inability to meet the needs of modern industrial and commercial development. In addition, the number of small and medium-sized enterprises serving various large and medium-sized enterprises is limited, which is unable to provide more mid to low-end employment positions for these enterprises, thereby reducing the employment rate of the low-end population and forming a vicious cycle. On the other hand, the fit of technical skills is relatively low. Since most enterprises in Djibouti are built with foreign investment, the coupling degree between enterprises and local vocational education is not high from the beginning of construction, resulting in the poor compatibility between the high-skilled talents required by positions and the talents cultivated by vocational education in the process of enterprise localization. Due to the lack of local skilled talents, to a certain extent, the development of enterprises in Djibouti has been affected, and at the same time, the employment rate of secondary vocational education students is very low, all of which can be summarized as "poor export" causing the "weak import".

8.3 Chinese-Funded Enterprises Collaborating with Chinese Vocational Education for "Going Global"

8.3.1 The Necessity of Chinese Vocational Education Supporting International Production Capacity Cooperation of the Cooperative Country

1. Determined by the Main Issues Faced by the Social Development of The Cooperating Countries

(1) Population

In the past decade, the population of Djibouti has grown by an average of 1.8% annually, showing two main characteristics. One is youthfulness. Although the youthfulness of the population structure is an opportunity for Djibouti's future development, due to insufficient employment opportunities in the labor market, the population dividend cannot be realized in time. The other is urbanization. Djibouti's healthcare level, education and housing conditions cannot maintain a positive correlation with the surge in urban population, resulting in the emergence of a large number of slums and a sharp increase in contradictions. The drawbacks of unbalanced urbanization have become increasingly prominent.

(2) Employment

In terms of the unemployment rate, divided by education level, the unemployment rate for those with basic education is 35%, for those with secondary education is 27%, and for those with higher education is 16%. By age, the unemployment rate for young people aged 15 to 24 is 86%, and the unemployment rate for young people aged 15 to 34 is 65%. From this, it can be seen that education level is an important factor affecting employment, and the high unemployment situation in Djibouti has seriously affected its economic and social development.

In terms of employment-population distribution, in 2021, the proportion of people engaged in the primary and secondary industries was 25% and 13% respectively, showing a decreasing trend annually. The proportion of people engaged in the tertiary industry was 62%, showing an increasing trend annually. According to data released by the National Bureau of Statistics of Djibouti, the employment population in the tertiary industry is mainly concentrated in industries such as administration, housekeeping, construction, public engineering, transportation, communication, post and telecommunications. It can be seen that the tertiary industry is the engine of Djibouti's economic and social development, and high-level technical and skilled talents are especially required. However, due to the lack or low level of vocational skills, some young workers can only enter low-end industries and the informal sector for employment.

2. Determined by the Lack of Vocational Education Systems in Partner Countries

Before 2019, graduates of senior secondary vocational and technical colleges can only enter ordinary institutions of higher education if they want to continue their studies, while Djibouti has only two schools to choose from, namely the University of Djibouti and Djibouti Medical College. Factors such as high admission barriers, limited practical teaching, and lack of close alignment with job requirements led to the vast majority of students giving up further education and directly entering society for employment. In addition, the majors of vocational colleges are concentrated in civil engineering, mechanical maintenance, office automation, tourism, construction, computer applications, etc., without involving the transportation, logistics, communication, post and telecommunications industries in the tertiary industry that contribute to the gross national product, resulting in a talent gap in these industries.

On March 28, 2019, the construction of the Luban Workshop in Djibouti set a precedent for higher vocational education in Djibouti, while filling the gap in the absence of railway-related majors in the country. The workshops are aimed at the Addis Ababa-Djibouti Railway and the Djibouti Port, cultivating railway and commercial talents, and achieving the localization practice of the apprenticeship system with Chinese characteristic featuring "enrollment means recruitment and graduation means employment". It can be seen that China's vocational education is indispensable in serving the process of production capacity cooperation between China and Djibouti.

3. Determined by the Demand for Localized Technical and Skilled Talents of Chinese-Funded Enterprises Stationed in Djibouti

At present, due to the differences in function, scale, industry, and management mode among Chinese-funded enterprises stationed in Djibouti, there are also differences in the training methods for local employees. It mainly includes setting up training institutions or training centers by the enterprise itself, entrusting schools, colleges and universities in Djibouti to train employees, adopting apprenticeship systems to train employees on the job, and sending employees to China for training. The training provided by China to Djibouti's local employees has made certain contributions in improving the quality of employment, providing human resources titles, and promoting the development of local technical talents.

However, the training of localized technical skills requires close cooperation between schools and colleges, and enterprises in order to play a greater role. Enterprises conducting training in Djibouti mostly adopt the on-the-job training mode, and the training content is about the improvement of basic professional quality and the cultivation of basic vocational skills. The training duration is mostly short-term, lacking long-term systematic training. The President unit of the China-Djibouti Chamber of Commerce and the Overseas Chinese-funded enterprises Survey project team of Yunnan University have made statistics on the training content and training market of local employees of Chinese-funded enterprises in Djibouti. The specific data are shown in Table 8–8 and Table 8–9.

Table 8–8 Main Distribution of Training Content for Employees by Gender

Training Content	Male	Female
Management Skills	16.67%	12.50%
Interpersonal Skills	8.33%	37.50%
Writing Ability	5.00%	12.50%
Professional Ethics	8.33%	12.50%
Chinese Reading and Writing	33.33%	12.50%
English Reading and Writing	6.67%	12.50%
Computer Skills	16.67%	25.00%

continued

Training Content	Male	Female
Technical Skills	26.67%	37.50%
Safe Production Knowledge	23.33%	12.50%
Other	1.67%	12.50%
No Training	8.33%	0

Table 8–9 Distribution of Training Duration by Gender

Training Duration	Male	Female
1–6 days	23.73%	62.50%
7–29 days	40.68%	37.50%
1–3 months	27.12%	0
3–6 months	8.47%	0
Total	100.00%	100.00%

8.3.2 Internationalization of Chinese Vocational Education in the Cooperative Country

In recent years, relying on China's aid of human resource training programs, academic degree education programs, and the Luban Workshops, China and Djibouti have continuously strengthened cooperation in the field of human resources in various industries such as transportation and logistics, public management, agriculture, forestry, animal husbandry, fishing, health, and social security, effectively improving Djibouti's employment ability.

1. Training and Resource Construction of Chinese Vocational Education in Djibouti

In the process of vocational training in Djibouti, Chinese vocational colleges have accumulated rich experience in helping international production capacity cooperation, and conducted 690 days of training in total, benefiting nearly 3,000 employees. Table 8–10 shows some training situations between China and Djibouti.

Table 8–10 Participation of Chinese Colleges in Training and Resource Construction in Djibouti

Start Time	Training Theme	Training Units	Number of Trainees (person)	Training Duration	Training Method
2014.5	Railway business knowledge training conducted by the Ethiopian Railway Company of the Addis Ababa-Djibouti Railway	Tianjin Railway Technical and Vocational College	254	6 months	Centralized training in Tianjin

continued

Start Time	Training Theme	Training Units	Number of Trainees (person)	Training Duration	Training Method
2015.6	Railway business knowledge training conducted by Djibouti Railway Company of Addis Ababa-Djibouti Railway	Tianjin Railway Technical and Vocational College	100	6 months	Centralized training in Tianjin
2018.5	Djibouti monitoring equipment and maintenance technical training	Hunan International Business Vocational College	29	7days	Centralized training in Hunan
2019.7	Djibouti IT engineers training	Beijing ChangPing Vocational School	4	4 days	Centralized training in Beijing
2019.10	Overseas training course on operation technology for the Ethiopian Railway of the Addis Ababa-Djibouti Railway	Beijing Jiaotong University entrusts Tianjin Railway Technical and Vocational College to undertake	150	40 days	Centralized training in Labu Station on the Addis Ababa-Djibouti Railway
2019.10	Electric locomotive driver training of the Addis Ababa-Djibouti Railway	Zhengzhou Railway Vocational and Technical College	200	6 months	Centralized training in Zhengzhou
2019.11	Djibouti bridge and pavement road maintenance training in 2019	School of Continuing Education at Central South University and Hunan International Business Vocational College	18	21 days	Centralized training in Hunan
2019.11	African jewelry processing technology training in 2019	Hunan International Business Vocational College	24 including Djibouti and 5 other countries	50	Centralized training in Hunan
2021.11	Construction of training resources for types of work on the Addis Ababa-Djibouti Railway (recorded courses)	Tianjin Railway Technical and Vocational College and Zhengzhou Railway Vocational and Technical College	2000	—	Online training
2022.4	Djibouti state administration management training	Jiangxi College Of Foreign Studies	11	21 days	Online training
2022.6	Overseas training course on locomotive application technology of the Addis Ababa-Djibouti Railway	Shanxi Railway institute	100	7 days	Online training

continued

Start Time	Training Theme	Training Units	Number of Trainees (person)	Training Duration	Training Method
2022.9	The first training camp of African youth innovation and entrepreneurship center	China Merchants Bureau, Djibouti Port and Free Trade Zone Management Bureau, Djibouti-China Chamber of Commerce, China Merchants Shekou Industrial Zone	26 outstanding young entre-preneurs from 4 countries including Djibouti	8 days	Centralized training in Djibouti

2. International Education Practice of Tianjin Railway Technical and Vocational College in Djibouti

The international educational forms carried out by Tianjin Railway Technical and Vocational College in Djibouti are mainly divided into social training and academic education. In terms of social training, in 2015, the college conducted a 6-month skill training program for 100 employees of Djibouti Railway Company, covering four majors: railway engineering, railway signaling, railway rolling stock, and railway transportation. After carefully researching the needs of enterprises and the socio-economic development of Djibouti, the college has developed a "five stage" training method, which includes training for students in the adaptive learning stage, basic knowledge stage, theoretical learning stage, special on-site internship stage, and professional course learning stage. During this period, the college completed 4 professional training programs, more than 20 course outlines, and more than 20 English textbooks. After receiving training and returning home, the trainees have become the backbone of the operation of the Addis Ababa-Djibouti Railway and have been highly recognized by the Ministry of Transport of Djibouti and the Djibouti Railway Company.

During the COVID-19, in order to serve the landmark project of the " Belt and Road" — the Addis Ababa-Djibouti Railway, Tianjin Railway Technical and Vocational College won the bid for the online education and training service project of the Addis Ababa-Djibouti Railway in July 2021. Considering the poor network environment, low level of technical personnel, and limit-experienced managers in African countries, and combined with the specific needs of the project, the college has explored and formed a "graded and classified" training path around the training goal of "understanding, using, learning, and practicing well", which is presented through practical operation and virtual simulationg technology. Standardized and professional teaching resource templates are used to explain the structure cognition, operation process and other contents involved in eight types of work, such as line workers and signal workers, focusing on enhancing the safety awareness of students, teamwork and other professional qualities, and building a

"Three Service, Three Modernization, and Three Connection" system, completing 554 class hours of recording and broadcasting course videos. There are 554 PPTs in both Chinese and English, 8 textbooks and 500 question banks, achieving the sustainable development of localized talents.

In terms of academic education, in 2019, the college enrolled four Djibouti students to study railway engineering, aiming to train professional talents needed for the operation of the railway in Djibouti. During the pandemic, the college actively explored new ideas for online teaching, and outlined an online teaching map of "diversified combination, mutual teaching and learning, classified teacher-guided learning, student exploration, teacher-student interaction, and student participation". In addition, the dual-subject education model of school-enterprise joint training is adopted. The college and China Civil Engineering Construction Corparation in Djibouti jointly formulated a talent training program, and built a course system of "course, job, and certificate integration" based on the demand of railway transportation positions in Djibouti. Enterprises are involved in the whole process of talent cultivation, achieving the integration of course content and professional standards, as well as the integration of teaching and production processes.

8.3.3 Forms and Achievements of Internationalized Education

Regarding the effectiveness of vocational education in Djibouti by other countries, there are no relevant clues on the Internet. To this end, project team members called the Chief Inspector of Djibouti's National Education and Vocational Training Department, Mahdi. He stated that vocational education cooperation between Djibouti and neighboring countries such as Morocco, Ethiopia, Somalia, etc. only exists in the cultivation of international students and teacher exchange. Except for China, no other country has invested in constructing specialized vocational and technical education and training centers or platforms in Djibouti.

8.4 Tianjin Railway Technical and Vocational College's Support for International Production Capacity Cooperation in Djibouti

8.4.1 Current Situation Analysis

1. Overview of the Luban Workshop in Djibouti

In order to serve the development of the Addis Ababa-Djibouti Railway and the port of Djibouti, in April 2017, Tianjin Railway Technical and Vocational College proposed the preliminary idea of building Luban Workshop in Djibouti. In October of the same year, it reached an intention to jointly build Luban Workshop in Djibouti with China Civil Engineering Construction Corporation. In March 2018, the college signed a memorandum of cooperation with the Ministry of Education of Djibouti. On March 28th, 2019, Tianjin Railway Technical and Vocational College, Tianjin First Commercial School, Djibouti Business School, and China Civil Engineering Construction Corperation in Djibouti jointly built the first Luban Workshop in Africa— the Luban Workshop in Djibouti, offering four majors: railway transportation operation management, railway engineering technology, commerce and logistics. With a construction area of 1,000 square meters, the railway major has 5 teaching areas, such as the sand table of railway operation teaching area and the locomotive simulation driving teaching area. The business major has 5 practical training areas, such as the enterprise panorama perception training room and the enterprise simulation operation cognition training room. The workshop training base is located at Nagad Station on the Addis Ababa-Djibouti Railway.

Figure 8–6 Appearance of the Luban Workshop in Djibouti

2. Construction Content

(1) Construction of Teaching Resources

In accordance with the local economic and social development needs of Djibouti, combined with the national vocational qualification standards of Djibouti and the national teaching standards of China, with the cultivation of practical innovation ability as the core, and in response to the weak basic knowledge and operational skills of local students and employees in Djibouti, the job requirements and skill characteristics are aligned, and practical skills are emphasized. A concise, easy-to-understand, modular textbook is developed to meet the needs of academic education and in-service employee training. In the construction of teaching materials, emphasis is placed on the vocational orientation of professional courses, and three-dimensional, and information-oriented bilingual teaching resources are developed, achieving synchronous and homogeneous professional teaching between China and Djibouti, and connecting overseas courses with Chinese courses as well.

(2) Construction of Teaching Staff

Whether in academic education or skill training, the construction of teaching staff is a crucial element for the sustainable development of vocational education services for international capacity cooperation. Teacher training based on professional development is a necessary way to share China's advanced educational concepts and models with Djibouti institutions. Teacher training has always adhered to the approach of combining "inviting in" and "going global", as well as the combination of online and offline methods, and the cultivation goals of "four levels, five abilities, and four qualifications".

The "four levels" lay a solid foundation for teacher training, including "lectures", "practices", "assessments", and "certifications". The lectures are about teaching theoretical knowledge and practical operation. The Practices refer to practicing professional skills and educational teaching skills. The assessments means testing theoretical knowledge and practical operational skills. And the qualifications implies obtaining a completion certificate and qualification certificate. The "five abilities" help promote teacher training, including enhancing teachers' professional practical abilities, teaching abilities, resource development abilities, information technology application abilities, and self-learning abilities. The "four qualifications" enable continuous empowerment in teacher training, aiming to cultivate a high qualified teaching team with an international perspective, international empathy, international knowledge, and international competence.

Figure 8–7 Chinese Colleges Providing Railway and Business Teacher Training for Djibouti

(3) Construction of Site

The cooperation between vocational colleges and Chinese-funded enterprises stationed in Djibouti to build an international internship and training base that integrates practical teaching, social training, enterprise real production, and social-technical services is a fundamental project to ensure the smooth implementation of academic education and skill training. During the construction of the Luban Workshop in Djibouti, China Civil Engineering Construction Corporation in Djibouti provided certain funds for site decoration and equipment procurement, and provided the Nagad Station of the Addis Ababa-Djibouti Railway as the Luban Workshop Training Base, which fully meets the needs of workshop teaching and practice, skill training, and pre-job training.

Figure 8–8 Part of the Teaching Areas of the Luban Workshop in Djibouti

(4)Academic Education

In terms of enrollment, college-enterprise cooperation in enrollment and joint cultivation has reached an organic linkage between talent cultivation and employment, as well as effective integration of talent supply and demand, achieving the "enrollment is recruitment and graduation is employment". In terms of talent cultivation, colleges and enterprises collaborate to establish teaching standards and develop teaching resources. Taking the Luban Workshop in Djibouti as an example, based on careful research on the job requirements of the Addis Ababa-Djibouti Railway and the Djibouti Free Trade Zone, Tianjin Railway Technical and Vocational College and Chinese enterprises in Djibouti, based on documents such as the *China Higher Vocational Education Standard Professional Talent Training Plan* and *China Higher Vocational Education Professional Teaching Standards*, determined talent training goals, restructured curriculum system, and improved teaching methods according to the actual situation of local students and employees. Also, they have formulated localized and effective international professional teaching standards, curriculum standards, and assessment and evaluation standards.

(5) Skills Training

There are three main ways for vocational colleges to collaborate with Chinese-funded enterprises in Djibouti to carry out employee training:

① Select employees to China for training. Before conducting training, Chinese-funded enterprises stationed in Djibouti will select vocational schools and colleges and training venues in China, and these vocational schools and colleges will arrange systematic training and related internships. Training in China is conducive to presenting Chinese standards, Chinese technology, and Chinese equipment more intuitively to enterprise employees, broadening their international perspectives, and effectively improving their overall qualities and skill levels. The disadvantage lies in the high cost of training.

② They send excellent teachers from Chinese vocational colleges to Djibouti to provide skill training for enterprise employees. In order to carry out targeted training the teachers need to have a deep understanding of Djibouti's cultural environment, laws and regulations, training methods, and specific content of cooperation projects before conducting training. The deficiency lies in the limited duration of training provided by Chinese teachers in Djibouti.

③ They carry out internal training in the enterprise. Specifically, it is divided into two stages. In the construction stage, enterprises carry out short-term simple skill training, and in their work, teachers and apprentices are often used to further improve their skill levels to meet the needs of rapid employment. In the operation and maintenance stage, it is necessary to carry out refined operation and maintenance of facilities and equipment, and put forward higher requirements for employees' business level and professional literacy. In the operation and maintenance stage, it is necessary to carry out detailed operation and maintenance of facilities and equipment, and put forward higher requirements for employees' business level and professional quality. At this time, it is also important for enterprises to cooperate with vocational schools and colleges to conduct systematic staff training, to facilitate the sustainable improvement of employees' abilities, and to develop standards, teaching resources and skill level certification systems that meet the needs of the project. In the post-epidemic era, schools, colleges and enterprises usually develop digital teaching resources or record and broadcast courses to coordinate training.

8.4.2 Education Models

1. Overview of the Partners

(1) Chinese Schools and Colleges

Tianjin Railway Technical and Vocational College (TRTVC), founded in 1951, is a public vocational college with a distinct industry focus and extensive international exchanges. It aims to cultivate highly skilled technical professionals for the railway and urban rail industries both within China and abroad. Since 2001, TRTVC has provided training for over 1,100 railway personnel from countries such as Tanzania, Zambia, Ethiopia, and Djibouti. In addition, TRTVC has established the Thailand Luban Workshop Center, Djibouti Luban Workshop, and Nigeria Luban Workshop. Tianjin First Commercial School is one of the first national secondary vocational schools specializing in commerce. It has been recognized as a national key secondary vocational school, one of the first batch of national demonstration schools, an advanced collective in the national education system, a national advanced unit of vocational education, and an excellent vocational education school at the fourth Huang Yanpei Vocational Education Award. The school currently offers programs in finance and commerce, business technology, electromechanical technology, and art and design. In 2019, it participated in the establishment of the Luban Workshop in Djibouti.

(2) Djibouti Schools and Colleges

Djibouti Business School is located in Djibouti City, the capital of the Republic of Djibouti. It was built by China Civil Engineering in 1993. It is the largest vocational school in Djibouti, offering 40 majors and with more than 1,700 students. The school has ten professional teaching areas, including civil engineering, building facilities, mechanical and electrical, electronic and electrical, refrigeration, and automotive driving and maintenance areas.

In accordance with China's higher vocational education standards, Djibouti's economic and social development needs, and the employment needs of enterprises, four majors have been established, namely railway traffic operation management, railway engineering technology, commerce, and logistics. All four majors of Luban Workshop in Djibouti have been approved and certified by the Ministry of Education of Djibouti, and have been officially incorporated into the national education system of Djibouti.

(3) Chinese-Funded Enterprises in Djibouti

China Civil Engineering Group Co., Ltd. is one of the earliest Chinese enterprises to enter the international market, and it was merged into China Railway Construction Corporation in 2003. At present, it has developed into a large state-owned enterprise with special qualification of general contracting of railway engineering construction in China, and has been listed among the top 100 of the world's largest 250 international contractors for 19 consecutive years. China Civil Engineering Group entered the Djibouti market in 1981, and has implemented more than 100 projects such as the building of the Ministry of Foreign Affairs of Djibouti, the National Stadium, and the Industrial and Commercial School. As the two-term chairman of China-Djibouti Chamber of Commerce, it is one of the longest, most influential and largest Chinese-funded enterprises in Djibouti.

The Djibouti Luban Workshop mainly serves the development of the Addis Ababa-Djibouti Railway and the Djibouti port economy undertaken by China Civil Engineering Group. In terms of academic education, it recruits railway students as needed every year, with an enrollment scale of 10–20 people per major. It cultivates high-quality technical and skilled talents who master frontline positions such as railway passenger transportation, freight transportation, and operation work, railway lines, highways, and housing construction and maintenance. The annual enrollment scale of business and trade majors is about 20 people, cultivating high-quality technical and skilled talents with knowledge in market planning and analysis, business negotiation, international trade, warehousing, transportation, packaging, distribution, and other fields.

2. Cooperation Mode and Organizational Structure

(1) Cooperation Mode

The Djibouti Luban Workshop adopts the cooperation mode, including governments, enterprises, and schools and colleges, as shown in Figure 8–9. This mode is supported by policies provided by the Tianjin Municipal People's Government, the Ministry of Education of Djibouti, and other government agencies in China and Djibouti. Teaching resources and teacher training are supported by Tianjin Railway Technical and Vocational College and Tianjin The First Commercial School, and teaching venues are supported by the Djibouti Business School. The China Civil Engineering Group in Djibouti, a Chinese-funded enterprise, will provide practical training sites and living support for Chinese construction personnel. At the same time, the "governments, enterprises and schools and colleges" tripartite cooperation to build a "4+2+1+1" mode. The "4" is four standards including professional standards, curriculum standards, competition standards, and evaluation standards; the "2" means two teams, a team of teachers who understand Chinese and Chinese technology and standards, and a team of unified management talents; The two "1s" respectively represent the research and development achievements of a complete set of rail transit training base and a set of skill competition equipment.

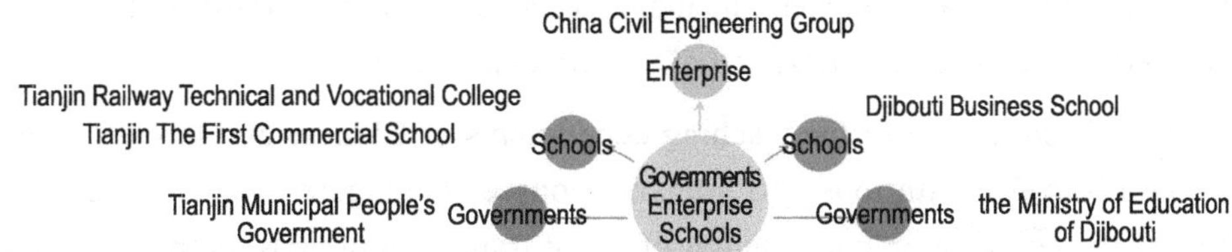

Figure 8–9 Cooperation Made of Djibouti Luban Workshop

(2) Work Sharing and Cooperation

In March 2019, Tianjin Railway Technical and Vocational College, Tianjin The First Commercial School, Djibouti Business School and China Civil Engineering Group in Djibouti signed the *Djibouti Luban Workshop Four-party and Co-construction Agreement.* Relying on Djibouti Luban Workshop, all parties explore the way for large and medium-sized state-owned enterprises to actively participate in the international cooperation in vocational education, serve the "1+N" development strategy of China Civil Engineering Group in Djibouti, help international production capacity cooperation, and gradually establish an "all-round, deep-level, and multi-form" effective mechanism for the integration of production and education, and school-enterprise cooperation.

(3) Organizational Framework

During the construction and operation of the Luban Workshop in Djibouti, an organizational structure consisting of decision-making, guidance, and execution was formed, as shown in the figure below 8–10.

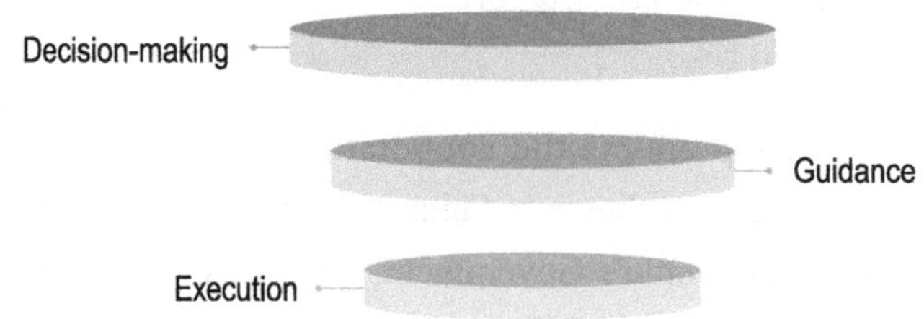

Figure 8–10 Organizational Structure of the Luban Workshop in Djibouti

Decision-making: It consists of Chinese and foreign governments, heads of Chinese and foreign vocational colleges, and heads of enterprises. It is responsible for the top-level design, including determining the training concept of Djibouti's technical talents, the organic integration path of on-the-job staff training and youth education training, and the method of carrying out cooperation between domestic and foreign schools, colleges and enterprises, with Djibouti Luban Workshop as the plateform.

Execution: It is composed of professional teachers from Chinese and foreign colleges and leaders of relevant key projects of enterprises. They are mainly responsible for the specific implementation of collaboration content, including teaching resources construction, training base construction and operation, and localization of modern apprenticeship.

Guidance: It is composed of the teaching departments of Chinese and foreign schools and colleges, second-level institutions and human resources managers of enterprises. They are responsible for the connotation construction of talent training programs, curriculum standards, and staff technical level standards.

8.4.3 Institutional Mechanism

1. Main Systems

With the completion of the construction task, Tianjin Railway Technical and Vocational College has shifted its focus to operation and maintenance. It has promptly established and revised rules and regulations such as the *Measures for the Operation and Management of Luban Workshop of Railway College* and the *Measures for the Management of Construction funds of Luban Workshop of Railway College*. The focus of the work has been moved down to secondary institutions, and gave full play to their main role. It is clear that the school and enterprise should carry out all-round cooperation in the selection of majors, the development of teaching resources, and the certification of skill levels, coordinate the offline training and the production of online recording and broadcasting courses, and constantly explore and practice new paths for the sustainable development of Luban Workshop, to achieve both social and economic benefits.

2. Operation Mechanism

(1) Government

The foreign government, led by the Ministry of Education of Djibouti, signed a *Memorandum of Understanding and Cooperation* with Tianjin Railway Technical and Vocational College in March 2018, confirming cooperation between the two sides in railway industry-related work and training appraisal, construction of Luban Workshop, training of Djibouti railway staff, implementation of training courses, training of academic students, and exchange and sharing of advanced technology and teaching equipment. A work promotion group composed of the Chief Inspector of the Ministry of Education of Djibouti, the Director of Djibouti Education Bureau, the President of Djibouti Business School, and the Dean of Tianjin Railway Technical and Vocational College was established. The group holds a working meeting at the beginning of each year to determine the annual work plan and important events for cooperation, and conducts regular inspection and supervision of the work carried out in the cooperation. In terms of the participation of the Chinese government, in September 2019, Tianjin established a leading group for the promotion of Luban Workshop headed by the municipal leader, to coordinate, lead and accelerate the construction of the workshop. Tianjin Education Commission has repeatedly given guidance on the construction plan and construction progress of Luban Workshop, ensuring the smooth implementation of the project.

(2) Colleges

In May 2018, Tianjin Railway Technical and Vocational College established the Luban Workshop Construction Organization, including the College Luban Workshop Construction Leading Group and Luban Workshop Construction Office. The construction office consisted of five special working groups, namely external communication, professional construction, training base construction, publicity, and scientific research. According to the requirements of "five factors in place" for equipment, site, standard, teaching materials and teachers, the construction of workshops was promoted.

(3) Enterprise

Since October 2017, China Civil Engineering Group Co., Ltd. and Tianjin Railway Technical and Vocational College have reached a consensus on the cooperation of jointly building Djibouti Luban Workshop, and have given strong support to personnel training, standard construction, practical training site construction, equipment customs clearance and accommodation during the construction process.

3. Evaluation Method

The Djibouti Luban Workshop Construction Evaluation Group is composed of the Chief Inspector of the Ministry of Education of Djibouti, the heads of Chinese and foreign vocational colleges, and the heads of Chinese enterprises stationed in Djibouti. At the end of each year, the evaluation team conducts a survey on the satisfaction of workshop students, trainees, and teachers, summarizing opinions and suggestions from all parties in order to further optimize the operation of the workshop. Figure 8–11 shows the questionnaire of the evaluation team to investigate the training quality of the trainees.

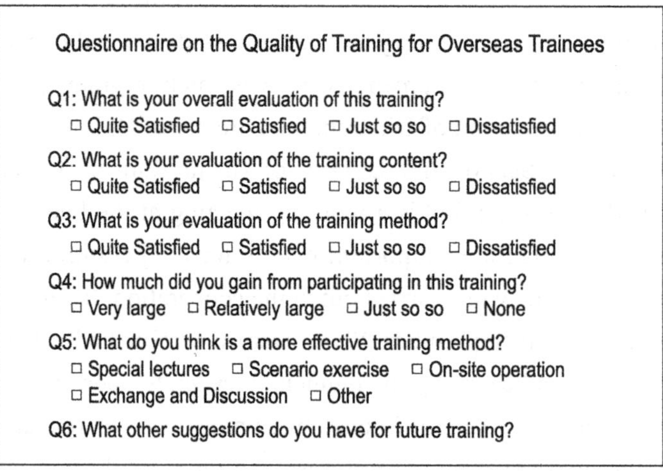
Questionnaire on the Quality of Training for Overseas Trainees

Q1: What is your overall evaluation of this training?
□ Quite Satisfied □ Satisfied □ Just so so □ Dissatisfied

Q2: What is your evaluation of the training content?
□ Quite Satisfied □ Satisfied □ Just so so □ Dissatisfied

Q3: What is your evaluation of the training method?
□ Quite Satisfied □ Satisfied □ Just so so □ Dissatisfied

Q4: How much did you gain from participating in this training?
□ Very large □ Relatively large □ Just so so □ None

Q5: What do you think is a more effective training method?
□ Special lectures □ Scenario exercise □ On-site operation
□ Exchange and Discussion □ Other

Q6: What other suggestions do you have for future training?

Figure 8–11 Questionnaire on Training Quality of the Trained Teachers in Luban Workshop

8.4.4 Main Achievements

1. Main Achievements

(1) Build a Platform for Sustainable Development of School-enterprise Cooperation

In order to further promote the innovative development of Luban Workshop and enrich the connotation construction of Luban Workshop, on April 29th, 2021, Luban Workshop Production-education Integration Development Alliance was established. The nature of the alliance is a national, non-profit cooperative organization with the participation of enterprises, colleges, research institutions and social organizations. It follows the basic principle of "joint construction and development, and sharing results", explores and deepens the international integration of industry and education development model of "serving the construction of the 'Belt and Road', helping the overseas development of enterprises, and expanding the space for school cooperation". It provides platform and resource support for the high-quality sustainable development of Luban Workshop, and provides skills training and technological innovation services for the overseas development of Chinese enterprises. At present, the members of the alliance have developed into 35 cooperative enterprises and 21 vocational colleges participating in the construction of Luban Workshop. Through participating in international conferences such as the World Conference on the Development of Vocational Education and China's International Import Expo, schools and colleges and enterprises continue to closely cooperate in expanding the professional construction of Luban workshops and adding new ones. The members of the alliance have joined forces to help international production capacity cooperation become a new normal.

(2) Enriched the Talent Path for Localized Technical Skills

Before the opening of the Luban Workshop in Djibouti, the two majors, namely railway engineering technology and railway traffic operation and management, were certified by the Ministry of Education of Djibouti, and it was agreed that China's higher vocational education at the specialist level could be held in Djibouti. The two majors of commerce and logistics have also successively obtained confirmation letters from the Ministry of National Education and Vocational Training of Djibouti for vocational education (See Figure 8–12), which has improved the academic level of Djibouti Business School and filled the gap in Djibouti's national education.

吉布提共和国
团结-平等-和平

吉布提国民教育与职业培训部

جمهورية جيبوتي

وزارة التربية الوطنية والتكوين المهني

28/3/2019

部长

الوزير

359

至
天津市教育委员会
天津铁道职业技术学院

主题：同意天津铁道职业技术学院开设铁道类专业的确认函

吉布提国民教育与职业培训部对天津铁道职业技术学院提交的铁道工程技术、铁道交通运营管理两个专业人才培养方案进行了严肃、细致的审查，认为专业人才培养方案能够针对吉布提鲁班工坊学生实际情况，并结合相关企业就业需求。

两个专业的人才培养方案培养目标及就业岗位明确，课程体系结构合理，教学模式理念先进，专业建设及发展目标符合企业实际需求。

为满足吉布提对铁路运输方面的技术技能需求，吉布提国民教育与职业培训部认证批准举办中国高等职业教育专科层次，同意开设两个铁道类专业，学生学习期满，成绩合格，同意颁发高等职业教育（专科）毕业证书。

吉布提国民教育与职业培训部部长
穆斯塔法·默罕默德·马哈穆德
MOUSTAPHA MOHAMED MAHAMOUD

RÉPUBLIQUE DE DJIBOUTI
Unité - Égalité - Paix

MINISTÈRE DE L'ÉDUCATION NATIONALE
ET DE LA FORMATION PROFESSIONNELLE

جمهورية جيبوتي

وزارة التربية الوطنية والتكوين المهني

Djibouti le 28/3/2019

LE MINISTRE

الوزير

N° 359 /MENFOP

A
La commission de l'Éducation de la municipalité de Tianjin,
Université Professionnelle de Tianjin pour les Techniques Ferroviaires.

Objet : Lettre de confirmation pour la création de spécialités ferroviaires

Le Ministère de l'Éducation Nationale et de la Formation Professionnelle a procédé à un examen approfondi sur les programmes de formation des spécialités suivantes de niveau Baccalauréat professionnelle +3ans:

- Ingénierie et technique ferroviaires,
- Exploitation et gestion ferroviaires.

Soumis par l'Université Professionnelle de Tianjin pour les Techniques Ferroviaires, ces programmes de formation peuvent être enseignés dans les ateliers Luban de Djibouti (Lycée Industriel et Commercial) en partenariat avec les entreprises du secteur de transport ferroviaire.

En outre, les conditions d'enseignement et de mise en œuvre permettent d'approuver la mise en place de ces formations.

Les objectifs de formation, les postes de travail, la structure du programme d'étude et de certification ainsi que le modèle d'enseignement répondent aux besoins réels de nos entreprises.

Afin de répondre aux besoins en compétences techniques dans le secteur de transport ferroviaire, le Ministère de l'Éducation Nationale et de la Formation Professionnelle valide et homologue le diplôme de licence professionnelle (Baccalauréat professionnelle +3ans) de l'enseignement professionnel supérieur Chinois.

Nous sommes convenus de mettre en œuvre les deux programmes de formation des spécialités ferroviaires et de délivrer un diplôme de licence professionnelle (Bac pro+3) de l'enseignement professionnel supérieur pour les candidats qui valident les examens de fin de formation.

Le Ministre
MOUSTAPHA MOHAMED MAHAMOUD

Figure 8–12 Professional Certification Letter

The Djibouti Luban Workshop has trained 148 students and 69 teachers. Four Djibouti international students will graduate in July 2022, and the first 24 students will soon graduate in September 2023. 150 international standards, textbooks, training guides and other materials have been compiled, 3 textbooks have been officially published, online teaching resources have reached 1,412 class hours, and more than 150 times have been reported by 34 mainstream media at home and abroad, including *CCTV News*, Xinhua News Agency, and Djibouti *National News*. In 2019, under the radiation influence of the Luban Workshop in Djibouti, Tianjin Railway

Technical and Vocational College was commissioned by Beijing Jiaotong University to undertake the Ethiopian Railway Operation Technology Overseas Training Project sponsored by the Ministry of Commerce of China. Four teachers were selected to conduct a 40-day employee training program in Ethiopia, with a total of 95 trainees. In 2021, Tianjin Railway Technical and Vocational College won the bid for the online training project for local employees of the Addis Ababa-Djibouti Railway Operation and Maintenance Project Company. The teaching team completed the recording of teaching videos for 8 types of work, including line workers, communication workers, and signal workers, totaling more than 550 class hours, benefiting more than 800 employees. In the future, the promotion stage will benefit more than 2,000 employees.

2. Main Features

The main features and innovation of China's vocational colleges in serving the international production capacity cooperation between China and Africa can be summarized as the "Eight Initiatives", which have created a new pattern of demonstration and leadership in China-Djibouti vocational education cooperation, and are one of the earliest landmark achievements in implementing the "Capacity Building" action of the Eight Major Actions on China-Africa Cooperation. It has created a new situation of implementing the instructions of the leaders of the two countries, serving national strategies, promoting economic cooperation between countries, improving people's livelihood and promoting employment of the young people. It has created a new model of cooperation between the two governments, joint construction of vocational schools and colleges on both sides, and full participation of Chinese "going global" enterprises. It has created a new mode of cooperation between Chinese and higher vocational colleges to build Luban Workshops. It is the first time for Djibouti to organize higher vocational education. It has created a new path to complete the professional certification in the country of arrival, filling the gap in Djibouti's national education. It has created a new mode of combining the teaching area inside the school and the training base outside the school. It has created an international school-enterprise cooperation on jointly implementing national projects, pushing the integration of industry and education, as well as school-enterprise cooperation, to a new height.

8.5 Existing Problems and Development Recommendations

8.5.1 Existing Problems and Analysis of Causes

1. The Cooperation Platform has Not Been Fully Established Yet

To support the international production capacity cooperation of Chinese-funded enterprises in Africa, China's vocational education needs to establish a relatively stable and mature cooperation platform. The platform should be jointly built by the governments of China and the partner countries, vocational education colleges or institutions and Chinese-funded enterprises. In the process of playing the functions of the platform, the cooperation projects, contents, objectives and implementation ways of multi-party cooperative entities should be solidified. Otherwise, the connection between Chinese vocational education resources and Chinese-funded enterprises in the partner countries will be blocked, and the project implementation subject can not gather strength and coordinated development. At the early stage of the construction of Luban Workshop in Djibouti, due to social, cultural and other differences, the college encountered a lot of resistance in the process of direct communication with institutions in the partner countries, because these institutions did not know much about the project objectives and specific implementation plans, and also did not realize that the project would have a positive impact on economic and social development and improvement of people's livelihood after implementation, resulting in very slow progress in the project. Subsequently, Chinese-funded enterprises stationed in Djibouti and joined the project, with their accumulated experience in production capacity cooperation through years of deep cultivation in Djibouti, assisted Chinese colleges in connecting government departments such as the Chinese Embassy in Djibouti and the Ministry of Education of Djibouti. They also assisted Chinese colleges in actively communicating with partner institutions, and provided strong support in talent cultivation, standard construction, training venue construction, equipment clearance, and accommodation provision during the construction process, forming a tripartite force of "the government, enterprises, and colleges", and reversing the situation that cooperation resistance was greater than motivation.

2. The Cooperation Mechanism has Not Yet Been Fully Formed

Chinese vocational colleges and Chinese-funded enterprises belong to the international integration of industry and education in their partner countries. Although the entities involved in the integration of industry and education are all cooperative entities in China, mechanisms for co-discussion, co-construction, co-management, sharing, and win-win situations should also be established on the basis of cooperation platforms overseas. Although the ultimate goal and fundamental interests of Chinese vocational education in cultivating localized highly skilled employees for partner countries overseas are consistent, as a school-enterprise cooperation project, it should follow the industrial policy environment of partner countries, and implement the principle of "sharing interests and mutual benefits" according to the characteristics of overseas cooperation. The practice has proved that it is not enough for overseas industry-education integration and school-enterprise cooperation to rely on domestic and host country policies and systems, and appropriate overseas "support" and "cooperation" mechanisms should be established. If there is no consensus on cooperation content, cooperation mode, cooperation goals and expected results, the efficiency of Chinese vocational education in supporting Chinese-funded enterprises in international production capacity cooperation abroad will be reduced. Tianjin Railway Technical and Vocational College, together with China Civil Engineering Group in Djibouti, has always attached importance to mechanism construction in the construction of the Luban Workshop in Djibouti, and they have jointly built 4 standards, 2 teams, 1 series of rail transit training bases and 1 set of skill competition equipment research and development achievements overseas. For example, in terms of jointly building training bases to assist in the cultivation of technical talents, on the afternoon of March 28th, 2019, the Luban Workshop Training Base in Djibouti was officially unveiled. China Civil Engineering Group in Djibouti incorporated its integrated construction and operation of the Nagad Station on the Addis Ababa-Djibouti Railway as the training base for the Luban Workshop. The first 24 railway students from the Luban Workshop in Djibouti conducted on-the-job internships at the training base in accordance with the talent training program certified by the Ministry of Education of Djibouti. In the process of talent training, we adhere to the coordination of "learning and testing", pay attention to on-site operations and situational teaching, strengthen practical training and mentoring, conduct professional practical operations every morning, teach theoretical knowledge in the afternoon, organize a test and expert Q&A on Saturdays, and finally conduct a final exam, exploring the path of overseas practice of China's modern apprenticeship system.

3. Information Communication Is Not Completely Smooth

Under the platform construction and mechanism, overseas cooperation between schools and enterprises should pay more attention to information communication to avoid information loss and asymmetry. For Chinese vocational education to train localized high-skilled talents for Chinese-funded enterprises, it should, with the support of Chinese embassies and consulates and institutions abroad, keep the information on the needs of China and foreign countries in cooperation in running schools unblocked, eliminate blind ideas and enhance the efficiency of integration and cooperation through fixed channels in terms of training mode, positioning and service targets. For example, in the process of teacher training at the Luban Workshop in Djibouti, both schools and enterprises, with the support of the Chinese Embassy in Djibouti and its business office, guided local teachers to construct a talent training model and positioning that serves the economic and social development needs of Djibouti, the technical and skilled talent needs of the Addis Ababa-Djibouti Railway positions, as well as the comprehensive quality improvement needs of students in cooperative countries. Before formulating the teacher training plan, based on the principle of adapting to local conditions, a thorough investigation was conducted on the job requirements of Chinese-Djibouti enterprises, as well as the specific situation of the Addis Ababa-Djibouti Railway line and crossings. Considering the high temperature in Djibouti throughout the year and the urgent need to enhance local safety awareness, the training focused on introducing safety precautions such as line maintenance and crossing guards under the influence of high temperature. Also, considering the fact that seamless tracks have not yet been popularized in Djibouti, the training process focused on introducing knowledge about the maintenance of jointed tracks and the improvement of rail-joint defects, achieving the goal of "seamless connection of tracks with joints".

4. Policy Support Has Not Yet Been Fully Implemented

The support of Chinese vocational education for international production capacity cooperation among Chinese-funded enterprises is a characteristic and advantage of China's support for African countries. The practice has proven that sustainable development can only be achieved through sustained construction, which requires policy support from both China and Africa. When building a community with a shared future between China and Africa in the new era, the continuous cooperation and construction of China's vocational education require policy support from the Chinese government as well as from the partner countries, thus placing China's vocational education support for international production capacity cooperation among Chinese-funded enterprises in a good policy ecosystem. For example, in terms of customs clearance for equipment at the Luban Workshop in Djibouti, due to the fact that Djibouti only provides tariff preferences to member countries of the Common Market for Southeast Africa (COMESA), certain tariffs have been imposed on the equipment and facilities of the Luban Workshop, such as the import raw material tax rate is 33%, the metal product tax rate is 33%, and the average tax rate for mineral and glass products is 24%. Because of lacking corresponding reduction and exemption policies for partner countries of the Djibouti government, The economic cost of China's vocational education "Going Global" is relatively high. In addition, there is a lack of effective and reasonable promotion policies for international production capacity cooperation between China and Djibouti, and the protection measures for overseas investment by Chinese-funded enterprises stationed in Djibouti also need to be strengthened.

8.5.2 Recommendations for Further Development

1. Build a China-Africa Vocational Education Cooperation Community

China has always been committed to promoting the building of the China–Africa community of desting in the new era, and the building of the China–Africa Vocational Education Cooperation Community is an important part of it. The support of Chinese vocational education for international production capacity cooperation among Chinese-funded enterprises will play a role in both industry and vocational education. Chinese vocational schools and colleges have joined hands with Chinese enterprises to enter Africa and cooperate with vocational colleges and enterprises from African countries. Under the role of community mechanisms and functions, the number of cooperation subjects has increased, the advantages of cooperation complement each other, and the scope of cooperation has widened. The cooperation benefits of all parties have improved, and the sustainable development ability and prospects are more in line with national strategies. This has enabled China-Africa vocational education cooperation to stand at a new starting point, adopt new mechanisms, take new steps, and achieve new leaps.

2. Create an Ecological Rainforest for Chinese Vocational Education to Support International Production Capacity Cooperation among Chinese-Funded Enterprises

In building a community with a shared future for vocational education in China and Africa, it is necessary for the cooperating countries to have an ecological rainforest suitable for cooperation among multiple parties. In addition to the socio-economic, industrial, and educational environment, it also includes cultural similarity, integration, and consistency in vocational education concepts between the two countries. Chinese vocational education and Chinese-funded enterprises should develop in African countries, achieve international integration of industry and education, and adapt to the ecological environment of the partner countries. In accordance with the needs and policies of the partner countries, Chinese vocational education should focus on supporting Chinese enterprises. In the partner countries, different models and mechanisms from domestic school-enterprise cooperation should be adopted, and efforts should be made to build a China-Africa community from both industrial and vocational education perspectives.

3. Continuously Explore and Innovate the Mode of China's Vocational Education Supporting International Production Capacity Cooperation among Chinese-Funded Enterprises

At present, the basic functions of the Luban Workshops established by Chinese vocational colleges in Africa include supporting international production capacity cooperation among Chinese-funded enterprises, but the support models are different. For example, the Luban Workshop in Egypt adopts the model of establishing a Chinese-funded enterprise employment park. The Luban Workshop in Uganda has established the Mbale Chinese-funded Enterprise Industrial Park in the vicinity of cooperative universities based on well-known domestic enterprises. The Luban Workshop in Uganda has trained nearly 300 local employees for 23 Chinese-funded enterprises in the park, effectively solving the shortage of highly skilled talents in Chinese-funded enterprises in the area, and also forming the characteristic of cooperative education between Chinese-funded vocational education and Chinese enterprises in African countries. The Djibouti Luban Workshop relies on domestic leading enterprises to collaborate and "going global", establishing the "government, enterprises, and schools" cooperation mode. The policy is provided by the Chinese government, the teaching resources and teacher training are provided by Chinese vocational colleges, the venue is provided by foreign colleges, and the training venue guarantee and the living support of Chinese construction personnel are provided by Chinese-funded enterprises stationed in Djibouti. Currently, it has trained 148 students, benefiting more than 2,000 employees of the Addis Ababa-Djibouti Railway. It has played an important role in benefiting the people's well-being of Djibouti and assisting regional economic development.

Chapter Ⅸ

Reports on Vocational Education Collaboration Serving China-Ghana Production Capacity Cooperation

The Republic of Ghana is located on the west coast of Africa, 750 km north of the equator, and on the northern coast of the Gulf of Guinea. It borders the Ivory Coast to the west, Burkina Faso to the north, Togo to the east, and the Atlantic Ocean to the south. The coastline stretches for 562 km and its land area is approximately 238,500 square kilometers. Ghana, with its vast territory, excellent location and abundant natural resources, has historically been known as the "Gold Coast". The Republic of Ghana was founded on July 1, 1960. It has since enjoyed a peaceful and stable political environment with globally recognized democratic politics. Currently, Ghana has a pragmatic, pluralistic, active and neutral foreign policy with economic diplomacy as its priority. While developing positive ties with developed Western countries, it has also strengthened mutually beneficial cooperation with China. Ghana officially established diplomatic relations with China on July 5, 1960. In 1966, following a military coup, the junta unilaterally severed diplomatic relations with China. Ghana restored diplomatic relations with China in 1972. Since then, bilateral relations between China and Ghana have steadily grown as the two countries share many common views on political issues, such as safeguarding international peace and regional security while working together to establish a peaceful, just and equal international order.

9.1 Economic & Industrial Situation and the Development of Vocational Education in Ghana

9.1.1 Breaking Away from Aid Dependence and Exploring the Path to Economic Independence

Ghana regards vigorously promoting economic development as a top priority in the overall development of the country. In recent years, the Ghanaian government has taken a series of effective measures for national economic development, including leveraging geographical advantages to expand the market for investors, attracting foreign investment, pursuing economic liberalization, gradually improving the legal system, creating a relatively open market environment, and formulating loose policies to attract investment. These efforts made by the government of Ghana have led to steady economic and social development, effectively improving people's livelihoods. As a result, Ghana has successfully positioned itself among African countries with better economic adjustment and reform, and has been praised by the World Bank as "the center of African Economic Renaissance".

In recent years, Ghana's total GDP and GDP per capita have remained stable, placing it at the forefront of Africa. According to the World Bank database: from 2017 to 2021, Ghana's total GDP increased by $17.18 billion, and GDP per capita increased by $371, indicating a trend of sustained growth in Ghana's economy (See Table 9–1). In 2020, Ghana's annual GDP growth rate plummeted to just 0.51% due to the impact of the COVID-19 pandemic and fluctuations in international oil prices. However, despite these challenges, Ghana remains one of the few countries where the economy continues to grow. Ghana's economy has begun to recover since 2021 due to the global economy recovery, relaxation of pandemic control, rise in oil prices, and acceleration of economic restructuring and transformation within Ghana itself. According to a report released by Globaldata, Ghana has been ranked as Africa's fastest-growing economy in 2021. Furthermore, it is expected that Ghana's economy will grow by 5% annually over the next five years driven by growth in the service sector and exports, according to Myjoyonline, a Ghanaian electronic media outlet. Overall, Ghana's economy is on an upswing with huge potential and room for development.

Table 9–1 Macroeconomic Data of Ghana in 2017–2021

Year	GDP (USD)	GDP Ranking in Africa	Per Capita GDP (USD)	Per Capita GDP Ranking in Africa
2017	60.41 bn	9	2,074.3	18
2018	67.30 bn	9	2,260.9	17
2019	68.34 bn	9	2,246.6	18
2020	70.04 bn	8	2,254.2	17
2021	77.59 bn	8	2,445.3	18

Source: World Bank Database

To boost the economy, the Ghanaian government has implemented several economic development plans. In 2006, the Ghanaian government formulated a ten-year economic development plan that aimed to vigorously develop the manufacturing sector, modernize agriculture, and enhance the construction of transport and communications infrastructure. After assuming office as president in January 2017, Nana Akufo-Addo made economic recovery the top priority of his administration. Specific measures included promoting economic transformation and industrialization, implementing policies of significant tax cuts and employment stimulus, issuing treasury bonds, rectifying the financial sector, and improving the business environment. In 2018, the Ghanaian government once again issued a seven-year national development plan that accelerated flagship projects for economic development such as "One district, One factory", "One village, One dam", and "Planting for Food & Jobs". Tenders were opened for several new oil fields, resulting in a significant increase in oil and gas production. Guided by the construction of "Aid-free Ghana", great effort has been made to change traditional aid-receiving models by attracting foreign investment with aspirations to become an economic and financial hub in West Africa. In recent years, Ghana has introduced the Beyond Aid plan which aims to transform it from a developing country into a developed nation that is prosperous confident and self-reliant while actively participating in global trade and investment competition. To implement Beyond Aid plan on the ground, Ghanaian leaders have consistently promoted intra-African trade. Ghana, which was the first country to sign the African Continental Free Trade Area (AfCFTA) Agreement that came into effect in January 2021, has also become home to its secretariat.

9.1.2 Developing Diversified Industries and Creating an Open and Business-Friendly Environment

Ghana is rich in natural resources such as agriculture, minerals, forestry and fisheries. Its stable political situation, sound legal system, open policies, and diverse economic development make it one of the most attractive countries in Africa for foreign investment. These factors have created favorable conditions for industrial development in Ghana.

Ghana's economy is dominated by agriculture, mineral industries, and the service industry. Petroleum, gold, and cocoa are the top three industries that earn foreign exchange. Figure 9–1 illustrates the current situation of these industries.

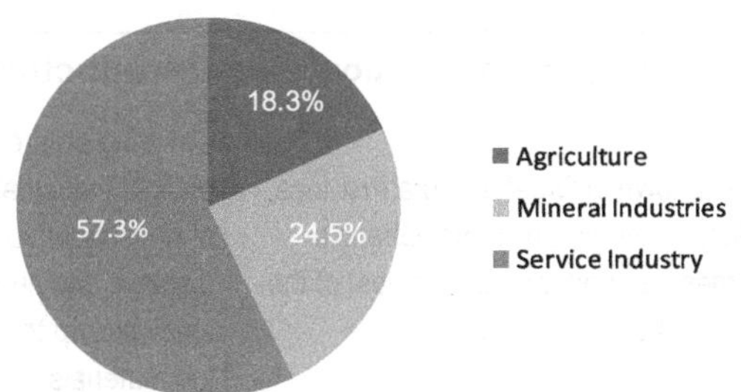

Figure 9–1 Current Situations of Industries

Source: CIA World Factbook

Agriculture is the foundation of Ghana's economy, accounting for 56.2% of the country's employment. The agricultural sector in Ghana is divided into four sub-sectors: crop farming, livestock, fisheries, and forestry. Cash crops grown in Ghana include cocoa (beans), grains, cassava, and tropical fruits. Livestock raised mainly includes goats, sheep, cattle, rabbits, pigs and poultry. The fishery is known for catching tuna, tilapia, and red seabream, the majority of which are commercially raised. Approximately 2.6 million Ghanaians (10% of the population) depend on the fishery for their livelihoods. Forestry is the fourth-largest export earner behind minerals, petroleum, and cocoa. Ghana has been exporting timber for nearly a century, and the upgrading of its wood processing industry has increased the volume of exported wood products. With a weak industrial foundation relying on imports for raw materials, Ghana's industries have recently focused on extracting gold, diamonds, manganese, and bauxite. Industries such as textiles, cement, wood processing, and electricity are relatively weak. Ghana's service industry also plays an important role in the national economy, accounting for about half of GDP in terms of output value. Sectors such as healthcare and information & communications have experienced rapid growth. Thanks to the absorption of FDI funds, Ghana's industrial structure has become increasingly diversified with sectors like renewable resources, financial services, and real estate emerging alongside traditional sectors like cocoa, oil and gas sectors.

To promote the rapid development of Ghana's industry, the Ghana Free Zones Scheme (GFZA) was formulated in accordance with the *Free Zone Act, 1995 (Act 504)*, an Act of Parliament. The scheme aims to attract foreign direct investment and promote exports of processing and manufacturing, and service trade. Private institutions operate the free zones independently, while the administration is solely responsible for coordinating and managing the relationships between developers, operators, and businesses within these zones. Currently, there are four free trade zones in Ghana as listed in Table 9–2.

Table 9–2 Industrial Parks in Ghana

Zone & Parks	Geographic Location	Introduction and Product Features
Tema Export Processing Zone, TEPZ	Tema town in Greater Accra Province, close to the port of Tema, Ghana's largest seaport, and 25 km east of the capital Accra	Covering an area of 485.6 hectares, it focuses on light industrial projects such as the production of household appliances, solar products, LED displays and neon lights, small diesel generators, small pickup truck assembly, and decorative building materials.
Sekondi Industrial Park	Sekondi-Takoradi, Ghana's second largest port	Covering an area of 880.3 hectares, it is designated for heavy industry, light industry and storage.
Yabin / Shama Land Bank	Shama District, Western Region, Ghana	Covering an area of 1,133.12 hectares, it is an export industrial park dedicated to the petroleum and petrochemical industry, mainly attracting downstream enterprises in the oil and gas industry

continued

Zone & Parks	Geographic Location	Introduction and Product Features
Ashanti Technology Park, ATP	Boankra, Ashanti Region, Central Ghana	Covering an area of 444.7 hectares, the park mainly attracts companies in information and communication technology, cocoa processing, light industrial manufacturing, heavy industrial manufacturing, warehouse logistics services, social service centers, and biotechnology research and development.

In addition to government support, Chinese-funded enterprises have been involved in the establishment of the four free trade zones in Ghana. Hualong (Ghana) Group, a subsidiary of China Gansu International Economic and Technical Cooperation, has invested in the Tema Export Processing Zone, and several Chinese multinational companies have invested in the Sekondi Industrial Park. With the support of the Ghanaian government and Chinese-funded enterprises, Ghanaian industry has received strong guarantees and is developing rapidly.

9.1.3 Comprehensive Education System and Underdeveloped Vocational Education

1. Comprehensive Education System and Vocational Education Framework

Vocational education is an integral part of the education system. Ghana's education system consists of three parts: first, basic education, which includes pre-schools, kindergartens, and junior high schools; second, three-year senior high schools; and third, higher education, which includes training colleges, technical colleges, and public and private universities. Additionally, there are specialized educational institutions in the public sector. Currently, basic education is divided into six years of primary education and three years of junior secondary education (collectively referred to as basic education). All Ghanaian children receive free and compulsory education up to grade nine. Upon completion of basic education, students can either progress to senior high school or pursue vocational education (TVET). High school lasts for three years, while vocational education school lasts three or four years. Higher education offers standard four-year university courses. Therefore, the Ghanaian education system can be summarized as a "6+3+3+4" system. According to the International Standard Classification of Education (ISCED), ISCED1 and ISCED2 encompass non-formal apprenticeship education. The education system in Ghana is shown in Figure 9–2.

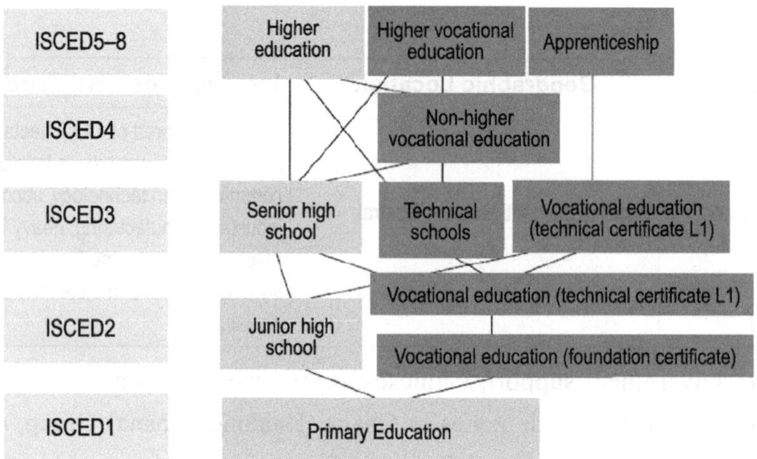

Figure 9–2 Education System in Ghana

Source:https://unevoc.unesco.org/

Currently, with the operation of this education system, basic education has been popularized and the administrative capacity of the public education sector has significantly improved. Although education management is seen as a model of best practice, it still faces significant challenges such as low enrollment of female students, poor student performance, few qualified teachers, over-sized classes, and inadequate teaching resources. To address these issues, the Ghanaian government is taking proactive measures to increase female enrollment rates, reduce inequality among schools, strengthen teacher training, and expand the number of teachers in order to achieve quality education.

In 2012, Ghana piloted the National TVET Qualifications Framework (NTVETQF), a technical and vocational education and training (TVET) framework system. The NTVETQF consists of eight levels, ranging from secondary school to doctoral level, which is overseen by the Council for Technical and Vocational Education and Training (COTVET) in Ghana. Table 9–3 shows the framework.

Table 9–3 National TVET Qualifications Framework (NTVETQF)

<table>
<tr><th>NQF Levels</th><th colspan="2">General/Academic National Qualification Framework</th><th colspan="2">NTVETQF</th><th>NTVETQF Levels</th><th>Education Levels</th></tr>
<tr><td>10</td><td colspan="2">Doctor's degree</td><td colspan="2">Technical Doctorate</td><td>8</td><td rowspan="5">Higher education</td></tr>
<tr><td>9</td><td colspan="2">Master's degree</td><td colspan="2" rowspan="2">Technical Master's degree</td><td rowspan="2">7</td></tr>
<tr><td>8</td><td colspan="2">Postgraduate diploma</td></tr>
<tr><td>7</td><td colspan="2">Bachelor degree</td><td colspan="2">Technical Bachelor's degree</td><td>6</td></tr>
<tr><td>6</td><td colspan="2">Higher education diploma</td><td rowspan="3">ABCE</td><td>Higher national diploma</td><td>5</td></tr>
<tr><td>5</td><td colspan="2">General national diploma</td><td rowspan="2">National certificate II</td><td rowspan="2">4</td><td rowspan="3">Secondary education</td></tr>
<tr><td>4</td><td>High school diploma</td><td>Higher GCE</td></tr>
<tr><td>3</td><td colspan="2">General GCE</td><td>GBCE</td><td>National certificate I</td><td>3</td></tr>
</table>

continued

NQF Levels	General/Academic National Qualification Framework	NTVETQF		NTVETQF Levels	Education Levels
2	Junior high school diploma	—	National ability II	2	Basic education
1			National ability Level I	1	

Source: Ghana's NQF in the making, 2020

TVET educational institutions in Ghana are divided into private and public institutions. According to COTVET's early survey data, there are a total of 578 vocational training institutions, including 223 public vocational education and training institutions and 355 private ones. According to recent statistics from UNESCO, the number of vocational training institutions in Ghana has increased to 795, including 395 public vocational education and training institutions and 400 private ones. The number of public education institutions has increased by 172, representing an increase of 69%, indicating strong government investment in vocational education. The TVET institutions and administrative departments in Ghana (2018 data) are shown in Table 9–4.

Table 9–4 Ghana's TVET Institutions and Management Departments (2018 data)

Administrative Departments	Type, Name and Number of Institutions
Ministry of Education	GES technical institutions, 47
Ministry of Employment and Labor Relations	National Vocational Training Institute (NVTI) centers, 34 Opportunity Industrialization Centers, 3 Integrated Community Centers for Employable Skills (ICCES) , 62
Ministry of Youth and Sports	Youth Leadership Training Centers, 11
Ministry of Trade and Industry	Business Advisory Centers for National Board for Small Scale Industries, 161; Rural Technology Facilities (RTFs), 15; Ghana Regional Appropriate Technology Industrial Service (GRATIS),9
Ministry of Environment, Science and Technology & Innovation	Suame Intermediate Technology Transfer Unit (Suame-ITTU), 1 Suame Magazine Automatics Technical Institute (SMATI), 1
Ministry of Food and Agriculture	Agricultural training institutions (Colleges of Agriculture: Adidome, Asuasi and Wenchi), 8
Ministry of Gender, Children and Social Protection	Social welfare training Centers and reformatories, 18
Ministry of Local Government and Rural Development	Community Development centers, 24
Ministry of Roads and Highways	Road and Highways Training Center (Kaneshie, Accra),1
Private Sector	Private institutions, non-governmental organizations, fixed operating bases, private individuals, 400
Ministry of Tourism, Arts and Culture	Hotel Catering and Tourism Training Institute (HOTCATT), 1

Source: UNESCO-UNEVOC https://unevoc.unesco.org/home/

Public vocational colleges have gone through several stages of development. The history of Kumasi Technical University demonstrates that the transformation and upgrading process of Ghana's public vocational education institutions can be divided into four phases. Founded in 1954 as Kumasi Technical Institute (K.T.I.), it initially offered technical and craft courses. In 1963, the institute was converted by the Ghana Education Service (GES) into a non-higher polytechnic institute, providing technical diplomas and professional courses. *The Polytechnic Law, 1992 (PNDC L.321)* elevated the institution to higher education system, serving as catalysts for technological development and training high-level technical personnel in manufacturing, business, science and technology. *The Technical Universities Act, 2016 (Act, 922)* restructured Kumasi Technical Institute into Kumasi Technical University, with a focus on providing higher education in technical and vocational training across basic disciplines such as engineering, applied arts, and science and technology. Currently, the university has evolved into a prominent vocational training center not only in Ghana but also in Africa. It offers junior college programs, as well as bachelor's and master's degree education, along with vocational and technical training for Ghanaian students and those from other African countries. It comprises 9 faculties, including Engineering and Technology, Applied Sciences and Technology, Health Sciences, Architecture and Natural Environment, Creative Arts and Technology, Business School, Entrepreneurship and Enterprise Development, as well as the Graduate School.

2. Low Social Recognition and Female Participation

According to UNESCO, Ghana had a total population of 31.7 million in 2021, with 76,800 students enrolled in vocational education. However, only 26.7% of these students were female. Additionally, 1.8% of adolescents and adults attended formal and non-formal education and training in the last twelve months, while 1.3% of individuals aged 14 to 25 participated in TVET training programs. Furthermore, the 2013/2014 EMIS data released by the Education Management Information System (EMIS) revealed that there were a total of 41,065 enrollment in vocational education and training institutions (35,349 in public institutions and 5,716 in private institutions), compared to a total enrollment of 750,706 in senior high schools across both public and private sectors. Therefore, the ratio between vocational students and senior high school students is approximately 1:18. In summary, although there has been an increase in enrollment for vocational education over the years, however, the number of individuals choosing vocational education remains low when compared to general education.

The *Notification of 2021 CTVET Certificate II Core and Elective Exams, Access Course, Technician, Advanced and Diploma Examinations* issued by the Commission for Technical and Vocational Educational and Training (CTVET) states that a total of 28,834 candidates (73% males and 27% females) from 175 public and private technical institutions in Ghana took the qualification exam at 120 centers across the country. However, the proportion of females taking the exam was less than one-third of that of males. As previously mentioned, the female enrollment rate for 2021 is 26.7% indicating a relatively low representation of women in vocational education.

According to the 2013/2014 data released by the Education Management Information System (EMIS), there are a total of 3,730 teachers in vocational education and training institutions (3,074 in public institutions and 656 in private institutions). Among these vocational education teachers who have recieved formal training, 73.3% are male, while only 26.7% are female. The proportion of female teachers is relatively low.

3.Government Initiating Various Reforms to Promote the Development of Vocational Education.

The Ghanaian government is currently implementing the *Education Strategic Plan (ESP 2018–2030)* to "empower the next generation". The plan emphasizes equity and accountability in education, aiming to ensure that the education system adapts to the environment and the ages, technology advances, industry changes, creativity, and the knowledge economy. The new measures aim to establish clear standards for teaching, learning, assessment, and grading of students while promoting professionalization of teaching and enhancing teaching standards. These measures are reflected in the TVET sector by focusing on improving teacher competence through establishing a professional qualification system for teachers in pre-tertiary education/vocational education as well as a career development framework oriented towards skills and competency improvement.

In addition, the Ministry of Education in Ghana is pushing forward the restructuring of the TVET education management body, formulating a five-year strategic plan for TVET, implementing the *TVET Services Bill*, amending COTVET legislation, establishing the National Vocational Training Institute (NVTI), and creating the National Board for Professional and Technical Examination (NABPTEX).

The Ministry of Education has also implemented three initiatives. Firstly, the Development of Skills for Industry Project (DSIP) is initiated with support from the national financial system. The project aims to increase equal access for women to public institutions and improve the quality and applicability of TVET education. Secondly, national skill competitions are held to raise public awareness about the importance of TVET, showcase various vocational skills to young people, and enhance vocational education's attractiveness. Thirdly, infrastructure construction is underway as part of government commitment to building at least two state of the art TVET centers in each district. These centers will serve as headquarters for technical and vocational training, equipped with advanced machinery and training tools.

9.2 Status Quo of International Production Capacity Cooperation in Ghana and Challenges Faced by Chinese-Funded Enterprises

9.2.1 Status Quo of International Production Capacity Cooperation in Ghana

1. Actively Participating in International Production Capacity Cooperation and Striving to Reduce Reliance on International Aid

The Ghanaian government emphasizes international economic cooperation and promotes economic development through participation in multilateral and regional economic cooperation. It has successively joined the World Trade Organization (WTO), the Economic Community of West African States (ECOWAS), and the Organization for Economic Cooperation and Development (OECD) to engage in various economic activities. It has been decided during the 12th Extraordinary Summit of the African Union that Ghana will be the Secretariat of the African Continental Free Trade Area (AfCFTA), indicating Ghana's commitment to driving Africa's economic development.

In terms of international economic cooperation, Ghana's major trading partners are China, the European Union, the United States, South Africa and the United Kingdom. China's position in Ghana's foreign trade has continued to rise in recent years and surpassed that of the European Union in 2015 as Ghana's largest trading partner. Ghana primarily exports gold, petroleum, and cocoa while importing automobiles, foodstuffs (such as rice, wheat, frozen fish, and poultry products), industrial products, cement, and fertilizers.

In recent years, the Ghanaian government has attached great importance to promoting economic and social development by absorbing foreign investment. According to the United Nations 2020 World Investment Report, Ghana attracted $2.32 billion in foreign investment in 2019, with a total foreign investment stock of $38.45 billion in the same year. Currently, major multinational companies investing in Ghana include Vodafone, Millicom, Coca-Cola, Pepsi, Unilever, Procter & Gamble, GOLDFIELDS, AngloGold and others. Investments are concentrated in telecommunications, beverages, cosmetics, gold mining and oil development.

Ghana's economy also relies on international aid, with bilateral aid mainly from Japan, the United States, Germany, the United Kingdom, and France; while multilateral aid comes mainly from the World Bank, the European Union, and the International Monetary Fund (IMF). In March 2012, the World Bank allocated $100 million to finance Ghana's agricultural trade. In August 2014, the United States and Ghana signed an aid agreement totaling $498.2 million within the framework of the Millennium Challenge Corporation (MCC). In April 2015, IMF approved a three-year special drawing right of 664.2 million *yuan* (equivalent to $918 million) for Ghana. The Ghanaian government withdrew from IMF's Extended Credit Facility (ECF) in April 2019. In April 2020, IMF approved a $1 billion loan to help Ghana fight against COVID-19 pandemic under Rapid Credit Facility. However, Ghana's chronic dependence on international aid has hindered its ability to achieve independent development, resulting in more drawbacks than benefits.

2. Industrialization is Slowly Progressing, and the Food Crisis Remains

In recent years, the Ghanaian government has actively strengthened infrastructure construction, vigorously promoted industrialization, deepened the level of processing for export products, attempted to transform the economy from one reliant on raw material exports, and strived to move away from an economic development model that depends on foreign aid. Ghanaian President Nana Akufo-Addo met with Chinese President Xi Jinping at the 2018 FOCAC Beijing Summit. President Xi Jinping stated that China supports Ghana's vision of "Beyond Aid" and encourages Chinese companies to invest in Ghana, making good use of the flagship projects initiated by the Ghanaian government, such as "One District, One Factory", "Planting for Food & Jobs", and infrastructure development initiatives, particularly in roads, railways, and the energy sector.

Unemployment in Ghana has remained high in recent years, and the country is facing a severe food crisis. According to the 2022 survey data from the Ghana Statistics Service (GSS) and the Ministry of Food and Agriculture, about 5%, or 1.2 million Ghanaians, faced food problems in 2009. In 2020, about 11.6%, or 3.6 million Ghanaians, did not have enough food to eat, indicating that the food crisis in Ghana has been worsening. Agriculture serves as the foundation of Ghana's economy, contributing 17.3% to GDP in 2019 and employing around 56.2% of the country's workforce figures. The total land area of Ghana is approximately 23.8539 million hectares, out of which 13.628 million hectares are suitable for agricultural cultivation, accounting for about 57% of the entire available land area for farming purposes. However, the actual agricultural acreage under cultivation is only 5.3 million hectares, which accounts for about one-third of the total arable land area in Ghana. The country heavily relies on food imports, with rice alone constituting 82% of the total imports and exceeding $1 billion in import value. In 2019, the Ghanaian government launched the "Planting for Food & Jobs" project to "promote local production" and meet domestic demand. Nevertheless, the results have been unsatisfactory so far, highlighting the urgent need for agricultural modernization to address Ghana's food crisis.

9.2.2 Development Foundation and Bottlenecks of Chinese-Funded Enterprises in Ghana

1. Extensive Investment in Various Areas, and Rapid Growth in Bilateral Trade Volume

Chinese investors have made extensive investments in Ghana. Chinese-funded enterprises are diverse, encompassing agriculture, fishery, real estate, building materials, furniture, food and beverage, ceramics, iron and steel, pesticides, footwear, wood processing, as well as textiles and clothing. Aviation, electricity, automobiles, daily chemicals, and foodstuffs have been hotspots for investment in recent years.

About 30,000 to 50,000 Chinese now reside in Accra, the capital of Ghana, as well as Tema and Kumasi. According to the latest data from NIA, Non-citizen Ghana cards were issued to 161,007 foreigners from 202 countries, of whom around 35,400 (22%) were Chinese. The Chinese population holds the largest number of Non-citizen Ghana cards. Over 300 Chinese companies have registered in Ghana, of which more than 50 large Chinese-funded enterprises employ about 6,000 individuals.

In recent years, Chinese-funded enterprises' invest in Ghana has grown significantly, with bilateral trade volume soaring from less than $100 million in 2000 to $7.5 billion in 2019. Data from Huajing Industry Research Institute shows that in January and February 2022, the import and export volume of bilateral goods between China and Ghana was $1,497.506 million, representing an increase of $206.963 million compared to the same period in 2021, which accounts for a growth rate of 15.9%. China has become Ghana's largest source of imports and an important trading partner.

2. State-Owned Enterprises have Settled in to Boost Local Development and Employment

New cooperation projects have been launched between China and Ghana, and numerous assistance, financing, investment, and project contracting initiatives have been implemented. Dozens of large Chinese central and state-owned enterprises have entered Ghana, including SINOHYDRO Corporation Limited, China Gezhouba Group, Hunan Construction Engineering Group, Shenzhen Energy Corporation, Sinopec, and China Railway Construction Engineering Group. These enterprises have adopted the model of "two concessional facilities," commercial loans, and PPP investments. They have successfully operated and implemented a large number of projects, including the Bui hydroelectric dam, Kpong Water Supply, Northern Grid Extension, Tema LNG Terminal, Takoradi NGL Terminal, and Cape Coast Trade Market. The total contract value of these projects exceeds $2 billion. According to April 2020 statistics, nearly 60 projects are currently under construction by members of the Chamber of Commerce for Chinese-funded enterprises in Ghana, resulting in the creation of 15,000 jobs for Ghanaians and effectively boosting local employment opportunities as well as economic development. Representative investment projects can be seen in Table 9–5.

Table 9–5 China's Representative Investment Projects in Ghana

Fields	Chinese Companies	Investment Projects	Project Brief
Railway	The First Construction Co., Ltd. of China Construction First Group	Ghana's transportation system improvement project—N1 Highway (Tatale to Yendi section)	The total construction length of the project is 61.6 km, which includes road design, roadbed and pavement work, drainage work, and maintenance work.

continued

Fields	Chinese Companies	Investment Projects	Project Brief
Waterway	SINOHYDRO Corporation Limited	Road project in Cape Coast City	The project started in December 2019 and was announced to be completed by September 26, 2022. It aims to upgrade 25 local urban roads with a total length of 22.4 km.
Aviation	Hainan Airlines Group	Africa World Airline (AWA)	Eight domestic and West African regional routes and charter flights
Healthcare	China Urban Construction Design&Research Institute; Nantong Si Jian Construction Group	Phase II project of University of Health and Allied Sciences, Ho	The project officially began on September 10, 2021. It involves the construction of a school administration building, nursing and midwifery college building, duty room, and equipment room with a total construction period of 36 months.
Resources	Shandong Gold Group	Namdini Gold Project	The project has a confirmed and credible gold reserve of 157.2 tons, as well as a proved and controlled resource of 203.1 tons. It will take 27 months to complete construction, with an annual production capacity of 8.9 tons of gold.
Renewable Energy	Power China International Group Limited	Sinohydro Corporation --Ghana Government Priority Infrastructure Project I	The project is a centerpiece of the Scaling-up Renewable Energy Program (SREP-IP) and plays a significant role in enhancing power generation capacity and increasing the proportion of renewable energy.

3. Lack of Talent and Multiple Bottlenecks Lead to Limited Development.

(1) Policy

In general, Ghana is friendly to foreign investment. However, some areas are not yet open to foreign investors, such as gambling except for soccer, pharmaceutical sales, and beauty and hairdressing. Foreign investors can establish businesses in the form of sole proprietorship or joint ventures. If a joint venture is established, the registered capital should not be less than $200,000, while the registered capital of a sole proprietorship should not be less than $500,000. Except for mining and oil and gas companies, the general corporate tax rate is 25%, and export companies in free zones can enjoy preferential tax policies for 10 years.

(2) Business Environment

Due to Ghana's small population and limited sales market, many companies lack in-depth research into the local market. This results in that foreign investors know little about the local market and their products do not meet local needs, leading to losses. Moreover, settling debts in Africa is challenging and demands a lot of effort. Furthermore, trade fraud is frequent in Ghana with various methods used, resulting in many companies being defrauded.

When developing in Ghana, Chinese-funded enterprises should pay attention to risk prevention and control and cautiously expand trade and investment cooperation. The African market offers huge business opportunities as well as substantial risks. The arrears in government projects are relatively severe, so Chinese enterprises should take precautionary measures in advance to avoid exchange rate risks and cross-border RMB settlement shall be adopted as far as possible under trade items.

(3) Lack of Talent

With the rapid development of economic exchanges between China and Ghana, the number of Chinese-funded enterprises in Ghana is increasing, as well as the demand for talent. According to the *Ghana Investment Promotion Center (GIPC) Act* passed by the Ghanaian Parliament in 2013, foreign companies can only employ a corresponding number of foreign employees based on the immigration quota set according to their investment amount. The number of Chinese employees is limited; therefore, Chinese enterprises can only hire local Ghanaian employees.

In addition to the policy and business environment factors mentioned above, talent is also one of the factors that limit the development of Chinese-funded enterprises in Ghana. Several things can be learned through interviews: Firstly, Chinese-funded enterprises increasingly require local employees who understand Chinese, but there is still a lack of professionals in Ghana who can speak, read and write Chinese, which unable to meet the occupational demand of Chinese-funded enterprises. Secondly, Ghanaian graduates prefer working in the public sector and are reluctant to work in businesses. Thirdly, managing local staff becomes challenging due to Ghana's slower pace of life. The habits of the natives, inherited from when Ghana was part of the British Commonwealth, differ from the industrious style of the Chinese laborers. Local employees have clear boundaries for their work and will not go beyond their duties or work overtime. This poses a significant management challenge for Chinese enterprises. Not only must the duties of each position be distributed fairly and scrupulously, but also the work contents of all personnel must be properly planned in advance to ensure regular production. All these factors affect the deepening and sustainable development of Chinese enterprises "going global".

9.3 Chinese-Funded Enterprises Collaborating with Chinese Vocational Education to Support China-Ghana Production Capacity Cooperation

9.3.1 The Necessity of Collaboration between Chinese-Funded Enterprises and Chinese Vocational Education

1. Ghana's Vocational Education Does not Align With It's Industrial Development

(1) A Narrow Specialty Setting is Unable to Meet the Industry's Needs

During the course of development, vocational education in Ghana should adapt to the transformation of economic patterns and the adjustment of industrial structure. It should also align with the basic skills and specialized knowledge required by emerging industries. Ghana's industry is dominated by agriculture, industrial and mineral sectors, as well as services; communication and financial services are also experiencing rapid growth. Currently, vocational education in Ghana focuses on trade-related courses, which plays a crucial role in promoting trade development. However, the curriculum is relatively narrow and does not meet the industry's demand for talent.

COTVET has identified TVET's goal of developing a globally competitive workforce through quality and demand-oriented learning for national development. However, according to the COTVET report on TVET in Ghana, vocational education has long been considered "uncoordinated, supply-driven (not demand-oriented), with weak linkages to businesses and industries, neglected informal sector apprenticeship, and a large number of unrecognized, unaccredited and ineffective skills in informal sectors."

(2) School-Enterprise Cooperation is Inadequate, and the Educational Accomplishments are not Recognized

Cooperation between vocational education institutions and enterprises in Ghana is inadequate, leading to several issues: lack of recognition for the accomplishments of vocational education by enterprises; and mismatched skill sets acquired by students with actual requirements. Both local and Chinese-funded enterprises in Ghana are facing a shortage of talent. The absence of a strong connection between industrial enterprises and technical and vocational education sectors results in numerous students enrolled at technical or polytechnic institutes failing to learn essential practical skills necessary for their future careers. As a result, graduates from these institutions possess limited job prospects due to reduced marketability, as well as an absence of entrepreneurial skills that hinder them from starting their own ventures; thus they rely on government employment support.

(3) Employment Situation is Not Optimistic, and the Quality of Education Needs to Be Improved

In recent years, influenced by Ghana's own national conditions and the global economic environment, Ghana's employment and entrepreneurial market has faced severe shocks. The outbreak of COVID-19 in 2020 and recent changes in the international situation have added to uncertainties in the national economic environment, leading to a more prominent structural contradiction in employment. As a result, there has been an increase in employment pressures, job losses, rising unemployment rates, and a severe employment situation in Ghana.

According to the Ghana Statistical Service (GSS), the unemployment rate in 2021 stands at 13.4%, with 32.8% of the population aged 15–24 being unemployed, compared to 6% in 2011. The sixth World Bank Economic Review report on Ghana, titled *Securing the Future: The Rising Challenge of Youth Unemployment*, states that in 2021, while 36% of the country's population is young, a staggering 75% of its young people are unemployed. It is evident that the employment market outlook in Ghana is not promising.

In addition to the international environment, Ghana's own situation constantly affects employment and unemployment. As of 2021, Ghana's population has reached 31.7 million. The Trades Union Congress (TUC) once pointed out that 400,000 people enter the job market in Ghana every year, facing severe employment pressure, especially among young people, which poses a serious challenge to social stability. Pressure from a growing population and an oversupply of labor has created a shortage of jobs. In addition, there are prominent structural contradictions in employment among young people and increasing market demand for high-quality skilled talent. Unsuited skill types and levels for job positions make it difficult for young people to meet job demands, resulting in poor quality and low employment stability.

2. Chinese-Funded Enterprises Are in Dire Need of Local Talent, While the Employment Rate of Local Youth is Low

The young labor force in Ghana has been expanding year by year (Figure 9–3), and with abundant labor resources, it is of great significance to the localization of talent in Chinese-funded enterprises. According to the Huajing Industrial Research Institute, the total workforce of Ghanaians aged 15 and above was 12.917,1 million in 2019, which increased by 305,500 from the previous year. In training localized talents, Chinese-funded enterprises should focus on improving their employees' professional skills and production efficiency while emphasizing "quality" rather than "quantity" in vocational education.

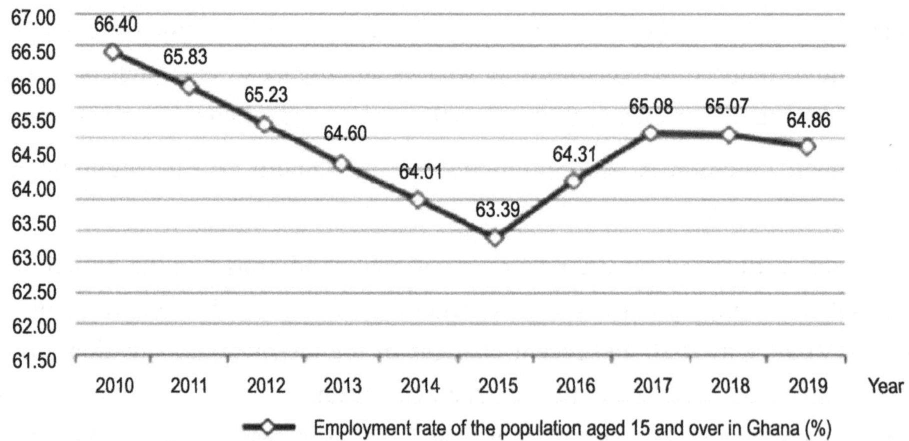

Figure 9–3 Employment Rate of the Population Aged 15 and Over in Ghana in 2010–2019

Source: World Bank. Compiled by Huajing Industry Research Institute.

Therefore, Chinese-funded enterprises should build on the realities of Ghana and promote the localization and diversification of talent by strengthening vocational skills training for local Ghanaians. Targeted training should be provided to professional and technical personnel, while also increasing language and social service training.

In view of the above analysis, to address the shortage of local talent in Ghana, Chinese-funded enterprises can start with the following aspects of vocational training: First, provide training opportunities for young people. There is a mismatch between the skills provided by schools and those needed in the Ghanaian workplace, with young people failing to acquire the vocational skills required by employers. Therefore, Chinese-funded enterprises should train young people to fit their actual situation and hiring needs. The second aspect is to enhance the enterprises' sustainable competitiveness. Training should be carried out in a top-down order. Managers should first improve their cross-cultural management ability and professional skills, with a focus on fostering employees' sense of belonging and business identity. In addition to Chinese language courses, the training content should be enriched to include general courses in management, business, and other related subjects as well. The third aspect is finding a talent-training model that works for local people, such as apprenticeships where experienced employees serve as mentors for new employees who acquire knowledge or skills under their guidance. This approach helps reduce training costs effectively. Fourth, women in Ghana have low employment rates and do not have an advantage in professional competition. However, there is huge potential for women in sectors such as services and electronics industries. The industry cooperation should therefore provide women with skills training specifically tailored for the electronics industry in order to create employment opportunities for them.

3. Vocational Education Serves Chinese-Funded Enterprises and Enhances the Well-Being of People in Partner Countries

Vocational education, as a type of education, possesses distinct advantages in "going global" through school-enterprise collaboration and in serving disadvantaged groups, effectively alleviating poverty and promoting employment. With the goal of sharing Chinese standards, technologies, and services, vocational colleges have fully utilized their training advantages in specialized fields to establish a systematic and professional training system. They have also assisted countries along the "Belt and Road" by providing skilled personnel through overseas training or technical guidance. Simultaneously, vocational colleges actively collaborate with enterprises to carry out high-level internationalized skills training with the aim of supporting Chinese enterprises' efforts of "going global", while nurturing highly competitive technical talents on an international scale. Chinese vocational colleges abroad contribute talent to the economic development of countries along the "Belt and Road" while facilitating the localization of Chinese-funded enterprises. This endeavor also lays a solid foundation for constructing vocational colleges with both Chinese characteristics and world-class standards.

9.3.2 Two Collaboration Models between Chinese-Funded Enterprises and Chinese Vocational Education

Vocational education supports industries, promotes employment, and plays an important role in facilitating international production capacity cooperation conducted by enterprises. Chinese enterprises are leading the globalization of vocational and technical education, while vocational and technical education is in turn meeting the labor demand of overseas Chinese-funded enterprises. Chinese-funded enterprises are usually directly involved in China-Africa vocational education cooperation, assuming two roles: educational agents and cooperative agents.

1. Enterprises Acting as Educational Agents

Educational agents refer to enterprises that independently organize vocational education or training, such as vocational training institutions, engineering institutes, and enterprise schools. It is an important initiative for enterprises to train people and develop local talent resources by conducting vocational skills training independently according to their own circumstances and with a view to their business development. For example, since 2013, Huawei has established the Huawei ICT Academy, which provides training, certification, competitions and other services in 72 countries around the world, benefiting tens of thousands of students each year. Since entering the African market in 1998, Huawei's operations have covered 54 countries in Africa, serving two-thirds of the African population, while training more than 50,000 ICT talents and creating tens of thousands of jobs.

2. Enterprises Acting as Cooperative Agents

Cooperative agents are enterprises that cooperate with higher vocational colleges or participate in vocational education, engaging in deep school-enterprise cooperation, training process, training base construction, technical skills innovation, teaching faculty construction, and quality assessment. There are two types of cooperative agents in vocational education. First, enterprises collaborate with higher vocational colleges to support their internationalization is one of the forms of "going global". The Luban Workshop is one example of school-business collaboration abroad. Luban Workshops cooperate with overseas enterprises and conduct vocational education with overseas vocational colleges or institutions to train skilled personnel for local enterprises. Second, alliances for vocational education. In 2018, initiated by the China Center for International People-to-People Exchange Ministry of Education (CCIPE) and Manufacturing Engineering and Related Services Sector Education and Training Authority (MerSETA) of South Africa, 58 units including relevant government departments, academies, and enterprises from both countries jointly launched the China & South Africa Technical and Vocational Education Cooperation Alliance. In 2020, supported by the Hunan provincial government, Hunan International Business Vocational College established the China-Africa Economic and Trade Cooperation Vocational Education Industry Alliance, which includes vocational colleges working with Africa as well as enterprises and the Hunan Business Association in Africa. The inaugural congress of the China-Africa Vocational Education Alliance and the first plenary session of the Alliance's Council were held successfully in Jinan in 2021. Attending members include more than 70 Chinese institutes and enterprises, and over 20 African institutions of higher education. The meeting further consolidated and strengthened educational cooperation among higher vocational colleges, local enterprises, and local governments in Africa. In the process of "going global" with higher vocational colleges, Chinese enterprises can provide support not only for the internationalization of these institutions through practical aspects like hardware facilities and equipment, practical training, technical innovation, and employment opportunities but also offer reference to higher vocational colleges in terms of their specialty setting.

9.3.3 The Achievements of International Production Capacity Cooperation between Chinese Vocational Education and Chinese-Funded Enterprises in Ghana

In 2007, the African Union issued the *Strategy to Revitalize Technical and Vocational Education and Training in Africa*, which made vocational education a key focus of education policies in African countries. China adheres to an internationalization path for vocational education that combines "bringing in" and "going global". It expands vocational education platforms and raises the level of cooperative education between China and other countries. Cooperation in vocational education between China and Ghana has developed in depth with the mode of cooperation changing from single aid to diversified collaboration. The important form of current China-African vocational education cooperation involves vocational colleges "going global" with cooperative enterprises, aiming to help Africa train technical talents, improve young people's employability and enhance national economic efficiency. China's assistance to Africa takes various forms, including conducting vocational and professional training, providing teaching equipment, sending experts and teachers for professional instruction, as well as assisting in the construction of vocational education institutions.

1. Carrying out Vocational Education Training in Africa (Ghana)

With the support of the School of Automotive Engineering's professional teachers at Henan Mechanical and Electrical Vocational College, a training class for the "Belt and Road" overseas vocational education project was launched in Ghana in collaboration with China National Electronics Components & Equipment Corp. Trainees underwent intensive 5-day courses such as "Diagnostic Instruments and Testing Methods for Automotive Electronic Control Systems", "Working Principles and Circuit Connections of Various Sensors and Actuators for Electronic Controlled Gasoline Engines", "Theory of Automotive Construction and Chassis Systems", and "Practical Operations of Automotive Construction and Chassis Systems" to cultivate skilled vocational education talents for Ghana.

2. Online and Offline Teacher Training or Technical Instruction

The Training for Managers and Key Teachers of African Vocational Colleges is the first training program for managers and key teachers of African vocational colleges, jointly organized by the China Education Association for International Exchange (CEAIE) and the Association of Technical Universities and Polytechnics in Africa (ATUPA). Weifang Vocational College has undertaken one-on-one training for Kumasi Technical University, which is divided into online and offline trainings. In collaboration with CEAIE and AVIC International Holding Corporation, Weifang Vocational College has sent three expert teachers from its mechanical and electrical engineering as well as automobile specialties to Ghana. These teachers provide technical training such as computer graphics and CNC lathes to teachers from universities such as Kumasi Technical University.

3. Assistance in the Construction of Vocational Education and Training Institutions

China has assisted Ghana in the construction of its educational infrastructure and provided scholarships and training opportunities. On November 15, 2014, the expansion project of Ghana's vocational and technical colleges, with Chinese assistance, was completed and put into operation. The total construction area is 4,500 square meters and includes teaching buildings for vocational colleges as well as primary and secondary schools.

In April 2022, a Chinese-assisted project to upgrade vocational and technical education and training in Ghana was completed. AVIC International Holding Corporation was contracted to build the project, which commenced construction in November 2019. It mainly consists of one examination center for the Ministry of Education of Ghana and 15 vocational college training centers. Additionally, the coorporation has provided 69 units of modern vocational training equipment to 23 Ghanaian vocational colleges covering five specialties: mechanical processing, electrical and electronics, welding, automotive repair, and civil engineering. The coorporation will also offer five years of after-sales service and assistance with operating the equipment. Furthermore, it has collaborated with several Chinese higher vocational colleges to train Ghanaian faculty members. The completion of this project will promote vocational and technical education in Ghana, facilitate the training of more professional and technical personnel, as well as boost Ghana's economic and social development.

4. Carrying out Project Cooperation to Establish an International Brand for Chinese Vocational Education.

In 2019, Binzhou Polytechnic partnered with Binzhou Re-intelligent Manufacturing (Zai Zhizao) International Trade Co., Ltd. to jointly implement the project "Intelligent Special Engineering Machinery + Industrialization of Luban Workshop" in Ghana. The goal is to achieve the "eight major initiatives" proposed at the Beijing Summit of FOCAC in 2018, with the aim of promoting Africa's development. The plan includes constructing the Binzhou Re-intelligent Manufacturing (China) Trade Center, establishing a China-Africa technical personnel growth platform and a German craftsmen training platform, as well as implementing the industrialization plans for intelligent engineering equipment manufacturing and training programs for African craftsmen. Through the construction and training program of the Luban Workshops, China aims to cultivate an echelon of talents in the machinery industry for African countries, thereby promoting better and faster economic development in Africa.

President Xi Jinping proposed the implementation of the "Future of Africa—a project for China-Africa cooperation on vocational education" at the opening ceremony of the 8th Ministerial Conference of the Forum on China-Africa Cooperation in 2021. The project is led by the Ministry of Education of the People's Republic of China and organized and implemented by the China Education Association for International Exchange (CEAIE). The organization form involves the joint training of technical personnel by Chinese and African insitutions. Mechatronics and architectural engineering is the initial pilot specialties, with a total of 14 insitutions selected throughout China. The project comprises two parts: one is a student training project, following the "1+2+1" (for African undergraduates, who study in Africa in the first year, study in China in the second and third years, and return to Africa in the fourth year to complete academics) model. Students receive undergraduate degrees in African studies as well as junior college degrees and associated certificates from Chinese institutions. Participating institutions may also choose to adopt flexible approaches such as "1.5+1+0.5", depending on their specific circumstances. The second is backbone teacher training, with Chinese institutions offering one-on-one training to educators from foreign institutions.

9.4 Practical Support from Weifang Vocational College for China-Ghana Production Capacity Cooperation

9.4.1 Background Analysis of Vocational Education's Participation in China-Ghana Production Capacity Cooperation

Currently, China-Africa relations are at their peak, and the African Union's Agenda 2063 and China's "Belt and Road" Initiative have become powerful engines for the development of China-Africa cooperation. The Forum on China-Africa Cooperation (FOCAC) is undoubtedly the highest-level mechanism leading China-Africa cooperation. Since its establishment in 2000, FOCAC has developed a mature operational mechanism with fruitful outcomes, providing a policy basis for the development of China-Africa cooperation and guiding its direction. The African Union has introduced several policies to promote Africa's development, such as the *New Partnership for Africa's Development (NEPAD) (2001)*, *Accelerated Industrial Development for Africa (AIDA) (2007)*, *Programme for Infrastructure Development in Africa (PIDA)*, and *Agenda 2063 (2013)*. All these policies emphasize accelerated industrialization as an important path and key element in promoting Africa's development.

The Chinese government has closely followed Africa's development demands and proposed corresponding cooperation programs with Africa. In May 2014, Premier Li Keqiang visited Ethiopia, Nigeria, Angola, and Kenya in Africa and put forward the "461" Framework for China-

Africa cooperation, which consists of four principles, six major projects, and one platform. In January 2015, the Chinese government and the African Union signed a memorandum on "three networks and infrastructure industrialization" to enhance transportation and infrastructure in Africa. In December 2015, President Xi Jinping unveiled the Forum on China-Africa Cooperation (FOCAC)—Johannesburg Action Plan at the Johannesburg Summit, proposing "five major pillars" and "ten cooperation plans" for China-Africa cooperation from 2016 to 2018.

Table 9–6 Major Projects of China-Africa Cooperation

Time & Events	Cooperation Policies of China and Africa	Specific Contents
In May 2014, Li Keqiang visited Ethiopia, Nigeria, Angola, and Kenya in Africa.	"461" Framework	Four principles: equality, solidarity/mutual trust, tolerance in development issues, and innovative cooperation. Six major projects: industrial cooperation, financial cooperation, poverty alleviation cooperation, environmental protection cooperation, civil and cultural exchanges cooperation, peace and security cooperation. One platform: FOCAC.
In January 2015, the Chinese government and the African Union signed a memorandum.	"Three Networks and Infrastructure Industrialization"	Three networks: high-speed railways, expressways, and civil aviation covering the entire African continent. Infrastructure industrialization.
In December 2015, Johannesburg Summit, the Forum on China-Africa Cooperation (FOCAC)—Johannesburg Action Plan	"Five Major Pillars" and "Ten Cooperation Plans"	Five major pillars: equality and mutual trust in politics, win-win cooperation in economy, exchanges and mutual learning among civilizations, mutual assistance in security, and unity and coordination in international affairs. Ten cooperation plans: industrialization plan, agricultural modernization plan, infrastructure plan, financial plan, green development plan, trade and investment facilitation plan, poverty reduction plan, public health plan, cultural and people-to-people plan, and peace and security plan.
In 2018, Beijing Summit of FOCAC, The Beijing Declaration	"Eight Major Initiatives"	Eight major initiatives cover the fields of industrial promotion, infrastructure connectivity, trade facilitation, green development, capacity building, healthcare, people-to-people exchanges as well as peace and security.
In November, 2021, the 8th Ministerial Conference of the FOCAC, China-Africa Cooperation Vision 2035	"Nine Programs"	China would work closely with African countries to implement the nine programs, which are the medical and health program, the poverty reduction and agricultural development program, the trade promotion program, the investment promotion program, the digital innovation program, the green development program, the capacity building program, the cultural and people-to-people exchange program, and the peace and security program.

With the deepening of the "Belt and Road" construction and the building of a community with a shared future for mankind, China-Africa vocational education cooperation has entered a new period of development. In 2018, President Xi Jinping clearly put forward at the Forum on China-Africa Cooperation Beijing Summit that China-Africa cooperation would implement the "eight major initiatives" in the next three years, promised to set up 10 Luban Workshops in Africa to provide vocational skills training for local young people, offer opportunities for education in China, exchange and training programs, as well as scholarships to 100,000 people to enhance African development capacity. In November 2021, at the opening ceremony of the 8th Ministerial Conference of the Forum on China-Africa Cooperation, President Xi Jinping proposed "Future of Africa — a project for China-Africa cooperation on vocational education". Based on this project, China will organize employment activities for African students in China while continuing to cooperate with African countries to establish Luban Workshops. Furthermore, Chinese enterprises in Africa will be encouraged to provide no less than 800,000 jobs and jointly implement "Nine Programs". As a result, China-Africa vocational education cooperation faces unprecedented development opportunities.

9.4.2 Basic Models of Weifang Vocational College's Participation in China-Ghana Vocational Education Cooperative Projects

Since Weifang Vocational College joined the "Future of Africa — a project for China-Africa cooperation on vocational education" in 2021, it has become one of the first batch of pilot colleges and has steadily promoted the "China-Africa joint training of applied talents". It has successfully completed one-to-one training for faculties and backbone teachers in African vocational colleges, as well as sent experts to Ghana to carry out the upgrading project of technical secondary schools and junior colleges. Additionally, Weifang Vocational College has shared a number of professional standards on internationalization, conducted research on vocational education that serves international production capacity cooperation, teacher training for Africa, and other related topics. As a result, it has achieved a series of positive outcomes in serving China-Africa vocational education cooperation and the building of the "Belt and Road".

1. Upgrading Vocational and Technical Education and Training in Ghana Through School-Enterprise Cooperation

The Chinese government's assistance in upgrading vocational and technical education and training in Ghana is an important step towards boosting Ghana's economic and social development, as well as deepening bilateral cooperation in the education sector. AVIC International Holding Corporation constructed the project in Kumasi, Ghana's second-largest city. Construction began in November 2019 and was completed in April 2022, which includes one examination center for the Ministry of Education and 15 vocational college training centers. This project aims to upgrade vocational education in Ghana by providing laboratory equipment, curriculum design, teacher training, school buildings and supporting services to technical colleges and secondary schools in Ghana. Its goal is to improve the quality of Ghana's vocational education, train more professional and technical personnel for Ghana, and contribute to its national development.

Ghana has been one of the African countries with the highest number of students studying in China for many years, and China has also become the largest provider of personnel training in Ghana. China has further deepened cooperation in the field of human resources by implementing vocational education and training upgrading programs to help Ghana train more outstanding talents needed for national construction and development, as well as assisting Ghana in industrial development, and economic restructuring and upgradating.

2. Stabilizing Quantity and Ensuring Quality, and Implementing Joint Training Programs for Technical and Skilled Personnel.

The joint training of applied talents between China and Africa is a sub-project under the "Future of Africa — a project for China-Africa cooperation on vocational education" framework. Weifang Vocational College and Rizhao Polytechnic are collaborating with Kumasi Technical University to provide joint training in high-level mechatronics and architectural engineering technology majors, using the "1+2+1" model for academic education. In response to Ghana's demand for human resources in infrastructure construction and early stages of industrialization, as well as job requirements of Chinese-funded enterprises, these institutions have developed talent cultivation plans and professional curriculum standards that meet both Chinese standards and Ghana's needs through multiple communications. Weifang Vocational College and Rizhao Polytechnic have admitted 30 students from Kumasi Technical University in related majors. This project aims to cultivate high-quality technical personnel skilled in mechatronics and architectural engineering, which are urgently needed for Ghana's economic and social development.

3. Integrating Online and Offline Approaches for One-to-One Teacher Training among Institutions

The training of vocational college managers and key teachers, which is a sub-project of the "Future of Africa — a project for China-Africa cooperation on vocational education", is sponsored by the China Education Association for International Exchange (CEAIE) and the Association of Technical Universities and Polytechnics in Africa (ATUPA). The offline teaching program for managers and key teachers of vocational colleges in Africa, undertaken by AVIC International, was held at Kumasi Technical University in April 2022. The project consists of two parts: online training and offline teaching. The training targets school leaders, heads of teaching, and related specialists in Ghanaian vocational colleges. The content includes theoretical knowledge, cutting-edge technology, educational concepts, teaching methods, curriculum design, and evaluation. The offline education venue is located at the new campus of Kumasi Technical University with 25 trainees receiving skills training in civil engineering and electromechanical fields. Through this training program, the practical skills and technical capabilities of managers and teachers in Ghanaian vocational colleges have been improved while strengthening exchanges between Chinese and African teachers. Furthermore, it has greatly expanded the breadth and depth of cooperation in vocational education between China and Africa.

4. Sharing International Standards and Expanding Curriculum Development and Academic Research in Vocational Education between China and Africa

Through in-depth participation, development, and sharing of international electromechanical curriculum standards, as well as specialized skills training in practical teaching, equipment operation, and vocational skills training capabilities of Ghanaian vocational teachers have been greatly improved. With a view to the education and teaching system of Ghana and the vocational education cooperation between China and Africa, related research has been jointly carried out with African colleges. The project "Exploration and Research on the Teacher Training Model of African Colleges in China-Africa Vocational Education Cooperation", initiated by the China Education Association for International Exchange (CEAIE), takes the Kumasi Technical University cooperation project as a pilot to timely popularize, which improves the effectiveness and pertinence of teacher training.

9.5 Existing Problems and Development Recommendations

International production capacity cooperation is an important desicion and initiative proposed by Chinese government inline with global economic development. As early as the end of 2014, Li Keqiang proposed the concept of "international production capacity cooperation". Since the establishment of diplomatic relations, China and Ghana have maintained friendly ties. China's experience in industrialization aligns with Ghana's development needs, creating huge potential for cooperation between the two countries. A large pool of industrial and technical talent forms the foundation for deep capacity cooperation between China and Ghana. Vocational education provides talent support and technical assistance for production capacity cooperation, serving as an important pathway for industrial output.

9.5.1 Theoretical Basis of Vocational Education Serving International Production Capacity Cooperation in the Context of Globalization

With the globalization of the world economy and the liberalization of trade, education has increasingly become internationalized. This is evident in the reasonable distribution of educational resources across borders and the global exchange and sharing of educational factors. The concept of internationalization of education has been defined differently by experts and academics. It is generally believed that the internationalization of education involves exchanging and learning educational concepts, methods, systems, and models among different countries. The main purpose is to promote the global flow of knowledge and talent, enhance the quality of education, and facilitate globalization. The internationalization of education focuses on procedure, internationality, purpose or functionality, which are conducive to governments and schools absorbing international experience and enhancing international influence. Vocational education, as an important type of education, also bears the mission of the new era. UNESCO has issued a number of documents suggesting that countries should strengthen the internationalization of education. It emphasizes that "vocational education should promote international understanding and tolerance, and cultivate citizens with a global vision and sense of responsibility", advocating for strengthened international cooperation in vocational education. Some international organizations and countries around the world have increased their support and investment in vocational education, promoted digital technology, enhanced international cooperation, reformed the certification system, and strengthened sustainable development. As a result, vocational education has experienced further development.

China has constructed the world's largest vocational education system, and has basically established the development path and model of vocational education with Chinese characteristics. The appeal, influence, and competitiveness of vocational education in China has been steadily increasing, undergoing historic transformation and pattern changes. Practical exploration has demonstrated that the advancement of vocational education in China must embrace an internationalization approach and promote reform through opening-up. By closely integrating its strategic plan of opening-up with the "Belt and Road", China has formed a regionally characterized model of internationalized vocational education.

Since the "Belt and Road" initiative was put forward, the Chinese government has issued several documents to accelerate the development of vocational education. In July 2016, the Ministry of Education formulated the *Education Action Plan for the "Belt and Road"* (hereinafter referred to as the Education Action), which points out that China is willing to shoulder more responsibilities and obligations within its capacity in deepening education cooperation with countries along the route, reflecting a sense of educational responsibility. Especially when facing most African countries with a relatively backward level of education, the Chinese government has taken proactive measures to demonstrate its responsibility as a major country by establishing various forms of "free ride" aimed at promoting Africa's human resources development. The cooperation in vocational education between China and Africa, initiated by the Chinese government, usually takes on an aid nature. It serves as an important means for helping African countries to improve their capacity for independent and sustainable development through "teaching people how to fish." China is playing an increasingly significant role in promoting is construction of a community with a shared future for mankind.

In the process of international production capacity cooperation, vocational education plays a crucial role. By collaborating with key industries in international production capacity cooperation, vocational education provides Chinese standards, international talent, information, and other support required for enterprises to "going global". There are both opportunities and challenges in China-Africa production capacity cooperation. We must not only pay attention to political, economic, diplomatic, and public opinion issues but also grasp the development pattern of China-Africa relations. When entering Ghana, Chinese vocational education services should be carried out in the long-term and overall interest in building friendly relations that align with the characteristics of the new era while giving full play to the positive and active role of vocational education.

9.5.2 Cooperative Achievements and Realities of China's Assistance to Africa

Currently, China-Africa educational exchanges and cooperation have established a multi-level, multi-field, and multi-agent model. High-level reciprocal visits at the government level, exchanges and cooperation in higher education institutions, international student education, sending teachers and volunteers to Africa, developing human resources in Africa, vocational education cooperation, as well as teaching and research in the Chinese language have achieved remarkable results.

1. Vocational Education Cooperation

Over the past few decades, China has trained more than 300,000 practical talents for Africa in 17 fields, including agriculture, forestry, environmental protection, public administration, transportation, and healthcare. In order to better meet the needs of African countries and cooperate with Chinese enterprises in "going global" and international production capacity cooperation, some Chinese vocational education institutions actively attempt to carry out vocational education overseas. The Luban Workshop is one of the representatives. So far, China has built and operated 12 Luban Workshops in Africa and opened 23 professional courses in 7 categories including additive manufacturing, new energy, mechatronics, and railway operation, thus promoting the development and innovation of vocational education in Africa.

2. Chinese-Funded Enterprises Collaboration with Local Institutions Based in Africa

Chinese-funded enterprises continue to expand their business and training, actively cooperate with local governments, and set up departments and institutions engaged in vocational education in Africa. For example, AVIC International Complete Equipment Co., Ltd. (hereinafter referred to as "AVIC International") has been operating in Africa for many years, gradually developing a professional business team engaged in the vocational education in Africa. It has undertaken top-level planning, civil construction, curriculum design, teacher training, management consulting, and other businesses related to vocational education in multiple African countries. AVIC International has partnered with the governments of Kenya, Gabon, and Uganda to implement a wide range of vocational education programs. For example, from 2012 to 2018, AVIC International provided curriculum design services as well as training, operations, and maintenance services to nearly 150 Kenyan schools. They trained 26,000 individuals with an employment rate of 80%. In addition, AVIC International is also conducting the Africa Tech Challenge (ATC) in Kenya, which provides cash rewards and study abroad opportunities for winners while offering commercial orders to winning colleges. AVIC International has gradually developed into an influential Chinese-funded enterprise specializing in the field of vocational education in Africa.

3. Education for International Students

China surpassed the United Kingdom and the United States to become the second-hottest destination for African students after France. According to UNESCO statistics, the United States and the United Kingdom each receive approximately 40,000 African international students annually. In 2014, China overtook these two countries with a total of 41,677 African students, making it the second most popular destination for African students studying abroad, only behind France. Over the past two decades, China has provided government scholarships to approximately 120,000 African students. According to statistics from the Ministry of Education of the People's Republic of China, in 2018, the total number of African international students reached a record high of 81,562, accounting for 16.57% of all international students studying in China. In 2019, that number increased to 87,409.

9.5.3 Problems and Challenges Faced by Vocational Colleges and Partnering Enterprises

From the perspective of China's aid scale development to Africa, assistance and cooperation in vocational education have been considered effective ways to improve vocational education level and develop human resources of African countries. Consequently, they have gained increasing attention from both Chinese and African governments. However, when considering China's current practice and situation regarding assistance and cooperation in vocational education in Africa, it is evident that the internationalization of Chinese vocational education is still at an early stage, which poses challenges for China's efforts.

1. A Deep-Seated Mechanism for Assisting Africa in the Field of Vocational Education Has Yet to Take Shape

(1) The Forms of Vocational Education Assistance for Africa Need to be Diversified

In the past, vocational education assistance to Africa mainly consisted of vocational and technical training based on the traditional government assistance programs and technical cooperation, and various bilateral or multilateral training courses coordinated by the Ministry of Commerce. In recent years, vocational colleges have partnered with enterprises to run overseas schools and conduct short-term human resources training programs in Africa. They have also explored joint training initiatives. Short-term training typically includes expert lectures, hands-on instruction, and on-the-spot investigations, which have the advantages of flexibility, ease of organization, and targeted learning and training. However, the short-term training makes it difficult to provide systematic learning as the content only covers the entry stage, and lectures and training have limited effectiveness. The lack of formal, systematic, campus-based vocational and technical education is the main problem. Overall, providing aid to Africa through educational institutions and businesses is still an exploratory practice without established experiences for reference.

(2) The Scope of Vocational Education Assistance to Africa Needs to be Expanded

At the 2015 Johannesburg Summit, China offered to provide on-the-spot training for 200,000 professional and technical personnel in Africa, as well as an opportunity for 40,000 individuals to study in China. However, based on the practice of Chinese vocational colleges actively exploring assistance and cooperation in Africa, only 40 out of the 1,298 Chinese vocational colleges have participated. There are still a large number of qualified vocational colleges that have not yet participated. Therefore, there is still significant room for development in China's practical assistance to Africa in the field of vocational education.

(3) The Quality of Vocational Education Teaching Needs to be Improved

Most Chinese enterprises engaged in vocational education in Africa are poorly equipped with teachers, limited teaching conditions and resources, and the quality of teaching is affected by differences in teaching hours and teacher levels. The lack of teachers and experimental equipment has resulted in African students learning more theoretical studies than practical operations. Vocational and technical education conducted by enterprises for the purpose of serving production exhibits a clear bias and selectivity in its teaching content, while problems such as language communication barriers, uneven teaching capacity, and ineffectiveness persist in methods like apprentice ship system. One key factor in improving the quality of vocational teaching is to find vocational and technical teachers with high levels of professional skills who can teach fluently in foreign languages, and attract them to teach in Africa. The low quality of education hinders local young workers from meeting the technical requirements of their posts. Issues such as the low employment rates and underutilization of human resources in Africa have yet to be addressed.

2. Lack of an Overall Layout for China-Africa Vocational Education Exchanges and Cooperation

(1) The Management Mechanism for China-Africa Cooperation Needs to be Strengthened

Since China-Africa international assistance and cooperation has long been managed by various departments such as the Ministry of Commerce, the Ministry of Foreign Affairs, the Ministry of Education, the Agency of International Economic Cooperation, China Scholarship Council and others, there is currently no specialized agency established to coordinate and harmonize the cooperation. This leads to issues with absent or multiple management which hinders the wholeness and coherence of China-Africa cooperation. As China's aid practices in

Africa continue to expand, they involve several sectors from different industries or the same field. In this regard, there is still a lack of mechanisms for cooperation among multiple parties to promote synergy. This is unfavorable to the full utilization of resource advantages from all parties and the formation of synergies in education.

(2) The Fund Guarantee Mechanism Needs to be Strengthened Further

Compared with general education, assistance for vocational education in Africa places more emphasis on specialized equipment, practical training sites, and teachers, which require large and sustained financial investments. Part of China-Africa vocational education cooperation is different from previous unilateral assistance. In this model, African students are financed according to the relevant training programs by the African side and trained by Chinese vocational colleges. However, this arrangement is often affected by the shortage of funds from the African side, leading to the postponement of the training programs. For example, when Changzhou College of Information Technology received its first batch of South African students, there were four designated internship units; however, after the second batch, only one remained. Beyond the language issue, the more important reason is a lack of funding.

African countries and regions vary in terms of their levels of development, legal systems, business practices, and technical regulations. Furthermore, inadequate support measures and a lack of capacity-building mechanisms continue to pose challenges for Chinese enterprises seeking to participate in infrastructure development in Africa. Additionally, there is a lack of strategic project funding and policy support at the national level, significant initial investment in infrastructure projects, long benefit and return cycles, limited financing capacity of enterprises, as well as a shortage of funding for overseas education projects led by enterprises or higher vocational colleges.

9.5.4 Recommendations for Vocational Education Colleges Serving China-Africa Production Capacity Cooperation

1. The Concept of "Extensive Consultation, Joint Contribution and Shared Benefits" Should be Established

In 2017, President Xi Jinping proposed and systematically explained the concept of "extensive consultation, joint contribution, and shared benefits" to jointly build a community with a shared future for mankind. In the process of promoting China-Africa production capacity cooperation, vocational colleges should also embrace the concept of "extensive consultation, joint construction, and shared benefits". The goal of the cooperation is to serve and benefit more people in various regions and countries while achieving common development.

First of all, when carrying out production capacity cooperation and vocational education cooperation with partner countries in Africa, it is necessary to clarify the demands of all parties through equal and in-depth exchanges and consultations. This should be done in light of the diverse backgrounds of African countries and the complex international situation. The aim is to reach a consensus on the form, content, action, and responsibilities of cooperation in order to ensure joint participation within the framework of mutual consultation and deliver benefits to all involved. China and Ghana have a solid foundation for cooperation. However, different interests make it difficult to promote, manage and develop cooperation in the process. Following the concept of "extensive consultation, joint construction, and shared benefit", vocational education serves Ghana's production capacity cooperation. Colleges, enterprises, industries, and governments should reach a willingness to cooperate through consultations during the initial phase of the project. During operations, problems should be detected and disputes should be discussed and negotiated in a timely manner to ensure that the project is carried out on th basis of good cooperation and communication.

In addition, due to differences in the education systems between China and Ghana, there are still barriers regarding post-high school education, vocational education, college and undergraduate education, mutual recognition of degrees and professional qualifications. While continuously improving the level of vocational education and developing a professional qualification framework, Chinese vocational colleges should actively engage in negotiations and cooperation with foreign parties to expand the scope of mutual recognition of educational achievements and professional qualifications while aligning better with international standards. Simultaneously, it is necessary to strengthen curriculum standard exchanges as well as teacher-student exchanges between the two countries to deepen understanding and jointly cultivate skilled individuals with international perspectives and competitiveness.

2. The Content of the Cooperation Should Align With the Two Countries National Strategies and Adhere to the Demand Orientations

In the process of carrying out production capacity cooperation with Ghana, it is necessary to adhere to the basic principle of "providing what is needed locally" and ensure a strong connection between specialty settings of vocational education and the local regional industrial structure. Firstly, production capacity cooperation and higher vocational colleges should align with the priority development needs and goals of partner countries, including clarifying whether the direction and specialty of cooperation are prioritized by partner countries.

In 2013, the Ghanaian Parliament passed the *Ghana Investment Promotion Center (GIPC 2013) Act*, which stipulates that foreign companies can only employ a corresponding number of foreign employees based on the immigration quota set according to their investment amount. Industries in Ghana that encourage foreign investment include: information sector, mining, oil and other energy sectors, infrastructure construction, agriculture and agricultural product processing, tourism, and services. From the perspective of the Ghanaian government's development plan, production capacity cooperation should begin with sectors that Ghana desperately needs, such as infrastructure construction, information industry and product processing.

3. Optimizing the Mode of Cooperation Among Government, Enterprises and Vocational Colleges

The three main bodies of international production capacity cooperation are the government, enterprises and higher vocational colleges. Under the premise of adhering to market laws, these three parties should form an inseparable and mutually supportive relationship as well as an operating mechanism.

(1) The Government Should Play a Guiding, Promoting, and Coordinating Role

The government plays the role of advocate and guarantor in international production capacity cooperation. Its role has gradually shifted from being a leader to an advocate, establishing platforms and channels for enterprises and vocational schools, as well as encouraging and leading their participation in international production capacity cooperation. Simultaneously, the government ensures the normal operation of international production capacity cooperation. In general, it, at the national level, formulates directions and plans for cooperation, enacts rules and regulations, and guides and provides institutional guarantees for international production capacity cooperation while also protecting the rights and responsibilities of enterprises and colleges involved. Therefore, adhering to the principle of "government playing a guiding role while non-government entities act as the main body", it is crucial for the government to fully exert its guiding role.

(2) Enterprises Play a Specific Role in Implementing and Executing China-Africa Production Capacity Cooperation

In China-Africa production capacity cooperation, enterpries output their production capacity and realize their own economic benefits through collaboration. Enterprises and vocational colleges jointly participate in international production capacity cooperation. Higher vocational colleges can provide technical talent to companies, which can assist in the implementation of enterprise cooperation projects and the construction of economic zones. They need to possess a high level of technology and international management capabilities. During the process of production capacity cooperation, they must also actively collaborate with higher institutions to fully communicate regarding employee vocational skills training and the cultivation of vocational and technical talent, thereby connecting industries with specialties for successful cooperation.

4. Vocational Colleges Should Deepen Cooperation with Enterprises and Implement Internationalized Education

Vocational colleges need to establish strong partnerships with enterprises in order to effectively carry out internationalized schooling based on the integration of industry and education, serving production capacity cooperation. This requires higher vocational colleges to have a high level of school management, preferably with experience in international school operations, and the ability to handle complex and evolving situations and issues in international school operations, in order to carry out effective cooperation.

First, vocational colleges should actively collaborate with key industries and enterprises to "going global". In terms of international production capacity cooperation, vocational colleges should leverage their unique characteristics to provide training, technical support, and translation services to Chinese enterprises overseas. For instance, Henan Mechanical and Electrical Vocational College partnered with China National Electronics Components & Equipment Corp., to conduct a training class for the "Belt and Road" overseas vocational education project. They relied on the expertise of the backbone teachers from the School of Automotive Engineering to provide professional training for trainees specializing in equipment integration within the field of overseas vocational education.

Second, vocational education should develop professional, industrial, and curriculum teaching standards that are applicable in partner countries. Promoting the connectivity of academic degree certification standards is one of the important components of the "Belt and Road" education action plan. Its essence lies in linking talent training standards. Vocational colleges should actively promote the internationalization of local high-quality vocational education resources and attach importance to the promotion and application of professional and industrial standards within the international scope. Rizhao Polytechnic has developed and shared 5 international curriculum standards for building materials and engineering surveying, as well as conducted special teaching training for teachers from Kumasi Technical University, Cape Coast Technical University, Sunyani Technical University, Tamale Technical University, and Bolgatanga Technical University.

Third, vocational colleges should establish a "cognitive community" to foster mutually beneficial and win-win consensus. People-to-people bonds are crucial for the success of the building of "Belt and Road". China and Ghana have distinct cultural backgrounds and values. Vocational colleges should enhance international exchanges, facilitate harmonious dialogues, promote in-depth interactions between Chinese and foreign industrial enterprises as well as vocational colleges, and effectively portray China's vocational education story. Jinan hosted the China (Shandong) —Ghana Dialogue on Friendly Cooperation and Development. Weifang in China has established friendly cooperative relations with Kumasi in Ghana. Weifang National Agricultural Comprehensive Zone has made deep contributions to the building of "Belt and Road" by signing international agricultural cooperation projects with Ghana. The vocational colleges should further advance practical bilateral cooperation, unlock new collaboration potential, and bring tangible benefits to both countries. Weifang Vocational College leverages its advantages in agricultural development and unique characteristics to organize the "Meeting at 'Chinese Bridge' to embark on a journey into the Chinese garden culture" project.

5. Fostering a Cooperative Policy Environment for Sustainable Development

International production capacity cooperation is a new area of cooperation among governments, enterprises, and vocational colleges. The success of Chinese enterprises in "going global" urgently requires top-level design, mechanism improvement, and introduction of policies, regulations, and standards. China is striving to create a favorable policy environment for China-Africa production capacity cooperation. In 2015, the State Council of China issued the *Guiding Opinions on Promoting International Production Capacity and Equipment Manufacturing Cooperation*, which set higher requirements for industries and enterprises. However, there are only a few documents that encourage and provide guidelines for vocational colleges to contribute to international production capacity cooperation. Moreover, there is no document addressing the management and standardization of international education cooperation specifically for vocational colleges. Therefore, it is urgently necessary to issue relevant policies and standards to ensure institutional guarantees for vocational colleges' involvement in production capacity cooperation.

In addition, the government should strengthen its management and supervision functions to prevent misbehavior by Chinese-funded enterprises doing business overseas from adversely affecting the country. As enterprises, they must prioritize national interest and refrain from gaining corporate advantage at the expense of national interest. The government may consider establishing a "blacklist" system, which would prohibit blacklisted enterprises from engaging in overseas business cooperation for a certain period of time. Simultaneously, vocational colleges should strengthen the education and training to teachers sent abroad, particularly in terms of fostering international understanding. Teachers should earnestly comply with local laws, respect local customs, treat local people equally and friendly, and build a positive image for their home country.

Chapter X

Reports on Vocational Education Collaboration Serving China-Rwanda Production Capacity Cooperation

The Republic of Rwanda, commonly referred to as Rwanda, is located in the central-eastern part of Africa. It's a landlocked country bordered by Tanzania to the east, Burundi to the south, the Democratic Republic of the Congo to the west, and Uganda to the north. With an area of 26,338 square kilometers, its population is approximately 12.96 million. Most of the nation experiences a tropical savanna climate and a tropical highland climate, and it's relatively scarce in natural resources. The year 1994 serves as a significant turning point in Rwanda's history. Particularly under the leadership of its current president, Paul Kagame, Rwanda has witnessed prolonged political stability, rapid economic growth, commendable public security, and ever-increasing international and regional influence. It has set a model for African countries and even nations worldwide bearing the weight of developmental rejuvenation. Consequently, Rwanda has earned accolades as the "Switzerland of Africa" and the "Singapore of Africa". It's considered one of the safest countries in Africa and currently stands out as one of the most open and rapidly developing economies in the south of the Sahara. An increasing number of individuals and enterprises regard Rwanda as a prime investment destination. Additionally, several economists and sociologists have coined the term "Rwanda Model" to express their affirmation of Rwanda's developmental trajectory.

10.1 Overview of Rwanda

10.1.1 Economic Development

As a developing nation, Rwanda, in recent years, has reaped the benefits of effective economic policies introduced by its government, thus undergoing a rapid process of industrialization. Since the year 2000, Rwanda has witnessed exponential economic growth and a significant improvement in the standard of living for its people. Under the leadership of President Paul Kagame, numerous policies aimed at attracting foreign aid, stabilizing the political climate, reducing corruption, and favoring investors have been rolled out. These policies have significantly contributed to Rwanda's economic surge. The accomplishments in Rwanda's economic development over the past three decades can be primarily summarized in the following aspects:

The swift progression of the service sector, industry, and manufacturing has been a backbone of Rwanda's economic upswing. Data from the World Bank reveals that from 2001 to 2015, Rwanda's Gross Domestic Product (GDP) experienced an average annual growth rate of 8%. Except for the year 2020, which saw a setback due to the impact of the COVID-19 pandemic with a GDP growth rate of –3.4% and a per capita GDP of $846, Rwanda's GDP for nearly 27 years has predominantly showcased an upward trend. In June 2022, the World Bank's "Global Economic Prospects" report predicted Rwanda's GDP growth rate for 2022 to be 6.8%, which is expected to rise to 7.2% in 2023.

Table 10–1 Major Economic Indicators of Rwanda for the Years 1994, 2016–2021

Year	1994	2016	2017	2018	2019	2020	2021
GDP (hundred million of US dollars)	7.54	86.90	92.50	96.40	103.60	101.80	110.70
GDP Real Growth Rate	–50.2%	6.0%	4.0%	8.6%	9.5%	–3.4%	10.9%
GDP Ranking in Africa	36	33	34	35	35	33	34
GDP Per Capita (US dollar)	176.0%	744.8%	772.3%	783.8%	820.2%	786.3%	833.8%
World Ranking of GDP Per Capita	185	163	188	189	186	185	191
Ranking of GDP Per Capita in African	42	37	38	39	37	38	39
Growth Rate of GDP Per Capita	–47.5%	3.2%	1.3%	5.7%	6.6%	–5.8%	8.2%

Source: World Bank, Rwanda National Bureau of Statistics

External trade volume has seen an uplift. According to the World Trade Organization data, Rwanda's goods export value in 2020 stood at $1.409 billion, marking an increase of 13.7% year-on-year. The import value was $3.106 billion, with a year-on-year growth of 15%. In the first nine months of 2021, the export value of traditional dominant products, including coffee, tea, cassiterite, and tungsten ore, rose by approximately 35%, further expanding the scale of foreign trade.

Receiving international aid and attracting foreign capital: The 2021 edition of the African Top Ten Investment Attractiveness Rankings, released by Rand Merchant Bank, placed Rwanda in fourth place, a leap of five positions from 2020. With the enactment of the *Economic Special*

Zone Law and the completion of the Kigali Economic Special Zone, over 80 enterprises from countries such as the United States, China, Germany, and India have invested and launched businesses in the Kigali Economic Zone. Following Rwanda's accession to the East African Community, the Southeast African Common Market, the Central African Economic Community, and the African Continental Free Trade Area, the investment environment in Rwanda has been improved significantly, drawing more foreign capital into the country.

Rapid development in the Information Technology and Communications sector, establishing the country as the "pacesetter" in Africa's digital economy: In October 2018, under the framework of the Electronic World Trade Platform (EWTP), the Chinese Alibaba Group reached a consensus with the Rwandan government to jointly develop Africa's first EWTP pilot. Alibaba, through its digital platform, aids in the export of local specialty products, fosters e-commerce awareness among Rwandan farmers, SMEs, and women, creates local employment opportunities, and assists in building digital governance, incrementally elevating the level of digital development in Africa. Consequently, Rwanda's e-commerce has hit the "fast track", with its digital economy sector making significant strides forward.

On one hand, Rwanda has been actively pushing forward its economic transformation strategy, shifting from an agriculture-dominated economy to a knowledge-based economy primarily centered on the development of the service industry. Successive visions such as "Vision 2020" and "Vision 2050" have been unveiled, all dedicated to Rwanda's economic development. The aim is to have Rwanda join the ranks of lower-middle, upper-middle, and high-income countries by the years 2020, 2035, and 2050 respectively. On the other hand, in alignment with these developmental strategies, the Rwandan government has rolled out plans for infrastructure development, digital economy growth, and green economy progression to promote national economic and social development.

10.1.2 Industrial Environment

In 2020, agriculture in Rwanda accounted for 26% of the total GDP, contributing a 0.2% growth rate to the economy. Industry constituted 19% of the GDP, dragging down the economic growth rate by 0.8%. The service sector represented 46% of the GDP, pulling down the economic growth rate by 2.6%.

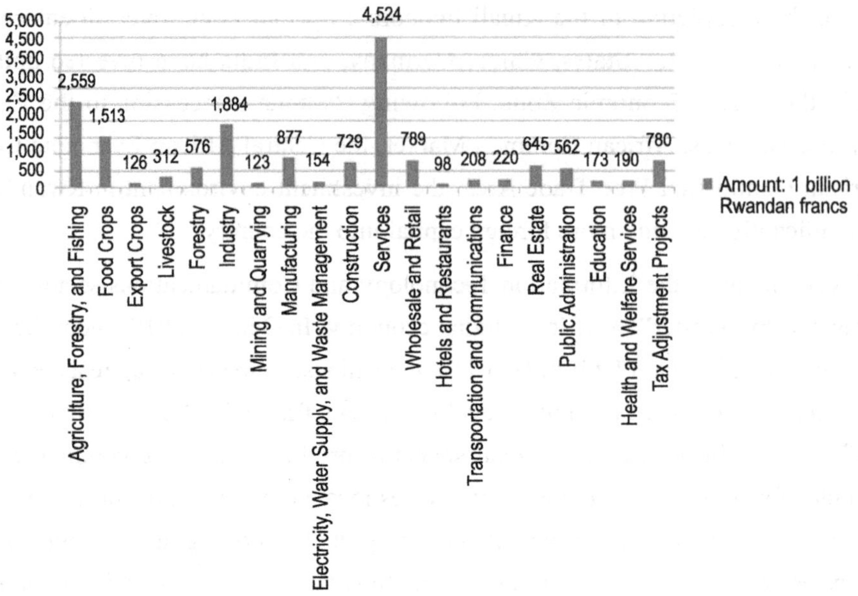

Figure 10–1 Industrial Output of Various Sectors in Rwanda for 2020

Rwanda's key characteristic industries are developing as follows:

Agriculture: The majority of Rwanda's trade exports are agricultural products, with tea and coffee being the primary products, accounting for over 80% of the total export value.

Mining: The main mineral exports include tungsten, tin, and tantalum-niobium ores. The Rwandan government is continually increasing its efforts to explore and develop resources such as petroleum. It is actively attracting foreign investment for mineral exploration and development.

Tourism: In 2019, Rwanda's tourism industry generated an income of $56 million, providing 11.1% of job positions. Currently, there's a severe deficiency in tourism facilities in Rwanda. Out of 250 hotels and lodges nationwide, only 10 are high-end, failing to meet the growing demand of international tourists. The Rwandan government is making significant efforts to attract foreign investment in the tourism sector, aiming for a diversified development of the industry.

Communication Industry: The Rwandan government has identified the communication industry as a key national sector and has set up a technology park in its special economic zones, aiming to become the information industry hub of the East African region. In recent years, the sector has seen rapid growth, attracting investments exceeding $500 million. In November 2014, Rwanda, in collaboration with the South Korean telecommunications company, launched the 4G network in Kigali. As of 2020, 70.6% of Rwandan households have mobile phones, and the mobile signal coverage has reached 99% of the population.

Transportation and Logistics Industry: The Rwandan government has always prioritized the construction of road transport infrastructure. One-tenth of the annual fiscal budget is allocated to the infrastructure sector. Rwanda boasts one of the best road network systems in East Africa, with 1,145 kilometers of paved roads and 3,562 kilometers of unpaved roads. The country has registered over 88,000 motor vehicles of various types. According to the Central Bank of Rwanda, the total revenue of the transportation and logistics industry reached 556 billion Rwandan francs in 2020.

Construction and Real Estate Industry: The construction and real estate sectors in Rwanda have witnessed rapid growth. According to the Central Bank of Rwanda's data, the total value of the real estate industry in 2020 was approximately 729 billion Rwandan francs, accounting for 8% of the GDP. In 2017, the Rwandan Ministry of Infrastructure announced an investment of 206 billion Rwandan francs (equivalent to $200 million) for the construction of affordable houses. This initiative aims to encourage citizens with monthly incomes between 300,000 and 700,000 Rwandan francs to purchase these affordable houses.

Rwanda has been vigorously promoting the development of special economic zones, yet its manufacturing industry hasn't seen significant progress. The reasons behind this include the country's lack of skills related to manufacturing, meaning that manufacturers have to incur substantial training costs. Moreover, due to lower demand and the higher opportunity costs of establishing manufacturing hubs in Rwanda compared to Kenya and Tanzania, the manufacturing sector faces challenges. Given Rwanda's population is under 13 million, the domestic market is relatively small, making it crucial for investments to focus on exports. For Rwanda, regional markets, especially in Burundi and the eastern part of the Democratic Republic of Congo, are increasingly important. Rwanda can capitalize on preferential trade agreements like "Everything But Arms" and the "African Growth and Opportunity Act" to access global markets.

10.1.3 Status Quo of Rwanda's Vocational Education

Since October 2020, Rwanda's Technical and Vocational Education and Training (TVET) system has been overseen by the Technical and Vocational Education and Training Committee (RTB). Currently, the country has a total of 368 institutions offering TVET education. These include: 344 Vocational Training Centers (VTCs) and Technical Secondary Schools (TSSs) offering levels TVET 1 to TVET 5 education. 8 Integrated Polytechnic Regional Centers (IPRCs) offering levels TVET 6 to TVET 7 education. In addition, there are 16 Teacher Training Colleges (TTC) responsible for training educators.

Table 10–2 Number of TVET Schools and Institutions in Rwanda

Schools and Institutions	2019	2020/2021	Difference
Teacher Training Colleges (TTC)	16	16	—
TVET Levels 1–5 (TSSs, VTCs)	331	344	+13

continued

Schools and Institutions	2019	2020/2021	Difference
Regional Polytechnic Institutes (RP-IPRCs)	10	8	–2
Total	357	368	+11

In 2008, the Rwandan government introduced a framework for the integration of vocational and general education in both horizontal and vertical directions. Guided by the Rwanda TVET Qualifications Framework (RTQF), the focus was to construct an industry-oriented flexible vocational education system. The government has designed clear entry and exit pathways for different levels of TVET and various TVET programs. All learners have the option to pursue further studies, and TVET graduates have the right to higher education. This has played a pivotal role in ensuring mobility, developing skills at all levels, and categorizing for all economic sectors.

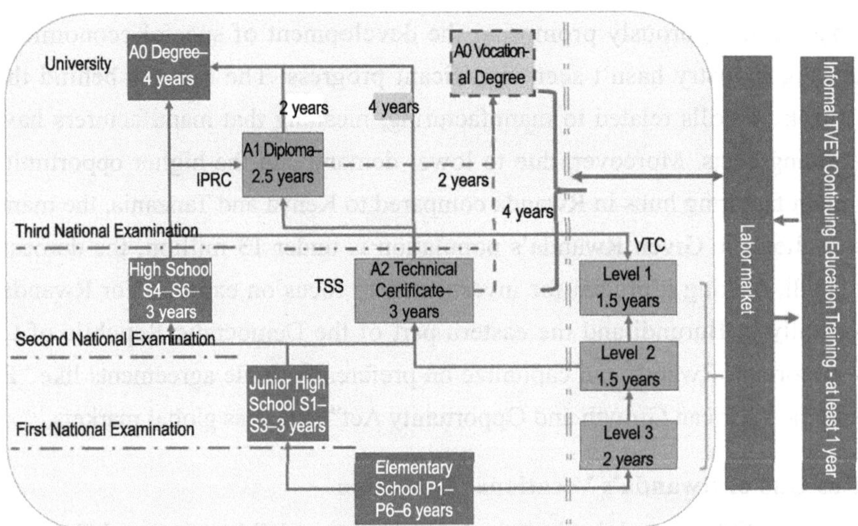

Figure 10–2 Structure of Vertical and Horizontal Integration between TVET and General Education in Rwanda

The Rwandan government has made significant efforts to expand the scale of TVET through a combination of domestic and foreign investments. This has resulted in a trained labor force that is both skilled and capable, nurturing a team of TVET teachers and considerably improving TVET facilities. However, the supply of vocational education in Rwanda is visibly inadequate in terms of both quantity and quality. The development status of vocational and technical education and training is not optimistic. A major challenge for the development of TVET in Rwanda is improving the alignment between vocational training supply and employer demand. Due to the prevalence of the informal economy and the high volatility in the labor market, there's a mismatch between the available skills of the labor force and the requirements of Rwanda's economic development.

10.1.4 Vocational Education and Industry

A report released by the Rwanda Human Resources and Institutional Capacity Development Bureau highlighted that there's a significant shortage of skilled technicians across various sectors in Rwanda. With the deepening of regional integration, competition in the broader market for skilled labor has intensified. As such, vigorously developing vocational education and cultivating a large number of adept vocational technicians is imperative for Rwanda. Presently, Rwanda's labor market is facing a substantial skill gap, manifested in the following ways:Firstly, there's a need to enhance the alignment between students' job capabilities and the market's demands. Approximately 50% of registered students in TVET institutions receive training confined mainly to construction and traditional technical skills. Recent surveys indicate that most students prefer pursuing advanced diplomas in architectural technology and electronics and telecommunications. This is followed by preferences for electrical and automotive technology, hotel management, and manufacturing technology specialties. This preference aligns with Rwanda's relatively weak industrial and agricultural sectors and its dedication to the development of the service industry. Secondly, the social recognition of TVET needs improvement. TVET is commonly perceived as a pathway for students with limited academic potential. It's often viewed as a last resort for those who aspire to further their studies after tertiary education (Maringa & Maringa, 2013). Hence, it's called the "second choice". The potential of TVET has not been fully realized, leading to an inability to effectively address the prevalent skill gap in Rwanda. Figure 10-3 shows the Rwanda TVET student distribution. Thirdly, TVET requires enhancement in terms of educational facilities, institutional strength and conditions, practical training quality, and the quality of talent cultivation. Due to constraints from a feeble economy and other factors, Rwanda relies heavily on the engagement of more stakeholders in the TVET educational system. By doing so, it aims to elevate the standard of educators, improve the quality of TVET education, and inherently raise the social recognition of TVET. Lastly, in comparison to the rapid progression of the knowledge-based economy era, the content of Rwanda's TVET curriculum seems somewhat outdated and needs to be improved. Although there has been a considerable expansion in course content and quantity, the depth and relevance of the curriculum don't completely align with contemporary technology and labor market demands. Many courses and programs don't undergo timely updates. Due to students' lack of genuine production experience and limited exposure to real-world production environments, there's a low integration of theory and practice. Moreover, some courses, planned at the national level, aren't effectively implemented due to a shortage of qualified instructors. This results in inadequacies in both the quantity and quality of trained labor to meet enterprise hiring needs. For instance, the wildlife management specialty, with high employer demand, has low enrollment rates. This can be attributed to the fact that the wildlife management specialty offers only two levels and boasts merely one professor of international wildlife management. The irrigation and drainage specialty is just a new project from the International Irrigation Research Center. In recent years, the employment and unemployment situation in Rwanda is shown in Table 10–3.

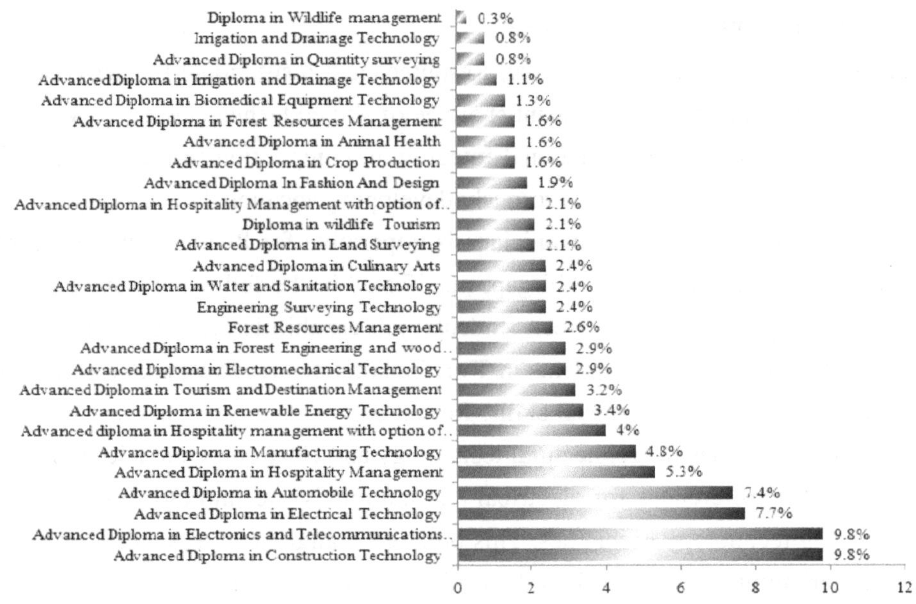

Figure 10–3 Rwanda TVET Student Distribution Diagram

Table 10–3 Employment and Unemployment Situation in Rwanda from 2016 to 2021

Year	2016	2017	2018	2019	2020	2021
Labor Force Participation Rate (%)	50.6	53.4	54.2	53.4	56.4	54.0
Employment Rate (%)	41.1	44.2	46.0	45.3	46.3	42.6
Unemployment Rate (%)	18.8	17.3	15.1	15.2	17.9	21.1
TVET Graduates Unemployment Rate (%)	18.0	18.7	17.4	15.4	—	20.3
General Education Graduates Unemployment Rate (%)	20.0	18.8	17.2	16.9	—	23.2
Youth Unemployment Rate (%)	20.9	21.3	18.7	19.4	22.4	26.5

10.1.5 International Economic Cooperation

Rwanda's foreign aid primarily originates from the World Bank, the United Kingdom, the European Union, the African Development Bank, Germany, the Netherlands, and Belgium, among others. The Rwandan government hopes to gradually reduce its dependence on foreign assistance. As of now, the Rwandan government's fiscal reliance on foreign sources has declined from 85% in 2000 to 34% in 2015. Simultaneously, Rwanda actively encourages foreign investments, having established investment promotion agencies and implemented a series of policies to attract foreign capital. In 2017, Rwanda drew in direct foreign investments amounting to $1.04 billion, marking a year-on-year growth of 70%. As per the World Bank's *Doing Business Report 2019*, Rwanda ranks 29th globally in terms of business environment services, second only to Mauritius in Africa.

Currently, the Rwandan government is vigorously expanding its global partnerships, aiming to improve the country's educational system. From July 1, 2020, to June 30, 2021, the Rwanda Institute of Technology maintained close collaborations with institutions and enterprises such as Germany's Koblenz and South Korea's Handong Global University. Although these efforts are undeniable, Rwanda still has a long way to go in achieving standard employment skills within its educational system. Economic and trade cooperation between China and Rwanda has been progressing smoothly. China is Rwanda's largest engineering contractor, a primary trade partner, and one of the significant sources of investment. The Chinese government offers Rwanda zero-tariff treatment for the vast majority of its exported goods.

According to data released by China Customs, in 2020, the trade volume between China and Rwanda amounted to $320 million, representing a growth of 6.9% year-on-year. Specifically, China's exports to Rwanda reached $283 million, marking an increase of 6.6%. Conversely, imports from Rwanda stood at $38 million, indicating a growth of 9.1% (See Table 10–4). Rwanda's trade volume with China ranks 43rd among African countries. In 2020, Chinese-funded enterprises signed new construction contracts in Rwanda amounting to $574 million, achieving a turnover of $318 million. By the end of 2020, China's direct investment stock in Rwanda was $191 million.

Table 10–4 China-Rwanda Bilateral Trade Statistics from 2016 to 2020 (Unit: $10,000)

Year	Total Import and Export	Year-on-year Growth (%)	China Exports	Year-on-year Growth (%)	China Imports	Year-on-year Growth (%)
2016	1.42	-14.6	1.09	-11.2	0.33	-23.9
2017	1.57	11.0	1.28	18.3	0.29	-13.0
2018	2.05	30.1	1.66	28.7	0.39	36.2
2019	3.00	46.4	2.65	60.0	0.35	-10.8
2020	3.21	6.9	2.83	6.6	0.38	9.1

Source: China Customs

10.2 Cooperation between Chinese-Funded Enterprises and International Production Capacity

10.2.1 Industrial Development in Rwanda and its Demand for Foreign Investment

In recent years, Rwanda has accelerated its drive towards modern agriculture, vigorously developed the information industry, focused on developing the conference and tourism industry, intensified its efforts to attract foreign investments, sought solutions to alleviate energy shortages, promoted "Made in Rwanda", and propelled national economic growth. Owing to the influence of the COVID-19 pandemic, Rwanda's health and social work sectors have witnessed rapid development, with a growth rate of 16%. Furthermore, as one of the nations in East Africa with a favorable marketing environment, Rwanda pursues an open economic policy. The majority of its economic sectors welcome foreign capital injections, particularly in areas like water conservancy, electricity, communications, roads, and other infrastructural domains where the demand for foreign capital is substantial.

Agriculture employs over 85% of Rwanda's workforce and contributes 26% to its GDP (2020). Rwanda's climate and environment are highly conducive to agriculture. Potential agricultural products for development include avocados, pineapples, and flowers, with primary exports being coffee, tea, pyrethrum, and chili peppers. Notably, its high-altitude black tea boasts exceptional quality with significant market potential, urgently necessitating foreign investment.

The Rwandan government has identified the information and communication sector as a pivotal national industry. As of 2020, Rwanda had 7.886 million internet users, with an internet penetration rate of 62.3%. Mobile network users stood at 5.627 million, with a mobile network penetration rate of 58.2%. The 4G network coverage reached 96.6%, the mobile phone penetration rate was 73.9%, and there were approximately 9.69 million mobile phone users. The country has constructed a backbone optical fiber network connecting various regions within the country and neighboring nations. However, Rwanda only has three telecommunications companies, namely MTN, TIGO, and Airtel, operating mobile communication and network services. Due to its landlocked location, Rwanda mainly relies on Indian Ocean cables relayed through neighboring countries for its external information exchange, resulting in slow internet speeds and frequent disconnections. In recent years, the information and communication sector has attracted over $500 million in annual investments.

The Rwandan government has always prioritized road and transport infrastructure development. Yet, most of its infrastructure project funding comes from the World Bank, the African Development Bank, and Arab national funds as loans. To date, Rwanda boasts one of the most impressive highway networks in East Africa, though it lacks railways. There are plans to increase its annual air passenger capacity from the current 500,000 to 3 million within the next five years.

With the rise in population and urbanization, the construction and real estate sectors in Rwanda have witnessed rapid growth. Between 2013 and 2022, the housing demand in Kigali city reached 4.6 million units. To meet this essential demand, there is an urgent need for foreign investment to expedite development and construction.

Looking at the mining industry, Rwanda primarily exports tungsten, tin, and tantalum-niobium ores. The country is actively seeking foreign investments for exploration and development to boost export earnings.

10.2.2 Status Quo and Development of Chinese-Funded Enterprises

Since the establishment of the Forum on China-Africa Cooperation (FOCAC) in 2000, China-Africa collaboration has taken significant strides in a comprehensive, multi-level, and wide-ranging direction. Given the international developmental context, the opportunity to capitalize on Africa's demographic dividend, the benefits arising from Africa's urbanization, and the golden period for manufacturing, the prospects for Chinese-funded enterprises in Africa appear promising. According to statistics from China's Ministry of Commerce, by the end of 2020, China's direct investment stock in Rwanda stood at $170 million. Over 30 Chinese businesses, including Zhongtu Group, Zhongdi Group, Beijing Construction Engineering, Huashan International, Henan International, Jiangxi International, Shangcheng Group, Beijing Henghua, Sinohydro, C&D Clothing Factory, and Zhongchen Steel Structure, are operating in Rwanda. These businesses span sectors such as telecommunications, construction, infrastructure, digital television, and e-commerce. Their main operations encompass road construction, building, farmland improvement, engineering consultancy, communication, digital TV, e-commerce, and mobile phone assembly. While there isn't an established overseas economic and trade cooperation zone for Chinese companies in Rwanda, private enterprises like the Sinohydro 13th Bureau, Beijing Construction Engineering, C&D Clothing Factory, and Zhongchen Steel Structure have settled in the Kigali Economic Zone. Furthermore, some Chinese private enterprises have invested in constructing accessory processing factories in the Kigali Economic Zone with a total investment of approximately $10 million (See Table 10–5).

Table 10–5 Direct Chinese Investment in Rwanda from 2016 to 2020 (Unit: $10,000)

Year	2016	2017	2018	2019	2020
Flow	–919	988	4,542	1,701	–655
Stock (by year-end)	8,936	9,925	14,682	16,751	17,080

Data sourced from China's Ministry of Commerce, National Bureau of Statistics, and State Administration of Foreign Exchange's *2020 Statistical Bulletin of China's Outward Foreign Direct Investment*

Currently, the primary channels through which Chinese companies in Rwanda obtain information on Rwandan engineering projects are mainly Rwandan media outlets (newspapers, Rwandan television stations, etc.), official websites of various Rwandan government departments, and the Rwandan Tendering Bureau. As of the end of 2020, China's aid projects in Rwanda mainly included: rice cultivation, sugar factories, the Kigali-Rusumo highway, development in the Rubengera and Rwamagana rice regions, a cement plant, a stadium, two rural primary schools, an agricultural technology demonstration center, Kigali General Hospital, and Musanze Integrated Polytechnic.

Table 10–6 Information on Major Chinese-Funded Enterprises in Rwanda

Enterprise Name	Type	Business Scope	Local Technician Demand
China Road and Bridge Corporation Rwanda Office	State-owned enterprise	Engaged in domestic and international road, bridge, port, railway, airport, tunnel, hydraulic engineering, municipal, dredging, and other engineering contracting, while also handling investment, industry, trade, leasing, and other services	General construction workers, masonry workers, construction equipment operators, etc
Rwanda Sida Media Co., Ltd.	Private enterprise	Large-scale broadcasting and television system integration, network investment and operations, program integration, translation, production and distribution and R&D of core technology of digital TV	workers engaged in TV network installation, maintenance, advertising, business, etc
Henan International Rwanda Managerial Department	State-owned enterprise	International engineering contracting, international engineering consulting, international labor cooperation, undertaking state foreign economic aid projects, mining investment and management, agricultural investment and management, international trade, network information services, and other foreign-related businesses	General construction workers, masonry workers, construction equipment operators, etc
Zhongtu East Africa Co., Ltd. Rwanda Managerial Department	State-owned enterprise	Mainly contracting projects, design consultation, labor cooperation, with real estate development, import and export trade, industry investment, and hotel management	General construction workers, masonry workers, construction equipment operators, business professionals, hotel management and project management professional, technicians, etc
Zhejiang China Small Commodities City Group Corporation Ltd.	State-owned enterprise	Purchasing, order following, commodity inspection, booking space, transportation, customs declaration, as well as import and export agency, foreign trade consulting, processing with imported materials; freight transport, warehousing, distribution, and freight information consulting	E-commerce, logistics, ICT and warehousing professionals
Beijing Henghua Weiye Technology Co., Ltd.	Private enterprise	Service provider for BIM platform software, industry digitalization application, and operations; smart grid, smart energy, smart water, smart transport. Also offers skill training services	Drone operators, construction machinery instructors, and basic coders
Zhongdi Group Rwanda Company	State-owned enterprise	Construction, investment operations, agriculture, water services, etc	Project management, technicians
Zhongchen Steel Structure Rwanda Company	State-owned enterprise	Prefabricated steel civil buildings, steel industrial buildings, and steel bridges	Project management professionals and technicians

continued

Enterprise Name	Type	Business Scope	Local Technician Demand
Huawei Rwanda Subsidiary	State-owned enterprise	Data services	ICT and management personnel
Beijing Construction Engineering Group Rwanda Branch	State-owned enterprise	Construction projects	Construction management, personnel and technicians
Huashan International Engineering Rwanda Company	State-owned enterprise	Construction projects	Construction management, personnel and technicians
Henan International Rwanda Company	State-owned enterprise	Engineering contracting, international engineering consulting, mining investment and management, agricultural investment and management, international trade, network information services, etc	Construction management, personnel, trade professionals, ICT professional, etc
Jiangxi International Rwanda Company	State-owned enterprise	Construction, foreign labor cooperation, foreign trade, architectural design, etc	Construction management, technicians, trade professionals, etc
China Hydropower Rwanda Company	State-owned enterprise	Hydropower industry	Technicians and management personnel
C&D Clothing Factory	Privatel enterprise	Clothing industry	Clothing designers, tailors, etc

The data from Table 10–6 shows that Chinese-funded enterprises in Rwanda are primarily state-owned enterprises (SOEs) supplemented by private firms. The primary sectors they operate in are construction, with a few in the apparel industry, trade, telecommunications, and more. There's a significant gap in technical workers, especially in the fields of construction, trade, telecommunications, and logistics. Moreover, these Chinese-funded enterprises have earned recognition from both the Rwandan government and private stakeholders for their management capability and construction quality. However, there are some challenges that hinder their growth in Rwanda.

Firstly, investment policy instability. In recent years, the Rwandan government has adopted various measures to encourage investment, making the investment threshold low and the process simplified. However, Rwanda has strict requirements when it comes to taxation and environmental protection. The enforcement is strong, often leading to substantial fines for foreign enterprises. The frequent changes in officials responsible for approvals also add to the instability of governmental policies. The lack of internal coordination presents a level of policy risk.

Secondly, trade credibility issues. Direct trade between China and Rwanda is relatively limited. There's minimal business interaction between the banks of the two countries, leading to potential trust crises in trade and difficulties in bank transactions. Merchants in Rwanda tend to focus excessively on transaction prices, often sidelining product quality. Thus, during trade interactions, there's a need for a heightened focus on detailed product quality clauses and other specifications.

Thirdly, shortage of skilled technicians. One of the major issues highlighted is the scarcity of skilled technical workers in Rwanda. The reasons behind this shortage include a lack of adequate educational infrastructure and a mismatch between educational content and job requirements. This has led Rwanda to rely heavily on skilled technicians introduced from neighboring countries. While Rwanda aims to integrate itself into the global economic chain and has set a long-term goal of transitioning to a knowledge-based economy with a highly-skilled workforce, there remains a pressing need to address the lack of skilled workers. This issue also severely restricts the localization of staff in Chinese-funded enterprises operating in Rwanda.

10.2.3 Chinese-Funded Enterprises' Demand for Vocational Education

Rwanda has an abundance of general labor, with supply surpassing demand. However, the overall quality of this labor force is low, and there's a pronounced shortage of technical workers. Adding to the challenge, the Rwandan government maintains strict controls on work visas, encouraging enterprises to hire locals to boost employment opportunities. According to statistics from China's Ministry of Commerce, in 2020, Chinese enterprises dispatched 455 various types of workers to Rwanda. By the end of the year, there were 1,001 Chinese workers in Rwanda. They primarily undertook roles in construction site supervision, hydroelectric installation, equipment setup and debugging, e-commerce, TV network installation, maintenance, advertising, business operations, logistics, ICT, warehousing, drone operations, teaching construction machinery, and basic coding. To reduce operational costs, Chinese-funded enterprises in Rwanda need to employ local staff. Therefore, there's an urgent need for the training and development of the aforementioned technical talents to support the localization efforts of Chinese-funded enterprises in Rwanda.

Moreover, when considering the fields of study offered by Rwanda's Vocational Training Centers (VTCs), Technical Secondary Schools (TSSs), and Integrated Polytechmic Regional Colleges (IPRCs), it's evident that there's a mismatch between Rwanda's technical and vocational education system and its transition to a knowledge-based economy. This leads to issues such as insufficient course offerings and a severe lack of trained professionals ready for employment. For instance, even though the ICT programs tailored for the development of the information and communication industry have been introduced in both TSSs and IPRCs, they suffer from a severe shortage of hands-on training equipment, unstable electricity and network connections, and challenging practical operations. As a result, the practical abilities of students are notably low. Furthermore, while Rwanda launched e-commerce services in 2018, the first batch of students specializing in e-commerce only began their studies in March 2022, lagging significantly behind the country's economic needs. Moreover, the logistics industry, which serves e-commerce development, has yet to introduce a corresponding logistics program, leading to an acute shortage of skilled professionals in logistics.

In conclusion, the development capacity of Rwanda's TVET cannot meet the demands for skilled workers in positions like construction site supervision, hydroelectric installation, equipment setup and tuning, television network setup, maintenance, advertising, logistics, warehousing, drone operation, machinery instruction for construction, and basic coding required by Chinese enterprises in Rwandan. There is an urgent need for vocational assistance from China to fulfill the localized development needs of technical workers for Chinese-funded enterprises there.

10.2.4 Adaptability of Rwandan Vocational Education to the Development of Chinese-Funded Enterprises

Rwanda's education policy, known as the Education Sector Plan (ESP), emphasizes the importance of technical and vocational training. The goal is to develop the Rwandan population into a human capital base that meets the country's development needs through skill teaching. They aim to produce a sufficient number of well-trained graduates. However, Rwanda still heavily relies on importing technical workers from neighboring countries like Kenya, Tanzania, and Uganda. The main reasons for the misalignment between Rwanda's vocational education and industry needs are:

1. Limited Social Recognition Hindering the Growth of Technical Workers

Rwanda's Education Department's strategic plan proposes that by 2024, 60% of high school graduates should enter TVET, and 40% should opt for general high schools and universities. However, Rwandan youth have a strong preference for white-collar jobs and perceive TVET education as a secondary or inferior choice. Between 2019 and 2021, the student ratio between general education and TVET shifted from 3 : 1 to 3.46 : 1 (See Table 10–7).

Table 10–7 Status of Rwandan Students in University from 2019 to 2020/2021

Indicator	2019 (Count of Students)	2020/2021 (Count of Students)	Difference (Count of Students)
TVET Short-term Training	9,932	8,561	–1,371
IPRCs	14,078	13,172	–906
General Higher Education	72,128	75,276	3,148

Source: *Rwanda Education Annual Report (2021)*

2. Insufficiency and Lower Quality of Teaching Staff Restricting TVET Development

There's a significant imbalance between the demand and supply of TVET teachers, and the quality of these teachers is not up to the mark, making it one of the major reasons for the inability to produce competent workers. As the enrollment rate in TVET institutions grows, the demand for professional teachers also rises. As shown in another unspecified table (presumably Table 10–8), even though the number of TVET schools and institutions has been adjusted multiple times since 2017, decreasing from 402 to 352, the number of students has increased by 3,453. In contrast, the teaching staff increased by only 449. This discrepancy highlights a significant issue in Rwandan TVET education: the lack of qualified and experienced TVET instructors. Furthermore, according to data from Rwanda's Education Board (REB), in 2012, only 15.4% of teachers held advanced diplomas. By 2021, teachers with a Master's degree or higher made up just 5% of all teaching personnel.

Table 10–8 Numbers of Rwanda TVET Schools and Teacher-Student Ratio from 2016 to 2020/2021

Indicator	2017	2018	2019	2020/2021
Number of TVET Schools and Institutions	402	360	341	352
Number of Students	107,501	102,485	107,167	110,954
Number of Teachers	6,929	6,607	6,711	7,219
Ratio of All Teachers to Students	1:15.5	1:15.5	1:16.0	1:15.4
Number of Teaching Staff	4,807	4,767	4,834	5,256
Ratio of Teaching Staff to Students	1:22.4	1:21.5	1:22.2	1:21.1

Data source: *Rwanda Education Annual Report (2021)*

3. Low Satisfaction Levels of TVET Courses Hindering Quality of Education and Improvement of TVET Satisfaction

In 2021, a student satisfaction survey in Rwanda (See Table 10–9) revealed that most TVET graduates were satisfied with their courses, academic and social services, modes of learning, and teacher-student interactions. However, they felt there was room for improvement regarding lab equipment, ICT infrastructure, internet facilities, sports venues, and industry-attached standards. When compared to the requirements of a knowledge-based economic transformation, Rwanda's TVET course content appears outdated. There's a mismatch between the curriculum and the current labor market needs. Many courses and programs aren't updated or innovated promptly.

Table 10–9 Factors Affecting the Competence of TVET Graduates in Rwanda in 2021

Elements of Educational Quality	Very High	High	Average	Low	Very Low
Training Equipment, Tools, Machinery	10(2.8%)	122(33.6%)	107(29.5%)	90(24.8%)	34(9.4%)
Safety During Training Sessions	11(3%)	106(29.2%)	132(36.4%)	80(22%)	34(9.4%)
Boarding and Lodging	11(3%)	94(25.9%)	168(46.3%)	66(18.2%)	24(6.6%)

continued

Elements of Educational Quality	Very High	High	Average	Low	Very Low
Environmental and Sanitation Facilities	16(4.4%)	100(27.5%)	142(39.1%)	48(13.2%)	57(15.7%)
Training Institution Infrastructure	22(6.1%)	109(30.0%)	112(30.9%)	80(22.0%)	40(11.0%)
Instructor Qualifications	13(3.6%)	142(39.1%)	85(23.4%)	60(16.5%)	63(17.4%)
Classrooms and Training Venues	9(2.5%)	120(33.1%)	130(35.6%)	63(17.4%)	41(11.3%)
Training Cost	10(2.8%)	95(26.2%)	168(46.3%)	67(18.5%)	23(6.3%)
Parental Support	30(8.3%)	79(21.8%)	107(29.5%)	91(25.1%)	56(15.4%)
Cultural Pressure	8(2.2%)	86(23.7%)	104(28.7%)	87(24.0%)	78(21.5%)
Total	139	931	1,255	642	370
Total Percentage	4.2%	27.9%	37.6%	19.2%	11.1%

Source: *Rwanda TVET Graduate Employability and Employer Satisfaction Survey Report (2021)*

4. Low Alignment Between Students' Employability Skills and Market Needs, Restricting Enhancement of TVET Graduate Employment Quality

From the 2021 survey on Rwanda TVET graduates' employability and employer satisfaction (See Table 10–10), it is evident that while TVET graduates expressed satisfaction with academic and social services provided by IPRCs, they voiced dissatisfaction regarding education in communication skills, stress resistance, negotiation, and leadership. Employers' feedback revealed that TVET graduates typically lack in areas such as communication, practical application, and innovative thinking.

Table 10–10 Satisfaction Levels of Rwanda TVET Graduates Regarding Educational Quality in 2021

Educational Quality Factors	Very Satisfied (Number / Percentage)	Satisfied (Number / Percentage)	Average (Number / Percentage)	Dissatisfied(Number / Percentage)	Very Dissatisfied(Number / Percentage)
Relevance to the Labor Market	69(19.0%)	171(47.1%)	86(23.7%)	37(10.2%)	—
Teachers and Teaching Methods	25(6.9%)	244(67.2%)	83(22.9%)	11(3.0%)	—
Curriculum Content	32(8.8%)	241(66.4%)	77(21.2%)	13(3.6%)	—
Learning Environment	34(9.4%)	219(60.3%)	101(27.8%)	9(2.5%)	—
Focused Student Learning	13(3.6%)	230(63.4%)	117(32.2%)	3(0.8%)	—

continued

Educational Quality Factors	Very Satisfied (Number / Percentage)	Satisfied (Number / Percentage)	Average (Number / Percentage)	Dissatisfied(Number / Percentage)	Very Dissatisfied(Number / Percentage)
Student Workload	29(8.0%)	229(63.1%)	96(26.4%)	9(2.5%)	—
Institutional Management	57(15.7%)	220(60.6%)	75(20.7%)	11(3.0%)	—
Practical Training and Experiments	33(9.1%)	167(46%)	107(29.5%)	20(13.8%)	6(1.7%)
Student Expectations and Conditions	15(4.1%)	196(54%)	140(38.6%)	12(3.3%)	—
Total	307	1,917	882	155	6
Total Percentage	9.4%	58.7%	27.0%	4.7%	0.2%

Source: *Rwanda TVET Graduate Employability and Employer Satisfaction Survey Report (2021)*

Based on the survey results concerning the TVET's Social recognition, the quality of educators, curriculum satisfaction, student employability, and employer satisfaction, it's evident that Rwanda's TVET education has entered a rapid developmental phase. The number of students and qualified teachers, educational quality, graduates' employability, and employer satisfaction have all shown significant increase. However, compared to the ambitious developmental goals of the Rwandan government, there's room for enhancement in TVET's educational facilities, institutional strength and conditions, practical training quality, and the quality of talent cultivation. To address these challenges, it's imperative to involve more stakeholders in the TVET educational system, elevating the standards of teaching and improving the quality of TVET education. This will inherently boost social recognition of and satisfaction towards TVET. As the Rwandan government is keen on developing a knowledge-based economy, they anticipate a swift growth in the number of e-commerce professionals to support the development of the digital economy. Opportunely, Jinhua Polytechnic, in collaboration with the Rwanda Institute of Technology, has developed an e-commerce curriculum standard (Levels 6–7) which has been successfully incorporated into the Rwanda Educational Qualifications Framework (REQF). The inaugural enrollment plan was for 30 students, but they admitted 60, and classes commenced in March 2022.

10.3 Chinese-Funded Enterprises Collaborating with Chinese Vocational Education for "Going Global"

10.3.1 The Necessity of Chinese Vocational Education Supporting International Production Capacity Cooperation

Owing to its weak infrastructure and frail economy, Rwanda remains one of the underdeveloped countries in the world. As of the end of 2020, Rwanda's public debt stood at 695.31 billion Rwandan Francs, constituting 71.3% of its GDP. The central government's external debt balance was 511.44 billion Rwandan Francs (accounting for 52.5% of GDP and 73.6% of the total public debt), while the internal debt was 133.88 billion Rwandan Francs (13.7% of GDP). Given that a tenth of Rwanda's annual budget is allocated to infrastructure development and that more than $500 million are invested annually in the telecommunications industry and other sectors aiming for growth, it is evident that there is an acute need for foreign investment and enterprises in Rwanda to realize its vision of transitioning to a knowledge-based economy.

Looking at the development of Rwanda's telecommunications sector, available data suggests that the ICT infrastructure in Rwanda has been growing rapidly. Its integration with other service sectors, as well as the agricultural and industrial departments, is relatively tight, playing a positive role in propelling its growth. In terms of regional competitiveness, the comprehensive development index of Rwanda's ICT industry has reached a medium level in Africa, trailing behind countries like Kenya, Zambia, and Uganda in East Africa. In 2019, Rwanda's domestic enterprise, Mara Group, launched two smartphone models, marking the first-ever African-made smartphones. Nevertheless, this has not altered the foreign-dominated landscape of Rwanda's telecommunications industry. The primary companies in the Rwandan telecommunications sector are six in number: MTN (South African investment, dominating over 70% of the wireless market share), BSC, INCH OF GOLD INTERNATIONAL, Liquid Telecom (Kenyan investment, primarily involved in fixed communication and broadband services), TIGO (invested by Rwanda's Sombor) and Airtel (Indian investment, holding 10% of the wireless communication market share). This landscape indicates that foreign companies hold a majority stake in Rwanda's telecommunications sector. Meanwhile, the Chinese-funded enterprises Huawei has a relatively small market share and there's a stark shortage of skilled technicians to meet the demands of the growing telecommunications industry.

Considering the development of Rwanda's tourism and e-commerce industries, there has been a consistent growth trend in the number of tourists visiting Rwanda in recent years. However, the number of hotels in Rwanda decreased from 360 in 2011 to 250 in 2020, of which 10 are high-end hotels. As for its impact on the national economy, the tourism industry's revenue in Rwanda amounted to $56 million in 2019, providing 11.1% of the nation's job positions. In terms of regional competitiveness, Rwanda's tourism industry scored a comprehensive competitiveness index of 3.2 in 2019. The environmental and policy conditions received a higher scores, surpassing the African average. Notably, Rwanda's ground and port infrastructure significantly outpaces the African average. Looking at the Meetings, Incentives, Conventions, and Exhibitions (MICE) tourism sector, Rwanda hosted 26 international conferences in 2018, making its capital, Kigali, the second-largest host city for international conferences in Africa. Although tourism is one of the fastest-growing industries in Rwanda, its industry chain has yet to be fully established.

In terms of the quality of Rwanda's workforce, as of 2019, the working-age population (16 years and above) stood at 7.2 million, with only 45% being employed. Data from the Rwanda National Bureau of Statistics indicates that (as illustrated in Figure 10–4), in 2020, the agricultural population accounted for 85% of the total, with agriculture contributing 27% to the nation's Gross Domestic Product (GDP).

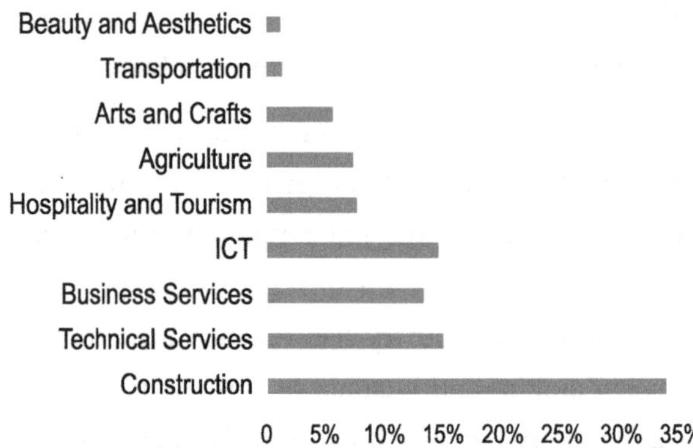

Figure 10–4 Registration Ratio of Students in Rwanda's TVET by Specialization

Note. From National Institute of Statistics of Rwanda (NISR) (2019).

From the above data, it's evident that by updating TVET curriculum content and enhancing farmers' skills, a substantial economic impact can be made, significantly improving agricultural output (Ngatia & Rigolini, 2019). While there have been significant advancements in the Information and Communications Technology (ICT) sector, Rwanda lags in digital skills, largely due to inadequate coverage of the TVET curriculum. Furthermore, TVET institutions in Rwanda predominantly offer learners technical skills in construction, failing to sufficiently focus on current technological trends. This leads to a misalignment between the skills supplied by Rwanda's employment sector and the skills that are in demand.

Besides being out of sync with its economic structure, the quality of Rwanda's TVET curriculum also raises concerns. According to Rukundo (2015), most non-agricultural jobs in Rwanda are concentrated in the informal sector, a sector that is not completely captured in Rwanda's official economic statistics in terms of trade and employment. Currently, the informal sector dominates most economic sectors, especially in manufacturing, commerce, and finance. It employs the highest number of people in Rwanda, accounting for 64% of the total industrial output. Trade-related occupations, such as street vending and micro-retailing, are among the most common activities in the informal sector. The vast majority of workers in this sector have received little to no formal or vocational training in their respective fields (Procknow, 2017). Consequently, there is an urgent need in Rwanda for a large number of skilled technicians and robust technical support.

From the perspective of China's vocational education strength and development trajectory, in the past few decades, China has trained over 300,000 practical talents for Africa, spanning 17 sectors including agriculture, forestry, environmental protection, public administration, transportation, and health. These short-term training sessions typically combine expert lectures, hands-on operations, and field observations, which are flexible in execution, relatively easy to organize, have a strong focus on learning content, and yield good results. Training non-Chinese-funded enterprises employees has become another primary method of China-Africa vocational and technical education collaboration. Specifically, it involves companies establishing their own training institutions, commissioning local universities for employee training, implementing a China-Africa employee apprenticeship system, and selecting outstanding employees for training in China. Such training achieves a win-win situation for both the company and the employees. Through providing training for local African employees, Chinese-funded enterprises not only bolster their own human resources, but also assist Africa in cultivating more skilled technicians, thus enhancing employment quality. African nations also send students to study in Chinese vocational institutions, which is a vital component of bilateral vocational education cooperation. Between 2017 and 2021, South Africa sent over 1,200 students to study in more than 20 vocational schools in China.

Rwanda's *Vision 2020 for Economic Development and Poverty Reduction* emphasizes that good governance, human resource development, a knowledge economy, a private-sector-led development strategy, infrastructure construction, market-oriented high-yield and efficient agriculture, as well as regional and international integration, are the directions the government should strive towards. The Rwandan government hopes to transition the nation from an agriculture-based economy to a knowledge-based economy by vigorously developing the information and communication industry. In conclusion, for the economic and social development of Rwanda, there is an urgent need for foreign investments and enterprises. For Chinese-funded enterprises operating in Rwanda, the rapid development of the business urgently requires Chinese vocational education to "going global", providing the enterprises with talent and intellectual support for sustainable growth.

10.3.2 Internationalization of Chinese Vocational Education in Rwanda

In service of the building of "Belt and Road", outstanding Chinese companies actively "going global" to serve international production capacity cooperation. The emerging Chinese vocational education should take its responsibilities and play its role by actively "going global" to serve Chinese-funded enterprises and international production capacity cooperation.

1. The Presence of Chinese Vocational Education in Rwanda's Education Field

As early as 2008, the China Civil Engineering Construction Corporation (CCECC) built the Hope Primary School in the Rulindo District of Rwanda's Northern Province. This was aimed at providing learning facilities for local school-age children. Subsequently, with funds secured from Rwanda's Ministry of Education, student dormitories and a canteen were specially built, upgrading it to a higher vocational and technical school for girls.

In 2016, the Beijing Forever Bright Technology Corporation undertook the "National Electric Power Geometric Network Modeling" project in Rwanda and was commissioned to train a group of electric grid technicians to meet future system maintenance needs. This led to the establishment of the Forever TVET Institute. In 2021, through the Skills Development Fund (SDF) set up in Rwanda, an inaugural six-month skills training program was launched for out-of-school Rwandan youths. Following that, in collaboration with institutions such as the Shaanxi Railway Engineering Vocational and Technical College and the German BIWE organization, they actively carried out information technology-based teaching, international talent training, BIM technology application training, and construction machinery operator training.

In November 2021, the University of Rwanda and the Rwanda Polytechnic, both signed a memorandum of understanding with Huawei in the capital Kigali, jointly establishing the Rwanda-Huawei Information and Communication (ICT) Institute. This collaboration aims to provide regular talent training for Rwanda's digitalization transformation.

2. Jinhua Polytechnic's Schooling Practices in Rwanda

In 2013, commissioned by the Rwandan government, Jinhua Polytechnic began training academic students for the Rwandan government's sponsored programs. As of now, in response to Rwanda's pressing needs in areas such as communication networks and devices, IOT application technology, automobile testing and maintenance technology, and tourism and hotel management, a "1+3" (one year of language learning and three years of skills training) talent training model has been adopted. This has trained a total of four cohorts with 99 individuals. In July 2017, at the invitation of Rwanda's Ministry of Education, Jinhua Polytechnic collaborated with Rwanda's Musanze Integrated Polytechnic to establish the Rwanda Musanze Integrated Polytechnic International College.

Since its establishment, institutions like Jinhua Polytechnic have become key participants and steadfast implementers under the framework of the Forum on China-Africa Cooperation (FOCAC). However, they still face new situations, challenges, and issues that urgently require governmental research and solutions. The main challenges include:

Insufficient protection and policy support. It's recommended to establish global vocational education institutions strategically and scientifically while "going global". A series of supporting policies should be developed, including those concerning accompanying enterprises in "going global" education, providing educational equipment support for "going global", and selecting exemplary projects for "going global" education. These would elevate the internationalization level and effectiveness of vocational education. Lack of funding. It's proposed that overseas education initiatives by vocational colleges should be timely incorporated into the national foreign aid funding plan. Concurrently, local governments should offer financial support, ensuring abundant funds for the "going global" initiatives of vocational education. Resource constraints and platform enhancement. The government should support and even proactively introduce platforms to relevant vocational colleges, differentiating them based on their tier. This would increase the participation of vocational colleges on related platforms and promote the high-quality and efficient development of overseas education.

10.3.3 Forms and Achievements of Internationalized Education

To attract more stakeholders to the system, Rwanda's TVET made unprecedented efforts. Taking the Rwanda Polytechnic (RP) as an example, from July 1, 2020, to June 30, 2021, RP closely collaborated with several enterprises and institutions, such as Koblenz from Germany and Handong Global University from South Korea. (See Table 10–11 for details)

Table 10–11 Overview of RP's Collaborations

No.	Project Name	Funding Source	Cooperation Field/Project	TVET Collaborative Units	Collaboration Outcomes
1	Priority Skills Development Project	Rwanda Finance Ministry, World Bank	Priority Skills Development Project / Technology Development Fund: 1. Energy 2. Agri-product processing 3. Logistics and transportation	Joint project of RP & RTB	1. Student admissions: RP increased student enrollment from 143 to 200 across 3 study programs as follows: i. IPRC Huye: 54 in Animal Health, 38 in Agri-product Processing ii. Musanze Integrated Polytechnic: 54 in Food Processing, 54 in Agri-product Processing. 2. The initial goal for 7 majors such as Airport Management, Railway Engineering, Aircraft Maintenance, Logistics & Supply Chain Operations, Food Processing, and Agri-product Processing was to enroll 295 students. This goal hasn't been achieved due to RP not introducing some of the programs yet.

continued

No.	Project Name	Funding Source	Cooperation Field/Project	TVET Collaborative Units	Collaboration Outcomes
2	Koblenz, Rhine-Land-palatinate region	Germany	1. Dual training programs 2. Capacity building 3. Expert exchanges 4. Implementation of workshop learning policies	Joint project of RP & RTB	1. 20 individuals trained in solar energy. 2. 125 individuals underwent tailoring and painting internship skills training through dual training programs at Engma Vocational Technical College.
3	Korean Project	South Korea	Strengthening and developing the Rwanda TVET system through capacity building	Joint project of RP & RTB	1. 2,281 individuals were trained and certified. 2. Developed the Rwanda TVET Qualification Framework (RTQF) training manual (levels 3–5).
4	Swiss Development Cooperation	Switzerland	1. Support the establishment of 5 vocational training centers in 5 districts of the Western Province 2. Provide capacity-building support for RTB 3. Implement industry-based dual training	RTB	1. Support for renovating IPRC Karongi's Nyamishaba campus. A feasibility study has been completed. 2. The preliminary phase of dual training has begun.
5	EDC-AKAZI KANOZE	USA	1. Support for the development and integration of pre-job courses 2. Support for entrepreneurship course development and integration 3. Promotion of entrepreneurship and youth employment	Joint project of RP & RTB	1. Provision of pre-job courses and training manuals for the Rwanda TVET Qualification Framework (level 2). 2. Support for the formulation of RP's strategic plan.
6	IOM TVET Project	UK	Promotion of skills and knowledge transfer, involving skilled Rwanda diaspora as part of the skill development agenda	Joint project of RP & RTB	1. Support for student innovation projects. 2. Technical development for the dispersed population.
7	AFD TVET Project	France	1. Aid construction of IPRC Tumba and four other TVET schools in Rulindo region 2. Renovation of existing facilities and equipment provision	Joint project of RP & RTB	1. Development of a project implementation manual. 2. Tenders called for the construction project of Mechatronics College of IPRC Tumba and four TVET schools in Rulindo region.

continued

No.	Project Name	Funding Source	Cooperation Field/Project	TVET Collaborative Units	Collaboration Outcomes
8	Strengthen Education for Agriculture Development (SEAD) Project	Netherlands	Skills development and capacity building in the agricultural sector	Joint project of RP & RTB	1. Formulated 8 policies for RP, pending activation. 2. Leadership and management training and certification for RP's middle management. 3. Support for the formulation of a horticulture curriculum outline, pending certification. 4. Construction of a potato seed multiplication greenhouse. 5. Construction of leguminous plant and fruit greenhouses at IPRC Huye. 6. Construction of a potato warehouse. 7. Provision and installation of equipment. 8. Construction of a poultry workshop with related equipment.
9	China TVET Aid Project	China	Expansion of IPRC Musanze	RP	1. 90% expansion and provision of equipment for Musanze Integrated Polytechnic. 2. Joint construction of Luban workshops. 3. Joint construction and launch of electrical automation technology and e-commerce majors with the first enrollment of 124 students. 4. Teacher training initiated. 5. Construction of 5 practical training rooms.

Source: *Rwanda Education Annual Report (2021)*

As shown in the table, it is evident that the main collaborative partners for Rwanda RP include Germany, South Korea, Switzerland, the United States, the United Kingdom, France, the Netherlands, and China. Examining the history and models of collaboration, developed nations like Europe and the United States hold dominant positions, with many having colonial legacies or leading with national institutions. For instance, Germany and France, with their colonial ties, have inherent advantages. The UK's strength lies in Rwanda's adoption of the Commonwealth system, which offers a shared benefit. Both South Korea and Japan's vocational education assistance are spearheaded by consortiums, offering a more flexible operational level. China's vocational education support, while led by the state in infrastructure construction, is carried out independently, lacking follow-up plans for software development. Such aid from China often stems from the independent actions of educational institutions and has less reliance. Compounded by the generally small scale of Chinese companies in Rwanda, China's vocational education faces significant challenges in the country. There is an urgent need for more national policies and financial support to assist its growth.

10.4 Jinhua Polytechnic's Support for Rwanda's International Production Capacity Cooperation

The Forum on China-Africa Cooperation (FOCAC) presents opportunities to deepen educational collaborations between China and Africa. Consequently, Chinese vocational schools in Africa have stepped onto a fast track of development. With an increasing number of vocational institutions "going global", the types of educational engagements are diversifying. These institutions have significantly contributed to the building of "Belt and Road", promoting China-Africa cultural exchanges, and cultivating skilled personnel. Jinhua Polytechnic actively responds to the "Belt and Road" Initiative and the concept of the China-Africa shared future. They are keen participants in FOCAC's action plans, aiming to serve the developmental needs of Chinese-funded enterprises in Rwanda, and Rwanda's transformation into a knowledge-based economy along with the development of its key industries. Through joint program development, constructing Luban workshops, faculty training, resource building, and skills training, Jinhua Polytechnic is dedicated to nurturing local Rwandan skilled talents. The institution actively explores a collaborative model between government, academia, and industry for vocational education aid, pushing for a profound and concrete collaboration in vocational education between China and Rwanda.

10.4.1 Educational Models: "Government&College-College&Enterprise-College & College" Collaboration for "Going Global"

Musanze Integrated Polytechnic is one of the eight institutions affiliated with Rwanda Polytechnic. It stands as the largest vocational and technical education and training center in Rwanda's Northern Province and is a Chinese foreign educational aid project in Rwanda. The first phase of this project was completed in March 2015, starting its admissions and accommodating up to 1,200 students. By 2021, the second phase was finished, raising its student capacity to 4,000. In 2017, the International College was officially inaugurated at the Musanze Integrated Polytechnic. The establishment of the International College signifies the substantial steps Jinhua Polytechnic has taken to promote vocational education "going global," serving the cultivation of African skilled talents, contributing to the construction of the China-Africa shared future, and supporting national strategic needs. With a focus on national foreign aid in education and international collaboration in vocational education, the construction and development of the International College have garnered significant attention and support from both the Chinese and Rwandan governments. Concurrently, the institution collaborates with Chinese-funded enterprises in Rwanda, not only cultivating talents that Rwanda urgently requires but also stabilizing and enhancing the performance of these Chinese-funded enterprises. (See Figure 10–5 for details)

In 2020, Jinhua Polytechnic signed a comprehensive collaboration agreement with Rwanda Polytechnic, extending the collaboration from Musanze Integrated Polytechnic to all eight institutions under the Institute's jurisdiction. The development of the International College has explored the "Government-School–School-Enterprise–School-School" collaborative model of international vocational education, a unique Jinhua Polytechnic example.

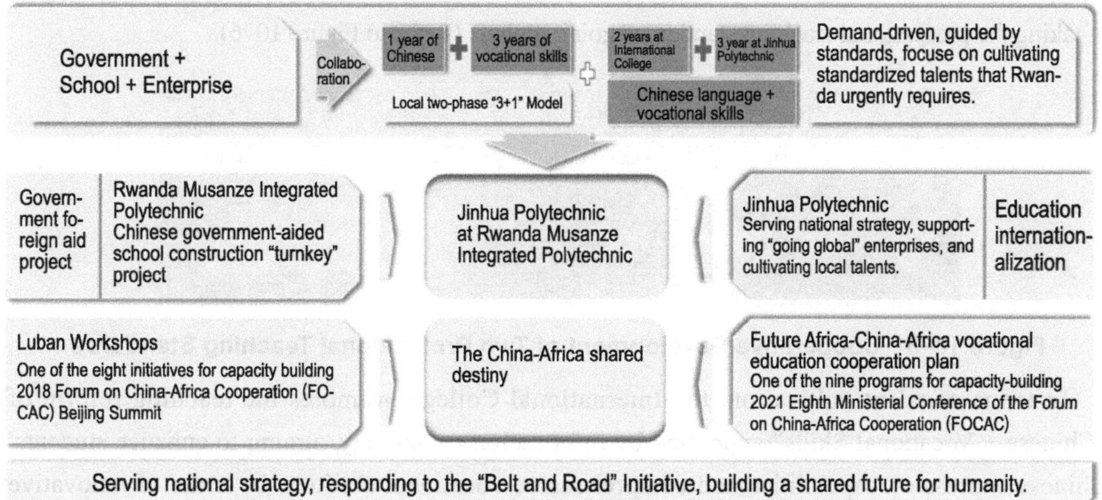

Figure 10–5 The "Government-School - School-School - School-Enterprise" Collaborative Model for Vocational Education Aid

10.4.2 Educational Approach: Demand-Oriented + Standard-Guided

In the advancement of the intrinsic development of the International College, we consistently adhere to the practical path of being "demand-oriented and led by standards".

Demand-oriented: This means focusing on Rwanda's priority industrial developments and training urgently needed skilled talents for those industries as the logical starting point for the development of the International College. In its initial stages, Jinhua Polytechnic dispatched teachers to Rwanda to conduct research on industrial development and the labor market, so as to understand the demand for skilled talents. The digital economy is a strategic emerging industry for the Rwandan government's 2030 economic plan. It's also Zhejiang province's primary project for economic development and Jinhua city's primary industry. Zhejiang China Small Commodities City Group Co., Ltd. has set up an overseas warehouse in Rwanda, and Alibaba has established its cross-border e-commerce platform, eWTP, in the country. Therefore, the International College selected e-commerce and automation as the two initial disciplines for cooperation, systematically planning the college in terms of areas of collaboration, functional positioning, operational mechanisms, and shared standards.

Criteria-Led: Building on the demand-oriented approach, the development of intrinsic specialties, such as course resources, teaching teams, and practical training bases, is led by the sharing standards of professional courses. After nearly a year, in collaboration with partner schools, the *Teaching Standards for the E-commerce Specialization (Levels 6–7)* and the Teaching Standards for *Electrical Automation Technology Specialization (Levels 6–7)* were completed, totaling nearly 400,000 words. In 2021, both of these standards were certified by Rwanda's Workforce Development Authority (WDA) and Higher Education Council (HEC) and were formally incorporated into the Rwandan Educational Qualifications Framework (REQF), truly realizing the goal of taking the professional teaching standards "going global" (Refer to Figure 10–6).

Figure 10–6 Cooperative Development of Two Professional Teaching Standards

In terms of talent cultivation, the International College promotes the teaching reform of "Chinese + Vocational Skills" supported by information technology, aiming to enhance students' Chinese expression capabilities and comprehensive vocational abilities. In terms of innovative talent cultivation models, for degree-seeking students sponsored by the government, a local two-phase "1+3" model has been adopted since 2013. In 2022, for the two specialties with which the International College cooperates, while cultivation is based on professional standards certified by the Rwandan Ministry of Education, an innovative practice of a two-phase "2+1" model, which combines "Chinese + Vocational Skills", was introduced. This means students spend two years studying at the International College and the last year at Jinhua Polytechnic. The first batch of 124 students officially started their education under this new talent cultivation model in March 2022. The project was selected for the "Future Africa-China-Africa Vocational Education Cooperation Plan" (See Figure 10–7).

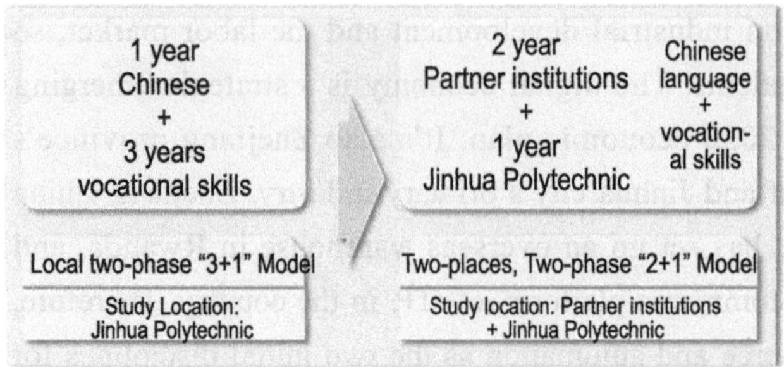

Figure 10–7 Exploring Innovative Talent Cultivation Models Based on "Chinese + Vocational Skills"

Regarding course resource development, and centering on the professional teaching standards, a team was organized to develop an online learning platform, completing a set of bilingual courses, bilingual textbooks, and skill training packages. At the same time, retaining the inherent characteristics of the Rwandan system, high-quality resources from the school's "double high" construction were integrated to develop serialized teaching resources. In terms of practical training infrastructure, to serve Chinese-funded enterprises in Rwanda and cultivate localized skilled talents, practical training rooms such as Huawei ICT certification, automation, live-stream e-commerce, and Chinese language training were co-established with national brands (enterprises) like Huawei and Zhejiang China Small Commodity City Group Co., Ltd., according to the professional teaching standards. Collaborative efforts were made to develop a series of practical training teaching standards. Jinhua Polytechnic organized a professional team using modern communication network technology to develop a remote reality-based experimental platform. This platform can carry out remote programming and modeling and conduct online real-world practical training on actual devices within China, innovating the practical teaching model (See Figure 10–8).

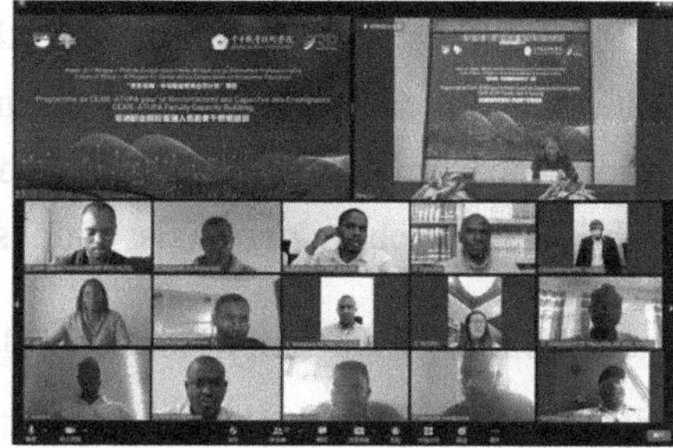

Figure 10–8 Development of Serialized Teaching Resources and Remote Reality-Based Training Platform

Regarding faculty development, we uphold the philosophy of "teaching a person to fish" and prioritize the cultivation of Rwandan local teaching capabilities, striving to enable local faculty to quickly undertake the teaching organization and implementation of cooperative professional teaching standards. To achieve this, we use three methods for training. First, dispatching core teachers to reside in Rwanda and provide hands-on training to Rwandan teachers. Second, annually receiving Rwandan core professional teachers to China for on-the-job learning. And third, the school uses the online learning platform to carry out one-on-one paired faculty training. Through the aforementioned multiple methods, continuous improvement in local faculty's teaching philosophy, practical skills, and teaching level is sought (See Figure 10–9).

Figure 10–9 Adhering to the Philosophy of "Teaching a Man to Fish" in Training Rwandan Teachers

10.4.3 Key Achievements

1. Shared a Batch of Standards and High-Quality Teaching Resources

Co-developed professional teaching standards for two specializations at levels 6 and 7, which have been officially incorporated into the Rwandan Education Qualification Framework (REQF). Established the Moodle course learning platform and created a dedicated learning space for international academy students on the "ChangXueJinZhi" platform. Moreover, 36 bilingual courses, 16 bilingual teaching materials, and 9 skill training packages were developed.

2. Cultivated a Batch of Urgently Needed Talents and High-Quality Teachers

Around specialties like hotel management and communication networks & devices, using the "3+1" model, four cohorts totaling 99 students were trained. The first batch of 124 students from the "2+1" model commenced their studies in Rwanda this March. Additionally, nearly 5,000 individuals were trained in local urgently needed vocational skill areas. Through various forms, 43 core teachers were trained for Rwanda. A group of local teachers with new teaching philosophies and strong capabilities effectively supported the implementation of shared professional teaching standards.

3. Jinhua Polytechnic was Selected for a Series of National Platforms for Cooperation with Africa

Jinhua Polytechnic was successively selected for the "Future Africa—China-Africa Vocational Education Cooperation Program" and became the deputy director unit of the Luban Workshops Construction Alliance. Since 2019, Jinhua Polytechnic has been involved as a hosting institution in organizing the China (Zhejiang) China-Africa Trade Forum and the China-Africa Cultural Cooperation Exchange Week, responsible for hosting parallel forums such as the China-Africa Vocational Education Forum. They have also integrated school and enterprise resources and launched initiatives with Chinese-funded enterprises in Africa, such as establishing the China-

Africa Digital Economy Vocational Education Industry-Education Collaboration Alliance. In 2022, Jinhua Polytechnic was approved for the first batch of national Luban Workshops operations projects (only 5 overseas), the first batch of Zhejiang Province's "Belt and Road" Silk Road Academy, Zhejiang Province's Standard International Cultivation Base, and one "Chinese Bridge" online group exchange project.

4. Received High Praise from Leaders and Media from Both Sides

The International Academy has always enjoyed robust support and high appreciation from the Chinese Embassy in Rwanda. The then ambassador to Rwanda, Rao Hongwei, visited the International Academy annually, met with on-duty teachers, and provided a lot of guidance on bilateral cooperation. In March 2019, during the commencement of the second phase, Ambassador Rao Hongwei visited the school. Using four "Rights" (Right Time, Right Partner, Right Person, Right Place), he highly affirmed the achievements of the International Academy. In 2019, the then-governor of Zhejiang Province, Yuan Jiajun, visited three African countries. During his visit to Rwanda, he and his delegation viewed an exhibition showcasing the achievements of the aid to Rwanda. This exhibition was jointly organized by Zhejiang Provincial Department of Science and Technology, Alibaba, and Jinhua Polytechnic. Governor Yuan gave high praise to the educational results Jinhua Polytechnic achieved in Rwanda. Through international vocational education cooperation, the bonds and connections between cities have been strengthened, promoting the bridging of friendly cities between China and Rwanda. In 2019, during the third Zhejiang (Jinhua) China-Africa Cultural Cooperation Exchange Week and the China-Africa Economic and Trade Forum, Jinhua City and Musanze City signed an intention letter for establishing friendly cities. The same year, the newly appointed Rwandan ambassador to China, James Kimonyo, visited Jinhua Polytechnic just a month after taking office. He met with students trained on behalf of the Rwandan government and highly commended the quality of education provided to these international students. Additionally, the International Academy's educational initiatives have been covered in-depth by more than 30 mainstream media outlets from both China and abroad.

10.4.4 Development Vision: "11131" Project

To actualize the harmonious vision of a joint China-Africa community of shared destiny, Jinhua Polytechnic is poised to promote the "One Plan, One Platform, One Workshop, Three Alliances, and One Center" project, known succinctly as the "11131" development initiative. One Plan refers to the rigorous implementation of the "Future Africa–China-Africa Vocational Education Cooperation Plan." One Workshop denotes leveraging the selection and establishment of the Luban workshops to iteratively upgrade the "Chinese Language + Vocational Skills" Silk Road Institute. One Platform is premised on the 2021 elevation to a national-level forum of the China (Zhejiang), China-Africa Trade Forum and the China-Africa Cultural Cooperation Exchange Week. Jinhua Polytechnic will annually host the China-Africa Vocational Education

Forum on this platform, sharing insights and drawing from the experiences of vocational education expansion into Africa. Three Alliances signify the commitment to deepening China-Africa vocational education cooperation by joining forces with the Luban Workshops Alliance, the Africa International Chinese Education Alliance, and the China-Africa Digital Economy Vocational Education Industry-Education Collaboration Alliance. By tapping into the quality resources of these alliances, the cooperative efforts are continually enriched. One Center emphasizes the creation of the China-Africa Vocational Education Research Center, harnessing the research prowess and resources of the Zhejiang Provincial Modern Vocational Education Research Center and the African Research Institute of Zhejiang Normal University. The focus is on the growth and collaboration of China-Africa industries and vocational education, with scholarly research being a pivotal facet, thus further deepening the International College's foundations (Refer to Figure 10–10).

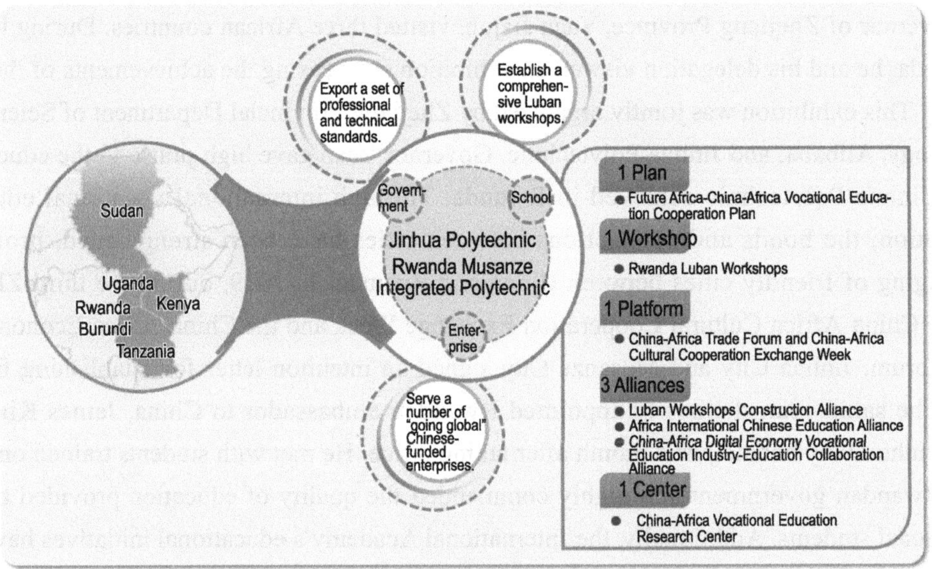

Figure 10–10 "11131" Development Initiative

10.5 Existing Problems and Development Recommendations

10.5.1 Existing Problems and Analysis of Causes

1. Insufficiency in Policy Framework and Country Studies

China's vocational education started relatively late, with limited practical experiences, and the related policies and regulations for "going global" are not well-developed. Since 2010, China has introduced over 30 policies related to the internationalization of education, such as the *Decision on Accelerating the Development of Modern Vocational Education*. However, most of these policies remain theoretical. On the one hand, there is a lack of comprehensive, multitiered planning across sectors like education, business, diplomacy, and culture. On the other hand, specialized policies and regulations are scarce, lacking supporting operational guidelines. Establishing educational institutions "going global" still faces numerous challenges, such as differing educational environments and backgrounds, distinct educational systems, and the fact that existing regional and country study bases are scattered across universities without a cohesive force.

2. Sluggish Development of an Internationalized Faculty Team

Currently, there's a noticeable gap between the internationalization level of faculty teams in specialized institutions and their development needs. Firstly, in terms of language, there's a shortage of professional teachers who can undertake bilingual teaching, especially those proficient in less-common languages spoken in countries and regions along the "Belt and Road". Secondly, in the context of international vocational qualification certificates, only 21% of our teachers possess vocational qualification certificates recognized by international professional organizations. The professional standards of these teachers are not internationally recognized, which affects the development of internationalized teaching.

3. Lagging Digital Skills in Overseas Teaching

Compared with the blended digital skills training widely conducted domestically, the degree of digitalization in the training methods of our vocational colleges overseas is relatively low. Teaching plans, curriculum standards, examination assessments, and other aspects are lack of necessary digital technology support, resulting in a less standardized teaching and training approach. Especially under the impact of the COVID-19 pandemic, the traditional joint schooling model involving domestic vocational colleges collaborating with overseas local institutions faces challenges in digital transformation. There's an urgent need to utilize digital means to establish an efficient skill training model.

4. Lower Stability and Rentability of Overseas Institutions

Due to limitations in the resources and development levels of partner countries, overseas vocational education faces various challenges including unstable faculty and weak profitability. Specifically, many outstanding domestic educators do not adapt well to the overseas environment, resulting in a prevalent issue of retention; the training cycles for foreign students coming to China for vocational training, as well as for faculty training in partner countries, are short, making it difficult to nurture high-quality educators in a brief period; the operational costs of overseas schools or training bases are high, with a large uncertainty in student enrollment, leading to poor operational sustainability.

10.5.2 Recommendations for Further Development

1. Strengthen Cooperative Principles and Lead in the Right Direction

(1) Highlight Ideological Guidance. We should follow President Xi Jinping's strategic ideas on African diplomacy, adhering to the principles set out in the various editions of the Forum on China-Africa Cooperation (FOCAC), integrating production and education, and opening up education. This will guide the China-Africa vocational education cooperation in the right direction. President Xi Jinping's critical judgments on China-Africa relations and his diplomatic policies towards Africa align with the essence of China-Africa friendship and basic norms of international relations. They reflect the solid bond between China and Africa and serve as the foundational principles for the everlasting friendship between the two.

(2) Optimize Top-level Design. The "going global" strategy for vocational education is a systemic project and will become a crucial content and significant measure for the current and future development of vocational education. At the national level, there should be a systematic plan for vocational colleges to serve companies "going global." We should strengthen policy guidance and financial input, enhance process management and monitoring, establish the "Belt and Road" vocational education research center, introduce guiding policies for companies "going global", clarify the strategic positioning and role of the "going global" initiative, and specify its nature, purpose, and operational scope. For companies participating in vocational education, we should draft favorable "going global" measures, encouraging these companies to allocate a portion of their investment or operational funds towards vocational education.

(3) Deepening Integrated Development. We must remain sincere, treat each other with honesty, and pursue win-win cooperation. Vocational education should be better integrated with industrial exports, and with the needs of African countries. Through the integrated development between various specialties within China-Africa and between specialty groups and industrial chains, we can better adapt to the rapid iterations of vocations brought by new technologies and enhance the capability of vocational education services.

(4) Resource Platform Integration. The advancement of China's vocational education faces the challenge of how to plan, optimize, coordinate, and integrate resource connectivity among different disciplines. Addressing this issue not only facilitates the better execution of tasks but also aids in the construction of shared resource platforms, the optimization and integration of resources from all sides, thus reducing difficulties encountered during the vocational education advancement.

For instance, consider establishing a high-level vocational college alliance for China-Africa vocational education cooperation. This could help in refining the educational model, broadening educational approaches, realizing resource complementarity, and expanding spaces for educational cooperation like talent cultivation and pedagogical research. By promoting the idea of vocational colleges "going global" as a group, we can enhance their educational strengths. Another consideration could be the establishment of a China-Africa vocational education industry-education alliance, effectively creating an enterprise "going global" service platform. This would better explore the deeply integrated talent cultivation model of vocational education with production and education, bolstering cooperation and exchanges among governments, schools, enterprises, and sectors. This also promotes scientific research, teaching development, funding integration, etc., to realize the advantage of resource consolidation.

2. Innovate Internationalization Pathways, Expand Domains for Stability.

(1) Active Promotion of In-depth Cooperation. Strengthen exchanges and cooperation with international organizations and professional institutions in the field of vocational education. Build think tanks, alliances, forums, and research bases related to vocational education. Actively participate in the governance of African vocational education, deeply involved in the formulation of African vocational education rules, standards, and evaluation systems.

(2) Actively Explore Overseas Education. The newly revised *Vocational Education Law* suggests that the nation encourages foreign exchanges and cooperation in the field of vocational education, supports the introduction of high-quality resources from abroad for vocational education development, and promotes qualified vocational education institutions to set up schools abroad. It also supports the mutual recognition of vocational education learning outcomes in various forms. China-Africa vocational education should strengthen cooperation and exchanges in terms of mutual recognition of degrees, standard intercommunication, and mutual learning from experiences, establishing talent training bases and primarily addressing issues like lack of talent utilization and suitability.

(3) Actively Innovate Cooperation Models. The Confucius Institute serves as a significant platform for promoting the Chinese language and culture abroad. In Africa, the combination of "language culture + vocational and technical education" is an effective model for the Confucius Institute to enhance its educational standards and levels.

3. Deepen Intrinsic Development, Emphasize Quality for Excellence.

(1) Adhere to Demand Orientation. Based on the demand orientation of China-Africa regional economic development and industrial transformation and upgrading, follow the principle of "what locals want, we provide." Thus enhance the connection between specialized programs and the local industrial structure. According to the needs of Chinese-funded enterprises, support African vocational education in launching relevant training courses with precision, crafting distinctive service platforms and brands, optimizing staff allocation to the fullest extent, and achieving higher economic and social benefits.

(2) It's essential to align with international standards. Establishing a "going global" standard

system for vocational education will showcase the Chinese vocational education brand. The aim of Chinese vocational education "venturing into Africa" is not merely to address the talent shortage faced by Chinese-funded enterprises and local enterprises in Africa. More importantly, it seeks to introduce China's vocational education standards, techniques, and culture to Africa, further elevating the brand of China's vocational education development.

(3) It's crucial to strengthen the construction of the teaching faculty. Educators are the implementers of vocational training towards Africa. Only teachers equipped with the "going global" capability can ensure the thriving development of Chinese vocational education in Africa.

(4) A firm commitment to quality is indispensable. A comprehensive quality assurance mechanism for vocational education cooperation with Africa should be established. By drawing from the successful experiences of developed countries in the internationalization of vocational education, relevant oversight measures should be implemented. This includes organizing specialized departments for educational quality audit and supervision, periodically reviewing the quality of education, ensuring that the educational standards of Chinese vocational institutions meet the developmental requirements of the host African countries

4. Establish Collaborative Frameworks to Ensure Sustainable Progress

(1) Strengthen Policy Guidance. Leverage the influence of policy as a catalyst, intensify the link between industrial and educational policies, support eligible schools and enterprises in their collaborations with vocational education institutions in African countries, explore the establishment of an educational evaluation system that reflects the direction of integrated international cooperation between industry and education, encourage tertiary vocational institutions to actively serve and deeply integrate into international regional cooperation and industrial development, and promote innovative integration of industry and education.

(2) Refine Collaboration Mechanisms. Perfect a cross-departmental coordination mechanism that involves the Ministry of Education, Ministry of Foreign Affairs, Ministry of Commerce, National Development and Reform Commission, Ministry of Finance, and the Office of Chinese Language Council International, among other related departments and national industry organizations. Gather educational resources through various channels and jointly lay out the "going global" strategy.

(3) Consolidate Collective Efforts. Harness the roles of various groups and communities, such as the youth, women, overseas Chinese, and other organizations, with a primary focus on vocational and technical education training for African youth. Assist them in expanding their employment and entrepreneurship platforms and offer vocational skills and medical Chinese training to Chinese-funded enterprises, local governments, and hospitals.

(4) Enhance the intrinsic motivation for "going global". Guide and encourage vocational

institutions to adopt the model of "where the enterprises go, vocational education follows". By streamlining the approval processes for overseas assignments and providing a "green channel" for title evaluations and preferential compensation for dispatched teachers, the enthusiasm of vocational schools for "going global" can be amplified.

Chapter XI

Reports on China-Senegal Capacity Cooperation in Vocational Education Cooperation Services

The Republic of Senegal (La République du Sénégal) is located in West Africa, with a land area of 196,700 square kilometers. It borders the Atlantic Ocean to the west and has a coastline of about 700 kilometers. The country has a tropical savanna climate. There are 14 regions containing 45 provinces, with a population of 16.3 million (2020) and the capital is Dakar.

China established diplomatic relations with Senegal in December 1971, but the diplomatic ties between the two countries were suspended from January 1996 due to Senegal's resumption of diplomatic relations with "Taiwan". The two countries did not restore ambassadorial-level diplomatic relations until October 2005. In recent years, the bilateral relationship between Senegal and China has developed smoothly. In September 2016, China and Senegal established a comprehensive strategic partnership. During the period of maintaining diplomatic relations, China has assisted Senegal in building projects such as the Friendship Stadium, the Afiniam Dam, and the National Grand Theater.

11.1 Overview of Senegal's Economy, Industries, and Education

11.1.1 Economic Situation

Senegal is one of the least developed countries. In 2014, the Senegalese government launched the Emerging Senegal Plan (PSE), which aims to improve the investment and business environment, strengthen infrastructure construction, promote the development of small and medium-sized enterprises, encourage the development of high value-added and labor-intensive outward-oriented economy, etc. In recent years, influenced by investment and agricultural production, Senegal's economy has shown some resilience. In 2021, Senegal's gross domestic product (GDP) was about $27.625 billion, a year-on-year increase of 6.06%[a]. It is expected that the total GDP in 2022 will be $28.435 billion (ranked 111th in the world), and the per capita GDP

---

a https://www.imf.org/en/Publications/WEO/weo-database/2022/April

will be $4,092 (ranked 158th)[a](See Table 11–1).

Table 11–1 Gross GDP of Senegal for the Three Years 2020, 2021 and 2022 (Unit value: $1 billion)

Year	2020	2021	2022
At the average exchange rate	24.534	27.640	28.435
By purchasing power	58.665	64.810	72.341

Source: International Monetary Fund

Currently, agriculture remains the fundamental industry in Senegal, while the service sector has the most potential to drive economic growth. Due to the impact of the COVID-19 pandemic, the development of the country's oil and gas projects has been repeatedly delayed, and it is not expected to generate any economic benefits before 2035[b].

11.1.2 Environment for Industrial Development

1. Industrial Status

Senegal is one of the least developed countries according to the United Nations, with 56% of the population engaged in agricultural production and possessing a certain industrial foundation. The development of the tertiary industry is relatively fast. In 2020, the proportion of the primary industry, the secondary industry, and the tertiary industry in Senegal's GDP was 16.2%, 22.2%, and 50.7%, respectively (See Table 11–2).

Table 11–2 Senegal's Gross Domestic Product and Share of Industries, 2016–2020

Year	2016	2017	2018	2019	2020
Gross Domestic Product (ten thousand FCFA)	112,830	122,720	134,090	143,340	139,328
The Proportion of Primary Industry	16.1%	17.9%	18.5%	18.6%	16.2%
The Proportion of Secondary Industry	26.0%	25.2%	25.4%	25.2%	22.2%
Proportion of Tertiary Industry	57.9%	56.9%	56.2%	56.2%	50.7%
Annual Growth Rate	6.4%	7.1%	6.8%	6.6%	0.7%

Source: National Statistical Office of Senegal (ANSD)

Rice and peanut planting are the main agricultural productions, and the food supplies are not

a Department of Outward Investment and Economic Cooperation, Ministry of Commerce. (2022). Guide to Investment and Cooperation Countries (Regions) of the Ministry of Commerce: Senegal (2021 Edition).

b https//www.worldbank.org/en/country/senegal/overview

self-sufficient as well. Fisheries, phosphate exports, and tourism are traditional industries for earning foreign exchange. After President Sall took office, he prioritized the development of an outward-looking economy with high added value and labor intensity, promoted the development of small and medium-sized enterprises, attracted foreign investment, and attached importance to infrastructure construction. The International Monetary Fund believes that Senegal's revitalization and development plan has effectively promoted economic development[a].

2. Industrial Distribution

(1) Primary Industry

Agriculture remains the main economic pillar of Senegal, with about 60% of the population living in rural areas. The country has a cultivable land area of 3.8 million hectares, with cereal crops accounting for 41% of the sown area. Rice is the staple food of Senegal, and other cereal crops include millet, maize, and sorghum. Rice and millet together account for over two-thirds of the total cereal production (See Table 11–3). The major cash crops such as peanuts, cotton, sesame, tropical fruits, vegetables, and flowers are grown on a planting area of 920,000 hectares, accounting for 47% of the total cultivated land. Agricultural production is mainly dominated by household farming and informal sectors, which are highly susceptible to changes in rainfall conditions and soil quality, posing challenges to food self-sufficiency.

Table 11–3 Production of Major Cereals in Senegal in 2020

	Output (ten thousand tons)	Percentage
Rice	134.97	37.1%
Millet	114.48	31.4%
Maize	76.18	20.9%
Sorghum	37.73	10.4%
Foniomi	0.67	0.1%

Source: Food and Agriculture Organization of the United Nations

Animal husbandry in Senegal mainly focuses on raising cattle and sheep (See Table 11–4), with production methods including modern animal husbandry, settled animal husbandry, and extensive migratory animal husbandry. Among them, dairy products dominate the diet in Senegal and provide millions of job opportunities for the country[b].

a Department of Outward Investment and Economic Cooperation, Ministry of Commerce. (2022). Guidelines on Outward Investment and Cooperation by the Ministry of Commerce: Senegal (2021 edition).

b Xu Guannan, Wang Zhan. Analysis of Agricultural investment perspective in Senegal [J] Investment Africa.2022.9.

Table 11–4 Stock of Major Livestock Products in Senegal in 2020 (Unit: 10,000 Head)

Sheep	Goats	Cattle	Pigs	Horses	Poultry
742.63	640.52	371.27	47.81	57.88	8.84

Source: Food and Agriculture Organization of the United Nations

The fishery is another economic pillar of Senegal and the largest foreign exchange earning industry, accounting for 16% of the total exports. Senegal has a coastline of 718 kilometers with abundant marine fishery resources, while traditional fishing methods are still dominant with low mechanization level, resulting in relatively light pollution to the marine environment and promoting sustainable development of the fishery industry. There are nearly 120 seafood processing companies nationwide, and about 600,000 people are engaged in fishing, processing, sales, trade and other related professions. China Fisheries Corporation has established fishing companies and processing plants in Senegal, which is the leading enterprise in the local industry.

Overall, the primary sector of Senegal has shown a rapid growth trend since the 1980s (See Figure 11–1).

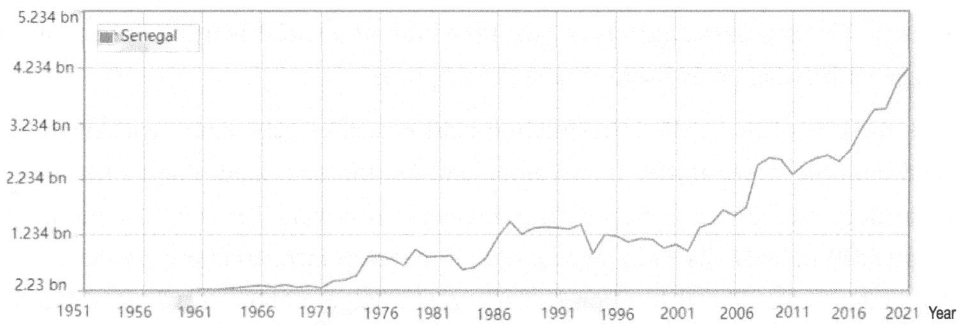

Figure 11–1 Trend of Value Added in Agriculture, Forestry, Animal Husbandry and Fisheries in Senegal (Unit: US Dollar)

(2) Secondary Industry

The secondary industry in Senegal mainly focuses on agricultural product processing, food, chemical industry, textile, leather, refining, building materials, and infrastructure. The industrial output value accounts for about 22% of the GDP, with more than 500 enterprises nationwide, and 85% of factory enterprises concentrated in the capital, Dakar. The food processing industry is the most important industrial sector, accounting for about 40% of the annual industrial added value. The chemical industry accounts for 12% of the annual industrial added value, mainly producing phosphates and fertilizers. In recent years, Senegal has vigorously promoted the development of energy and mining industries, especially the oil and gas industry, and it is expected to become a new growth point for the economic development of Senegal in the future[a].

Transportation industry. Highways: The total length of highways in Senegal is 16,495 kilometers, including 5,956 kilometers of asphalt roads and 10,539 kilometers of dirt roads. 83% of the asphalt roads and 57% of the dirt roads are in good condition. In addition, there are 216 kilometers of expressways; Railways: The total length of railways is 1,300 kilometers, with a main line length of 905 kilometers. However, due to long-term disrepair and insufficient capacity, safety accidents occur from time to time; Aviation: Senegal is the headquarters of African Civil Aviation, and is also an important aviation hub in West Africa. 28 airlines operate here, connecting Europe, America and more than 20 countries in Africa. In addition, second-tier airports such as Ziguinchor and Saint-Louis are also included in the government's plan.

Real estate industry. In recent years, the housing construction market in Senegal has been quite hot. However due to the construction of the new city Diamniadio, private property developers dominate the market, and there are few government bidding projects, leading to prominent issues in the standardization of the real estate industry. In addition, the complicated process of bank housing loans and the high cost of foreign investment limit the development speed of the real estate industry. The Senegalese government's promotion of a social housing project of 100,000 units has a potentially high risk due to restricted sale prices.

Overall, the size of Senegal's infrastructure market is relatively small, with many limiting factors and multiple uncertainties in development. On the one hand, due to factors such as multilateral debt, the government's budget investment is very limited, and public-private partnership (PPP) models has to be encouraged to develop infrastructure; on the other hand, Senegal's unique geographical location has attracted a large number of Chinese and foreign-funded infrastructure companies to settle in, and the competition in the infrastructure market is fierce (See Figure 11–2).

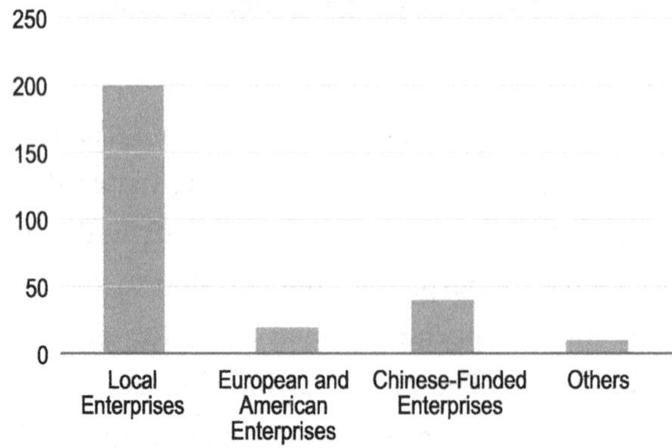

Source: The Reseach Project

Figure 11–2 Distribution of Infrastructure Enterprises in Senegal

a Research and Development Department of China-Africa Development Fund. Senegal [J] China Investment. 2020.9.

(3) Tertiary Industry

Tourism is one of the four pillars of Senegal's economy. Its advantageous geographical location, rich tourism resources, and convenient tourism transportation have made Senegal one of the most developed countries in West Africa and even Africa's tourism industry. The development of Senegal's tourism industry is not only benefited from its abundant tourism resources but also from its flexible tourism development strategies, such as developing multiple centers for seaside resort tourism, actively developing rural tourism, and fully utilizing national parks for sightseeing tourism[a]. Tourists mainly come from developed countries in Europe and America, with France, Italy, and Spain accounting for more than 50% of the total number of tourists. The main tourist attractions are concentrated in the Dakar, Thies, and Saint-Louis regions[b].

3. Education System

During the early period of independence, education in Senegal developed rapidly, but the education system was still the same as the former colonial power France. It was divided into four stages: preschool education, primary education, secondary education, and higher education. The diplomas obtained by students were also recognized by France.

In 2013, the enrollment rate for primary school in Senegal was 93%, for junior high school it was 89%, and for senior high school it was 29%[c]. There were 112,000 university students enrolled. There are 5 public universities, more than 10 higher vocational colleges, and over 80 private colleges and universities in the country. Among them, the University of Dakar, founded in 1957, is one of the institutions of higher education with a long history, with 21 faculties and more than 70,000 students currently enrolled.

Since 2014, the overall enrollment rate for preschool, primary and secondary education, as well as the proportion of those receiving higher education, have all increased. In terms of vocational and technical training, the enrollment rate has risen from 3.15% in 2012 to 13% in 2017. The proportion of young graduates in their careers has increased from 29% in 2013 to 36% in 2017. At the same time, the government has established vocational training clusters in the agriculture, poultry, and tourism sectors, as well as training centers specifically for the construction and mechanical industries. The Senegalese education system is mainly divided into preschool education, primary education, secondary education, and higher education. Vocational and technical training is mainly distributed in secondary and higher education (Figure 11–3). Education at all levels is the responsibility of the Ministry of National Education and the

---

a Zhang Jinluo. The Rapidly Developing Tourism Industry in Senegal [J]. Reference for Chinese Geography teaching. 2000(03):19-20.

b Research and Development Department of the China-Africa Development Fund. Senegal [J]. China Investment (Chinese and English) 2020(28):92-94.

c Department of Outward Investment and Economic Cooperation, Ministry of Commerce. (2022). Guidelines on Country (Region) for Outward Investment and Cooperation of the Ministry of Commerce: Senegal (2021 Edition).

Ministry of Higher Education, while vocational and technical education is the responsibility of the Ministry of Vocational and Technical Education and Training (MFPAI). Education funding is generally composed of national appropriations, local funds, and foreign aid.

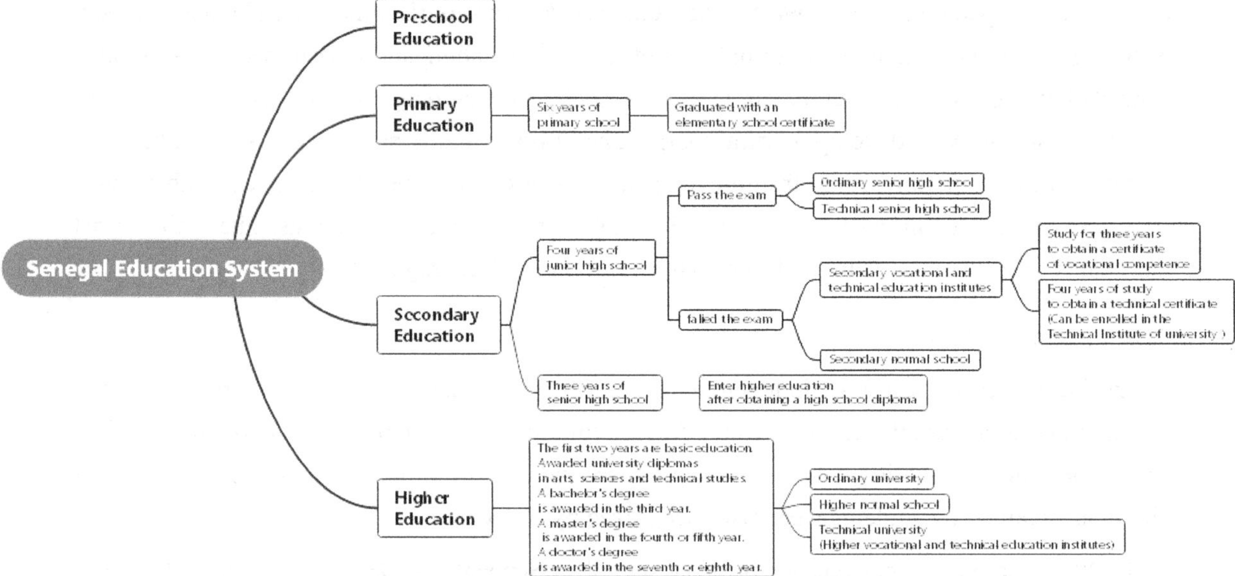

Figure 11–3 Senegalese National Education System

In the 1990s, Senegal began to improve the quality of vocational training to enhance the employ ability of all young people. Following the vocational training assessment conducted by the International Organization of La Francophonie in Bamako in 1998, Senegal organized a national technical education and vocational training assessment conference in 2001. Based on the recommendations of the Bamako assessment conference, the evaluation was a thorough reform of the country's technical and vocational education and training system. Subsequently, the Vocational Education Department was established in 2002. With the support of the French Cooperation Agency and the World Bank, Senegal's vocational education reform also promoted the establishment of the Vocational Training Development Foundation.

In 2003, the Ministry of Education emphasized that technical education and vocational training, like basic education, is a high priority in Senegal's education policy in response to the needs of economic and social development. The importance of strengthening school-enterprise cooperation was also emphasized. In 2006, the Ministry of Vocational and Technical Education and Training (MFPAI) pointed out that the development of technical education and vocational training should be the main competitiveness of Senegal's economic growth.

The main purpose of vocational training in Senegal is to provide students with theoretical knowledge and practical skills in specific fields. Vocational schools in Senegal offer initial or continuing vocational education, providing fixed-term courses in various fields, and the number of vocational schools is increasing day by day. Students can choose training courses of corresponding years according to their actual situation. And regardless of the type of course, they will receive corresponding diplomas after passing the assessment at the end of the course.

In Senegal, the National Agency for the Quality Assurance of Higher Education, Research and Innovation (ANAQ-Sup) inspects and trains schools on teaching quality; while the African and Malagasy Council for Higher Education (CAMES) is responsible for certifying diplomas issued by higher education institutions of the member states.

4. Vocational Education and Industry

According to statistical data, there are about 380 schools and training institutions at all levels in Senegal's education system, of which 126 are vocational and technical training colleges and institutions. This study analyzed the matching degree between Senegal's vocational education majors and the national industries. Only 6 colleges and institutions offer majors related to agriculture, animal husbandry and fishery, while 21 offer majors related to industry, transportation and infrastructure, and 99 offer majors related to commerce, finance, tourism, language training, etc. Overall, the situation of vocational colleges offering majors in Senegal is basically in line with the proportion of GDP in various industries. However, there is a significant shortage of vocational colleges offering majors related to the primary industry, and an oversupply of vocational colleges offering majors related to the tertiary industry. Therefore, Senegal has problems such as a mismatch between the current situation of vocational education majors and the industrial structure, single major types, and unreasonable major layout (See Figure 11–4).

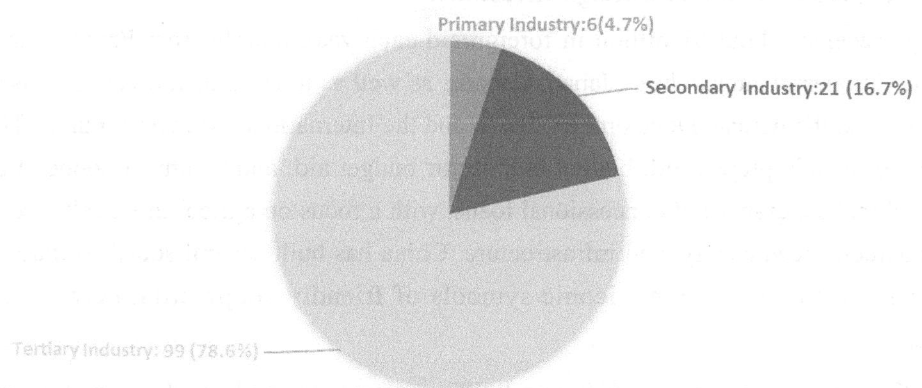

Figure 11–4 Matching Chart of Majors Offered by Vocational Colleges and Industries

5. International Economic and Trade Cooperation

France has always been Senegal's largest source of imports[a]. In 2017, Senegal's imports from France reached 1,294% of its exports to France. In terms of labor exports, France is the main destination for Senegal's overseas labor exports. The remittances brought by Senegalese

a Chen Lijuan, Obstacles to independent development faced by contemporary African countries: A case study of Senegal, French Countries and Regions Research, 2020(03):1–10+91.

immigrants account for 10% of the country's GDP, far exceeding the funds obtained from foreign direct investment, national debt, and development assistance.

Since 2019, Senegal's main import sources are France, China, Nigeria, India, and the Netherlands, while its main export destinations are Switzerland, Mali, Spain, Cote d'Ivoire, China, and Italy. France, China, and India are Senegal's top three trading partners.

Its main exports include non-monetary gold, seafood, cement, and phosphates, while its main imports include refined petroleum products, machinery and equipment, pharmaceuticals, and daily consumer goods. According to data from the Senegal Statistics Bureau, Senegal exported approximately $3.309 billion and imported approximately $7.049 billion in 2019, resulting in a trade deficit of approximately $3.74 billion[a].

Senegal is a formal member of the World Trade Organization since its foundation on January 1, 1995, one of the 15 member countries of the Economic Community of West African States (CEDEAO), a member of the West African Economic and Monetary Union (UEMOA), and a member of the Cotonou Agreement. Senegal is also a beneficiary country of the European Union's tariff preferences.

11.2 Cooperation between Chinese–Funded Enterprises and International Production Capacity

11.2.1 Senegal's Demand for Foreign Investment

Senegal receives about $1 billion in foreign aid each year, mainly from France, the United States, the European Union, China, Japan, Canada, as well as international organizations such as the World Bank, the African Development Bank, and the International Monetary Fund[b]. The main forms of aid include project aid, budget aid, sector budget aid, and technical cooperation. The types of aid include grants and concessional loans, with a focus on agriculture, health, education, water resources, green energy, and infrastructure. China has built several social welfare projects in Senegal, which have become iconic symbols of friendly cooperation between the two countries.

In 2008, China granted nearly 500 zero-tariff treatments to the least-developed countries in Africa (including Senegal)[c]. According to Chinese customs statistics, the total bilateral trade between China and Senegal in 2019 was $2.511 billion, a year-on-year increase of 10.58%.

---

a Department of Outward Investment and Economic Cooperation, Ministry of Commerce. (2022). Guidelines on Foreign Investment and Cooperation Countries (Regions) of the Ministry of Commerce: Senegal (2021 Edition).

b Ministry of Commerce of the People's Republic of China. Assistance to Senegal by various countries, international and regional organizations. 2013.

c The Central People's Government of the People's Republic of China. China granted partial product duty-free treatment to the least developed countries in Africa.2009.

Among them, China's total exports to Senegal were $2.211 billion, a year-on-year increase of 3.18%. China has become Senegal's second largest source of imports. China's total imports from Senegal were $300 million, a year-on-year increase of 133.9%. According to statistics from the Chinese Ministry of Commerce, the total trade volume between the two countries in 2020 was $2.88 billion, of which China's total exports to Senegal were $2.56 billion, and China's total imports from Senegal were $320 million. As of the end of 2020, China's direct investment stock in Senegal was $430 million (See Table 11–5).

Table 11–5 Statistics of Imports and Exports between Senegal and China (Unit: Hundred million US dollar)

Year	Total Trade	Chinese Exports to Senegal	Chinese Imports from Senegal
2016	23.56	21.94	1.62
2017	21.90	20.41	1.50
2018	22.71	21.43	1.29
2019	25.11	22.11	3.00

Source: Chinese Customs Website (www.hgsj.com).

China's main categories of exported goods to Senegal include: ①mechanical and electrical products, including machinery, electrical and electronic products, household appliances (refrigerators, air conditioners, washing machines, electric fans, microwave ovens, etc.); ②transportation equipment, including motorcycles and accessories, trucks, cars, bicycles; ③clothing and accessories; ④metal products, mainly including steel and aluminum; ⑤ceramic products, mainly including ceramic tiles for construction; ⑥footwear; ⑦furniture and its parts; ⑧food; ⑨bags; ⑩eyeglasses.

China's main categories of imported goods from Senegal include: ①peanuts and peanut oil; ②marine products, mainly frozen fish; ③zirconium ore and titanium ore sand. In addition, there are small amounts of sesame seeds and logs imported.

11.2.2 Development of Chinese-Funded Enterprises and Production Capacity Cooperation

Against the background of the building of "Belt and Road", international Production Capacity Cooperation, and Chinese companies "going global", China and Senegal established a comprehensive strategic partnership in 2016 and signed a memorandum of understanding on the building of "Belt and Road". In addition, the two countries also signed a memorandum of understanding on cooperation in the field of infrastructure, established a bilateral economic and trade joint commission, and confirmed preferential trade arrangements and cultural cooperation mechanisms. Currently, China is Senegal's second largest trading partner and the largest source of financing.

In September 2018, the government of Senegal and Sichuan Province, China signed an agreement to promote production capacity cooperation between the two regions, successfully establishing a new model of international production capacity cooperation called “one province connecting with one country”. Enterprises such as Sichuan Railway Investment Group, Sichuan Energy Investment Group, and Huaxi Energy participated in construction projects in Senegal related to transportation, energy, and environmental protection.

Chinese-funded enterprises in Senegal mainly engage in industries such as seafood processing, peanut processing and export, retail, and infrastructure construction. According to the Chinese Embassy in Senegal, there are about 8,000 employees of Chinese-funded enterprises and overseas Chinese in Senegal, mainly concentrated in the capital city of Dakar, engaged in contracting projects, commodity trade, processing and manufacturing, fishing, customs clearance logistics, catering and tourism, etc. According to the Chinese Ministry of Commerce, in 2019, Chinese-funded enterprises signed 35 new contracting projects in Senegal, with a new contract value of $1.025 billion and a completed turnover of $884 million. A total of 705 labor service personnel were dispatched, and there were 2,967 labor service personnel in Senegal at the end of the year. Large-scale contracting projects signed in 2019 include the Dakar BRT project undertaken by China Road and Bridge Corporation, the Enwo City project undertaken by Weihai International Economic and Technical Cooperation Co., Ltd., and the Senegal GRAND SICAP housing project undertaken by China Overseas Economic Cooperation Ltd. In 2020, Chinese-funded enterprises signed 35 new contracting projects in Senegal, with a new contract value of $1.489 billion and a completed turnover of $521 million. A total of 392 labor service personnel were dispatched, and there were 1,105[a] labor service personnel in Senegal at the end of 2020. Currently, China has established two Chinese business associations and communities in Senegal, and 63 major Chinese-funded enterprises and institutions are developing in Senegal (See Tables 11–6 and 11–7).

Table 11–6 Statistics on the Industries Involved in the Main Chinese-Funded Enterprises in Senegal

No.	Industry	Involvement Areas of Chinese-Funded Enterprises in Senegal	Number of Chinese-Funded Enterprises	Name of the Main Chinese-Funded Enterprises in Senegal
1	Primary Industry	Fishery	5	China Fisheries Co., Ltd.

a Ministry of Commerce of the People's Republic of China. [R]. Guide to Investment and Cooperation Countries (Regions) - Senegal, 2021.

continued

No.	Industry	Involvement Areas of Chinese-Funded Enterprises in Senegal	Number of Chinese-Funded Enterprises	Name of the Main Chinese-Funded Enterprises in Senegal
2	Secondary Industry	Engineering	36	China Road and Bridge Engineering Co., Ltd.
3		Mechanical	4	China National Machinery Import and Export (Group) Co., Ltd.
4		Manufacturing	2	Guangzhou Senda International Group Investment
5		Energy	2	Gezhouba Group Company
6		Aviation	2	China Aerospace Construction Co., Ltd.
7		Building Materials	1	Nanjing Atlantic Building Materials Co., Ltd.
8		Agricultural Processing	1	SSJ Peanut Processing Plant
9	Tertiary Industry	Communication	2	Huawei Technologies Co. Ltd.
10		Logistics	2	Greenford logistics
11		Scientific and Technological	2	Zhongan Technology Co., Ltd.
12		Transportation	1	China Heavy Duty Automobile Group Co., Ltd.
13		Media	1	China Startimes Group Co., Ltd.
14		Foreign Trade	1	Huafei International Trading Co., Ltd.
15		Financial	1	Export-import Bank of China

Table 11–7 Contracted Projects by China in Senegal from 2016 to 2020 (Unit: $100 million)

Year	New Contract Value	Completed Turnover
2016	10.41	6.00
2017	7.45	9.48
2018	4.04	11.43
2019	10.25	8.84
2020	14.89	5.21

Source: Website of the Ministry of Commerce of the People's Republic of China

Introduction to key industries of Chinese-funded enterprises in senegal:

In the field of fisheries, China National Fisheries Corporation plans to build new fish processing plants in important fishing ports such as Saint Louis and Casamance to help local fishermen expand their product sales, create employment opportunities, and modernize local fish processing, so as to promote comprehensive economic and social development in Senegal, and provide stable sources of income for local fishermen (See Table 11–8).

Table 11–8 International Production Production Capacity Cooperation Projects of Major Chinese-Funded Enterprises in Senegal's Aquaculture Industry

Name of Chines-Funded Enterprises	Name of Projects	Partner	Cooperation Time	Achievements
China National Fisheries Corporation	Establishment of the Senegal fishing Company	African Seafood Company	1994	Acquired the African Seafood Company to become a leading enterprise in fisheries processing in Senegal

In the field of engineering, Chinese infrastructure companies have built different career development channels for local employees, providing them with stable sources of income. Employees can unleash their potential and achieve career success in every position, and many local workers have grown into infrastructure technology experts. The completed projects have greatly promoted the social, economic, and cultural development of the local area (See Table 11–9).

Table 11–9 Overview of International Production Capacity Cooperation Projects of Major Chinese-Funded Enterprises in Senegal's Infrastructure Construction

Name of Chines-Funded Enterprises	Name of Projects	Partner	Cooperation Time	Scale
Wuhan Company of China Railway Seventh Group	The Fongioni Bridge	The city of Fongioni	2019	1,600 meters
Hunan Construction Engineering Group	Competitive wrestling in Senegal	The city of Dakar	2021	18,000 square meters, can accommodate 20,000 people, the first modern wrestling arena in Africa

This project is the most important supporting project for the expansion of the third production line of Sahel Cement Company, the largest cement production enterprise in Senegal. It adopts full European standard design and construction, and is equipped with heavy oil generators that can be converted into dual fuel mode. After completion, it will meet all the power needs of Sahel Cement Company, increase Senegal's installed capacity by about 5%, and help the development of the country's infrastructure construction (See Table 11–10).

Table 11–10 Overview of International Production Capacity Cooperation Projects of Major Chinese-Funded Enterprises in Senegal's Energy Industry

Name of Chinese-Funded Enterprises	Name of Projects	Partner	Cooperation Time	Scale
Gezhouba Group of Energy China	Sahel Cement Company dual-fuel power plant project	Sahel Cement Company	2020	55 megawatts

In the field of communication, Huawei Technologies Co., Ltd.'s "Smart Senegal" project was highly praised by the Senegalese government, believing that it will help the government to response to the epidemic more efficiently and timely; the establishment of an international data center means that Senegal will have data sovereignty. ZTE Corporation's "Promoting Digital Informationization in Remote Areas of Senegal" project will provide a platform for people living in remote areas to have the opportunity to use the internet and enjoy electronic information services (See Table 11–11).

Table 11–11 Overview of International Production Capacity Cooperation Projects of Major Chinese-Funded Enterprises in Senegal's Communication Industry

Name of Chinese-Funded Enterprises	Name of Projects	Partner	Cooperation Time	Achievements
Huawei Technologies Co., Ltd.	National Data Centre and the "Smart Senegal" project	Information Bureau of Segenal	2020	The national data center was built
ZTE Corporation	Promoting Digital Informationization in Remote Areas of Senegal	Ministry of Post and Telecommunications of Senegal	2016	The country will be digitized by 2025

China's aid to Africa's "Ten Thousand Villages" project has benefited 600 villages in Senegal, providing free satellite TV reception equipment for local residents in remote rural areas to watch TV and receive information from the outside world more conveniently. The establishment of the Senegal subsidiary of China Startimes Group Co., LTD is not only beneficial for the long-term operation and maintenance of the "Ten Thousand Villages Project", but also provides new TV service options for local viewers, which helps the development of local digital TV business (See Table 11–12).

Table 11–12 Overview of International Production Capacity Cooperation Projects of Major Chinese-Funded Enterprises in Senegal's Media Industry

Name of Chinese-Funded Enterprises	Name of Projects	Partner	Cooperation Time	Achievements
China Startimes Group Co., Ltd.	The second phase of the "Ten Thousand Villages Project" in Senegal	Department of Information, Ministry of Culture and Public Information, Senegal	2021	In Senegal, 300 villages have installed solar TV sets, solar projection equipment and digital set-top boxes in public areas and homes.
	Set up Startimes Group subsidiary internal		2022	180 TV channels are available

The completion of the ceramic production line is another witness to the high-level and high-quality development of the comprehensive strategic partnership between China and Senegal. As the first ceramic enterprise in Senegal, the factory directly employs more than 1,000 employees and indirectly drives more than 2,000 people to employment, with 95% of the production materials coming from Senegal. The products will be sold to neighboring countries such as Mauritania, Mali, Guinea, and Gambia, greatly promoting the development of the domestic ceramic industry (See Table 11–13).

Table 11–13 Overview of International Production Capacity Cooperation Projects of Major Chinese-Funded Enterprises in Senegal's Manufacturing Sector

Name of Chinese -Funded Enterprises	Name of Projects	Partner	Cooperation Time	Achievements
Guangdong Keda Clean Energy Co., Ltd. and Guangzhou Senda International Group investment	The Tefu Ceramics factory project	The city of Centia	2020	More than 50,000 square meters of ceramic products per day. The annual tax is estimated at $6 million

During the initial stage of the project, the Sichuan Branch of the China Export-Import Bank provided external contracting project loans to the construction enterprise Sichuan Road and Bridge Construction Group Co., Ltd., and issued guarantees in a timely manner to meet the requirements of commercial terms and solve the contractor's funding gap problem. It effectively played its functional role, actively participated in major projects of the "Belt and Road", and helped achieve greater results in the construction of the "Belt and Road" (See Table 11–14).

Table 11–14 Overview of International Production Capacity Cooperation Projects of Major Chinese-Funded Enterprises in the Financial Sector in Senegal

Name of Chinese-Funded Enterprises	Name of Projects	Partner	Cooperation Time	Scale
the Sichuan Branch of the Export-Import Bank	The second phrase of Gamnyagu Integrated Industrial Park in Senegal	The city of Gamnyajou	2021	306,300 square meters

11.2.3 Talent Needs of Chinese-Funded Enterprises and Industry & Education Cooperation

In 2015, the National Development and Reform Commission, the Ministry of Foreign Affairs, and the Ministry of Commerce jointly issued the Vision and Action Plan for Promoting the Building of the Silk Road Economic Belt and the 21st-Century Maritime Silk Road, proposing that infrastructure connectivity is a priority area for the construction of the "Belt and Road", and emphasizing the necessity of policy communication, facility connectivity, unimpeded trade, financial integration, and people-to-people bonds (the "Five Connectivities") between China and its partner countries. At the end of 2021, the Ministry of Education issued a letter in response to *Proposal No.2624 (Education No.091) of the Fourth Session of the 13th National Committee of the Chinese People's Political Consultative Conference*, which encouraged Chinese-funded enterprises to cooperate with vocational education to "going global" and serve the countries along the "Belt and Road" with "Chinese language + vocational skills" as the basis. With the encouragement and support of policies, the "going global" of Chinese-funded enterprises is a prerequisite for realizing international Production Capacity Cooperation, and cooperation with vocational colleges is an important way to optimize international Production Capacity Cooperation.

As mentioned above, Chinese-funded enterprises have wide coverage in the investment field in Senegal. Although the overall development trend is good, they still face difficulties. For example, the domestic market in Senegal is small and highly competitive, and the consumption level is low, resulting in poor infrastructure and engineering supporting capabilities and a lack of skilled technical workers. Chinese-funded enterprises need to introduce technical talents from China. The proportion of Chinese employees to local employees in Chinese-funded enterprises is about 7:3 (Figure 11–5), which leads to an increase in operating costs.

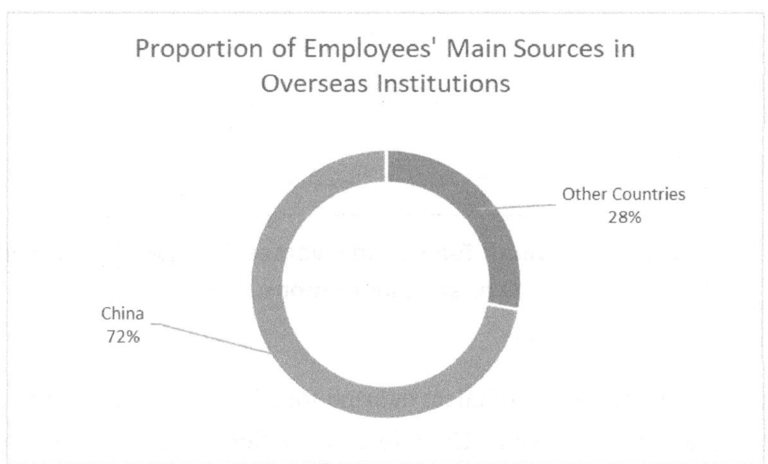

Figure 11–5 Proportion of Employees' Main Sources in Overseas Institutions

The Research Report on the Internationalization and Diversification Talent Strategy of State-owned Enterprises also pointed out the pain points of Chinese companies in serving the Belt and Road Initiative, which are difficult to access high-level talents and lack channels to find candidates. *The White Paper on Talent for the building of "Belt and Road"* conducted a survey on Chinese-funded enterprises serving countries along the "Belt and Road", of which 66% of enterprises believed that it was difficult to find high-level talents locally, and the job matching degree was low. The competitiveness of Chinese-funded enterprises in the local area is also low, reflected in the lack of competitiveness in salary and benefits (42%) and the lack of channels to find suitable candidates (36%) (Figure 11–6).

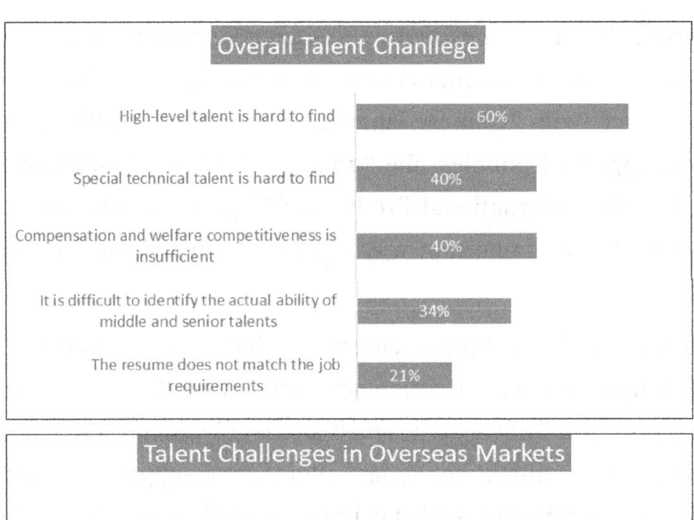

Figure 11–6 Proportion of Overall Talent and Overseas Market Talent Challenges for Overseas Institutions

Source: *White Paper on the "Belt and Road"*

To further confirm the pain points of talent demand for Chinese-funded enterprises in Senegal, our team conducted a survey on major Chinese construction enterprises in Senegal based on the professional characteristics of our college. The survey results showed that the cooperation between vocational colleges and Chinese-funded enterprises is not optimistic at present. All the interviewed enterprises have not carried out school-enterprise cooperation projects with domestic vocational colleges.

Based on the interview with Zhongdi Overseas Group[a]. The company believes that there are significant cultural differences and communication barriers with local employees, as well as differences in construction standards and regulations, making it difficult to establish a unified management mechanism. The company also mentioned in the survey that the Senegalese government has restrictions on the employment of foreign personnel by companies, therefore, a large number of Chinese skilled workers going to work in Senegal will greatly increase the

a Interview with the Head of China Geo-Engineering Corporation Overseas Senegal Branch, Location: Dakar, September 14, 2022.

company's cost pressure. Even though the localization of employees is the ideal result for all local Chinese-funded enterprises, it is still very difficult to achieve. The engineering industry is a labor-intensive industry with high personnel turnover, making it difficult to establish a sense of belonging among local employees.

Taking the example of the Diamniadio Industrial Park, which is funded by the government of Senegal and constructed by China Geo-Engineering Corporation International, it is located more than 30 kilometers east of the capital Dakar and is a highlight project of the *Plan for Emerging Senegal*. The construction of the industrial park aims to develop export-oriented industries rapidly by introducing foreign capital and technology. The construction of the park is supported by Chinese financing, and the project is undertaken by Chinese companies, with the operation of the park following the Chinese model. A vocational training and technical center has been established in the second phase of the park, which shows the urgent need for local high-quality skilled talents in Senegal[a]. According to the White Paper on the "Belt and Road" Initiative, the demand for senior technical talents ranks first (44%) in the recruitment of overseas talents by Chinese-funded enterprises (Figure 11–7).

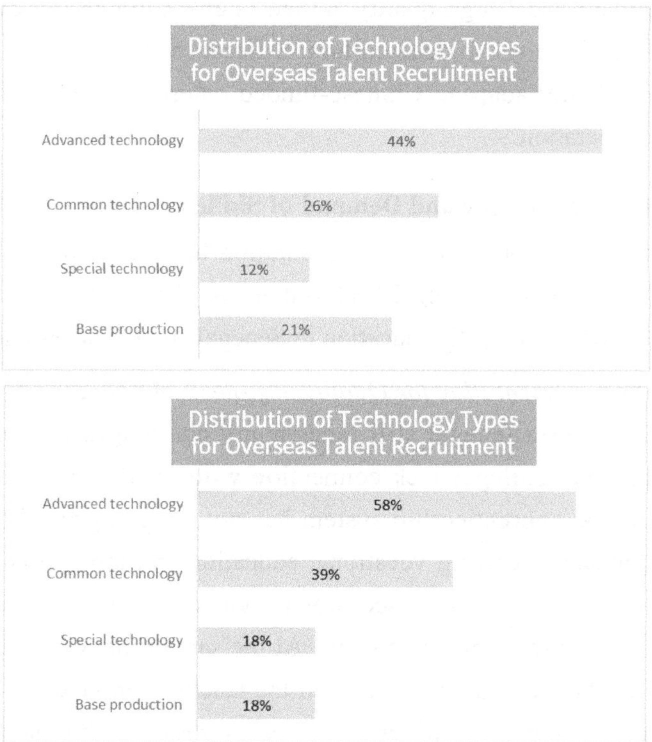

Figure 11–7 Distribution of Technology Types and Technology Level for Oversea Talent Recruitment

Source: White Paper on the "Belt and Road"

a Chen Zhan. Senegal Industrial Park Draws Lessons from China's Experience [CP/OL]. 2021–07–22

There are two main reasons why vocational colleges in China have very school-enterprise cooperation is the social responsibility of the enterprises little cooperation with Chinese companies. On the one hand, vocational colleges believe that school enterprises cooperation is the social responsibility of the enterprises, so they only advocate enterprises to participate in school-enterprise cooperation. However, in practice, as organizations that pursue profit maximization, it is difficult for the enterprises to actively participate in school-enterprise cooperation when their investment in vocational colleges is greater than their returns. This is especially true for enterprises in the countries along the "Belt and Road", who need to promote their own development and obtain the achievements of the "Belt and Road" through school-enterprise cooperation. Therefore, the advocacy-based school-enterprise cooperation model is difficult to attract these enterprises to participate deeply. On the other hand, there are many countries along the "Belt and Road", with different stages of development, different interests, and complex and intertwined conflicts, making it difficult to form an effective school-enterprise cooperation mechanism to serve international production capacity.

In this context, the governments of China and Senegal should further encourage Chinese-funded enterprises and vocational colleges to work together to increase joint overseas talent training projects, cultivate local high-quality skilled talents through the cooperation mode of government-school-enterprise and reduce cultural differences between China and Senegal, so as to help local talents better adapt to Chinese-funded enterprises, and promote international production capacity cooperation.

11.2.4 Imbalance between Supply and Demand of Skilled Talents

In addition to the reasons for the lack of cooperation between Chinese vocational colleges and Chinese-funded enterprises in Senegal analyzed above, there is still an asymmetry of talent demand between local vocational skills education in Senegal and Chinese-funded enterprises.

According to the *Improvement Plan for Quality, Fairness and Transparency in the Vocational Training Field (2013–2025)*, Senegal still faces many challenges in vocational education, for example the vocational colleges lack connection with local chambers of commerce and enterprises, the traditional apprenticeship system has not been improved, and the percentage of basic education graduates receiving vocational education and training is still below 30%. In Senegal, for example, traditional apprenticeships provided by the informal sector remain the most important way to acquire employable skills. At the same time, Chinese-funded enterprises in Senegal lack high-quality skilled personnel, and the teaching provided by the informal sector cannot meet the needs of enterprises, which is one of the reasons why the supply of vocational education personnel in Senegal does not match the talent demand of the Chinese-funded enterprises. Furthermore, Senegalese vocational schools lack cooperation with local enterprises. For example, "industry standards, joint training by schools and enterprises, and full government guarantees" should be the guarantee for training high-quality workers, but the lack of cooperation between local schools and enterprises has led to the teaching content and talent training mode formulated by vocational colleges cannot truly meet the needs of the labor market and achieve supply-demand balance.

In Senegal, regional, economic, and gender inequalities remain prominent, and students and women in some impoverished areas are unable to participate in skills training and to obtain corresponding qualifications, further exacerbating the shortage of skilled talent in Senegal. Due to economic issues, vocational and teacher training in Senegal cannot be widely implemented, and teachers' teaching abilities cannot be continuously improved, resulting in the outcome of vocational education cannot be guaranteed. In addition, the brain drain in Africa has also led to the asymmetry between vocational education in Senegal and the demand of Chinese-funded enterprises. In order to fill the gap of brain drain, African countries need to hire 150,000 foreign experts every year, with an annual expenditure of $4 billion, which means 35% of international development aid to Africa is used to pay for foreign experts[a]. Facing today's international talent flow, Africa is facing the problem of imbalance between talent inflow and outflow. Better living conditions and salaries abroad, unemployment, lack of social security, nepotism, tribalism, etc. are the main factors for brain drain in Africa. In this context, the number of high-quality skilled talents in Senegal cannot match the demand of Chinese-funded enterprises.

Although African governments are increasingly focusing on the development of vocational education, and the African Union issued the *African Strategy for the Revitalization of Technical and Vocational Education and Training* in 2007, Senegal's vocational education policies, systems, and models still need a lot of time to improve in order to meet the needs of the local labor market.

11.3 Exploration of Practical Collaboration between Vocational Colleges and Enterprises for "Going Global"

11.3.1 Development of Vocational Education in Senegal in the Context of International Aid

1. China's Assistance to Senegalese Vocational Education

Currently, China's assistance to Senegalese vocational education includes recruiting students to study in China, providing government scholarships, and supporting teachers and experts to provide online or offline teaching and training to the teachers and students in Senegalese vocational colleges. For example, in 2022, in the "Future Africa: Sino-Africa Vocational Education Cooperation Project" co-sponsored by the China Education Association for International Exchange and the Association of African Technical and Applied Universities and Colleges, 10 Chinese experts, including Professor Liu Yufeng and Professor Chen Mingkun,

a Li Zhiwei. The Loss of Talent, a Hindrance to the Development of African Society [CP/OL]. People's Daily. 2016-08-23.

and 14 higher vocational colleges across the country are invited to train teachers and students of African vocational colleges.

Among them are three faculty members and six students from the Saint Louis Institute of Technology in Senegal. In addition to the above conventional assistance models, the Chinese government also encourages Chinese vocational colleges to "go global" with local companies, and jointly serve international capacity cooperation with Senegalese vocational colleges through a "school-school-enterprise" approach. China's assistance to vocational education in Senegal mainly focuses on the construction industry, agriculture, and aquaculture. While providing financial and technical support to Senegal, China has also cultivated a batch of urgently needed talents for Senegal, to a certain extent, promoting the sustainable development of Senegal's economy and society.

2. Japan's Assistance to Senegalese Vocational Education

Japan's aid to Senegal began in 1991, focusing on two main themes 'Millennium Development Goals' and 'Sustainable Development'. The main aid projects include basic education, healthcare, rural drinking water and technical training. At the fifth Tokyo Conference, Japan pledged to train 30,000 Africans on the continent between 2013 and 2017 to help them find jobs. To achieve this, the Japanese government promised to establish Tokyo Conference on Business and Industry Human Resources Development Center in 10 locations and send employment-training experts to 10 African countries. Japan's aid in the field of vocational education mainly focuses on providing equipment to recipient countries and helping to establish vocational training centers.

Japan designated the Senegal-Japan Vocational Training Center as a model for educational assistance to Senegal. The center, jointly established by Japan and Senegal in 1984, aims to train intermediate and advanced technical personnel. Japan provides training materials, experts, and accepts trainees from Senegal. Currently, the center offers courses in electronics, electrical engineering, and automotive mechanics, and has trained a large number of technical talents for Senegal and other West African countries[a]. The center's students come not only from Senegal but also from other African countries where the official language is French. The center is considered one of the best technical training centers in West Africa. Finding the optimal balance between diplomatic strategy and economic development strategy is a key feature of Japan's foreign educational assistance.

3. French's Assistance to Senegalese Vocational Education

France is Senegal's largest bilateral aid donor. The strategic goal of aid to Senegal is to increase Senegal's economic competitiveness and promote sustainable and balanced growth of

a Economic and Commercial Office of the Embassy of the People's Republic of China in the Republic of Senegal. Japan's assistance to Senegal. 2013.

the national economy. As the leading contributor in the field of education in Senegal, France also supports Senegal's *Ten-Year Education Plan*, which plans to build various schools in the suburbs of Dakar and help Senegal become a beneficiary of the *Education for All* international fund[a]. In 2006, the two governments signed the *Framework Document for Partnership Cooperation.* In terms of vocational education, France will support the technological transformation of productive enterprises, especially private enterprises, and establish training centers to strengthen various vocational training.

In addition to the establishment of vocational skills training centers, France's vocational education effectiveness in Senegal also includes the construction of a long-term development system, capacity building, and assistance in the development of a local talent training system. For example, France participates in the formulation of vocational education policies, and helps establish vocational education governance systems to improve decision-making quality, efficiency, and governance levels. France also accepts Senegalese students to study or receive training in France and sends experts to Senegal for technical guidance. Unlike Japan's characteristics of foreign education assistance, France's foreign assistance is based on the dissemination of "soft culture", aiming to expand the scope of French language application, spread French culture, and enhance the influence of French intellectual culture, so that French education assistance can achieve longer-lasting benefits.

4. Germany's Assistance to Senegalese Vocational Education

Currently, Germany's vocational education assistance to Senegal is mainly based on the project plan *Supporting the Reform of Vocational Education and Training in Senegal* released by the Federal Ministry for Economic Cooperation and Development (BMZ) of Germany.[b] Germany will help provide vocational education and training opportunities for young people in Senegal from 2020 to 2024, in order to coordinate vocational education with the labor market demand, and promote sustainable economic growth and good employment prospects. The plan proposes that Germany's vocational education assistance to Senegal mainly focuses on four aspects: firstly, providing strategic advisory support to the Senegalese government to ensure that vocational education in Senegal can meet the market labor demand and improve the opportunities for women to participate in vocational training; secondly, helping to strengthen the cooperation between the government and the private sector; thirdly, developing the German "dual system" training model in Senegal.

In 2005, Germany invested 24.8 million euros in education aid for Africa, which increased

---

a Economic and Commercial Office of the Embassy of the People's Republic of China in the Republic of Senegal. Cooperation between the French Development Agency and Senegal. 2008.

b Bintou, D. (2022). Support to the reform of TVET in Senegal. Towards a technical and vocational Education and Training (TVET) offer for Young people That IS More Closely Aligned with the Needs of the Labor Market.

to 50.8 million euros high by 2013. From 2010 to 2012, Germany's aid for vocational education development in Africa increased from 56 million euros to 110 million euros. This shows that Germany's emphasis on vocational education aid to Africa is constantly growing. Germany's education aid to Africa is characterized by equality and fairness, emphasizing Africa's autonomy and building equal relationships between Africa, Germany, and the entire EU.

11.3.2 The Necessity of Chinese Vocational Education Assistance in Supporting Industrial Development in Senegal

Higher education bears the mission of providing talent and intellectual support for the national development strategy, constructing a modern education system that is compatible with the modern economic system, actively participating in global education governance, and achieving the goal of becoming an education powerhouse. As a type of higher education in China, higher vocational education must seize the opportunity of the high-quality construction of the "Belt and Road" under the new development pattern, align with the demand for international capacity cooperation, expand cooperation and opening up to the outside world, enrich the level and structure of talent cultivation, and cultivate internationally skilled professionals. The *2035 China Education Modernization* proposes to "achieve overall education modernization, enter the ranks of education powerhouses, and promote China to become a learning nation, a powerhouse of human resources, and a powerhouse of talent."

As an African country with a low level of industrial development and vocational education, Senegal needs high-quality skilled personnel to support its industrial development. Implementing the internationalization development strategy of vocational education and cultivating international technical and skilled talents are the development requirements for China to enhance its international human capital investment. It is necessary for China to accelerate the construction of modern vocational education system, enhance the ability to participate in the global vocational education governance system, and increase the development of international vocational education. Relying on international production capacity cooperation and cultivating international technical and skilled talents is the requirement of the internationalization of higher vocational education in the era.

11.3.3 Collaborative Educational Practices of Sichuan College of Architectural Technology in Senegal

Sichuan College of Architecture Technology (referred to as SCAT) is a public full-time higher education institution, affiliated with the Department of Housing and Urban-Rural Development of Sichuan Province. In 2019, the college was approved for the establishment of a high-level professional group under the national "Double High Plan", marking the beginning of a new journey of high-quality development for the college. With 65 years of experience in civil engineering vocational education and more than 10 years of international exchange and cooperation, as well as practical experience in Sino-foreign cooperative education projects, the college adheres to the concept of cultivating high-quality technical and skilled talents in the field of civil engineering for international capacity cooperation. Starting from the aspects of curriculum system, teaching resources, faculty team, and quality assurance, the college has built a vocational education international talent training system for civil engineering that promotes collaboration between domestic and foreign institutions and enterprises, providing a program and implementing it for the training of international talents in vocational civil engineering, with remarkable results.

On May 11, 2022, SCAT and Gaston Berger University Saint-Louis Institute of Technology signed a cooperation agreement for the *Sino-African Applied Talents Joint Training Program*. This program is a sub-project of the "Future Africa: Sino-Africa Vocational Education Cooperation Plan" announced by President Xi Jinping at the opening ceremony of the 8th Ministerial Conference of the Forum on China-Africa Cooperation in 2021. The program aims to cultivate applied talents in different professional fields through targeted cooperation between Chinese and African universities and Chinese-funded enterprises, help African youth master vocational skills based on universal industry standards, expand employment, and cultivate a young labor force and leading technical talents needed for the economic and social development of Africa.

According to the active negotiation between the two universities, the cooperative major is determined as the category of construction engineering technology (mainly for water supply and drainage, and also provides practical elective courses for civil engineering). International students, whose credits obtained will be recognized by both Chinese and Senegalese schools, are required to complete the prescribed courses and pass the exams, and they will receive diplomas from both schools. In the "1+1.5+0.5" joint directional training mode, SCAT organizes a high-level bilingual teaching team to tailor professional basic courses, professional core courses, and Chinese language and culture courses for 15 Senegalese students selected for the joint training project. As of October 2022, all teachers and students in the project have successfully completed the first phase of online training courses.

11.3.4 Experiences and Achievements of Vocational Education Cooperation between Sichuan College of Architectural Technology and Senegal

1. Situation Analysis

In May 2022, Sichuan College of Architecture Technology (referred to as 'SCAT' hereafter) signed an international cooperation agreement for education with the University of Dakar in Senegal and the Saint-Louis Polytechnic School of Gaston Berger University, and subsequently launched the degree education for international students.

In order to actively implement the spirit of the *State Council General Office's Opinions on Deepening the Integration of Industry* and *Education, the National Vocational Education Reform*

Implementation Plan, and other documents, vigorously promote the construction of the talent training project for Chinese enterprises' overseas projects, enhance the core competitiveness of construction enterprises, and improve the quality and level of education in schools, based on the advantageous professional background of civil engineering in Sichuan Construction Academy, the academy actively contacted the Chinese Embassy in Senegal and civil engineering Chinese companies in Senegal, successfully connected with Zhongdi Overseas Group Co., Ltd. in Senegal, and conducted preliminary research on school-enterprise cooperation.

Since entering the Senegal market in 2006, Zhongdi Overseas Group Co., Ltd. has successively completed the urban water supply pipeline renovation project of the National Water Company in Dakar, the construction of nearly 100 deep wells and more than 30 water towers, and the laying of about 800 kilometers of water supply pipeline network in villages by the Rural Water Conservancy Bureau. It has also completed over 3,000 hectares of farmland improvement projects and the civil construction of two pumping stations in the Senegal River Basin.

2. Educational Model

Based on the tripartite cooperation of SCAT, Senegalese institutions and multinational enterprises, with cross-border collaboration as the main method and win-win cooperation as the ultimate goal, it aims to jointly cultivate technical and skilled personnel who are proficient in language and culture, with rich teaching resources, complete teaching content, and perfect management system and evaluation methods.

Currently, the "school-school" education model has been established, focusing on the cultivation of vocational core competencies, comprehensive cultural literacy, and cross-cultural communication awareness for international students. It aims to stimulate students' interest in learning, improve their self-learning abilities, and enable them to master effective learning methods and strategies, laying a necessary foundation for enhancing their competitiveness in employment and future sustainable development.

Next, SCAT plans to cooperate with Zhongdi Overseas Group to support each other in talent cultivation. Both parties will jointly formulate talent cultivation plans that meet the needs of enterprises, and invite relevant management and technical personnel from enterprises to conduct teaching activities in the school. According to their needs, enterprises can carry out customized training such as 'order classes' and 'targeted students' in the school, giving priority to selecting outstanding graduates to work in the enterprise.

3. Project Mechanism

In the context of the building of "Belt and Road" and the expansion of international capacity cooperation, higher vocational education must strengthen its mission, innovate boldly, focus on solving the obstacles of industry-education integration and school-enterprise cooperation mechanism in the "going global" education, innovate the integration mode of industry and education, strengthen policy guidance, give full play to the leading role of enterprises, innovate diversified school-enterprise cooperation mechanisms, and use production capacity cooperation projects to jointly build integrated practical training bases. In addition, the recognition of academic qualifications and degrees between Chinese and African colleges and universities is also an important part of international production capacity cooperation. Establishing internationally comparable quality certification standards and mechanisms for Chinese vocational education overseas cooperation and education has important significance for promoting the sharing of vocational education resources, models, and experiences, as well as the sharing of human resources in China.

(1) Project Operation Mechanism

Taking SCAT's new model of "domestic and foreign cooperation, school-school-enterprise co-education" international technical skills training for higher vocational civil engineering talents as the project brand, the "school-school-enterprise" cooperation model among SCAT, Senegalese vocational colleges and Zhongdi Overseas Group is carried out:

①Standardized venue construction. It is planned to build a venue in the Senegal Comprehensive Industrial Park of Zhongdi Overseas Group to meet the needs of educational activities, including practical training and theoretical teaching.

②Standardization of practical training equipment. The practical training equipment used in the cooperative project is equipped according to the construction needs of the Sino-Senegal international cooperation professionals.

③Systematization of international teacher training. Professional teachers from SCAT provide comprehensive professional training for teachers from Senegal cooperative colleges, including theoretical teaching, practical teaching, and Chinese corporate culture, and apply them to local professional education.

④Internationalization of professional standards. SCAT takes civil engineering as its advantage backbone major, benchmarks the international cutting-edge technology standards of the industry in standard design, and benchmarks advanced educational concepts and teaching models in teaching organization and implementation.

⑤Relying on the existing cooperation with Australia's Melbourne Institute of Technology, SCAT has established a national virtual simulation training base for prefabricated buildings, a provincial BIM+VR virtual simulation training center, an exploratory intelligent training room, and an information technology training room. Based on the demand for technical and skilled talents in Senegal, it has built a teaching resource and practical platform with international standards.

(2) Project Work Mechanism

SCAT will form a project operation team to fully manage, operate and supervise the project.

① Establish a regular work system, which is responsible by the Foreign Affairs Office of the College. It is responsible for the daily management and routine work of the project, as well as coordinating and summarizing relevant information.

② Establish a special discussion system to conduct special investigations and research on specific issues during the project's progress, hold special meetings for discussion, which will be responsible by supporting working groups.

③ Establish a project supervision system, conduct regular inspections and research on cooperative projects, and include them in the annual evaluation and assessment.

④ Establish a risk warning system, which is responsible by the leadership group and implemented by the Foreign Affairs Office. Develop risk-warning plans and conduct project risk assessments annually or according to project progress.

(3) Policy Measures

To better serve the international production capacity cooperation projects, SCAT actively promotes the construction of internship and training bases in Senegal. The opening-up of education in the new era is not only a need for the development of vocational education, but also a need for national modernization. The college should attach great importance to the construction of overseas internship bases and closely link it with the national development strategy.

Increasing investment is the most direct and efficient measure to accelerate the construction of overseas internship bases. Firstly, dedicated personnel from universities and enterprises are required to be responsible for overseas internship projects, coordinating and communicating various issues encountered during the overseas internship process. It is also necessary to strengthen the construction of internship mentor teams and improve the management level of overseas internships. In the process of selecting internship mentors, not only should the teacher's knowledge reserve, professional quality, and teaching ability be emphasized, but also their foreign language proficiency, cross-cultural communication ability, adaptability to overseas work and life, and ability to cope with changes are important assessment indicators. Secondly, it requires investment in material and financial resources, mainly for the promotion and implementation of internship projects, and also for establishing incentive measures, including performance rewards, bonus points for title evaluation, and opportunities for overseas further study for teachers participating in overseas internship bases.

In addition, providing "Chinese language + skills" training courses for overseas employees is a necessary measure to serve international production capacity cooperation. With the increasing number of Chinese-funded enterprises in Senegal, the demand for communication and exchange between Chinese and Senegalese employees is constantly increasing. It is also necessary for Senegalese employees to learn Chinese and understand Chinese culture. Providing Chinese language and Chinese culture courses for Senegalese employees can help them better integrate into Chinese enterprises in Senegal and improve communication efficiency between Senegalese and Chinese employees. Chinese language teachers should not only cover daily language in the process of teaching Chinese to Senegalese employees, but also establish a curriculum system for professional Chinese, so that Senegalese employees can learn and apply it more quickly in practical work.

For teachers participating in the construction of overseas internship training bases and the online training course of 'Chinese language + skills', corresponding incentive measures should be established, and perfect guarantee policies should also be established. There are two guarantee policies:

One is an internal guarantee, which mean to establish a supervision mechanism within the college. The quality control department of the college should formulate performance quantification assessment plans for overseas internship mentors, conduct regular assessments, and check the teachers who participate in the 'Chinese language + skills' online training course. It should also regularly conduct satisfaction surveys on the trained Senegalese employees, and timely rectify and improve the training plan for any problems. Another guarantee method is to introduce third-party organizations for supervision, actively give play to the professionalism of third parties, to improve professional ability and guidance quality. This method can reflect the actual benefits of the international production capacity project to improve the accuracy of result application.

4. Main Achievements

Against the background of economic globalization and the construction of the "Belt and Road", SCAT intends to cooperate with Zhongdi Overseas Group. As the number of international engineering projects of state-owned large construction enterprises continues to increase, they face human resource management problems in the process of "going global". Both parties will establish and deepen the cooperation relationship of skills and talent cultivation between schools and enterprises based on the principles of mutual benefit and common development, starting from fulfilling the social responsibility of central enterprises and playing the leading role of industry "Double-High" vocational colleges in industrial services. The school-enterprise cooperation will combine the actual situation in Senegal to carry out more extensive local labor skills and overseas engineering project management personnel business training. In addition, both parties will continue to promote the construction of international skills and talent cultivation standards, certification standards, and curriculum systems, integrate high-quality resources of both parties, help enterprises transform and upgrade, effectively improve the quality of talent cultivation and the level of technological research and development, and provide all-round assistance to Chinese-funded enterprises in Africa to play a more important role. At the same time, they will enhance the international influence of SCAT and contribute to the "SCAT's proposals" for the development of world vocational education.

11.4 Exsiting Problems and Development Recommendations for Sino-Senegal Vocational Education Cooperation

11.4.1 Exsiting Problems

The model of Chinese vocational colleges serving Senegal's international production capacity cooperation is not yet sound, and the ability of vocational education to serve international production capacity cooperation is uneven. There are obvious phenomena such as low level of internationalization development of vocational education, slow development speed, the mismatch between internationalization scale and vocational college scale, low level of openness in running schools, and uneven and incomplete development. The way of vocational education serving international production capacity cooperation is relatively single. It mainly focuses on overseas schools, sharing professional teaching standards with target countries, lack of international skills competitions and construction of international cooperation and research platforms. The depth of vocational education serving international production capacity cooperation is not enough, and there are not many models like the Luban Workshop project that promote the cooperation between schools and enterprises to help enterprises "going global". Most of them are still in cooperation between schools and schools, schools and educational institutions or training institutions, schools and government institutions, etc. The mechanism and system of vocational education serving international production capacity cooperation are not sound, and there is a lack of planning, implementation opinions, and support policies specifically for the internationalization of education in Senegal. It is urgent to explore and build a vocational education cooperation mechanism that involves multiple subjects, multiple parties, and collaborative operations, including government institutions, domestic and foreign enterprises, vocational colleges, and industry associations, in order to eliminate the problems and costs brought by the asymmetry of domestic and foreign information for enterprises' "going global".

11.4.2 Recommendations for Further Development

1. Suggestions on How Vocational Colleges Can Serve Chinese-Funded Enterprises

Research shows that vocational colleges in China take talent cultivation as the core, and establish cooperative relationships with Senegalese Chinese-funded enterprises as service providers based on the outsourcing needs. Therefore, the following suggestions are proposed for the cooperation between vocational colleges and Chinese-funded enterprises: First, vocational colleges should fully evaluate their service capabilities, including the actual workload of outsourcing, their own degree of specialization, technological research and development facilities, and short-term reserve of human resources. Second, it is necessary to formulate outsourcing contracts that cover quality standards and cooperation norms. Third, we should execute outsourcing projects based on Senegal's domestic industry needs, complete the talent cultivation process, and provide deliverable outsourcing results for Senegalese Chinese-funded enterprises. Fourth, we should evaluate and provide feedback on the outsourcing results to promote the sustainable development of school-enterprise cooperation (Figure 11–8).

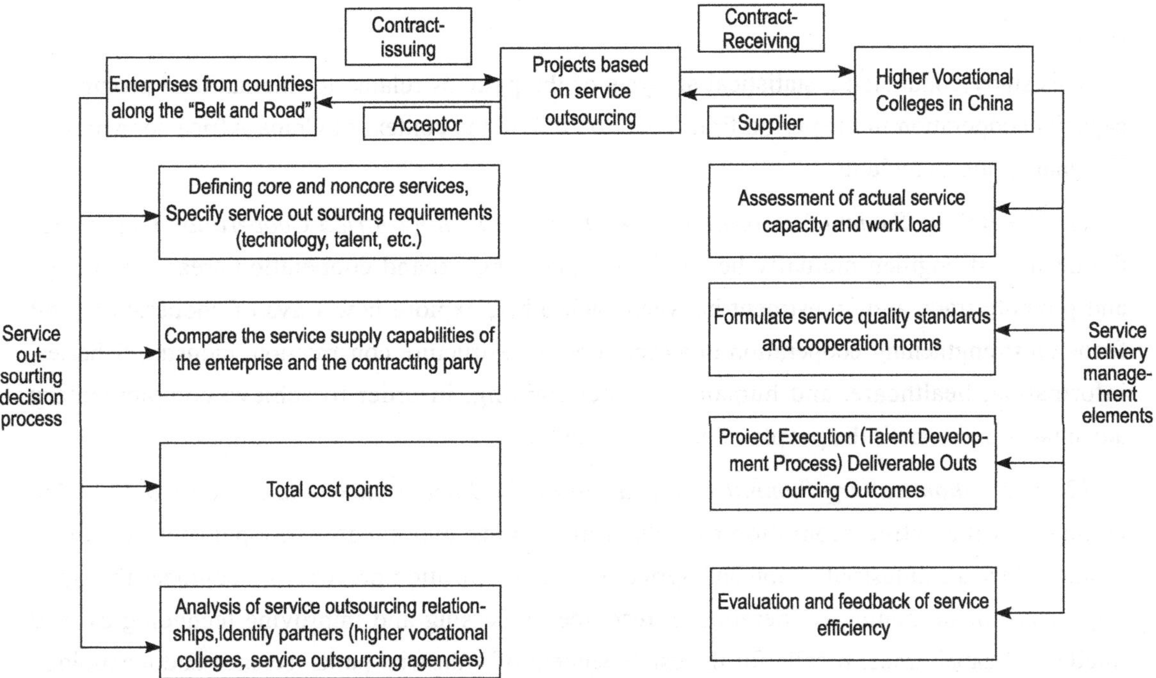

Figure 11–8 Construction of a Vocational College-Enterprise Cooperation Model Based on Service Outsourcing under the Building of "Belt and Road"(Wang Lan et al., 2020)

From the perspective of vocational colleges in China, the cooperation mode between vocational colleges and enterprises can be conducted in two ways. Firstly vocational colleges can participate in the production, service and operation activities of Chinese-funded enterprises in African countries through service outsourcing projects, integrate into the development process of enterprises, become the service provider of enterprises, and provide effective services mainly based on technology and intelligence for the differentiated development needs of enterprises. Chinese vocational colleges obtain talent-training resources from Chinese-funded enterprises in African countries through participating in service outsourcing activities. In order to obtain high-quality service outsourcing results, enterprises will invest resources mainly based on internship and training bases in vocational colleges, promote the integration of the teaching process and work process, improve the effectiveness of practical teaching, and enhance the quality of talent training. Secondly, it is the acquisition of teacher training resources. In the process of vocational college-enterprise cooperation based on service outsourcing, vocational college teachers are the key force responsible for service outsourcing tasks. Enterprises assign responsible persons to assist vocational colleges in completing service outsourcing projects and provide training opportunities for vocational college teachers. Thirdly, it is the acquisition of financial resources. Although vocational colleges in China are not profit-oriented, they will benefit from cooperation profits through the smooth development and final delivery of service outsourcing projects.

2. Proposal for International Production Capacity Cooperation in Vocational Education Services

This study conducted a statistical analysis of the policies related to international production capacity cooperation in the period from 2000 to 2022 in the context of China-Africa cooperation. The main policies include:

(1) *The Beijing Summit Declaration of the Forum on China-Africa Cooperation* emphasizes the need to strengthen mutually beneficial cooperation, expand cooperation areas, encourage and promote trade and investment between each other, explore new ways of cooperation, and focus on strengthening cooperation in agriculture, infrastructure construction, industry, fisheries, information, healthcare, and human resources training, in order to achieve complementary advantages and benefit the people of both sides (2006).

(2) *The Johannesburg Summit Declaration of the Forum on China-Africa Cooperation* emphasizes the active promotion of industrial docking and capacity cooperation to jointly promote Africa's industrialization and agricultural modernization process. It recognizes the equal importance of deepening cooperation in resource processing and improving technological and intellectual capabilities. It calls for the establishment of industrial parks, science and technology parks, economic zones, as well as training centers for engineering, technology, and management personnel, to enhance cooperation in the field of industrial production and increase added value (2015).

(3) *The Beijing Declaration on Building a Closer China-Africa Community with a Shared Future* emphasizes that China is willing to continue upholding the principle of mutual benefit and win-win cooperation. China will support Africa in cultivating endogenous growth capabilities that are not reliant on raw material exports, enhance Africa's production capacity in the secondary and tertiary industries, promote the transformation and upgrading of China-Africa economic and trade cooperation, and provide various types of assistance and support to Africa's development without attaching any political conditions. Africa reaffirms its commitment to pursuing a path of sustainable, diversified, and socially and economically coordinated development to ensure win-win outcomes (2018).

(4) The China-Africa Cooperation 2035 Vision emphasizes the deepening and expansion of production capacity cooperation. China and Africa will improve the manufacturing system,

cultivate the "Made in Africa" brand, and integrate into the international industrial and supply chains. China will support Africa in building a sound technical standard system and enhancing quality infrastructure capabilities. China will share its experience with Africa, help Africa promote the upgrading of the manufacturing industry, enhance industrial competitiveness, unleash the vitality of the private economy, and create more employment opportunities (2021).

Existing policies indicate that the policy support for vocational education services in international production capacity is still insufficient. The new version of the Vocational Education Law, which came into effect on May 1, 2022, emphasizes in Article 13 of the General Provisions that the state encourages international exchanges and cooperation in the field of vocational education, supports the introduction of high-quality overseas resources for the development of vocational education, encourages qualified vocational education institutions to establish schools overseas, and supports the mutual recognition of various forms of vocational education learning outcomes. Therefore, this study proposes the following suggestions for international production capacity cooperation in vocational education services.

(1) Introduce special plans to guide vocational education in serving international capacity cooperation. Relevant government departments need to further plan the internationalization of vocational education, enhance the importance of international exchange and cooperation, guide vocational education to serve enterprises in "going global", and support international production capacity cooperation.

(2) Develop supportive policies for vocational education services in international production capacity cooperation. Establish a working group for international production capacity cooperation services, coordinate with departments such as finance, taxation, development and reform, industry and information technology, and finance, comprehensively use financial and tax, land, credit and other means, encourage and support industry enterprises and social funds to actively participate in vocational education internationalization, cultivate technical and skilled personnel for countries along the "Belt and Road", and promote international production capacity cooperation.

(3) Establish a special fund for international production capacity cooperation in vocational education services. Provide financial supports for talent cultivation in vocational colleges, research institutes, and professional group construction. Provide awards, assistance, and loans for international students, teachers going abroad for academic visits, student exchange programs, and the introduction of foreign teachers. Create a favorable environment for internationalized education.

(4) Integrate advantageous resources from all parties and build a large platform to serve international production capacity cooperation. Integrate advantageous resources from vocational education and leverage the advantages of overseas Chinese to help enterprises "going global" and serve international production capacity cooperation. Explore the construction of a diverse

platform for international cooperation in vocational education, which involves multiple subjects, multi-party cooperation, and collaborative operation. The platform integrates government agencies, enterprises, vocational colleges, industry associations, overseas industrial (industrial) parks, overseas Chinese organizations, etc. Adhering to the concept of co-consultation, co-construction, and sharing, resources will be integrated and improved in terms of professional docking, curriculum standard setting, customized courses, teacher exchange visits, scientific research cooperation, international student training, skills training, and qualification certificate recognition, forming a replaceable and promotable international vocational education model.

(5) Innovate the mode and content of international production capacity cooperation, and highlight the characteristics. The form of vocational education serving international production capacity cooperation can shift from the "1+1" cooperation mode ("home institution + overseas institution", "home institution + overseas Chinese community", "home institution + Chinese-funded enterprises") to the "1+N" cooperation mode (home institution + government agencies + industry associations + social organizations + enterprises + research institutions, etc.).

Each partner country has obvious differences in economy and politics. Therefore, when promoting vocational education services to African enterprises, it is necessary to pay attention to studying the relevant situation of the target country, and not to generalize. It is recommended to promote the implementation path and quality assurance of school-enterprise cooperation corresponding to each country, so that Chinese vocational colleges can truly achieve international production capacity cooperation and cultivate high-quality skilled talents that are suitable for the development of the target country.

Chapter XII

Reports on Vocational Education Collaboration Serving China-Uganda Production Capacity Cooperation

Uganda is located in eastern Africa, with its capital city being Kampala. It is a landlocked country that spans the equator, bordered by Kenya to the east, Tanzania and Rwanda to the south, the Democratic Republic of Congo to the west, and it shares its northern border with South Sudan. The country has a land area of 241,550 square kilometers, consisting mostly of plateaus at an elevation of 1,200 meters, with forest coverage of 12%. Uganda enjoys a moderate climate and abundant rainfall. It is home to Africa's third-highest peak, Mount Rwenzori, as well as Lake Victoria, the largest lake in Africa and the second-largest freshwater lake in the world. Uganda also possesses abundant resources, including minerals, fisheries and oil. The country is known for its rich tourism resources.

In 1962, China and Uganda formally established diplomatic relations. In 2019, the China-Uganda relationship was elevated to a comprehensive partnership. Under the framework of the "Belt and Road" Initiative and the Forum on China-Africa Cooperation (FOCAC) Beijing Summit's "Eight Major Initiatives", the relationship between China and Uganda has continued to develop steadily with deepening political mutual trust. Trade and investment have been mutually beneficial, and the level of cooperation has been continuously improving. Uganda is the fourth largest destination for Chinese investment in Africa, and China is Uganda's third largest trading partner.

12.1 Overview of Uganda

12.1.1 Economic Development

Uganda has adopted a policy of economic liberalization and has maintained a relatively fast economic growth. In the past five years, the annual average GDP growth rate of Uganda has been around 4%. The GDP growth figures for Uganda from 2017 to 2021 can be found in Table 12–1, and the GDP rankings of African countries in 2021 are shown in Table 12–1.

Table 12–1 GDP Growth of Uganda from 2017 to 2021

Year	GDP (0.1 billions of US dollars)	GDP Growth Rate	GDP African Ranking
2017	307.44	3.1%	17
2018	329.27	6.3%	16
2019	353.53	6.4%	16
2020	376.00	3.0%	16
2021	404.30	3.4%	16

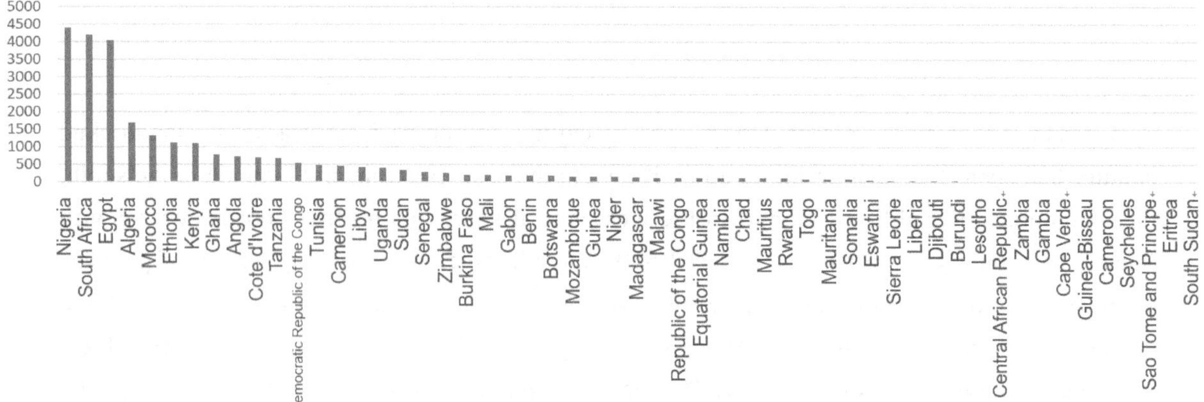

Figure 12–1 2021 GDP Rankings of African Countries (0.1 billion *yuan*)

Data source: World Bank Database https://data.worldbank.org.cn/indicator/NY.GDP.MKTP.CD?view=chart&locations=UG

According to Table 12–1, it can be seen that in 2019, the Ugandan economy experienced strong growth with a high growth rate of 6.4%. In early 2020, the COVID-19 pandemic broke out in multiple locations around the world and rapidly spread, causing a huge impact on the Ugandan economy and society. The growth rate dropped to only 3%, the lowest in nearly 30 years. In 2021, the total size of the Ugandan economy increased to $40.43 billion with a growth rate of 3.4%. In Africa, Uganda is considered an economically underdeveloped country, but over the past five years, its GDP has been ranked in the upper-middle range among African countries, showing slow overall growth.

Table 12–2 provides information on the per capita GDP growth in Uganda from 2017 to 2021. As for the ranking of African countries in terms of GDP per capita in 2021, you can refer to Figure 12–2.

Table 12–2 GDP Per Capita Growth in Uganda from 2017 to 2021

Year	GDP Per Capita (USD)	GDP Per Capita Growth Rate	GDP Per Capita Africa Ranking
2017	746.8	–0.7%	38
2018	770.6	2.4%	40
2019	798.6	2.7%	37
2020	822.0	–0.4%	37
2021	858.1	0.3%	37

Source of data: World Bank database https://data.worldbank.org.cn/indicator/NY.GDP.PCAP.CD?locations=UG

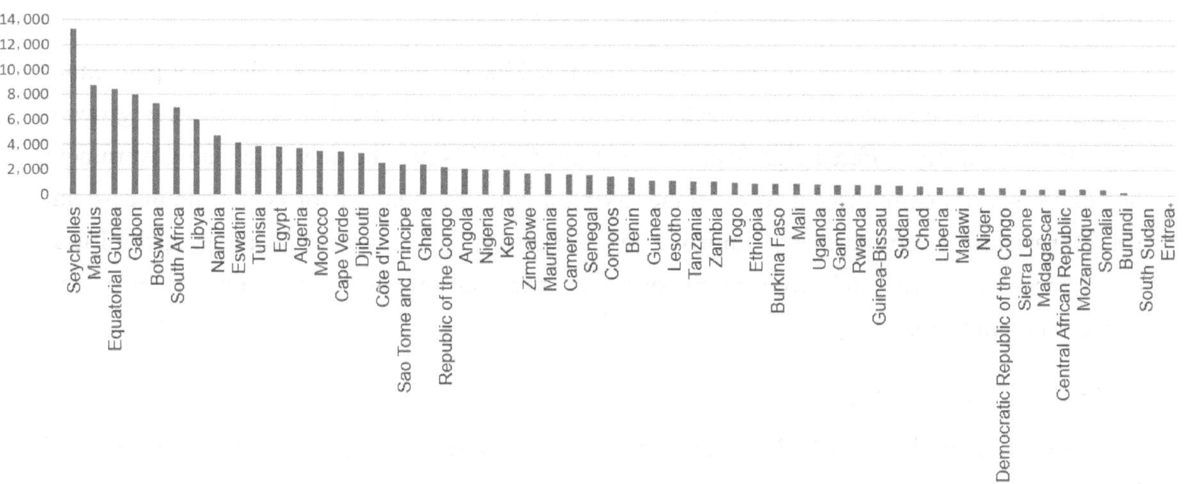

Figure 12–2 Ranking of African Countries by GDP per Capita in 2021

As shown in Table 12–2, Uganda's GDP per capita consistently ranks around the 40th position in Africa, indicating that it is a country with slow social development and is in the early stages of industrialization. In 2021, Uganda's GDP per capita increased to $858.1, achieving positive growth after experiencing negative growth in 2020. However, it is still far below the 2.7% growth rate in 2019.

12.1.2 Industrial Environment

1. Overview of Industrial Development

Uganda has a weak economic foundation and a single economic structure. Agriculture is the industry that employs the largest number of people in Uganda, but its productivity is low and there is an urgent need to introduce advanced agricultural production technologies and equipment to increase output and efficiency. The industrial sector is in its early stages of development, with manufacturing and construction as the main focus. The service sector contributes a significant proportion to the GDP, with trade, tourism, repair services, and education as the main components. In 2020, the proportions of the primary, secondary, and tertiary sectors in Uganda's GDP were 24%, 26.2%, and 43% respectively.

The proportion of each sector in GDP from 2016 to 2020 can be seen in Table 12–3.

Table 12–3 2016–2020 Industry Proportions in Uganda's GDP

Year	2016	2017	2018	2019	2020
Agriculture, Forestry, and Fishing	22.8%	23.5%	23.2%	23.1%	24.0%
Industry	26.3%	26.0%	26.1%	26.3%	26.2%
Services	44.2%	43.5%	43.5%	43.2%	43.0%

Data source: Uganda Bureau of Statistics http://data.un.org/en/iso/ug.html

According to Table 12–3, it can be seen that in 2020, in spite of the COVID-19 pandemic, agriculture was the least affected industry and the only industry to experience positive growth. The service industry suffered significant losses from COVID-19. The new Ugandan government has expressed its commitment to continue laying a solid foundation for economic and social transformation. It commited to improve infrastructure in key areas, promote agricultural development, and drive industrialization based on agriculture. Its goal is to maintain the current stable economic situation.

2. Key Featured Industries

Agriculture: In the 2019/2020 fiscal year, growth slowed down, mainly relying on bountiful harvests and livestock farming.

Industry: In the past decade, the industrial sector has steadily developed, with steel and cement manufacturing being the dominant industries in the country. However, in the 2019/2020 fiscal year, the growth rate significantly slowed down compared to the previous year. This was mainly due to the slower development in the manufacturing and mining industries.

Service sector: The growth rate in the service sector also slowed down in the 2019/2020 fiscal year. Within this sector, the information and communication industry grew by 34.3%, public services grew by 13.0%, and the technology industry grew by 4.4%.

Manufacturing industry: Steel and cement are currently the industries in Uganda that have a certain foundation for development. In Uganda, there are currently 11 steel mills established, including companies like Roofingsteel (invested by India), Tian Tang Group (invested by China), Ugandabaati (invested by India), Steelandtube (invested by India), Primukesteel (invested by India), etc. These manufacturers account for approximately 65% to 75% of the market share in Uganda.

Tourism industry: Uganda's wildlife conservation areas are the main destinations for tourists.

However, due to the COVID-19 pandemic, the tourism industry in Uganda has been severely affected and is expected to take at least two years to recover to pre-pandemic levels.

12.1.3 Status Quo of Vocational Education

1. Vocational Education System

The vocational and technical education system in Uganda consists of three levels: primary, intermediate, and advanced. Vocational and technical education institutions include community craft schools, vocational education and training schools, business colleges, technical colleges, and other types of institutions. Collectively, these schools are referred to as BTVET (Business, Technical, Vocational Education, and Training).

Basic Technical Schools mainly admit elementary school graduates. The duration of study is 3 years, with 40% of the curriculum dedicated to foundational courses and 60% to specialized courses. Upon passing the graduation examination, students can obtain a certificate for primary-level technical skills.

Intermediate Technical Colleges primarily admit junior high school graduates and graduates from junior technical schools. The duration of the program is 2 years, with English and humanities subjects accounting for 10% of the curriculum, and professional theory and practical training accounting for 90%. Upon passing the graduation exam, students can obtain a vocational certificate.

Advanced Vocational Colleges are divided into two types: 2-year Vocational Colleges and Higher Vocational Colleges. They primarily admit high school graduates and graduates from Intermediate Technical Colleges. After graduation, those who obtain a national diploma certificate can directly enter the second year or below of university for further studies, while those who obtain a national advanced diploma can directly enter the third year or below of university for further studies.

In the field of vocational education and training, technical colleges provide modular short-term courses (1–6 months) and informal skills training (a few weeks), charging certain training fees and external examination assessment fees. The areas of vocational education and training have expanded from traditional agriculture and crafts to fields such as telecommunications, construction, energy, and management, among others.

Uganda's vocational education system is shown in Figure 12–3.

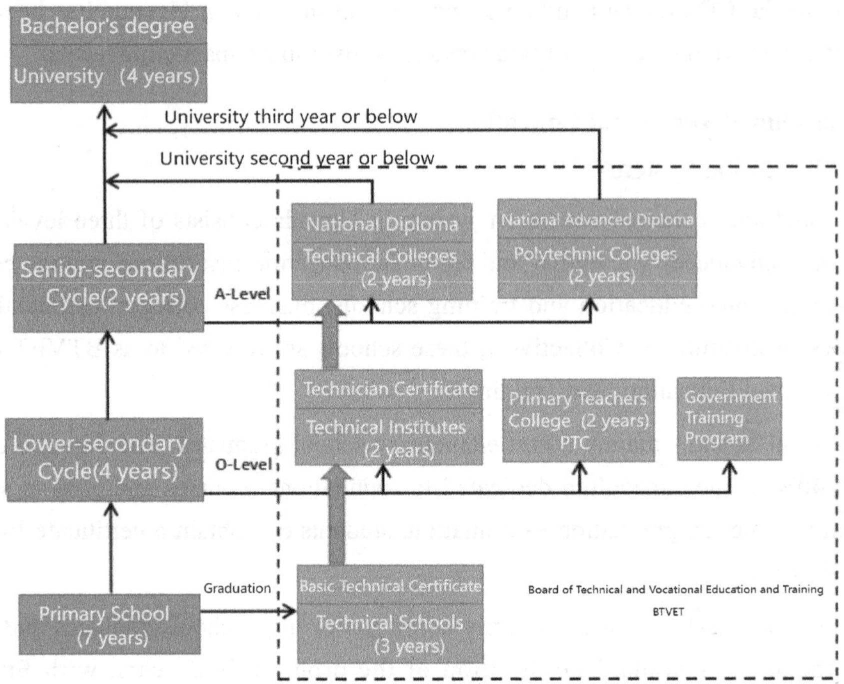

Figure 12–3 Ugandan Education System

According to figure 12–3, the Ugandan education system demonstrates the integration of vertical general education and horizontal vocational education. In Uganda, vocational education supports graduates from primary, secondary, and high schools to enroll in corresponding vocational schools for further studies. Additionally, graduates who obtain national diplomas and advanced national diplomas can proceed to university for further education and earn bachelor's degrees. This highlights the acceptance and recognition for vocational education by general education.

2. Establishment of Higher Vocational Colleges in Uganda

There are a total of 313 higher vocational colleges, and degree-granting, and certificate-granting institutions in Uganda, with 32.06% being public institutions. The distribution of these schools can be seen in Table 12–4.

Table 12–4 Distribution of Fields and Industries of Uganda's Higher Vocational Colleges

Industry	College Type	Quantity	Percentage	Public	Private
Primary industry (2.29%)	Agriculture, Fisheries, and Forestry	3	2.29%	3	0
Secondary industry (4.58%)	Technology	5	3.82%	5	0

continued

Industry	College Type	Quantity	Percentage	Public	Private
Tertiary industry (81.67%)	Surveying and Land	1	0.76%	1	0
	Business	58	44.27%	5	53
	Health Institutions	21	16.03%	13	8
	Meteorology	1	0.76%	1	0
	Media	4	3.05%	0	4
	Tourism	3	2.29%	2	1
	Normal Education	5	3.82%	5	0
	Aviation	1	0.76%	1	0
	Management	12	9.16%	2	10
	Law	1	0.76%	1	0
	Art	1	0.76%	0	1
Others (11.46%)	Religion	11	8.40%	0	11
	Cooperation	2	1.53%	2	0
	Others	2	1.53%	1	1

Source: Ministry of Education and Sports, Uganda. *Tertiary Institutions*

From Table 12–4, it can be seen that in Uganda's Higher Vocational College, the majority are business schools and health schools. Among them, there are 5 technical colleges representing the highest level of technical personnel training in the country, which belong to the secondary industry.

3. Course Curriculum

Uganda is currently in the early stages of industrialization, and the large-scale development of infrastructure has driven the construction and development of professionals such as civil engineering, hydraulic engineering, electrical engineering, mechanical engineering, and others. Technical vocational schools primarily offer courses in carpentry, electrical repair, ceramics, tailoring, and agriculture. Intermediate technical colleges focus on majors such as carpentry, masonry, motorcycle technology, agricultural machinery repair, and electrical equipment maintenance. Advanced vocational colleges, such as Elgon Uganda Technical College, mainly offer majors in industrial technology, including fields like construction and civil engineering, hydraulic engineering, electrical engineering, mechanical engineering, refrigeration and air conditioning engineering, architectural drafting, and information and communication technology. From the vocational education programs available in Uganda, it is evident that vocational education in Uganda is focused on supporting the industrial development of the country.

12.1.4 Vocational Education and Industry

According to the 2019 graduate survey conducted by the Uganda Higher Education Commission, a total of 4,037 graduates from 7 universities and 7 higher vocational colleges were recorded. The main employment sectors for these graduates were agriculture, trade, banking and finance, as well as healthcare.

Uganda currently has a population of 44.3 million people, and it is projected to increase to 86.5 million by 2050. Approximately 78% of the population in Uganda is made up of young people under the age of 30. In the fiscal year 2018/2019, the reported unemployment rate in Uganda was 9.2%. However, according to a survey conducted by the African Development Bank, the youth unemployment rate in Uganda is as high as 83%. Each year, approximately 400,000 students graduate from universities in Uganda, but there are only about 9,000 job opportunities available in the market. Due to abundant labor resources and underdeveloped industries, there are relatively few employment opportunities, resulting in a high unemployment rate.

As of 2021, the total labor force in Uganda reached 17,351,430 people, and it has been consistently growing for the past five years. The employment distribution across different industries from 2015 to 2019 is shown in Table 12–5.

Table 12–5 2015–2019 Industry Employment Ratios

Employment Industries (Percentage of Total Employment)	2015	2016	2017	2018	2019
Employment in primary industry	72.63%	72.84%	73.05%	72.88%	72.67%
Employment in secondary industry	6.79%	6.70%	6.58%	6.60%	6.60%
Employment in tertiary industry	20.58%	20.46%	20.37%	20.53%	20.73%

Data source: World Bank website.

From Table 12–5, it can be observed that the employment figures across industries remain relatively stable each year. Over the years, Uganda has had the highest number of individuals employed in the primary sector, accounting for around 70% of the total workforce. Employment in the tertiary sector constitutes approximately 20% of the total, while the secondary sector makes up less than 7%. In contrast, the GDP contributions of the three sectors in Uganda in 2019 were as follows: 23.1% for the primary sector, 26.3% for the secondary sector, and 43.2% for the tertiary sector. The disparity between the proportion of workers in each sector and their respective contributions to GDP is quite significant.

Uganda released the *Labor Force Survey Report for the 2018/2019* period in March 2021. This report includes the industry and occupation distribution of the employed population. Figures 12–4 and 12–5 show the proportions of the employed population in various industries and occupations in Uganda from 2018 to 2019.

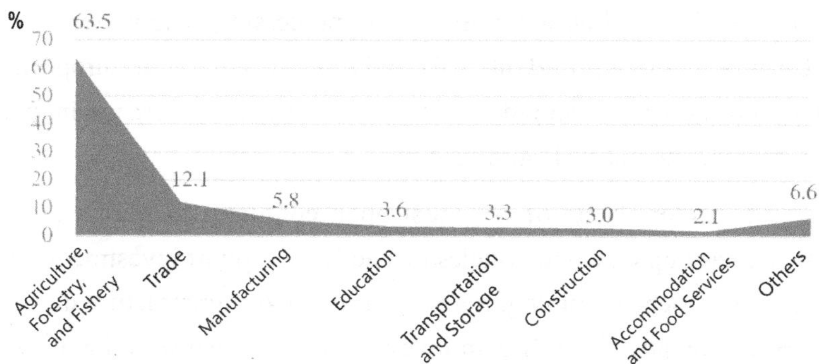

Figure 12–4 2018–2019 Employment Distribution by Industry in Uganda

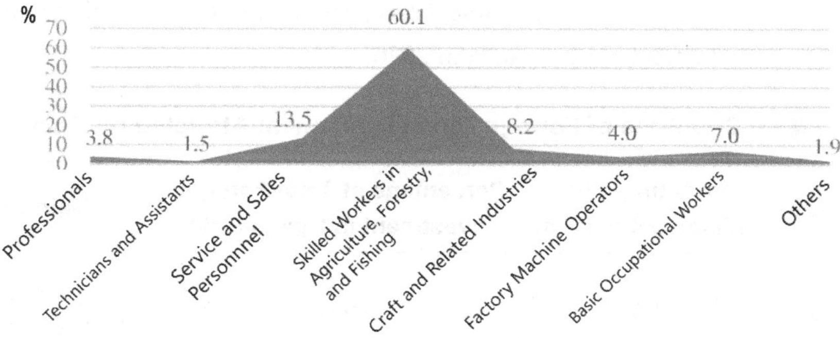

Figure 12–5 2018–2019 Employment Distribution by Occupation in Uganda

According to Figure 12–4, it can be seen that 63.5% of the workforce consists of workers in agriculture, forestry, and fishing, which is the largest share of workers in Uganda. The trade sector is the second largest employer, employing 12.1% of the workforce. According to the percentage of employment by occupation in Figure 12–5, 13.5% of people are service and sales workers, 7% are skilled workers, and only 3.8% are professionals and technicians. The research results further show that the proportion of workers in professions requiring higher education, such as professionals and managers, is relatively low. Uganda has a high demand for professional and technical personnel.

12.1.5 International Economic Cooperation

In 2020, Uganda recorded a total foreign trade volume of $12.399 billion, with exports amounting to $4.149 billion and imports totaling $8.251 billion, resulting in a trade deficit of $4.102 billion. Uganda's main exports include coffee, aquatic products, and maize, while its primary imports consist of machinery and high-tech products required for industrial development, including machinery, automobiles and parts, and petrochemical products, etc. The country's major trading partners for imports are China, India, Kenya, and the United Arab Emirates.

In 2020, Uganda attracted Foreign Direct Investment (FDI) of $520 million, which significantly decreased compared to the previous fiscal year. FDI primarily flowed into sectors such as manufacturing, construction, and agricultural product processing. The major sources of foreign aid received by Uganda are the World Bank, African Development Fund, European Union, China, the United States, and the United Kingdom. The main areas of assistance include agriculture, education, transportation, and public health services.

Uganda is now considered one of the most open countries in Africa for foreign direct investment (FDI) and has implemented policies that actively support investment. The government encourages foreign investment in mining, manufacturing, and infrastructure development. There is a particular emphasis on attracting foreign investment for the construction of industrial parks, with new companies investing in these parks enjoying a 10-year tax exemption on corporate income. However, there is some resistance to foreign involvement in sectors such as retail, which could compete with local employments. Table 12–6 presents the main countries and sectors of foreign direct investment attracted by Uganda in 2020.

Table 12–6 Main Countries of Foreign Direct Investment Attracted by Uganda in 2020

No.	Country	Investment (0.1 billion US dollars)	Percentage of Total Foreign Investment in Uganda (%)	Main Sectors
1	China	2.57	49.37	Energy and Minerals, Infra-structure Construction, etc.
2	United King-dom	0.57	10.92	Finance, Petroleum, Health-care, etc.
3	India	0.43	8.29	Pharmaceuticals, Steel, Power Equipment

From Table 12–6, it can be seen that China is the largest source of foreign direct investment (FDI) for Uganda, accounting for nearly 50% of the total FDI inflows. The investments are mainly focused on sectors that align with Uganda's industrial development.

12.2 Cooperation between Chinese-Funded Enterprises and China-Uganda Production Capacity

12.2.1 Industrial Development in Uganda and its Demand for Foreign Investment

Uganda boasts abundant natural, mineral, and tourism resources. Agriculture is the supporting industry, while the service sector contributes the largest share to the country's GDP. However, in order to break free from Uganda's current poverty and boost social and economic development, industrialization is seen as the only path forward. The proportion of industrial added value to Uganda's GDP has increased from 9.6% in 1986 to 27.1% in 2021, providing ample space for the establishment of more industries.

Uganda's national development plans related to industrial development mainly include the

Uganda Vision 2040 Development Strategy, *National Development Plan 2021–2025*, *Government Key Work for the 2021/2022 Financial Year*, COVID-19 Response Plan, and the industrialization policy formulated in 2020. The policies primarily focus on the development of various industrial sectors, as shown in Table 12–7.

Table 12–7 Uganda's Industrial-Related Policies

No.	Policy Name	Time of Introduction	Key Development Industries
1	2040 Vision Development Strategy	2013	1. Focus on making early investments in infrastructure related to the petroleum, energy, transportation, and ICT industries to maximize industrial potential. 2. Accelerate the process of industrialization by upgrading and diversifying industries to effectively utilize local resources.
2	National Development Plan 2021–2025	2020	1. Increase the contribution of the industrial sector to GDP to at least 25%. 2. Prioritize the development of the mining and manufacturing sectors.
3	Industrialization Policy 2020	2020	1. Agriculture-based industrialization; 2. Knowledge-based industrialization; 3. Export-oriented industrialization; 4. Import-substitution industrialization; 5. Resource-based industrialization; 6. Market-oriented industrialization.
4	Government Key Work for the 2021/2022 Financial Year	2021	1. In agriculture, promote industrialization development based on agriculture; nurture the private sector and improve the welfare and innovative work capacity of Ugandan people; encourage fishery development; increase the production of various types of food crops and expand the market for products such as sugar. 2. In industry, actively attract investment and promote the development of manufacturing, while incorporating youth and women into enterprises. 3. In transportation, continue to promote domestic road construction, including upgrading dirt roads, renovating old roads, and constructing overpasses. 4. In the financial sector, address the issue of loan rates by strengthening microfinance. Additionally, the government continues to encourage the public to purchase domestic products and services as much as possible to reduce imports and increase exports.
5	COVID-19 Response Plan	2021	Focus on developing the real economy, with core areas including grain, clothing, housing, medicine, national defense, infrastructure, healthcare, and education.

According to Table 12–7, the Ugandan government prioritizes the development of the real economy industries such as agriculture, petroleum, energy, transportation, mining, and manufacturing as key sectors. It aims to accelerate the industrialization process by effective utilization of local resources through strengthening infrastructure development, upgrading and diversifying industries. Specific industries that Uganda demands include household appliances, steel industry, construction and building materials, food processing, glass and plastics, automotive manufacturing and assembly, furniture, medical equipment, logistics and warehousing, textile and leather, agricultural product processing, and chemical industry.

In 2020, the COVID-19 pandemic severely impacted Uganda's economic development, resulting in a significant rise in unemployment and even pushing people back into poverty, thereby exacerbating social unrest. In response to the pandemic, Uganda has placed emphasis on developing a real economy, with agriculture as the foundation for industrialization and promoting the growth of the manufacturing sector. Key areas include food production, clothing, housing, pharmaceuticals, defense, infrastructure, healthcare, and education, etc.

The Ugandan government also actively invites foreign direct investors to take advantage of industrialization so as to bring employment opportunities. The main investment areas include the industrialization of agricultural products, import substitution, mineral-based industrialization, and export-oriented industrialization.

12.2.2 Status Quo and Development of Chinese-Funded Enterprises in Uganda

1. An Overview of the Development of Chinese-Funded Enterprises in Uganda

Since the first Chinese-funded enterprise was registered in Uganda in 1993, as of the end of 2020, over 600 ventures have been registered in Uganda. Chinese-funded enterprises in Uganda are involved in various sectors such as energy and mineral development, infrastructure construction, trade, digital television operation, agricultural development, leather processing, footwear and plastic product manufacturing, steel and other building materials production, and hotel industry. In June 2019, the governments of China and Uganda signed *Framework Agreement on Capacity Cooperation Between the National Development and Reform Commission of the People's Republic of China and the Ministry of Finance, Planning and Economic Development of the Republic of Uganda*. Both sides agreed to establish a capacity cooperation mechanism, with a focus on promoting cooperation in fields such as infrastructure, metallurgy and building materials, resource processing, equipment manufacturing, light industry and electronics, and industrial parks, etc.

Chinese-funded enterprises in Uganda support large-scale projects, such as the Karuma hydropower station, Isimba hydropower station, and the Kampala-Entebbe Expressway. These infrastructure developments create a favorable environment for Uganda and contribute to the development of industrial bases. Key Chinese companies in Uganda are about 50, including China Communications Construction Group Limited, China Water Resources and Hydropower Construction Corporation, China Water Resources and Electric Power Corporation, China Gezhouba Group International Engineering Co., Ltd., China Railway Fifth Group Co., Ltd., China Railway Seventh Group Co., Ltd., Chongqing Foreign Construction (Group) Co., Ltd., China Henan International Cooperation Group Co., Ltd., China Jiangxi International Economic and Technical Cooperation Corporation, ZTE Corporation, Huawei Technologies Co., Ltd., etc.

In 2020, a total of 1,081 Chinese workers were sent to Uganda, with 2,139 Chinese workers in Uganda by the end of the year.

2. Investment in Industrial Park by Chinese Companies in Uganda

Chinese companies have actively responded to the investment and factory establishment policies in Uganda and have invested in the construction of multiple economic and trade cooperation parks for the development of industries in Uganda. The specific details of each park are shown in Table 12–8:

Table 12–8 Industrial Parks Development Situation of Chinese Enterprise Investment

No.	Industrial Park	Investor	Establishment Date	Business Scope	Personnel Demand
1	TianTang Industrial Park	Tian Tang Group	2009	Industrial park construction; hotel catering, and tourism; production and manufacturing; real estate development; mineral resource development; machinery trading, security services	Steelmaking, ironmaking, chemical engineering, mechanical maintenance workers, intelligent equipment technicians, etc.
2	Shandong Industrial Park	China Shandong International Economic and Technical Cooperation Group Ltd.	2013	Telecommunications, textiles, plastic products, building materials, beverages, packaging industry, resin and oil, new energy, mining industry, construction, aluminum alloys for power, glass and hardware, etc.	Tiler, decorator, plumber, electronics and electrical worker, textile worker, intelligent equipment technician, mechanical maintenance workers, etc.
3	Liaoshen Industrial Park	Zhangs Group	2015	Automobile manufacturing and assembly, automobile parts, household appliances, construction materials, light industry, textiles, agricultural product processing and food, etc.	Mechanical installation and assembly, electronics and electrical appliances, construction, textiles, mechanical maintenance workers, automobile repair and manufacturing, etc.
4	Wuzheng Agricultural Industrial Park	Wuzheng Group	2016	Promotion of agricultural machinery and agronomic technology, breeding of superior varieties, demonstration of crop cultivation, application of plant protection machinery, promotion of agricultural materials, promotion of harvest and storage models, deep processing of agricultural products, agricultural product trading	Agricultural seed breeding, machinery maintenance, warehousing, logistics, etc.
5	China- Uganda Ke Hong Agricultural Industrial Park	Sichuan Ke Hong Group	2016	Crop cultivation, agricultural product processing, livestock and poultry farming and processing, agricultural machinery services, agricultural by-product trading, e-commerce logistics	Rice cultivation, rice processing and trading, laying hens farming and egg sales, beef processing and trading, etc.

continued

No.	Industrial Park	Investor	Establishment Date	Business Scope	Personnel Demand
6	Sino-Uganda Mbale Industrial Park	Tiantang Group	2018	Processing of agricultural products, metallurgical building materials, equipment manufacturing, daily necessities, clothing and textiles, power and electronics, and pharmaceutical and chemical industries.	Mechanical maintenance worker, steelmaking and ironmaking, chemical engineering, construction, mechanical maintenance workers, logistics, electrical and electronic
7	Guangzhou Dongsong International Industrial Park for Capacity Cooperation	Guangzhou Dongsong Energy Group	2018	Phosphatic fertilizers, refractory materials, ore beneficiation, and steel industry	Chemical engineering, steelmaking and ironmaking, tiling, etc.
8	Sino- Uganda Modern Economic Development Special Zone	China- Uganda Modern Economic Development Group Limited Company	—	industrial and agricultural sectors	Textiles, pharmaceuticals, agricultural processing, etc.

As seen from Table 12–8, the investors in the industrial parks constructed by Chinese enterprises in Uganda are mainly Chinese private enterprises, and their main business activities involve agricultural processing, minerals, steelmaking, equipment manufacturing, textiles, construction, etc. They closely align with Uganda's industrial development and provide tens of thousands of job opportunities for Ugandan youth. These investments have been highly welcomed and praised by the Ugandan government and the people. For instance, Tian Tang Industrial Park, the first industrial park established by China in Uganda, has provided numerous employment opportunities for Ugandan youth and women. It has also received visits from officials of both China and Uganda governments and has been recommended as a model enterprise to delegations visiting from China.

3. Main Challenges Faced by Chinese-Funded Enterprises in Uganda

The main bottlenecks faced by Chinese-funded enterprises in Uganda include:

(1) High Operating Costs

Uganda, being a landlocked country, faces disadvantages in terms of transportation costs. It relies mainly on road transportation, which is approximately five times more expensive than in China. Additionally, Uganda has an inadequate electricity supply and businesses need to self-generate power, resulting in electricity costs three times higher than in China. The lending interest rates in Uganda are relatively high, and the procedures are comparatively complex, which can be unfavorable for the long-term development of Chinese-funded enterprises. Furthermore, recent international circumstances have led to significant increases and fluctuations in sea freight prices, land transportation costs, and fuel prices.

(2) Lacking Skilled Technical Workers

Uganda's current policies still focus more on the supply side of the labor market rather than the demand side. Uganda has formulated policies such as the *Business, Technical, Vocational Education and Training Act*, *BTVET Strategic Plan 2011–2020 "Skilling Uganda"*, and *Vocational Guidance Handbook* to enhance vocational education in Uganda. However, there is a lack of research on labor market demands and a lack of demand-oriented approaches. As a result, the youth labor force available in the employment market does not align with the genuine requirements, leading to a severe mismatch between the supply and demand of skilled talent in Uganda.

12.2.3 Chinese-Funded Enterprises' Demand for Vocational Education

In 2022, Tianjin Industrial Vocational College conducted research on the employment demand in the China-Uganda Mbale Industrial Park using a survey questionnaire. Currently, there are 30 enterprises settled in the China-Uganda Mbale Industrial Park, creating over 3,200 direct job positions in the park and the distribution of employees in the China-Uganda Mbale Industrial Park is shown in Figure 12–6.

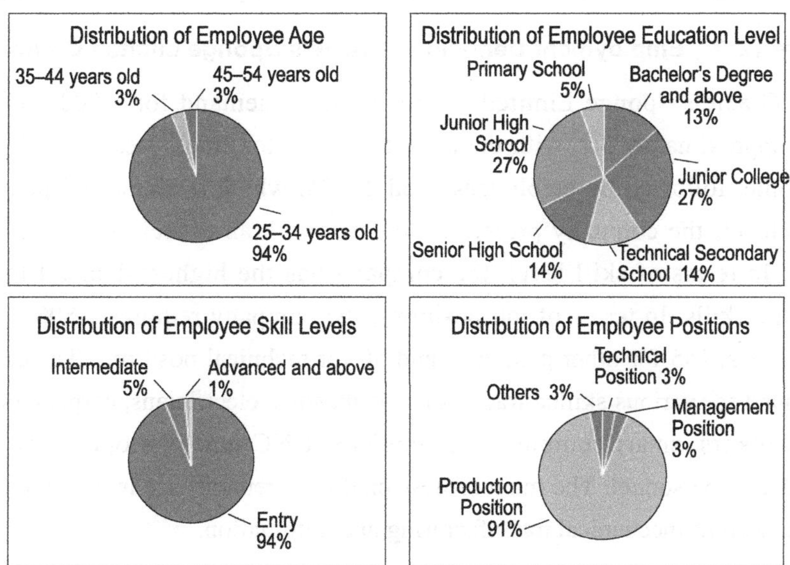

Figure 12–6 Distribution of Employees in China-Uganda Mbale Industrial Park

The research results show that the enterprises in the park are mainly from the agricultural, forestry, animal husbandry, fishery, construction, and manufacturing industries. The park currently has 3,200 employees, with the highest number of 3,000 employees in the age group of

25–34. Over 68% of the employees have a college or technical secondary school degree or above. 94% of the employees have a primary level of technical skills. The majority of the employees are from Uganda and are mainly engaged in production positions, with an average salary of 300,000 Ugandan shillings.

Based on the survey questionnaires sent to the enterprises in the park, it is found that Gris Sponge Limited Company, as an example, utilizes a mechanical production method and belongs to the manufacturing industry. Due to the need for expanding production and employee turnover, the company requires the recruitment of new employees. The employment demand of the company is shown in Figure 12–7.

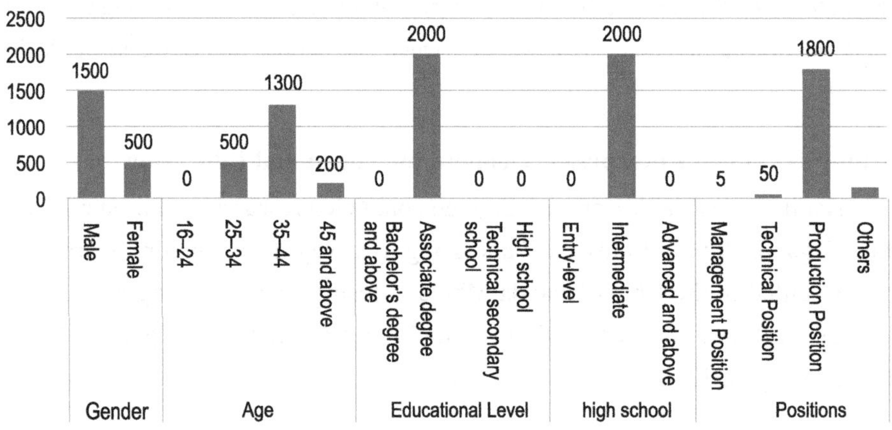

Figure 12–7 Employment Demand at Gracie's Sponge Limited Company

Currently, Gracie's Sponge Limited Company has a demand for 2,000 employees. The gender ratio is approximately 3:1, with the largest demand for employees aged 35–44, reaching up to 1300 people, followed by employees aged 25–34, which is about 500 people. In terms of educational level, the company prefers candidates with an associate degree for technical skill positions. In terms of skill level, the company has the highest demand for candidates with intermediate skills. In terms of job positions, the company requires 1,800 employees for production positions, 145 for other positions, and 50 for technical positions. The company has a significant demand for various skilled trades such as masons, electricians, carpenters, mechanical maintenance workers, smart equipment technicians, CNC machine operators, and various chemical production personnel. The main professional requirements are in safety technology and management, as well as mechanical manufacturing and automation.

In the future, China-Uganda Mbale Industrial Park plans to attract diversified industries to enter the African market. It aims to attract investment from over 80 productive enterprises, with the Ugandan production base as the core, to drive the development of diverse industries. Therefore, the park requires more skilled workers in various fields, including electronics, metallurgy, textiles, construction, chemicals, packaging materials, and others. The employment demand is expected to exceed 20,000 people.

12.2.4 Adaptability of Ugandan Vocational Education to the Development of Chinese Enterprises

The education system in Uganda lags behind, particularly in terms of the government's inability to allocate sufficient funds for vocational education to meet the needs of industrial development. Additionally, there is a long-standing bias among Ugandan society and people toward vocational education. Other factors that hinder the development of vocational education in Uganda include poor employment prospects for vocational education graduates, a lack of flexibility and practicality in vocational education curricula, a shortage of qualified teachers, and weak information technology infrastructure. These factors impede the development of vocational education in Uganda and constrain the development of professional and technical talent needed for capacity cooperation between China and Uganda.

Through the research on vocational education in Uganda, a problem tree that hinders the development of vocational education in Uganda has been formed through systematic review and data analysis, as shown in Figure 12–8.

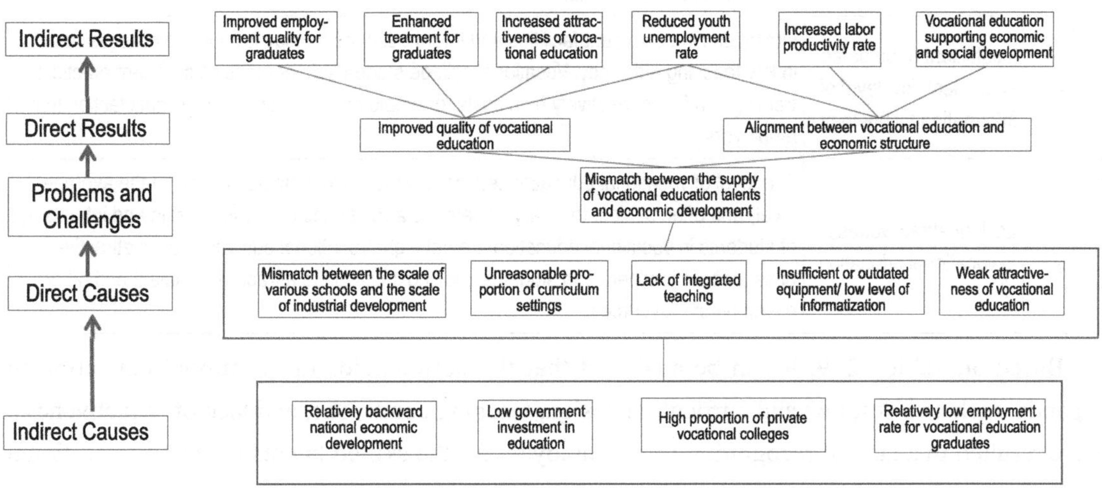

Figure 12–8 Problem Tree of Vocational Education in Uganda

By logically reasoning through the direct and indirect causes that affect the development of vocational education in Uganda, and then addressing the above problems through a reasonable approach, it is expected to enhance the quality of vocational education and improve the alignment with the local economic and industrial structure. Therefore, identifying the root causes of the direct causes is of guiding significance for proposing targeted solutions. The project team conducted an attribution analysis for vocational education in Uganda (Refer to Table 12–9).

Table 12–9 Attribution Analysis Table of Vocational Education Development Issues in Uganda

No.	Direct Reasons	Description
1	mismatch between the scale of various schools and the scale of industrial development	The proportions of employees in the primary, secondary, and tertiary industries are 72.67%, 6.60%, and 20.73% respectively, while the proportions of vocational colleges according to the relevant industries are 2.29%, 4.58%, and 81.67% for the primary, secondary, and tertiary industries respectively, not in line with their industrial development. The ratios of different types of vocational colleges do not match the industrial development and the distribution of labor force among different industries in Uganda.
2	Mismatch between curriculum design and job demand	Through research conducted on the Uganda Higher Education Commission, it has been discovered that both graduates and employers provide feedback that there is a need for improvement in the curriculum design of vocational education. Many graduates suggest the inclusion of additional courses in their field of study, while also pointing out that there is a lack of courses that are beneficial for their employment prospects.
3	Lack of integrated teaching	Due to limitations in resources, most vocational colleges lack integrated teaching, learning, and practical experiences. They only offer industrial visits, which results in insufficient practical exposure for students and makes it challenging to cultivate talents that meet the demands of the job market.
4	Insufficient or outdated equipment; low level of information technology	Limitations in equipment facilities and information technology level in the colleges result in low teaching efficiency. Vocational college students do not receive sufficient practical training, leading to relatively high costs for employment training and low satisfaction from employers.
5	Lack of attractiveness in vocational education	The level of vocational education teacher salaries is low (approximately at the average level) and often subject to salary arrears. As a result, the employment rate and job quality of students in vocational education are not high. Vocational education lacks attractiveness for both teachers and students, making it difficult to attract better talent and other development resources.

Based on Table 12–9, it can be analyzed that the deficiencies in vocational education in Uganda, such as institution and curriculum design, teaching conditions, and lack of attractiveness, have resulted in a lack of recognition from employers for the skilled talents trained by vocational education.

A survey conducted on China-Uganda Mbale Industrial Park also revealed that employers stated that employees need to undergo training before starting their jobs. They identified several prominent issues among employees in their actual positions, including weak management knowledge, inadequate technical skills, lack of industry-specific professional background knowledge, insufficient understanding of industry regulations and standards, a disconnect between learned professional knowledge and actual job requirements, narrow technical knowledge, and weak practical abilities, among others. It is hoped that graduates will receive sufficient practical training during their higher education and possess creativity, critical thinking, a spirit of teamwork, and a sense of responsibility. Therefore, vocational education in Uganda still cannot meet the demand for a large number of skilled workers for industrial parks and the labor market, which will hinder China-Ugandan production capacity cooperation.

12.3 Chinese-Funded Enterprises Collaborating with Chinese Vocational Education for Going Global

12.3.1 The Necessity of Chinese Vocational Education Supporting China-Uganda Production Capacity Cooperation

1. The Demand for Technical and Skilled Personnel in the Economic and Industrial Development of Uganda

Uganda is endowed with abundant natural resources, including vast mineral deposits. However, its agricultural sector suffers from insufficient technology and equipment, resulting in low productivity and efficiency. The Ugandan government aims to modernize agriculture through mechanization, scientific storage methods, and irrigation plans. It seeks to import advanced Chinese technology, top-notch equipment, and scientific production management practices to increase crop yield and enhance production efficiency. The industrial sector in Uganda has been slow to develop due to inadequate infrastructure and high production costs. To accelerate industrialization, the government plans to prioritize industrialization efforts across the country and invest in infrastructure development. The service industry is the fastest-growing sector in Uganda. The government is focused on developing knowledge-based industries and giving priority to sectors such as information and communication technology, human resources, tourism, and trade sectors.

Uganda's Vision 2040 Development Strategy aims for the country to become a middle-income country by 2040. The strategy is implemented through individual ten-year plans, six five-year national development plans, and other policy frameworks. Key development areas include oil and gas, tourism, minerals, information and communication technology, water resources, industry, and agriculture. In the first national development plan (2011–2015) and the second national development plan (2015–2020) of the vision implementation, Uganda successfully reduced the absolute poverty rate to 14.8%. However, due to the impact of the COVID-19 pandemic, the poverty rate in Uganda has risen to 22%, with 32% of Ugandan youth living below the poverty line. Therefore, in 2021, Uganda focused on industrial development in the formulation of the third national development plan (2021–2025), under the theme of "industrialization for inclusive growth, employment, and sustainable wealth creation," aiming to overcome the existing poverty levels in the country. In 2020, Uganda also introduced industrialization policies, focusing on utilizing its natural resources and basing industrialization on agriculture, resources, and knowledge, while following the path of export-oriented, import substitution, and market-driven industrial development.

Based on Uganda's industrial structure and strategic documents such as the *Vision 2040*

Development Strategy, National Development Plan 2021–2025, Government Priority Areas for the 2021/2022 Fiscal Year, and the *COVID-19 Response Plan*, as well as the industrialization policy implemented in 2020, it is evident that the Ugandan government prioritizes the development of key industries such as agriculture, manufacturing, construction, steel industry, oil and gas, transportation, and mining as part of its economic diversification efforts. The government aims to accelerate the industrialization process by strengthening infrastructure development, promoting industrial upgrading, and effectively utilizing local resources.

In May 2020, the latest report from the Uganda Investment Authority revealed that in the first three quarters of the 2019/2020 fiscal year, the Ugandan government created 23,055 job opportunities. Out of those, 7,716 jobs were created through domestic direct investment, while 15,339 were created through foreign direct investment. However, Uganda's current economy faces challenges in providing more job opportunities for the growing labor force, making it difficult to achieve the target of creating 60,000 jobs in the current fiscal year. In addition, the emphasis on industrial development in Uganda has further widened the gap between the supply and demand of human resources in the industrial sector. Therefore, Uganda urgently needs to attract more foreign investment to create more employment opportunities for its youth.

2. The Demand for Technical and Skilled Talent in China-Uganda Capacity Cooperation

Chinai is the largest source of direct investment for Uganda. Chinese-funded enterprises has built a large amount of infrastructure for Uganda, providing a solid foundation for its industrial development. The industrial areas of China-Uganda capacity cooperation are in line with Uganda's industrial development needs, primarily involving energy and mineral development, infrastructure construction, trade, digital television operation, agricultural development, leather processing, shoe and plastic product manufacturing, steel and other building materials production, and hotels. In the future, the focus will be on promoting cooperation in areas such as infrastructure, metallurgy and building materials, resource processing, equipment manufacturing, light industry and electronics, and industrial clusters. At the same time, Chinese-funded enterprises actively respond to Uganda's investment policies for industrial park construction and have established eight industrial parks, providing tens of thousands of job opportunities for Uganda. Among them, the China-Uganda Mbale Industrial Park, constructed by the Tian Tang Group, has successfully addressed the issue of employment for Ugandan youth and women, receiving great appreciation from the Ugandan government and people. The China-Uganda Mbale Industrial Park, invested and constructed by the Tian Tang Group, is an important achievement in implementing the "Belt and Road" Initiative and the Forum on China-Africa Cooperation mechanism. It is listed as a national-level industrial park in Uganda and is committed to attracting excellent Chinese enterprises to invest and produce in the park, providing a good platform for China-Uganda capacity cooperation and serving as an intellectual support platform for China's vocational education support to China-Uganda capacity cooperation.

Currently, there are 30 companies stationed in the China-Uganda Mbale Industrial Park, and it is expected to attract more than 80 companies in the future. Research conducted on the park shows that the companies stationed there, due to increasing production demands, may employ up to 20,000 employees, including talents from various fields such as electronics, metallurgy, textiles, construction, chemicals, and packaging. At the same time, the surveyed companies stated that employees need to undergo training before starting work and expressed the view that Ugandan employees have a low quality of education, lacking professional skills and a work ethic.

3. Insufficient Supply of Skilled Professionals in Uganda's Vocational Education for Specialized Technical Skills

In 2012, the Ugandan government introduced the "Skilling Uganda Programme" to incorporate vocational and technical courses into the regular education system and higher education curriculum, spanning the entire learning phase of students. This significant decision, taking into account the overall situation in Uganda, has played a role in alleviating the country's youth unemployment problem. However, there are still many issues with the professional and technical skills development in Ugandan vocational education, which hinder the provision of high-quality professional and technical talents for the country's economic and industrial development and pose obstacles to China-Uganda capacity cooperation.

The total labor force in Uganda exceeded 17 million in 2021, with over 70% of the labor force engaged in agriculture-related work, while only 20% were in the industrial sector. There is a significant shortage of professional and technical talent. Additionally, due to factors such as a mismatch between job opportunities and the skills taught in vocational education and poor teaching conditions, the quality of vocational education graduates in Uganda is not high.

There is a mismatch between job opportunities and the skills taught in vocational education. The number of higher vocational colleges in Uganda does not align with the country's current industrial planning. There are only five technical institutes, which are unable to provide the technical and skilled workforce needed for Uganda's industrialization efforts. Furthermore, according to a report from the Uganda Higher Education Commission in 2019, the majority of graduates surveyed (75.1%) and employers (54%) believe that the vocational education curriculum needs to be more aligned with the socio-economic development and occupational demands. They also suggest allocating more time during the curriculum implementation process.

There are poor teaching conditions in vocational education. Due to limited resources, most vocational colleges lack integrated teaching, learning, and practical components. The practical experience of students is insufficient, leading to difficulties in developing talents that meet job requirements. Furthermore, constrained by the conditions and level of information technology in institutions, teaching efficiency is low. Students in higher vocational colleges do not receive sufficient practical training, resulting in higher costs for employment training and low satisfaction from employers.

The quality of vocational education graduates is not high. Graduates from higher vocational education programs receive lower salary packages compared to university graduates, and their employment rates and quality are not high. Employers express relative satisfaction with the knowledge and skills acquired by students during their studies. However, they also note a mismatch between the students' academic performance and their actual output in the workplace. There is a lack of a strong work ethic among graduates. Employers hope for a quality assurance system for the university graduates.

In summary, Uganda urgently needs to promote its overall economic and social development through industrialization, and there is an urgent need for Chinese companies to enter Uganda to address the issue of youth unemployment. However, the current vocational education in Uganda cannot meet the demands of the labor market and provide professional and technical talents that are matched with job opportunities. It requires support from Chinese vocational education and collaboration with Chinese companies to provide technical expertise and talent support for Uganda's socio-economic development.

12.3.2 Chinese Vocational Education's Support for China-Uganda Production Capacity Cooperation

Under the framework of the "Belt and Road" Initiative and the Forum on China-Africa Cooperation, an increasing number of Chinese higher vocational education institutions are entering Uganda to collaborate with Chinese companies in supporting China-Uganda capacity cooperation. This collaboration mainly includes initiatives such as establishing the Uganda Luban Workshop, establishing China-Uganda vocational colleges, and conducting short-term training programs.

1. Uganda Luban Workshop

To serve the "Belt and Road" Initiative and implement the spirit of President Xi Jinping's speech at the Forum on China-Africa Cooperation, Tianjin Vocational Institute of Industry and Trade, together with Elgon Uganda Technical College and Tian Tang Group, jointly established the Uganda Luban Workshop to provide higher vocational education and skills training. On December 10, 2020, a virtual unveiling ceremony was held, with the Vice Mayor of Tianjin and the Minister of Science, Technology, and Innovation of Uganda in attendance. President Museveni of Uganda unveiled the plaque for the training base of the Uganda Luban Workshop. As one of the first operational projects among the Luban Workshops nationwide, the Uganda Luban Workshop will facilitate the international integration of distinctive professional clusters with advantageous industrial chains. It aims to effectively support Chinese enterprises to "going global," enhance the friendship between China and Uganda, inject new vitality into the social and economic development of Uganda as well as the East African and Central African regions, and enhance China's vocational education service capabilities for the "Belt and Road" Initiative.

During the construction process, the Uganda Luban Workshop strictly adhered to the "five in-place" requirements, including site construction, training equipment, teacher training, professional standards, and teaching resources, to ensure the smooth operation of the workshop. The workshop is guided by the needs of Uganda's economic development and construction, and offers programs in black metallurgy technology and key professional fields such as mechatronics. It aims to cultivate technical and skilled personnel in metallurgy, mechanical manufacturing, and electrical automation to support Uganda's industrialization development.

2. China-Uganda Vocational College

The vocational colleges established by China in Uganda mainly include Sunmaker Uganda Petroleum Institute, Shandong S&T International College in East Africa (Uganda), Uganda Technical Training Center, and Uganda College of Sichuan Architectural Vocational and Technical College.

Sunmaker Uganda Petroleum Institute was established by the Sunmaker Project team. It offers a comprehensive training system covering exploration, drilling, cementing, well completion, oil and gas production, oil and gas gathering and transmission, refining, and management. The college can issue internationally recognized certificates. Based on petroleum technology training, it aims to address the technical challenges arising from the significant untapped oil resources in Uganda.

Shandong Vocational College of Science and Technology, East Africa (Uganda) International College is jointly established by Shandong Vocational College of S&T, Uganda Sunmaker Textile and Garment Co., Ltd., and Sunmaker Uganda Petroleum Institute. It is located in Kampala. The college primarily offers professional training programs in computer application technology, textile and clothing, and mechanical processing. It also provides Chinese language training, expand the enrollment and systematically cultivating internationally specialized talents.

The Uganda Technical Training Center, cooperatively established by Weifang Vocational College and the Uganda Oil Training Institute, was officially established in November 2018. Weifang Vocational College provided over 30 sets of mechanical, automotive, and agricultural technical equipment to the Uganda Technical Training Center. They also shared a series of technical training standards, training materials, and other high-quality educational resources.

The Uganda College of Sichuan College of Architectural Technology is jointly established by Sichuan College of Architectural Technology, East Africa International University, and Sunmaker Uganda Petroleum Institute. It aims to cultivate architectural technical and skilled personnel for Uganda and East Africa.

3. Short-term Training Programs

The Wuhan-Uganda Entebbe Vocational Education Training Program is one of the important aspects of friendly exchanges between the Wuhan Municipal Government and the Entebbe Municipal Government. It has been held twice, training a total of 40 Ugandan students. The training program covers more than 20 disciplines, including early childhood education, tourism service skills, development and design of handicrafts, electronic information technology, carpentry skills, automotive maintenance, aquaculture, edible mushroom cultivation, mineral detection and development, engineering surveying, solar power generation (maintenance and repair), and e-commerce.

The 2016 Uganda Agricultural Planting Technology Overseas Training Program, sponsored by the Ministry of Commerce and organized by Shandong Foreign Trade Vocational College, was China's first foreign aid training program implemented in Uganda. It trained a total of 30 Ugandan technicians, with a focus on rice and millet planting techniques.

In 2018, the Training Program on Fruit Tree Cultivation Techniques for Developing Countries was launched at Shandong Foreign Trade Vocational College, with 28 participants from eight countries, including Uganda. After theoretical classes held at the Tai'an base, the participants visited major fruit production bases in Jinan, Shenzhen, and Qixia, learning advanced planting techniques in China and promoting agricultural development in their respective countries.

12.3.3 Forms and Achievements of Internationalized Education

Uganda, as one of the underdeveloped countries in Africa, has a relatively low overall level of economic development. The country faces challenges such as high rates of out-of-school and drop-out among children and youth, the need for improving comprehensive skills among workers, and a shortage of technical and skilled personnel in the process of industrialization. Uganda is one of the regions in urgent need for educational assistance.

Based on over 60 years of colonial rule, Uganda's education system bears a deep imprint of British influence. Over the years, Uganda has established and continued to follow an education system based on the British-style 7–4–2 system, which has had a profound impact on the development of education, including higher education. The development of education in Uganda still heavily relies on international assistance and cooperation and external financial aid and effective coordination of aid agencies are crucial. The main education aid agencies in Uganda include the World Bank, the United Kingdom, the United States, the Netherlands, and Ireland. The majority of international education aid funds that flow into Uganda are directed towards primary education, followed by secondary education, with very little direct funding allocated to higher vocational education.

The World Bank-funded Uganda Skills Development Project aims to meet the skill demands in agriculture, construction, and manufacturing. The project provides competency-based, high-quality training for craftsmen (low-level), technicians (mid-level), and artisans (high-level) through four schools: Uganda Technical College Bushenyi, Elgon, Lira, and Bukalasa Agricultural College. The training equips them with the skills required in relevant industries or professions in Uganda's manufacturing, construction, and agricultural processing sectors. The project supports the improvement of 12 public vocational training institutions through training, curriculum development assistance, and equipment procurement guidelines, with a focus on establishing networking relationships.

The Ugandan government, with funding from the World Bank, has developed the Aberdeen Area Sustainable Development Project. The project aims to train professionals in emerging industries, with a focus on the oil sector (petroleum operations, mechanical maintenance, electrical maintenance, and instrumentation) and artisans in the construction industry (carpenters, joiners, bricklayers, plumbers, electrical installers, scaffolders, welders, and fabricators). The project will support approximately 600 students from the region to undergo skill training lasting from six months to two and a half years at leading institutes in the country specializing in construction, agricultural processing, tourism, and nursing.

12.4 Tianjin Polytechnic College's Support for China-Ugandan Capacity Cooperation

Tianjin Polytechnic College actively serves the construction of the "Belt and Road" Initiative, implements the objectives of the speeches at the China-Africa Cooperation Forum, in accordance with the spiritual instructions of the Tianjin Municipal Education Commission, collaborates with Uganda Technical College Elgon and TianTang Group to jointly establish the Uganda Luban Workshop. It strives to support Chinese enterprises' "going global" strategy by co-building training bases with Chinese-funded enterprises, conducting overseas training, and achieving international integration between distinctive p rofessional clusters and local advantageous industrial chains.

12.4.1 Current Situation Analysis

The Uganda Luban Workshop is geared towards meeting the demand for technical and skilled talents in Uganda's industrialization, the demand for technical and skilled talents by companies in the China-Uganda Mbale Industrial Park and other industrial zones, and the demand for metallurgical and electromechanical professionals in Uganda. It provides talent services to Tian Tang Group, companies in the China-Uganda Mbale Industrial Park, and other Chinese-funded enterprises in Uganda. The workshop is jointly built by the college and enterprises, aiming to establish professional standards and share resources, in order to provide skills training for Ugandan employees.

Currently, the Uganda Luban Workshop has adopted the cooperative approach of "Universities

-Enterprise-Industrial park" and the construction model of "demand-oriented, standard-guided, all-round cooperation, continuous efforts". The workshop covers a total area of 1825 square meters and has four professional training labs and five specialized training areas. It offers programs in black metallurgy technology and electromechanical integration technology, and has developed two internationalized teaching standards and corresponding teaching resources tailored to the economic development of Uganda. The workshop has also established bilingual training resources for CNC lathe operators, organized three teacher training sessions with a total of 764 teaching hours, and provided training for 45 employees from companies in the training park.

12.4.2 Education Models

The Uganda Luban workshop adopts a "Universities-Enterprise-Industrial park" integrated construction approach, with two universities including Tianjin Polytechnic College and Uganda Technical College Elgon, the enterprise referring to the Uganda Tian Tang Group, and the park representing the China-Uganda Mbale Industrial Park. The four entities collaborate and engage in partnerships between universities and enterprises. In the construction and operation of the Uganda Luban workshop, Uganda Technical College Elgon provides the workshop venue, handles local admissions, recommends talent for enterprise development, and collaborates on organizing the Sino-Uganda Vocational Skills Competition. Tian Tang Group provides training base facilities, assists in site and equipment construction, participates in jointly developing professional standards and resources, offers internships, provides guidance and training, gathers feedback from enterprise demands, actively recommends enterprises and entrepreneurs, and facilitates local communication for the workshop construction. Tianjin Polytechnic College fully supports the professional development of the workshop, invests in equipment and instruments, provides skills training for the China-Uganda Mbale Industrial Park, and shares network resources with Uganda Technical College Elgon and the park enterprises.

The Uganda Luban workshop adopts a construction model of "demand-oriented, standard-led, four-party collaboration, and continuous efforts". It is driven by the demand for technical and skilled talents in the social and economic industries of Uganda. Based on Chinese professional teaching standards, vocational skills standards, equipment standards, and curriculum standards, combined with the local economic situation and industrial structure of Uganda, Luban workshop teaching standards are formulated, integrating into the vocational education system of Uganda. Following the construction approach of the "Universities-Enterprise-Industrial park" collaboration, Tianjin Polytechnic College, Uganda Technical College Elgon, and Tian Tang Group are the collaborating units. Leveraging the China-Uganda Mbale Industrial Park, they carry out international university-enterprise cooperation and integrate industry with education, continuously promoting the construction of the Luban Workshop to achieve sustainable development (See Figure 12–9).

During the construction process of the Uganda Luban Workshop, we have consistently adhered to the "five requirements" of site construction, training equipment, teacher training, professional standards, and teaching materials and resources. Our goal is to establish a high-quality Luban workshop and ensure its smooth construction and operation.

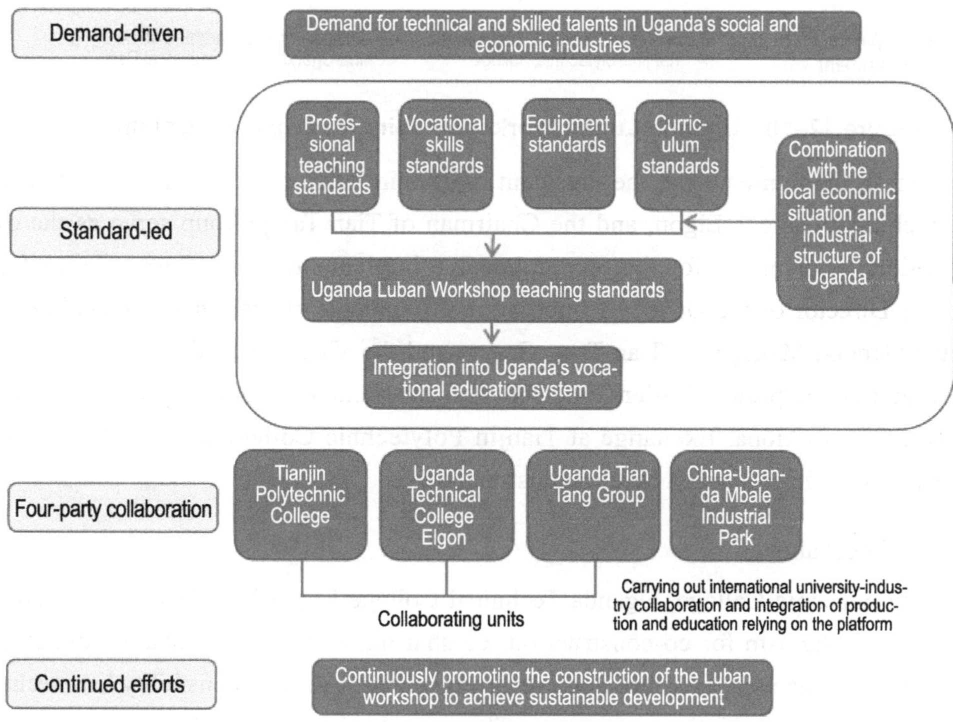

Figure 12–9 Construction Model of Uganda Luban Workshop

12.4.3 Institutional Mechanism

When Tianjin Polytechnic College, Uganda Technical College Elgon, and Tian Tang Group first established the Uganda Luban Workshop, the three parties signed a tripartite agreement called the *China-Uganda Vocational Education Tripartite Cooperation Agreement* and two school-enterprise cooperation agreements. Within the framework of these agreements, the management system and operation mechanism of the Uganda Luban Workshop were established.

1. Management System

Tianjin Polytechnic College, Uganda Technical College Elgon, and Tian Tang Group have dispatched dedicated personnel in charge of the Luban Workshop to form the Joint Management Committee of the Uganda Luban Workshop, responsible for the implementation of Sino-Uganda Vocational Education Exchange and Cooperation Projects. The structure of the Joint Management Committee of the Uganda Luban Workshop is shown in Figure 12–10.

Figure 12–10 Uganda Luban Workshop Joint Management Committee

As shown in the figure above, the President of Tianjin Polytechnic College, the Principal of Uganda Technical College Elgon, and the Chairman of Tian Tang Group serve as the overall project leaders, responsible for the comprehensive implementation and management of the project. The Director of the Office of International Exchange at Tianjin Polytechnic College, the Deputy General Manager of Tian Tang Group, and the Vice Principal of Uganda Technical College Elgon act as project leaders, and the main implementing departments are located in the Office of International Exchange at Tianjin Polytechnic College and the Administrative Department of the China-Uganda Mbale Industrial Park.

2. Operation Mechanism

Tianjin Polytechnic College, Uganda Technical College Elgon, and Tian Tang Group have established a mechanism for co-construction, co-sharing, and mutual consultation, a regular communication mechanism, an information reporting mechanism, a responsibility list mechanism, and a coordination and resolution mechanism. These mechanisms ensure the smooth operation of the Uganda Luban Workshop.

(1) Mechanism of Co-Planning, Co-Construction, and Co-Sharing

Tianjin Polytechnic College, Uganda Technical College Elgon, and Tian Tang Group have jointly planned and constructed the Uganda Luban Workshop, including the construction of the workshop venue and training base, the scientific planning of training rooms and areas, and the provision of corresponding training equipment.

The three parties prioritize resource integration and information sharing. The Chinese universities share quality majors and state-of-the-art technical equipment with partner countries. Based on this foundation, the collaborating enterprises combine talent development and practical production capabilities in line with the market demands of the partner country, incorporating new processes, technologies, concepts, and standards. In accordance with local education and teaching standards, the three parties jointly establish professional standards for the Uganda Luban Workshop, enhancing the expertise of teaching staff and sharing high-quality vocational education resources and achievements from China.

(2) Mechanism of Regular Communication

Tianjin Polytechnic College has established a mechanism of regular communication with Tian Tang Group. The President of Tianjin Polytechnic College and the Chairman of Uganda Tian Tang Group communicate at least once every quarter to provide guidance on the deep and smooth integration of industry and education in top-level design. The project leaders from the university and the responsible person of Tian Tang Group for the Luban Workshop communicate at least once every month to exchange information on the progress of the industry-education integration or address any issues encountered. The project implementation staff from the university and the workshop staff from Tian Tang Group have weekly communication to continuously monitor changes in Uganda's socio-economic development, keep up with new technologies and standards of "going global" enterprises, and continuously improve teaching standards, equipment and facilities, teacher training, and resource development based on international advanced professional technology, advanced process flow, and the latest international standards. These efforts enrich the service functions of the Luban Workshop and ensure its sustainable development.

(3) Mechanism of Information Reporting

Uganda Technical College Elgon collaborates with Tian Tang Group to submit various information required by the management system of the Luban Workshop. They also cooperate in conducting surveys on the demand for technical and skilled talents in Uganda, providing timely feedback on teacher training, student learning, and employee training. Additionally, they promptly report relevant information regarding the workshop and the training base, such as emergency situations regarding venues and equipment, media interviews about the workshop, and visits by domestic and foreign leaders.

(4) Responsibility List Mechanism

Tianjin Polytechnic College, Uganda Technical College Elgon, and Tian Tang Group signed the *China-Uganda Vocational Education Tripartite Cooperation Agreement* in February 2020, which stipulates the rights and obligations of the three parties. Based on this, the responsibility lists of the three parties are divided. Tianjin Polytechnic College is mainly responsible for supporting the construction of majors (standards, courses, resources, internships, and practical training), investing in equipment and instruments, providing skills training, and sharing network resources. Uganda Technical College Elgon is mainly responsible for providing Luban Workshop venues, local enrollment, training and recommending talents needed by enterprises, and jointly promoting the holding of skills competitions. Tian Tang Group is mainly responsible for providing training base venues, co-building professional standards and resources, assisting in venue and equipment construction, recommending enterprises and entrepreneurs, providing internships, guidance, and training, and doing local communication. The China-Uganda Mbale Industrial Park is mainly responsible for training base venues, feedback on needs from enterprises in the park, and guidance and training.

(5) Coordination and Resolution Mechanism

The Uganda Luban Workshop has encountered many problems during its construction and operation. Tianjin Polytechnic College, Uganda Technical College Elgon, and Tian Tang Group have adopted a method of negotiating and jointly solving problems, and successfully promoted the construction and operation of the workshop. In the case of minor issues, the three-party project implementation personnel negotiate to solve them; if they cannot be resolved, the project leaders negotiate; if the project leaders cannot solve them, the project general leaders negotiate to solve them, to ensure the continuous construction of the Uganda Luban Workshop.

12.4.4 Safeguard Measures

The "School-Enterprise-School" tripartite has jointly formulated more than 10 Luban Workshop series management systems, providing institutional guarantee for the smooth operation of the workshop. In addition, safety management systems and 8S management systems have been developed in the four training rooms and four training areas to ensure that the students who learn and practice in the workshop complete their learning and practical content safely and in accordance with the system requirements.

Tianjin Polytechnic College has participated in high-level research projects multiple times, forming a series of research results. Deeper research has been conducted on the social and economic industries of Uganda and even East Africa, laying the theoretical foundation for the construction of Uganda Luban Workshop.

12.4.5 Main Achievements

1. The Expanding Influence of Luban Workshop Promoting Deep Cooperation in International Production and Education Integration

On December 10, 2020, the Ugandan Luban Workshop was officially launched and was reported by 24 domestic and foreign media outlets. Africa LIVE and CCTV News broadcasted news about the workshop on the day of the 2021 African Industrialization Day. The Ugandan Luban Workshop welcomed the visit of the Chinese Ambassador to Uganda and the new Ugandan Ambassador to China, and as one of the achievements of the Luban Workshop construction, it exhibited its construction achievements at the first World Vocational Education Production-Education Integration Expo, which was welcomed by people from all walks of life and expanded its international influence.

The continuous expansion of the influence of the Ugandan Luban Workshop allows Ugandan teachers, students, and employees to deepen their understanding of the workshop, Chinese vocational education development, educational culture, and education models, which is conducive to improving the recognition of Chinese vocational education in Uganda and promoting production-education integration of the Luban Workshop in Uganda. At the same time, in the process of serving the production capacity cooperation between China and Uganda, Ugandan students and enterprise employees have deepened their understanding and recognition of Chinese vocational education, Chinese technology, Chinese products, and Chinese enterprises through training, which promotes the sustainable development of Luban Workshop. Therefore, the workshop and China-Uganda production capacity cooperation complement each other, promote each other, and are conducive to the sustainable development of both parties.

2. Setting Up the Training Base and Platform for Sustainable Production and Education Integration

The Uganda Luban Workshop Training Base covers a total area of 1080 square meters and has 5 professional training areas: CNC machining, fitter, electrical automation technology, industrial simulation, and mechatronics comprehensive training. The CNC machining training area is equipped with 4 CNC lathes, which can be used to learn the processing of shaft and disk parts, and complete the basic operations of CNC machining and CNC lathes. The fitter training area is equipped with fitter training tables and other equipment to cultivate technical and skilled personnel engaged in mechanical product assembly, commissioning, installation, and maintenance. The electrical automation technology training area is equipped with 4 electrician and electronic training tables and 4 advanced maintenance electrician training tables, which can train composite technical and skilled personnel for the positions of electrical installation, operation, and maintenance personnel of production equipment. The industrial simulation training area is equipped with 24 computers, with two sets of simulation training systems for continuous casting production simulation and small-section production simulation, which can simulate the production process of continuous casting and small-sections. The mechatronics comprehensive training area is equipped with mechatronics comprehensive training equipment for the national vocational college skills competition, which can connect with the international professional skills and core competence training of mechatronics technology, and also cultivate methodological abilities in occupational literacy.

All devices have been installed and debugged and can be put into use. All equipment at the Luban Workshop Training Base can provide skill training for employees of companies in the China-Uganda Mbale Industrial Park, and provide internship and training conditions for students at Uganda Technical College Elgon.

3. Joint Construction of International Professional Standards and Resources Between Schools and Enterprises

The teaching resources of the Uganda Luban Workshop are mainly in English. The international teaching standards for two majors and international course standards for nine core courses have been jointly developed. Nine bilingual textbooks for core courses and one bilingual training textbook have been published. The major of mechatronics technology is based on the international teaching standards approved by the Tianjin Education Commission, and the major of black metallurgical technology is based on the international teaching standards approved by the Nonferrous Metals Industry Association Committee. The three parties of "school-enterprise-school" have improved and revised two international teaching standards for two majors in line with the economic development in Uganda. Both majors completed professional certification approval and payment in 2021. After all certification procedures are completed, they will be incorporated into the Ugandan education system. At the same time, Uganda Luban Workshop has built and equipped a professional teaching resource library related to this major, including audio and video materials, teaching courseware, digital teaching case libraries, virtual simulation software, and digital textbooks, greatly enriching the three-dimensional teaching resources and ensuring the smooth progress of training for enterprise employees in the park.

Construction of the Black Metallurgical Technology professional teaching resource library follows the idea of "fragmented resources, structured curriculum and systematic design", with the goal of resource development and curriculum system construction as the mainline. It is built in a coordinated manner in three directions: resource management, learning management and portal management. Based on cutting-edge technology and new achievements in industry applications, the digital shared courses "Bar Production Technology", "Steel Production Technology", "Continuous Casting Production Technology", "Metallurgical Overview" and "External Refining Technology" are developed to greatly increase the quantity and type of construction, so that teachers can flexibly build courses for independent learning.

The Mechatronics Technology major constructs high-quality characteristic courses, develops stereoscopic textbooks, and builds the latest high-quality education resources integrating education, industry, and enterprises, including virtual processing, virtual assembly, text, pictures, audio, video, animation, electronic textbooks, courseware, exercises library, and test library, etc. The digital shared courses with self-learning and online communication functions include Numerical Control Machining Technology, Maintenance Electrical Skills Training, Mechatronics Innovative Intelligent Application Technology, and Electrical Control and PLC Application.

The bilingual training resources for CNC turning include one volume of CNC Turning Vocational Skills Training Course (Chinese-English version) and a series of micro-course resources.

4. Emphasis on Teacher Training, Laying the Foundation for Talent in China-Uganda Production Capacity Cooperation

During the construction and operation period of Uganda Luban Workshop, teacher training has always been valued to improve the practical teaching ability of Ugandan teachers and enable students trained by Ugandan teachers to possess the technical skills required by the enterprises in the industrial park. Uganda Luban Workshop has held two teacher training exchange conferences to address targeted teacher training issues and has organized three teacher training sessions, with 764 training hours in total. The specific training situation is shown in Table 12–10.

Table 12–10 Teacher Training Situation in Uganda

Training Session	Training Dates	Training Method	Training Hours	Number of Chinese Teachers	Number of Ugandan Trainees
1	January 11, 2021–February 7 (4 weeks in total)	Online Training (Email Communication)	288	11	17
2	September 13, 2021–December 12, 2021 (13 weeks in total)	Online Training (Email Communication)	380	11	17
3	February 28, 2022–May 3, 2022 (8 weeks in total)	Online Training (Tencent Meeting)	96	15	18

As seen in Table 12–10, teachers responsible for the nine courses in Uganda participated in every teacher training, and the third training session was conducted through centralized training. Chinese teachers utilized online meeting platform for on-site teaching, greatly improving the learning effectiveness of Ugandan teachers.

In November 2022, Uganda Luban Workshop held a series of teacher training thematic lectures, specifically introducing the connotation and construction of Luban Workshop, online resources for smart vocational education, EPIP teaching mode, etc. Ugandan teachers gained a deeper understanding of Luban Workshop, Chinese teaching concepts, teaching methods, and teaching resources, which will be conducive to deepening cultural exchanges between China and Uganda, facilitating Ugandan teachers in training Luban Workshop students, and promoting China-Uganda vocational education to serve production capacity cooperation.

5. Improving the Skills of African Employees

Uganda Luban Workshop actively serves the "Belt and Road" construction and China-Africa production capacity cooperation and continuously strengthens school-enterprise cooperation. Based on the enterprises in the China-Uganda Mbale Industrial Park, the workshop matches the types of training majors that Tianjin Polytechnic College can provide with the professional settings of Uganda Luban Workshop through research on the training needs of the park's enterprises, forming a training program for African employees in the park, providing technical and skills training for African young professionals, effectively supporting vocational education services for the "Belt and Road" construction and the socio-economic development of cooperative countries. By adopting remote education and training cooperation, international vocational education services, mainly technical and skills training, are provided for African employees.

In January 2022, Uganda Tian Tang Group trained 45 African employees, using Luban Workshop's professional equipment, effectively improving the professional technical skills of African young people. Their satisfaction with the equipment and training of the workshop was over 80%.

12.5 Existing Problems and Development Recommendations

12.5.1 Existing Problems and Analysis of Causes

1. Shortage of Ugandan Technical Talents Leading to Difficulties in Providing Chinese Vocational Education Services

From 2017 to 2021, Uganda's annual GDP growth rate was around 4%, with a GDP of only $40.43 billion and a GDP per capita of $848.1 in 2021. These two indicators ranked 16th and 37th respectively among African countries, making Uganda an underdeveloped economy. Agriculture is its pillar industry while the manufacturing industry is lagging. The Ugandan government intends to promote the development of more industries by accelerating the *industrialization* process. In 2019, the proportions of the first, second, and third industries in Uganda were 23.1%, 26.3%, and 43.2% respectively. The proportions of employees in the first, second, and third industries were 72.67%, 6.60%, and 20.73% respectively. The data shows that Uganda lacks personnel engaged in the second industry, which is inconsistent with Uganda's strategy of increasing economic growth by accelerating industrialization. There is a huge gap in the technical and skilled talents needed for Uganda's industrialization, which brings opportunities and challenges for China's vocational education support for China-Uganda production capacity cooperation.

The opportunity is that Chinese-funded enterprises have built a large number of infrastructure and industrial parks for Uganda's industrialization development, providing tens of thousands of job opportunities. However, Uganda's vocational education cannot provide professional skilled *talents with job-matching* capabilities for Uganda's industrialization development, which requires China's vocational education services to support China-Uganda production capacity cooperation and solve the problem of Uganda's shortage of technical and skilled talents. The challenge is that facing such a huge gap in skillful talents in Uganda, how can China's vocational education choose the field and professional direction to serve China-Uganda production capacity cooperation on the basis of Uganda's existing industrial structure and bring about economic growth and employment level improvement to Uganda.

2. Difficulty of Introducing Chinese Vocational Education into Uganda due to Inadequate attraction of Uganda Vocational Education

The recognition of vocational education in Uganda is low. Even though Uganda has issued policies to promote vocational education development, it has not effectively improved the quality of vocational education graduates, and cannot provide sufficient talent support for Sino-Ugandan production capacity cooperation. There are significant differences between Uganda and China in vocational education concepts, management functions, school standards, information technology infrastructure, etc., which will have an impact on the entry of Chinese vocational education into Uganda and serving Sino-Ugandan production capacity cooperation.

The main reasons are:

(1) Inability of Ugandan Vocational Education to Adapt to Industrial Development Due to Limited Government Investment

In the 2011 fiscal year, only about 3% of the GDP was invested in education, and the education funds used to support Ugandan business, technology, and vocational education accounted for only 3.4% of the national education funds. Insufficient funding has caused the development of vocational education in Uganda, especially in the field of technology, to be unable to match Uganda's policy direction of vigorously developing the industry.

(2) Small Scale of Vocational Education and Insufficient Teaching Staff

In 2017, vocational education institutions (BTVET and PTC) accounted for only 9% of the number of general secondary education (USE) institutions; the enrollment in vocational education was only 4.7% of the enrollment in general secondary education; and the number of teachers engaged in vocational education was only 7.7% of the number of teachers in general secondary education. At the same time, the income level of vocational education teachers in Uganda is low, and their interests are often not guaranteed. The channels for improving the teaching ability of vocational education teachers in Uganda are not smooth. Only limited teacher training courses are organized by the government (University Teachers/ Instructors Training Office) or commercial institutions during the long vacation or enrollment break from June to August each year.

(3) Lack of Flexibility and Practicality in Uganda's Vocational Education Curriculum

Ugandan vocational schools lack autonomy and flexibility in curriculum development, as they must strictly adhere to the courses set by the government-established authority - the committee. Due to the committee's corruption and inefficiency, the curriculum has become outdated, and the teaching standards and content updates are slow, leading to a significant gap with Uganda's existing enterprises (especially international enterprises) and standards.

(4) Lack of Quality Assurance System in Uganda's Vocational Education

According to feedback from Ugandan employers in surveys of graduates, they hope that graduates can receive sufficient practical training during their higher education to enable them to have creativity, critical thinking, teamwork, and a sense of responsibility. They also hope for a quality assurance system for university graduates, to ensure that their skills match the practical output of their work.

3. Poor Outcome of China's Vocational Education Support for China-Uganda Production Capacity Cooperation

Since 2020, facing complex international situations, China's vocational education "going global" to serve international capacity cooperation has encountered many difficulties.

Some companies that have gone abroad have only signed China-Ugandan capacity cooperation agreements but have not started work in a timely manner, making it difficult to cooperate closely with Chinese colleges and universities. China-Uganda Mbale Industrial Park plans to attract 60 companies to settle in, providing 20,000 job opportunities for Uganda. As of August 2022, more than 30 companies have signed contracts to settle in, but only 20 are actually in production or under construction. China-Ugandan capacity cooperation has not been fully carried out, and China's vocational education services for China-Ugandan capacity cooperation can only focus on teacher training and resource construction, and the degree of school-enterprise cooperation needs to be deepened.

The difficulty of international personnel mobility has caused some cooperative exchanges to stay online, affecting the teaching effectiveness of teacher training or employee training. From February to March 2022, Uganda's Luban Workshop carried out concentrated teacher training. Although the effect of teachers personally practicing equipment operation has improved, it still lags behind face-to-face training, and there is less communication between the two parties during training. In the future, the "school-enterprise-school" tripartite needs to increase cultural exchange activities to promote China's vocational education services for China-Ugandan capacity cooperation.

In addition, in the process of China's vocational education service for China-Ugandan capacity cooperation, there is a lack of a complete institutional mechanism and a comprehensive guarantee for China's vocational education to support China-Ugandan capacity cooperation.

12.5.2 Recommendations for Further Development

1. Focusing on the Demand and Adapting to the Direction of China-Ugandan Capacity Cooperation Development

China's vocational education services for China-Ugandan capacity cooperation should always be guided by the socio-economic and industrial development needs of Uganda, and always be guided by the talent needs of Chinese-funded enterprises that serve China-Ugandan capacity cooperation. Taking the Ugandan Luban Workshop as an example, it is necessary to deeply analyze and research the professional needs and key technologies of enterprises in China-Uganda Mbale Industrial Park, continuously adjust and optimize the professional layout and scope, and expand the professional extension to meet the development needs of the industrial park.

2. Expanding the Education Function of Luban Workshop Centered on Faculty Training

Based on the advanced equipment of the Luban Workshop platform and combined with the local enterprise characteristics, a training program for African vocational college backbone teachers and park enterprise employees will be jointly implemented with TianTang Group, teaching advanced production methods, production processes, technologies and more. With the help of the Luban Workshop platform and conducting school-enterprise cooperation with local enterprises, an overseas talent training and practical training base will be established. By integrating high-quality resources from multiple sources, teaching resource libraries, online video open courses, MOOCs, action-oriented textbooks, international teaching standards, and vocational standards will be developed. The existing Luban Workshop curriculum will be reformed to radiate to other colleges, drive the construction, reform, and improvement of Uganda's vocational education curriculum system, and support Uganda's industrialization process and China-Africa international production capacity cooperation.

3. Enriching Course Formats and Use Online Resources to Provide Flexible Training

Distance education will become a new trend in China's vocational education services for China-Uganda capacity cooperation in the future. China's vocational education should fully utilize online platforms, set up flexible course modules, create single or combined courses, and provide flexible training for African employees of Chinese-funded enterprises through micro-courses, so that African youth can learn anytime and anywhere and improve their learning effectiveness.

4. Building a Comprehensive Service Platform to Achieve Sustainable Development

Centered around China-Uganda capacity cooperation, a comprehensive service platform will be built for the joint construction and sharing among government, enterprises and schools. This will effectively integrate and connect Chinese enterprises and vocational colleges that are "going global" to increase their ability to resist various risks through joint development. Regional cooperation organizations such as the China-Africa Vocational Education Cooperation Alliance and the China-East Africa National Industry-Education Cooperation Alliance will be established, and forums and seminars will be used to form a "policy library, industry library, and vocational education database" for China-East Africa vocational education. These will lay a foundation for dynamically adjusting major settings, and focus on solving the problem of international capacity cooperation and the cultivation of technical and skilled talents.

5. Improving the Construction and Operation Mechanism of Luban Workshop

As a model of Sino-foreign cooperative education, Luban Workshop needs to continuously improve its construction and operation mechanism, establish risk prevention and mitigation plans, effectively avoid and prevent risks from various factors, and smoothly settle and take root in Uganda, so as to cultivate high-quality and high-skilled local talents for African countries and make domestic vocational colleges play an irreplaceable role in serving international production capacity cooperation.

The operation and management of Luban Workshop are mainly composed of Chinese partner universities and Ugandan cooperative enterprises, supplemented by Ugandan universities. The three parties form a joint management committee and improve the dialogue mechanism among the principals of the three institutions. With the deepening of cooperation, there are plans to establish an industrial college in the industrial park, build a China-Ugandan higher vocational college, and form a standardized institutional setting to ensure the ability of vocational colleges to serve China-Ugandan production capacity cooperation.

6. Diversifying Forms of Cooperation and Communication to Create a Positive Atmosphere for Serving China-Ugandan Capacity Cooperation

In order to better serve China-Ugandan capacity cooperation, the "school-enterprise-school" tripartite should always maintain good communication and diversify forms of cooperation and communication, mainly including academic and cultural exchanges, forums, competitions, etc. Every opportunity for communication should be fully utilized to expand the influence of Luban Workshop in Africa.

Luban Workshop can use international skills competitions to enable teachers and students from both China and Uganda, as well as employees of Chinese-funded enterprises, to continuously enhance their technical skills, broaden their international horizons, and fully reflect modern technology and traditional skills, promoting learning through competition and teaching, enhancing friendship, and creating a positive atmosphere for Luban Workshop to promote China-Ugandan capacity cooperation.